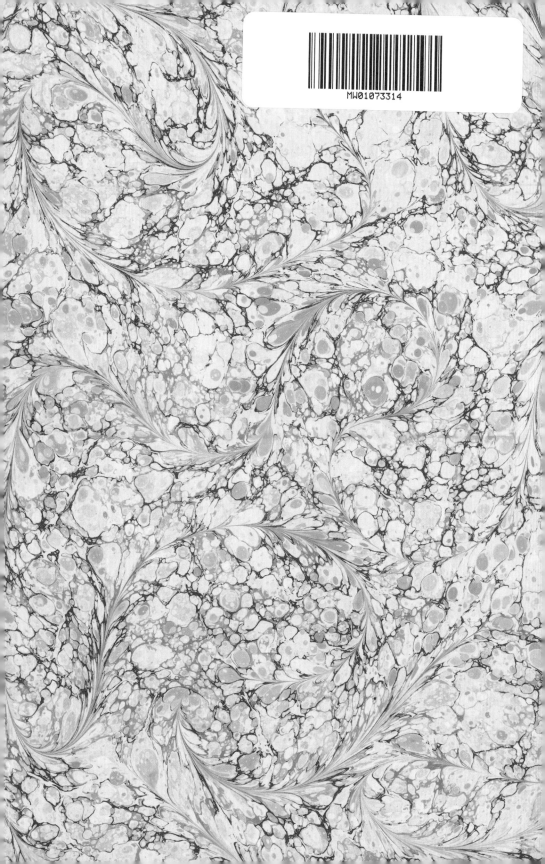

DYING HARD

Colonel French L. MacLean
United States Army, Ret.

DYING HARD

Company B, 39th Infantry Regiment, 9th US Infantry Division in WWII

Schiffer
Military History

Other Schiffer books by the author

The Fifth Field: The Story of the 96 American Soldiers Sentenced to Death and Executed in Europe and North Africa in World War II,
    978-0-7643-4577-7

American Hangman: MSgt. John C. Woods; The United States Army's Notorious Executioner in World War II and Nürnberg,
    978-0-7643-5815-9

Sitting Bull, Crazy Horse, Gold and Guns: The 1874 Yellowstone Wagon Road and Prospecting Expedition and the Battle of Lodge Grass Creek,
    978-0-7643-5151-8

Copyright © 2024 by French L. MacLean

Library of Congress Control Number: **2024932131**

Type set in Minion

ISBN: **978-0-7643-6829-5**
Printed in **China**

Published by Schiffer Publishing, Ltd.
4880 Lower Valley Road
Atglen, PA 19310
Phone: (610) 593-1777; Fax: (610) 593-2002
Email: Info@schifferbooks.com
Web: www.schifferbooks.com

For our complete selection of fine books on this and related subjects, please visit our website at www.schifferbooks.com. You may also write for a free catalog.

Schiffer Publishing's titles are available at special discounts for bulk purchases for sales promotions or premiums. Special editions, including personalized covers, corporate imprints, and excerpts, can be created in large quantities for special needs. For more information, contact the publisher.

We are always looking for people to write books on new and related subjects. If you have an idea for a book, please contact us at proposals@schifferbooks.com.

Them wuz his exack words—
"I envy th' way you dogfaces git first pick o' wimmen
an' likker in towns."
—Willie

This book is dedicated to every "Willie and Joe"—stock cartoon characters created by cartoonist Bill Mauldin—typical of infantrymen in Company B of the 39th Infantry Regiment, who fought all the way from the brawl at the Town Pump in Fayetteville to VE-day and composed this song to keep their spirits up in the Hürtgen Forest, sung to the tune of "The Wabash Cannonball":

Hear the One-Five-Fives a barking; Hear the angry shrapnel whine,
The airplanes they will help us; To saturate the swine,
We'll have our Christmas dinner; In a big Berlin hotel,
While Hitler and his buddies; All sweat it out in Hell.

It is also dedicated to all the "Willies" and "Joes" who fought everywhere else in that war around the world, and who have fought for this country since it was born, except now there are a lot of "Ginas" and "Flos" standing next to them too.

The American Army

Of 191,701 ground battle deaths during World War II, 142,962 were infantrymen. Of the US Army's 820,877 ground battle casualties of all types, infantrymen accounted for 661,059.

THE NINTH US INFANTRY DIVISION

A total of 304 days of combat; 4,581 killed in action, 16,961 wounded in action, and 750 missing in action—22,292 battle casualties and 15,233 nonbattle casualties, for 37,525 total losses—second heaviest of any US Army division in the war.

COMPANY B, 39TH INFANTRY REGIMENT

In total, 177 enlisted men assigned when formed in 1941; a soldier from this nucleus had only a 6.7 percent chance to survive and be in the company in May 1945. Many of the 93.3 percent of men not present in May 1945 had not gone gentle into that good night . . .

They had died hard.

CONTENTS

FOREWORD : The American Soldier   11

INTRODUCTION : "Things Ain't What They Used to Be"   13

PREFACE AND ACKNOWLEDGMENTS   17

CHAPTER ONE : Long Ago and Far Away, Ft. Bragg   21
School of the Soldier: Marksmanship Training; The Letter;
Goldbricking; Mess Halls

CHAPTER TWO : The Old Reliables: Algeria, Tunisia, Sicily, and England   35
School of the Soldier: Your Helmet; Private Snafu; Combat Fatigue;
Mustangs; Officers and Sergeants; Combat Infantryman Badge;
Bob Hope; The Army Way; Wounds

CHAPTER THREE : The Americans Are Coming! Across France and Belgium   57
School of the Soldier: Medics; Bazooka; Hooch; Sleep; Krauts, Jerries,
Huns, Heinies, and Fritz; IV-Fs and Jody; Tiger Tank; Guardian Angel

CHAPTER FOUR : The Hell of the Hürtgen   89
School of the Soldier: May Hosiery Mill; Navigating through
the Woods; C Rations and K Rations; German Discipline; M1s and
BARs; Mortars; Maps; Pneumonia; Sounds

CHAPTER FIVE : The Hohes Venn, Elsenborn Ridge (1), Merode Castle   129
School of the Soldier: Trench Foot; Unit Call Signs; Latrines; Gas Masks;
Deuce and a Half; Foxholes; Booby Traps; The Uniform; Foraging,
Scrounging, and Looting; Radios; Infantry Tactics; Penicillin; Malmedy

CHAPTER SIX : Battle of the Bulge, Elsenborn Ridge (2), Kalterherberg   171
School of the Soldier: Glenn Miller; Hey, Joe. Whaddya Know?; Spam;
Continental Stockade; Barbed Wire; Fruitcake; Victory Mail

CHAPTER SEVEN : Mac's War Stalag VI G   201
School of the Soldier: Dog Tags; Missing in Action; Typhus

CHAPTER EIGHT : Dying a Man at a Time   213
School of the Soldier: Repple Depots; Silver Star; Snipers;
Beware, Traitor . . . the Werewolf Watches

CHAPTER NINE: "Show Me the Way to Go Home" 241
School of the Soldier: Operation Downfall

CONCLUSION: "I won't forget the men who died, who gave 251
that right to me."

EPILOGUE: The Silent Generation 261

APPENDIX: Company B Personnel 287

ENDNOTES 306
BIBLIOGRAPHY 329
PERSONNEL INDEX 338

MAPS

MAP 1: 39th Regiment Landings, Company B, Algeria, 36
November 8, 1942

MAP 2: 39th Infantry Regiment, Company B, Northern Tunisia, 37
April 1943

MAP 3: Company B, 39th Infantry Regiment, Sicily 1943 42

MAP 4: Panzer Lehr Division Attack of Company B, Le Dézert, 61
Normandy, July 1944

MAP 5: 9th Infantry Division, Company B, Attack to Germeter, 94
Hürtgen Forest

MAP 6: Company B at Germeter, Hürtgen Forest, October 4–25, 1944 120

MAP 7: Company B Defense of Elsenborn Ridge, Hohes Venn, Belgium 174

MAP 8: Company B Attack of Siegfried Line, Kalterherberg, Germany 192

MAP 9: 9th Infantry Division, Company B Crosses Remagen Bridge, 223
March 10, 1945

MAP 10: Significant Company B Locations, Late 1944–45 236

The American Soldier

"Some say the American soldier is the same clean-cut young man who left home; others say morale is sky-high at the front because everybody's face is shining for the great Cause. They are wrong. The combat man isn't the same clean-cut lad, because you don't fight a kraut by Marquis of Queensberry rules. You shoot him in the back, you kill or maim him the quickest and most effective way you can with the least danger to yourself. He does the same to you. He tricks you and he cheats you, and if you don't beat him at his own game you don't live to appreciate your own nobleness.

"But you don't become a killer. No normal man who has smelled and associated with death ever wants to see any more of it. In fact, the only men who are even going to want to bloody noses in a fist fight after this war will be those who want people to think they were tough combat men, when they weren't. The surest way to become a pacifist is to join the infantry.

"I don't make the infantryman look noble, because he couldn't look noble even if he tried. Still there is a certain nobility and dignity in combat soldiers and medical aid men with dirt in their ears. They are rough and their language gets course because they live a life stripped of convention and niceties. Their nobility and dignity come from the way they live unselfishly and risk their lives to help each other.

"They are normal people who have been put where they are and whose actions and feelings have been molded by their circumstances. There are gentlemen and boors; intelligent ones and stupid ones; talented ones and inefficient ones. But when they are all together and they are fighting, despite their bitching and griping and goldbricking and mortal fear, they are facing cold steel and screaming lead and hard enemies, and they are advancing and beating the hell out of the opposition.

"They wish the hell they were someplace else, and they wish to hell they would get relief. They wish to hell the mud was dry and they wish to hell their coffee was hot. They want to go home. But they stay in their wet holes and fight and then they climb out and crawl through minefields and fight some more."

—Bill Mauldin, *Up Front*

"Things Ain't What They Used to Be"

O'er the land of the free and the home of the brave.
—Francis Scott Key, "The Star-Spangled Banner"

Once upon a time, the forces of evil came within a razor's edge of plunging the world into a second dark age. Many, many nations answered the call to defend civilization, but only one—the United States of America—could tip the balance of fate to victory for the defenders of what was good and right. And she did.

America won the war with a huge industrial base. She won it with a unity of effort seldom seen before, and never seen since. She won it by bringing women and minorities into the war effort. She won it with magnificent technology. She won it with a few senior leaders in each military service and in Washington, who had the remarkable foresight to comprehend the new character of this war and how it would be conducted. But most of all, she won it with a bunch of boys—soon to be men—who stood on godforsaken battlefields around the world and in their typical American brazen and cocky manner snarled at their foe: "Not today, Tojo; not today, Benito; not today, Adolf. Not today, not tomorrow; not ever. To get to where you want to go, Adolf, you have to go through us. And that ain't happening."

The cost of that victory was monumental—which is why we have so many monuments around the world to remember their sacrifice. Unlike in many other nations, however, most of America's monuments are not triumphal arches or palisaded promenades, but rather her military cemeteries, unfortunately filled to the brim with her heroes. In World War II, the United States of America lost roughly 407,000 military dead—enough that almost every city, town, and village lost loved ones. As to civilian deaths worldwide, the slaughter estimates range from forty-five million to ninety-five million—and the only reason America did not suffer millions of civilian deaths at home is because these same young Americans stopped the enemy before they could get here.

That conflict is called <u>World</u> War II, and no other nation on the planet lost soldiers, sailors, aircrew, or marines in virtually as many corners of the globe as did America. Above the Arctic Circle, forty American Merchant Marine ships sunk by enemy action suffered fatalities—sometimes the entire crew drowning in the icy waters. Flying the "Skyway to Hell" over "the Hump"—the sky-scratching Himalaya Mountains—so many Army Air Corps aircraft crashed that the route was dubbed the "Aluminum Trail," for the visible wreckage of C-47s and C-46s (dubbed "Flying Coffins")—because when a transport barrels into the side of a snow-covered peak at 10,000 feet, there are no survivors.

American service members died in the jungles of Bataan, and on the ensuing Death March in 1942; two years later, more Americans perished in these same Philippines at Leyte Gulf and Luzon when MacArthur returned. The Navy lost sailors hunting German U-boats in the North Atlantic, South Atlantic, Caribbean, and Mediterranean and lost sailors hunting Japanese submarines on the other side of the world. Marines fell assaulting Tarawa, Guadalcanal, Iwo, and countless other islands. Their sisters died too—some 543 in war-related incidents. Thirty-eight ladies of the Women Airforce Service Pilots (WASP) perished in service to their nation piloting military aircraft, flying almost everything their brothers did, including B-17 Flying Fortresses, one of which sported the feisty name of "Pistol Packin' Mama," because the "Air Janes" were just as saucy as the guys.

American soldiers bled to death in the sands of Africa, in the wild blue yonder over Germany and Japan, and from one end of the Pacific Ocean to the other. Bomber crews died at 20,000 feet in the air in flaming bombers, and the boys who ran silent and deep died hundreds of feet below the surface of the sea in the crushed hulls of their submarines. And they died by the bucketload on the ground in Europe—2,499 just on June 6, 1944, at Normandy, on the longest and last day of their lives.

And so it went around the world. A 2017 congressional research report lists deaths in battle as 234,874 Army, including 52,173 Army Air Corps, as well as 36,950 Navy and 19,733 Marines. And the infantry? Other historians have concluded that infantrymen accounted for 142,962 of the 191,701 deaths among American army ground battle casualties in the war—75 percent. Concerning Army ground battle casualties of all types, infantrymen accounted for 661,059 of 820,877—a staggering 80 percent.[1]

That's the "Big Picture." This work is written from a much-narrower point of view, where names are more important than numbers—one small unit—Company B, in the First Battalion (referred by the troops as "Battalion") of the 39th Infantry Regiment ("the 39th Infantry") in the 9th Infantry Division ("the 9th Infantry"). While reading this book, you are now a soldier in Company B. In Europe, your division is sometimes part of the VIIth US Corps and sometimes the Vth US Corps, both in the First US Army. You've heard of Gen. Dwight Eisenhower, supreme commander of the Army in Europe; Gen. Omar Bradley, commander Twelfth Army Group; and Lt. Gen. Courtney Hodges, commander of First Army, but you probably have never met them, or your corps commanders. You may have seen your division commander but probably have never talked with him.

Not so your commander of the 39th Infantry. If you were there with Col. Harry "Paddy" Flint, not only did you undoubtedly see him up close, but you knew that he created the AAAO on your helmet and you idolized him—in part because he was often out front during the fighting. Battalion commanders, company commanders, and platoon leaders came and went, because casualties were high for them. In fact, after your previous platoon leader was gravely wounded last month, your new platoon leader will die on a snowy hill in Germany trying to save your life.

You'll start your journey at Fort Bragg, North Carolina, where the division is formed. Then it's off to England in 1942, and then we're all going to Algeria, Tunisia, and Sicily; we'll see combat in each. After that, it's Normandy, France, and then we'll head east to Belgium. This fighting is tough, but you'll think the war will be over by Christmas. It won't be. Your next stop is the Hürtgen Forest. If you survive that, and a lot of us didn't, it's on to another miserable place, the Hohes Venn. Then it's off to Merode Castle and later Elsenborn Ridge. The castle, built in 1263, has five-story towers and a wide moat with 7-foot-deep, cold water. There is one entrance—a narrow bridge 12 feet wide, covered by machine gun fire. Getting into that castle, borrowing a phrase from poet Alfred, Lord Tennyson, you will be "stormed at with shot and shell."

In January 1945, we'll try to get warm and attack the vaunted Siegfried Line, where concrete bunkers have machine guns that we call "Hitler's buzz saws" or "Kraut bone saws," and when you hear them firing, you'll know why. Then you'll see the inside of a German POW camp. You'll lose a lot of weight here, be infested with fleas and lice, suffer constant diarrhea, get no hot showers, sleep three to a bunk, and see guys drop from typhus—while big, angry guard dogs try to bite you.

Along the way, you'll meet a few German units that fought against your division, because an army's achievements in war must be measured in terms of the ferocity of its enemy. Panzer Lehr Division is the most powerful unit in the Wehrmacht, their armed forces; you'll fight them twice—Normandy in 1944 and Germany in 1945. The 3rd Panzergrenadier Division, which you'll fight on Elsenborn Ridge in the Battle of the Bulge, had been at Stalingrad, and its veterans know every trick in the book. And the Luftwaffe's 3rd Fallschirmjäger Division, a paratrooper outfit, is waiting to kill you at Merode.

Company B keeps fighting to the end of the war in Europe. It's a rough time, and casualties continue at a frightening rate right through to the end. After that, although all you want is for the Army to "Show Me the Way To Go Home," not everyone will just pack up their gear and scram. What would happen with Japan, how long will the occupation of Germany last, what will be the system for a soldier to return home?

Finally, there is a conclusion and epilogue; save them for last. Some of the book is sad, but much is funny, which could be offensive to some readers. But no less an authority than famed war correspondent Ernie Pyle had this to say about humor in war:[2]

> It would be wrong to say that war is all grim; if it were, the human spirit could not survive two and three and four years of it. . . . As some soldier once said, the Army is good for one ridiculous laugh per minute. Our soldiers are still just as roughly good-humored as they always were, and they laugh easily, although there isn't as much to laugh about as there used to be.

At the end of most chapters, you'll find a total of over sixty special topics under the rubric "School of the Soldier," an old Army term that has to do with teaching a soldier the really important stuff in the Army—such as goldbricking, sleep, chow, and hooch—and how to survive.

Baseball is a thread throughout the book. Major League Baseball was the most popular professional team sport in America, with eight teams both in the American and National Leagues; there were also a handful of additional leagues for Black players, and these "Negro Leagues" were packing stadiums too. And in 1943, baseball execs Philip Wrigley, Paul Harper, and Branch Rickey, founded the All-American Girls Professional Baseball League, consisting of ten teams. But baseball is more than a sport during the war. If you are returning to friendly lines, for example, after a patrol and do not know the correct password, an outpost may ask you about baseball—since the Germans don't play it. So, if you do not know anything about the New York Yankees, Joe DiMaggio, or the St. Louis Cardinals "Gashouse Gang," you may have some "splainin'" to do.

History is the oxygen for storytelling, and storytelling is the essence of humanity. Once upon a time, your father, grandfathers, and great-grandfathers became part of that history, which fueled a legend that should never die—in part because so many of them did. Your mother, grandmothers, and great-grandmothers were legends too, sometimes in combat areas—such as the Philippines, where seventy-seven Army nurses, the "Angels of Bataan and Corregidor," were forced by the enemy on a 68-mile "death march" without food or water and in 100-degree temperatures—or back home, working in dangerous factory jobs building the Arsenal of Democracy. Now it is up to you whether that legend is passed down to your children and grandchildren, or whether you let that legend die. *Because legends don't die with a bang; they die with a whimper.*

You might ask, "Why is it up to me to keep their story alive?" Because you would fit right in with us in Company B. How do we know? When something in life knocks you down, and you get back up on your feet, wipe the blood off your nose with your sleeve, and say, "Is that all you've got?," you're in Company B. If people have told you that you were too small, or too slow, or too poor, or too anything, and you went out and proved them all wrong, you're in Company B, because a lot of us were too. If you ever saw someone bullied by a group of people bigger than you, and yet you jumped in to help that person, you're in Company B.

You love dogs? In 1942, a young soldier found a stray dog in the Aleutian Islands and took care of him until reassigned to the States. Putting the dog, named Buff, in his duffel bag, the trooper took him on the long journey. Months later, the soldier climbed aboard a troopship—Buff hidden again in his duffel bag—and sailed to Europe and Company B, where Buff served as a mascot and helped pull guard duty.[3] So if you love dogs, you're in Company B. And if you love to read about American soldiers, then you're in Company B too. So, rise and shine, grab your helmet, and follow us. And make sure your M1 rifle is loaded, because we're all going back to the line. But first we'll review a couple of pages of paperwork—because the Army runs on paperwork—and then we are going to Fort Bragg.

Preface and Acknowledgments

The nicest veterans…the kindest and funniest ones, the ones who hated war the most, were the ones who'd really fought.

—Kurt Vonnegut, *Slaughterhouse-Five*[1]

The men and women of America who fought World War II were notoriously reticent about discussing their experiences. Called "the Greatest Generation," they should also have been nicknamed "the Silent Generation." Not only were they closemouthed, many seemed proud that they "wouldn't talk," to the extent that their children and grand-children came to the conclusion that even if they waterboarded "Old Gramps"—which they would never do to such a beloved person—he wasn't talking, so why bother, because everyone was just going to get wet.

Maybe it was because a soldier in this work, my father, Myron "Mac" MacLean, was so closemouthed about the war that I wrote it. Once in a while, you could get a few grunts and groans out of the old man if you were lucky, but he was of the mind that the war was a chapter of life already finished and better off not to be reread. My brother and I would get a hint of his experiences when Dad stormed into our bedrooms each school-day morning, screaming at the top of his lungs in German to get out of bed, turning on every light, throwing back the curtains, pulling down a certain way on the shade so it would go flying back up when released, and, finally—when he was in a particularly charitable mood—fully opening the windows on frosty-cold mornings to ensure that you got out of bed. Quickly.

Dad had spent some "quality time" as a prisoner of war (POW) at some place in Germany called Stalag VI G and obviously wanted his two sons—who had designs on attending West Point—to get used to catching hell. To his friends he was Mac, but while reading *Up Front* by Bill Mauldin, I realized that Dad had a lot of Willie and Joe in him.

We are going to try to get their story right, in spite of their reluctance in life to talk much about the war. Of course, each one would insist that we not talk about his own efforts, but of his buddies instead, saying that they were the real heroes, and what they were able to accomplish together. All were unique, but as a team they made each other better. And so, it did—and they passed on from history. At the end of my re-searching this book, only one out of about thirty-five men known to be in the 3rd Platoon of Company B in the fall of 1944 was still alive, so gaps in the story seemed like chasms. Several people rode to the rescue—archivists at the National Archives in St. Louis, Missouri, and College Park, Maryland; Dwight D. Eisenhower Presidential Library at Abilene, Kansas; Donovan Research Library at the Infantry School; Army Heritage Center at Carlisle, Pennsylvania; College of the Holy Cross, Worcester,

Massachusetts; and Ike Skelton Combined Arms Research Library at Fort Leavenworth, Kansas.

Archives are mountains, and to get where you want to go you need "sherpas," including Dean Gall, Eric Kilgore, Holly Rivet, Tim Rose, Theresa Fitzgerald, Kayla Hays, Kevin Helenthal, and Whitney Mahar, at St. Louis. At Carlisle, Amanda Neal answered the call; Rebekka Bernotat at the Infantry School, John Dubuisson at Fort Leavenworth, and Kevin Baily at Abilene. At College Park, Marcus L. Bacher, and at Holy Cross, Abby Stambach and Corinne Gabriele helped immensely.

Edward Miller, expert on the US Army in the Hürtgen Forest, contributed, while Doug Nash—another expert author—did the same concerning German forces. Albert Trostorf of Merode, Germany, provided expertise on the Hürtgen. J. P. Speder, with the Missing in Action Project in Belgium, provided enormous help concerning SSgt. Warren Ridgeway. My longtime friend Manfred Sommer in Rohrbach, Germany, found Stalag VI G. Laverne Wilson helped at Peoria High School in Peoria, Illinois, as did Brittany Keegan at the Watkins Museum of History, Douglas County (Kansas) Historical Society. Wes Pietsch taught me how to fire an M1.

Then I found the "new" kid on the block, at least for me—artificial intelligence. Maybe it's just a form of AI, or maybe technically not AI at all, but Ancestry.com, Find a Grave, and the National Archives (NARA) World War II Army Enlistment Records online databases often made researching the hundreds of soldiers who passed through Company B just a couple of mouse clicks away. In short, every soldier mentioned in the conclusion and epilogue has information from one or more of these databases. And since the appendix (Company B Personnel) has each soldier's full name and service number, you can find even more data on them. As more info migrates to easily searchable databases, we may be entering a golden age for military history.

Finally, Army buddies Louis DiMarco, Hank Adams, Tom Veve, and Jack Pattison reviewed the draft, knowing that I couldn't let the soldiers in Company B down. Most importantly, then Sergeant First Class Willie Johnson, Master Sergeant Dexter McClanahan, and First Sergeant Eddie Clayton deserve my undying thanks. While West Point taught me how the Army was supposed to function, they taught me how the Army really worked—true professors in the "School of the Soldier."

As gifted as these archivists, historians, and friends are, none personally knew the soldiers herein. So, I turned to those who did—children and grandchildren, and slowly the blanks filled:

Nicholas Baccile / Lisa Baccile Navone: son/granddaughter,
    SSgt. Albert Baccile
David Basham: grandson, Pfc. Kenny Seaman
Louis Benoist: son, 2Lt. Louis Benoist
Scott Blanchard: son, Pvt. Edward Blanchard

Linda Wasnick Browning / Alex Wasnick: daughter/grandson,
   Pfc. Lloyd Wasnick

Sarah O'Connor Collins: granddaughter, Pfc. Manley Fuller

Anita Eannace: daughter, Cpl. Carmine Eannace

Carl Eichel: grandson, Pfc. Herman Eichel

Myra Elliott / Myranda Elliott: daughter/granddaughter, TSgt.
   Langley Turner

Billy Flowers: son, Pfc. Billie Flowers

James Gravino: grandson, 1Sgt. Joseph Gravino

James Holman / Matthew Holman: son/grandson, Sgt. Jay Holman

Kathy Jewell Schilmoeller / Glenn Jewell: daughter/son, 1Lt. Jack Jewell

Kelly Lieber / David Frankel: granddaughter/grandson, Pfc.
   Harry Nodell

Debra Kaye Lockridge Pitsenbarger: daughter, Pfc. Kermit Lockridge

Scott Lucas: grandson, 1Lt. Lucien Lucas

David MacLean: son, Pfc. Myron MacLean

James Pettigrew: son, Pfc. Robert Pettigrew

Judith Mills Porter / Anita Mills Thompson / Heidi Marie Thompson:
   daughters/granddaughter, 1Lt. Stanley Mills

Regan Pourchot: son, Sgt. Leonard Pourchot

Nancy Ridgeway: niece, SSgt. Warren Ridgeway

Alison Rush / Kathy Scroggins: daughter/granddaughter,
   SSgt. James Rush

Billie Joe Slaughter: son, Medic Jessie Slaughter

Anna White Blair / Lauriekim White: daughter/niece,
   Sgt. Willie S. White

Timmy Woods / Briny Woods / Dean Woods / Dr. Gerald Marks:
   wife / stepson / Briny's son / lifelong friend, Pfc. Jay H. Lavinsky
   (Lavin)

They began as information sources and progressed to friends and extended family, which I think would make our fathers, grandfathers, and great-grandfathers in Company B happy.

And thank you to millions of significant others nationwide, who didn't sit under the apple tree with anyone else till your soldier came marching home. After going through the Depression, you now sacrificed the best years of your life in raising the family and putting the interests of your spouse above yourself—and often your own careers. You raised the kids, maintained the home, and hugged your soldier boy whenever he woke up screaming at the war demons in the middle of the night. And during the day, you imposed good order and discipline with the dreaded phrase "Your father is trying to sleep" to the children—many of whom were truly little hellraisers, because, after all, they took after Dad.

And you became "golf widows" when your spouse hit the links every Saturday with his foursome—because walking with his friends through the countryside helped him remember the good things about the guys he had fought alongside.

And your reward for all this? Whenever the children would get an idea to do something crazy, and huddle around their father to ask permission, that same man—"El Jefe"—who had looked death in the face and never flinched all around the world during the war, would now shirk all paternal responsibilities and simply say, "Go ask your mother!"

CHAPTER ONE

Long Ago and Far Away, Ft. Bragg

The key to immortality is first living a life worth remembering.
—Bruce Lee

It was the best of times; it was the worst of times. It was the exhilaration of the Roaring Twenties; it was the despair of the Great Depression. It was the oppression of Prohibition; it was the liberation of the speakeasy. It was the hope of a League of Nations; it was the hopelessness of totalitarianism. It was the shackle of illiteracy; it was the freedom of a college education. It was a woman's place is in the home; it was Rosie the Riveter hammering hot steel in a tank factory. It was the humiliation of segregation; it was the jubilation of the Tuskegee Airmen. It was the blues; it was Ol' Blue Eyes. It was Kate Smith and "God Bless America," Duke Ellington and "Take the 'A' Train," Glenn Miller and "American Patrol" and "Snafu Jump," Tommy Dorsey and "Opus One," Count Basie and "One O'Clock Jump," Woody Hermann and "Woodchopper's Ball," and Benny Goodman and "Sing, Sing, Sing," and it was Lena Horne and Billie Holiday. And while it was a time for working hard and playing hard, very soon it would become a time for dying hard.

They come from all corners of America—teeming cities of the Northeast, rural South, golden sun of California, farms of the Midwest, coal country of Appalachia, cold country of Minnesota, and even from the Standing Rock Indian Reservation, somewhere on the endless Dakota plains. Some are illiterate, needing buddies to help them read letters from home; others are college boys from schools such as "Ole Miss," University of Maryland, Santa Monica Junior College, University of Kansas, and Bradley Polytechnic Institute.

But college boys are in the minority; most start work at an early age to help the family, and a lot of them are more familiar with hard manual labor than they ever wanted to be. A couple have dangerous jobs up in towering treetops as lumberjacks, or deep underground as coal miners. Several toil on hardscrabble farms, another hauls 100-pound sacks of coal up one flight of stairs after another. One stands in front of a hot plate, hoping someday to own a small restaurant; another crouches behind home plate, chasing his dream of playing catcher in the major leagues.

Some are married; some are spoken for; some think they are God's gift to women; a few are too shy to even ask a girl to dance. Born of Austrian, German, Czech, Italian, Russian, French, Scottish, Irish, Lithuanian, English, Danish, Hungarian, Canadian, Swiss, Mexican, Korean, Filipino, Yugoslav, Swedish, Romanian, Ukrainian, Greek, and Polish immigrant parents, they have nicknames such as Mac, Hawk, Kenny, Willie, Noodles, Timber, Doc, Vito, Candy, Greek, Buster, Bulldog, Porky, and Russian. Not all are born across the fruited plain, and they are more than happy to tell you about their "old country" of Scotland, Austria, Hungary, Ireland, Italy, Spain, Mexico, Poland, Philippines, Cuba, Greece, China, Norway, Canada . . . or Texas.

Most are young—anyone who shaves is considered old, and every old guy is called "Pop." The company commander, even though just twenty-two, is invariably termed "the Old Man." They all would give their eye teeth to see their mothers just one more time; ladies with names of Pearl, Anne, Fern, Edith, Eva, Pauline, Rose, Tarcila, Grace, Estelle, Felisa, Antonetta, Ruth, Lupe, Elena, Apie, Ella Fair, Margaret, Maria, Minnie, Neva Mae, Elizabeth Mae, and Lillie Mae, because every mother thinks that her own son is the cat's meow. And while each son would trade a few of his tomorrows to be sitting at Mom's kitchen table tonight, not a one of them one wants to become a Gold Star in her window.

Rich or poor—they are proud of their upbringing, whether it's in a famous big city, some small Podunk, or as a fifth-generation hillbilly with a PO box, which will lead to a scuffle every now and then, and sometimes a full-fledged brawl. They are mostly Protestant or Catholic, with several Jewish troopers—some churchgoers and some not—and maybe a few atheists, although Dwight Eisenhower will later declare: "There are no atheists in foxholes."[1]

At war's outset, the regiment is all White, the Army not truly integrating until 1948. The 39th Infantry moves faster than Uncle Sam, though, and by 1944 numerous Mexican American soldiers will fight and die in the company, two Korean Americans and a Filipino American soldier will be wounded, while a young man from the Lakota tribe and another young man from the Quechan tribe will leave their reservations to fight for all Americans. And in 1945, a Black soldier in the regiment will receive the Silver Star for gallantry in action from his division commander, while several others, led by a sergeant from Dallas, Texas, will serve as infantrymen in 3rd Platoon of Company B in combat.

None of their immediate officers are West Pointers; the first "Pointer" in their chain of command is their regimental commander. Theirs is a "meat and potatoes" infantry outfit, disrespectfully termed "cannon fodder" hundreds of years ago by some generals who didn't give a damn how many soldiers died taking this hill or that village. They aren't "purebred" commando units; they're mutts, who don't get a lot of ink, but without whom no war can be won. And while several first applied for the Army Air Corps, where the food is better, there's a bunk to fall into at the end of the day, and wearing those wonderful fleece-lined flight jackets just screams out that you are "somebody," they ultimately find themselves in a place that no one wants to be, doing a job that no one wants to do.

That all starts at Fort Bragg, North Carolina, where the 9th Infantry Division—created in July 1918—is reactivated on August 1, 1940, as is the 39th Infantry. While the division—as a whole—did not fight in France in World War I, the individual regiments did, with the 39th Infantry receiving the French Croix de Guerre with Gold Star for the capture of the Cresnes Wood and Noroy in July 1918. The initial batch of troops now contains many career soldiers; only in 1941 will units reach full strength. The men live in tents at Fort Bragg until Christmas 1940, when they move into new, wooden barracks. Francis W. Honeycutt, the first division commander, dies in an aircraft crash on September 21, 1940. His replacement will be Jacob "Jake" L. Devers, an artilleryman, who had graduated from West Point in 1909. Promoted to brigadier general five months earlier—over 474 more-senior colonels—Devers is the youngest brigadier in the Army.

Neither West Point nor any staff college can make a "battlefield general." That title is earned by an officer who has the soldiers' touch of understanding what goes on down on the line. Jake has that soldiers' touch. Arriving at the parade field to assume command of the division on November 15, 1940, he finds nine thousand soldiers shivering in a cold, howling wind. Jake sees that very few have overcoats. Not even a general can make overcoats fall from the sky, but Jake does the next best thing—he takes off his own coat and throws it to the ground. As the ceremony ends, Devers steps to the microphone and begins to talk—now to "his" soldiers:[2]

> You men have put on a good show. You look like soldiers. This is a fine division, and it will be a great division. I've been down through your area in the two days I've been here, and there is one thing I want to tell you. Next Saturday night you can have a hot bath. There will be heaters for water down there in your bathhouses. I don't know where I'll get them, but you will have a hot bath.

Six days later the men take hot baths. Perhaps Jake called in a few favors from his West Point classmates; perhaps unit scroungers "appropriated" every water heater not nailed down in North Cackalacky. Whatever it was, it worked. The troops had been without hot water for three months, but not now. *Their* general had come through for them.[3]

One of the first young men arriving in Company B is Langley Turner. A farm boy from Dema in Knott County, eastern Kentucky, born June 12, 1920, Langley stands 5'9" tall and weighs 155 pounds, with brown eyes and hair; he is the son of John M. "Johnnie" Turner—a farmer and a constable, who had been killed trying to break up a domestic dispute when Langley is eighteen months old—and Eliza Mary "Dank" Justice. Langley has four siblings: Oscar, Lummie, Bertha, and Silvia. He drops out of a two-room school in Salisbury Branch after eighth grade, becoming a farmhand. Langley enlists on August 21, 1940, at Fort Thomas, Kentucky, and is sent to the 39th Infantry at Fort Bragg.[4] Lang has skills the Army needs; he is soon licensed to drive a command car, ¼- and 1½-ton trucks, and even a halftrack, and he makes corporal. Tracking crafty raccoons over the hills back home, he knows land navigation and is also an excellent shot.

The regiment starts filling up with five hundred draftees from Camp Upton, Long Island, New York, led by Captain Van H. Bond, on January 16, 1941—several for Company B.[5] The next day, five hundred more arrive. For the first thirteen weeks, the men, restricted to their company area, receive a whopping $21 per month. Later, as "buck privates," pay increases to $30, not sounding like much, but a lot of dough for a kid from rural Kentucky.[6]

Like Chester McClurg. Born March 20, 1919, in Rowan County, Kentucky, he is the son of Andrew Marion McClurg and Elenora Netherly, who run a farm 30 miles east of Lexington. Chester finishes eighth grade, drops out of school, and becomes a farm laborer to help his older brother and three younger sisters, since his parents divorced in 1937. Farming isn't in his blood, and on August 16, 1940, Chester, 5'4" and 125 pounds, enlists in the infantry at Fort Thomas, hoping to be stationed at the Panama Canal.[7] The Army has other plans. Chester is in one of the first levies to fill up Company B. He also has a penchant for going over the hill. Although he will receive the Combat Infantryman Badge (CIB) for North Africa and Sicily, the award is later revoked due to his undisciplined behavior.

There are several other bad boys in Company B. That's OK; you don't want the Vienna Boys' Choir in an infantry platoon. Gen. George Patton knew that. In a tent during the 1941 Louisiana Maneuvers, a pensive Patton shared his thoughts on the war he knew would surely come:[8]

I'm worried because I'm not sure this country can field a fighting army at this stage in our history. We've pampered and confused our youth. We've talked too much about rights and not enough about duties. Now we've got to try and make them attack and kill. A big percentage of our men won't be worth a goddam to us. Many a brave soldier will lose his life unnecessarily because the man next to him turns yellow. We're going to have to dig down deep to find our hard core of scrappers. That takes time and time is short.

Joseph Gravino also rolls in. Son of Domenic Gravino (a laborer who emigrated from Italy in 1905) and Angelina Paone, also from Italy, Joe is born on January 28, 1919, in Newark, New York—just east of Rochester. Catholic, Joe finishes eighth grade of grammar school to pursue his dream and plays semipro baseball at age fourteen in 1933.

In 1938, Joe gets a contract from the Rochester Red Wings. He plays fifteen games with the Auburn Bouleys (Auburn, New York) in the Canadian American League; in twenty-one at-bats he has four singles and a double. The next year, Joe begins a two-year stint as a catcher with minor-league clubs of the St. Louis Cardinals, first with the Washington Redbirds (Washington, Pennsylvania). In sixty-seven games he bats .279, with thirty-seven singles, thirteen doubles, four triples, and a home run. In 1940, he splits time between the Portsmouth Redbirds (Portsmouth, Ohio) and the Fostoria Redbirds (Fostoria, Ohio), appearing in twenty-seven games, with thirty-two hits, seven doubles, two triples, and a home run.

Needing stable work, Joe drives a delivery wagon and cleans, presses, alters, and remodels clothes at Al Colacino's "The Man's Shop" in Newark in 1940. More importantly, Joe stays visible, since the store is a meeting place for major-league scouts visiting the area. The connection pays off, and Joe is invited to St. Louis with five hundred would-be major leaguers. He makes the cut and signs a $275 contract. Since the great Walker Cooper is currently their catcher, Cardinals manager Billy Southworth tells Joe to enlist in the Army, do his year, and then report to the club.

Joe is inducted into the Army at Syracuse on January 16, 1941. Soon after, he arrives at Fort Bragg, assigned to the 39th Infantry.[9] Not unexpectedly, Joe becomes the starting catcher on the company baseball team. Participating in athletics in the regiment allows the players to often skip reveille formation and just show up for practice at 0900 hours, allowing you to be a sack rat just a little while longer.[10] You also miss early-morning physical training of lots of sit-ups, pull-ups, and push-ups, and then a 300-yard run, or whatever the sergeants feel like doing.

Joe will be on the company team a bit longer than planned. Just weeks before his year in the Army is over, the Japanese bomb Pearl Harbor and Joe hears a new phrase: "in for the duration." Promoted to corporal, he becomes a squad leader. In early 1942, he makes staff sergeant (SSgt.) and is a platoon sergeant. Joe fights in North Africa and Sicily with Company B and is wounded in May 1943.[11] He is now the company first sergeant—a position often referred to as "Top"—ensuring that the company is fed and resupplied, that casualties are evacuated, and that good order and discipline are maintained. That is often difficult, since the American soldier probably does more griping and bellyaching than any other soldier in the world.

Every company needs a good supply sergeant (Army occupational specialty 821), and Company B has one in Albert Baccile. The son of Liberato Baccile and Elizabeth Scarinci—both from Chieti Province in central Italy, who immigrated to the US in 1912–13—Al is born at Coaldale, Pennsylvania, on December 26, 1915. The large family, with seven girls and five boys, moves between Pennsylvania and New York until the late 1920s. Al finishes freshman year of high school, leaving to become a construction laborer, like his father.

Al registers for the draft in Elmira on October 16, 1940, listed as 155 pounds, with a ruddy complexion, gray eyes, and brown hair, and employed by the O'Connell Contracting Company. Inducted on January 15, 1941, he soon finds himself in Company B at Fort Bragg. Al has a special skill that serves him well; he is a good boxer. The division boxing team—called the "Fighting Ninth"—wins the local Golden Gloves tournament at Lumberton on February 9, 1941. Little by little, the Army starts finding its scrappers. Able to grab a rifle, when necessary, Al will receive the CIB for combat in North Africa and Sicily. Fluent in Italian, Al will be particularly valuable in Sicily, serving as a translator for the company commander.

Over the next months, the regiments conduct individual and small-unit training. The 39th Infantry also conducts an organization day on June 9, 1941, including a relay race, hand-grenade-throwing contest, obstacle course race with full pack and equipment, softball game between the officers and noncommissioned officers, and a pie-eating contest, where there are no losers.

"An army marches on its stomach" is a phrase attributed either to Napoleon or Frederick the Great. Regardless of who coined it, every unit needs a good cook. Albert Paul DiRisio is larger than life. That's because he has a thankless job—the mess sergeant, senior cook, pan rattler in the unit. Even when the mess sergeant is competent, he is often termed a "hash burner." And when he has rocks for brains, those epithets are unprintable. Fortunately for all, Al is a good cook with a great sense of humor. And a cook needs to be a scrapper too. If you give too small a serving to the wrong soldier, you better be ready for a throw-down!

Born in Fairport, New York, on December 31, 1915, the son of Joseph DiRisio and Genevieve "Jennie" Polito, Al has six brothers; all will serve overseas during the war. Joseph, who emigrated from Italy in 1905, works in a vinegar factory; Jennie dies when Al is nine; the family is Catholic. Al attends Fairport High School; in school musicals he is a natural ham. Later, Al is a cook in a Fairport restaurant, and a waiter at the Cottage Hotel. During the hotel floor show intermissions, Al is coerced to play the piano. With some 250 people cheering wildly, Al plays his renditions of "Frankie and Johnnie" and "Barnacle Bill the Sailor," although no reviews exist indicating if he played the risqué versions of the songs when he tickled the ivories.

Life soon changes for Al. Enacted September 16, 1940, the Selective Training and Service Act of 1940 is the first peacetime conscription in the country's history. All American men aged twenty-one through forty-five must register for the draft; not all will be picked—the national lottery leaves it up to chance. A month later the first lottery numbers are selected—Al's number comes up. On January 16, 1941, it's time for Al to "Shuffle Off to Buffalo," New York, get a physical, and take a free train trip to Camp Upton. During the Great War, famed composer Irving Berlin, stationed at the camp, wrote a musical, *Yip, Yip, Yaphank*, including the prophetic song "Oh! How I Hate to Get Up in the Morning." Much in the Army, in addition to early rising, upsets Al:

> They herded us like cattle into this big building. A soldier looked at you, guessed what size you were, and threw World War I Army uniforms at you, at that time knickers with the wrapped leggings. When I put on my uniform, the sleeves ran six inches past my fingers; completely dressed, I was a sight for sore eyes.

Another train takes Al and his new friends to Fort Bragg. Because wooden barracks have yet to be built, the men sleep in tents. It is a new, painful land for Al. "With my big new army shoes and my flat feet, it wasn't long before the blisters got me to walk like a duck. I sure was disliking Army life already." Al then learns that the Army actually read his induction form. Al had listed cooking experience, in Army terms a "Cook Short Order-2-26.33," and immediately is thrown into a mess hall as a third cook.

Al soon gets his Army nickname of "Hawk" due to keen eyes: "The Hawk could not only distinguish a male from a female at a quarter-mile distance but also probably tell you who she was. And he could make the identification in the dark!" Hawk will need that keen eyesight at marksmanship training. He receives an M1 rifle and is told to report to the range; the officers and enlisted men are having a competition. Seeing the cook, his fellow soldiers begin laughing. What they do not know is that Al's favorite pastime back home is woodchuck hunting, and he estimates he has shot over 2,500. Al finishes first, firing 211 out of 220 possible points, but now there is a problem. Officers read the results of shooting competitions. And it isn't just some shavetail lieutenant; it's the division commander. Quite naturally, Gen. Devers asks, "Who is this DiRisio?" After being told that Private (Pvt.) DiRisio is a third cook, the general asks a second—and far more ominous—question: "What's he doing in the kitchen?"[12]

Those kinds of questions travel fast in the Army—really fast. For the next several marksmanship sessions, for reasons unknown, Al starts firing "Maggie's drawers," missing the target entirely. That ruse works for a while, but what Al needs is an ally; his prayers are answered as Capt. Oscar Thompson of Atlanta, Georgia, becomes the Company B commander. Oscar attended the Riverside Military Academy in Gainesville, Georgia; he served in the reserves until called to active duty in 1940 as a first lieutenant at the Infantry School at Fort Benning.[13] Al later said of his new commander: "He didn't smoke or swear, and he could have been a minister or preacher."[14]

That may have been true, but Oscar later would be a tiger on the battlefield, decorated for heroism, when, "subjected to severe machine gun and mortar attacks, Capt. Thompson voluntarily led numerous patrols across rugged terrain to recover the dead and wounded. His indefatigable efforts and absolute disregard for danger won him the admiration of all who witnessed his actions." However, this was all in the future. Now, the former Georgia Tech "Yellow Jackets" football player knows a good man when he sees one and, in the blink of an eye, squelches any possibility that Al will be ordered out of the kitchen due to his shooting prowess—he makes DiRisio the company mess sergeant and promotes him to staff sergeant.[15] And those marksmanship targets? What targets?

Hawk also learns a lesson in the kitchen—improvisation. Working with John Mittag, another cook, the two decide on "pigs in blankets" for lunch at Fort Bragg. Mittag, from New York City—who had worked on an ocean freighter before his Army service—is a natural storyteller and describes a voyage to Africa in such comedic detail that Hawk later says, "I got so excited about the story I kept handin' him the ingredients—blindly," as Mittag mixes them in a large stainless-steel bowl. "He was gonna mix dough into patties, wrap the patties around a hot dog, place them in big sheet pans, and slide them into the big black old stove oven." The pair slide the sheet pans into the oven and, when the dish was done, pull the sheet pans out of the oven.

There were fluffy pigs-in-blankets. They looked delicious. We each grabbed one and took a healthy bite. We almost died. Salt! I looked at the floor and there was an empty 10-pound salt bag. I should have used a 10-pound sugar bag. But bein' so engrossed in the stories, I grabbed the wrong bag. "My God, what will we do," Mittag hollered, so I hollered back—SOS! (cream beef on toast). We called all the KPs and chopped all the pigs-in-blankets into a Sloppy Joe mess. We threw bread on the top of the stove, toasted one side only because we had no time, and I made a quick white flour gravy with lukewarm water. The men came charging into the dining room, all 200 of 'em, lined up with their plates, and we threw a piece of toast on the plate, laid a scoop of Sloppy Joe on top of it, poured white gravy over, and they all sat down to eat. Believe it or not, out of 200 soldiers, only about 20 came to the kitchen to complain it was too salty.[16]

Maj. Gen. Devers is appointed in August 1941 as chief of the armored force, with the responsibility to expand the existing four armored divisions to sixteen—it is now clear that someone in Washington believes that the country may have to take on the panzer forces of Germany one day soon. So, the Army starts large-scale maneuvers, the first two in Louisiana. The 9th Infantry is part of huge war games in North and South Carolina, between October 6 and November 28, 1941, that pit the "Blue" First Army against the "Red" IVth Corps—a smaller but mechanized force.

Not everything runs smoothly. One battle rule is that a tank can be knocked out by an infantryman hitting it with a flour bag "hand grenade," bringing a rebuke by one general: "If hand grenades could destroy tanks, we would quit building them." And the food; chow consists mostly of early C rations, or prepared lunches of "one sandwich, ham; one sandwich, jam; one apple, eating." Thanksgiving falls during the maneuvers, but it's no feast: "A soldier who got a piece of fried chicken from a rolling field kitchen counted himself lucky."[17]

After Pearl Harbor, security codes are implemented. Company B becomes "Baker" and the 9th Infantry is coded "Notorious." The 39th Infantry, nicknamed "Fighting Falcons" in the Great War, is termed "Nudge." Twice, Company A and Company B get into no-holds-barred fistfights with hundreds of guys duking it out.[18] Had George Patton been informed of the incident, he probably would have asked, "And your point is?"

Another fighter arrives. Warren "Timber" Ridgeway is born on September 21, 1919, at Sandy Creek, New York, son of Anna Mary Daly and John Wesley Ridgeway, a teamster at a local lumber mill; Warren has six brothers and five sisters. Timber is a rootin' tootin' son of a gun, a natural leader to whom officer and enlisted alike will turn in moments of crisis—extremely outgoing and boisterous—a guy who yells a lot, will "take charge," and could have been an "action guy" in a movie.[19] After eighth grade, he becomes a lumberjack and also claims that he had been a hunting guide for Babe Ruth and Lou Gehrig, but that they were too drunk to shoot. In 1940, Ridgeway resided at Boylston, New York, making $300 a year. He enlists in Syracuse on January 17, 1941; he is 6'0" and 173 pounds.[20]

Timber is at Ft. Bragg when one of those seminal events happens in a young man's life—in this case, hundreds of young men. Future sports announcer Lindsey Nelson—a young public-affairs officer in the 9th Infantry—is present and describes the event in his down-home style:[21]

I was a member of the 9th Infantry Division from the peacetime days of August 1941 until July of 1945 when the war had ended in Europe. I got my first taste of combat at the Town Pump here in downtown Fayetteville, North Carolina. By then, I was already a veteran, however. I had been through minor skirmishes at the Brooklyn Spaghetti House and the Rainbow Restaurant. And I had spent dangerous and adventuresome nights in the Lafayette Hotel.

The Town Pump was an elaborate bar that had been constructed to take advantage of the soldier business. There were leather banquettes—or at worst imitation leather, it didn't matter—there were curved bars—and a lot of frosted plate glass windows. The 9th Division was getting ready to go overseas and had moved out into the field. Their barracks had been occupied by the 82nd Airborne. As a part of their indoctrination and training, the airborne soldiers were taught that they were the toughest people on the face of the earth. The 82nd Airborne had been well-trained, and they believed it.

There were other things that annoyed the soldiers of the 9th Division—the airborne fellows usually wore uniforms that were clean and sharply pressed. They wore highly polished jump boots and lacquered helmet-liners. Not only that—they got extra "jump" pay, which put them in a financial bracket above the dogface soldier. And let me hasten here to say that the term "dogface soldier" is one of endearment. To me, there is no higher accolade that one can bestow than to refer to an individual as a dogface soldier. That means a GI of the foot-walking, dirt-behind-the-ears—combat infantry, you can't do without us—soldier. Well, if you are living in a pup tent out there on Chicken Road and you come into town for a short beer at the Town Pump and you run into a paratrooper who is better dressed and richer—you may not take kindly to it. Especially if you've had two—maybe three—short beers.

So, on this particular night—a pitched battle broke out between the soldiers of the 9th and the 82nd. I saw it plainly. I was in one of those imitation leather banquettes up close. I didn't have any trouble leaving. There were rather quickly doors where doors had never been before—and there was a lot less of that frosted plate glass. I remember a lady who left just ahead of me. She wasn't touching the ground anywhere. She landed, relatively uninjured, out there in the rubble. And as she lay there stunned—one of our good old GIs—an opportunist to the end—asked her for her phone number.

We didn't give battle stars for the Town Pump campaign—but we should have. We were remembered in dispatches. When the 9th Division cut the Cherbourg Peninsula to seal off the port-city in the first great allied victory after the invasion of Normandy—a sign went up in the window of a storefront here in Fayetteville. It said, "Here's to the 9th Division—they fought all the way from the Town Pump to Cherbourg."

On July 24, 1942, Maj. Gen. Manton "Matt" Eddy takes command. Eddy is not a West Pointer; in fact, he looks more like a schoolteacher than a soldier. Looks are deceiving; Matt has the soldiers' touch, just like Jake. Born in Chicago in 1892, he is expelled from two high schools there, Lake View (called "Leg View" since the girls wore skirts) and Lane Tech. One of Matt's friends, newsman Westbrook Pegler, wrote how Matt was dismissed from Leg View:[22]

> There was a general *verboten* against fraternities in high schools in Chicago then, so Matt Eddy had joined one as a matter of course. It was his fate, though who would say his misfortune, to be called upon by the fully accredited brothers in the sacred, everlasting bond to get up on the rickety little stage of a nickel movie theatre on Clark Street, near Belmont, one night, and make a fool of himself by impromptu antics, at that fateful hour in the infinity of time which Professor Buck, the principal of Leg View, selected to cast an eye on that flickering novelty which was coming to be called the silent drama. In due course, Matt Eddy, the pledge, was called before Professor Buck and fired from Leg View High.

Matt then attends the Shattuck Academy in Minnesota, graduating in 1913, and in 1916 he enlists in the infantry; by 1918, Matt, a second lieutenant, deploys to Europe in the Great War, commanding a machine gun company in the 39th Infantry until he is wounded. He is later an instructor at the Infantry School and the Army Command and General Staff School and will see Europe again—but first has a gig in Africa.

In early 1942, attached to the Amphibious Corps of the Atlantic Fleet, the division conducts amphibious training, consisting of boarding ships in Chesapeake Bay and conducting mock amphibious assaults against Solomons Island, Maryland. Day after day, the troops negotiate rope ladders on the sides of swaying ships, carrying all their gear on beach after beach. In return, they are treated to canned or dried chow, bread, onions, and beans.[23]

After getting its feet wet, the Ninth returns to control of the Army ground forces. Meanwhile, some of the musically inclined soldiers put on their own vaudeville musical, *Whacky in Khaki*, at the Fort Bragg Community Theater, to packed houses. By early September 1942, latrine rumors are rampant. Gen. Eddy confirms that the unit is leaving, and that the infantry regiments would fight under other commands, but that the division would re-form before the end of the year. Fighting where? That's hush-hush. The 39th Infantry departs Fort Bragg first, on September 17, under Col. Benjamin Caffey, travels by train to Fort Dix, and then Staten Island, New York, where on September 25 it departs on six transport ships for Belfast, Northern

Ireland.[24] Shipboard life will be a "mouth-watering" experience.[25]

It became worse when men got seasick. Not having time to run above deck, they would vomit from their bunks, letting it go past the bunks below them. The heavier the swells in the ocean, the sicker the men became until you couldn't bear the sight and smell in the holds of the ship. It was then that I was thankful for having the top-most bunk. The weather changed completely for the worse. High seas and winds were buffeting us, causing our vessel to bounce around like a cork. At times, the bow of the ship would rise out of the water and come down on top of a wave with a clap like thunder. The impact of the ship meeting the water would send sounds and vibrations throughout the hull. In the berth below with me was Alfred Rowles, a skinny kid from Wisconsin. Sick, and with a green wax-like color, heaving over the side of his bunk, moaning and groaning, in between gags and gasps of "I wanna die; please God, let me die." But when the bow of the ship struck the water, again, he chickened out with "Not now God!, a little later."

Army, Navy, or Marine; puking, barfing, gagging, heaving, hurling, retching, spewing, or vomiting is no fun.

SCHOOL OF THE SOLDIER

MARKSMANSHIP TRAINING

There may have been a time in America's history when a majority of young men knew how to fire a musket or a rifle, but those days are long gone by this war. City slickers probably have never fired any rifle before, but even soldiers from rural areas may not have had much experience with a .30-caliber military rifle or firing at distances at which the Army trains. Marksmanship training is standardized in the Army with the July 20, 1941, issue of the War Department *Field Manual (FM) 23-5, Basic Field Manual: US Rifle. Caliber .30, M1*, which teaches four shooting positions: prone (most stable and accurate), sitting, kneeling, and standing (least stable and least accurate).

Instructors teach slow and rapid fire, at ranges of 200 and 300 yards, with a few targets at 500 yards. In rapid fire, a soldier has sixty to sixty-five seconds to fire sixteen rounds; slow fire has no time limit to fire four rounds standing, sitting, and kneeling at 200 yards, and eight rounds prone at 500 yards, but instructors won't coddle slow-pokes. They also teach soldiers to shoot a little low, resulting in telltale impacts, so they can adjust slightly upward—plus a ricochet might cause a nasty wound. Finally, the soldiers are taught how to distribute fire between targets, how to conduct advancing fire while moving forward (also called marching fire), and how to conduct suppressive fire to keep the enemy's heads down.[26]

THE LETTER

In January 1941, seven brand-new recruits are packed on a troop train en route from Fort Dix, New Jersey, to Fort Bragg. Feeling their oats, the young men collaborate to write two postcards, one to Gen. George Marshall, chief of staff of the US Army, highly critical of Army life and cheerfully signed "love and kisses, The Boys."[27] The recruits give the letter to a porter, who mails it to Washington, and down the road the general finally receives the stinging missive.

They then write a second card, addressed to "A. Schickelgruber, housepainter," intended for Adolf Hitler, Germany's chancellor. "Schickelgruber" is a derogatory swipe at Adolf's family lineage, since Hitler's father, Alois, was born out of wedlock to a Maria Anna Schicklgruber. In his youth, the German führer had been an aspiring artist, which foreign cartoonists ridiculed, characterizing Hitler as a house painter—and not a good one at that. The soldiers warn Hitler to retreat east across the Rhine River or they will come over and kick him back. It too is signed "The Boys," but whether the führer ever receives it is doubtful. Nonetheless, he finally did comply. At Fort Bragg, "The Boys" become part of Company G of the 47th Infantry Regiment in the 9th Infantry. Four years later, this unit, along with many others, including Company B, will fulfill that vow as they run under fire across a bridge at a place called Remagen, pushing the German army east over the Rhine. So, Adolf, how do you like them apples?

GOLDBRICKING

To some officers and sergeants, playing baseball on the company team falls into the category of "goldbricking," referring to soldiers not pulling their weight—just the opposite of an eager beaver, an enthusiastic helper for almost any project. But for many enlisted men, goldbricking is a fine art; it wasn't so much that you avoided hard work, but more importantly that you felt that you had pulled one over on the Army.

Goldbricking could involve a make-work detail picking up garbage or cutting grass; the uninterested young sergeant in charge sometimes leaves the men with the threat that when he returns, the job better be done. The junior enlisted men find the easiest way to do the task, finish quickly, and goldbrick the rest of the afternoon with a nap, rather than returning to headquarters, where they invariably would get more work to do. Stamping out goldbricking is well-nigh impossible, and really only when the senior noncommissioned officers had done a bit of it themselves and knew every trick before the privates ever thought of doing it. You can't goldbrick with Top Gravino, since he'll throw you out before you're halfway to first base. So, as Nat King Cole would say, just "Straighten Up & Fly Right."

MESS HALLS

Supposedly the word "mess" meant a portion of food in Old English, and that came from the Old French word *mes*, which meant "a dish." But, because of the French lingo, if you were thinking of *haute cuisine* in an Army mess hall, think again. Eggs? You can have them up or down. Scrambled? Sure, but only when the eggs are powdered. Omelets? Right, General MacArthur. Chipped beef? We call that SOS, and when you eat it, you'll know why. Pork chops today? No, Spam. Chicken today? No, Spam. Bacon today? No, Spam. OK, chow hound: we do have Army chicken (franks and beans), alligator bait (fried liver), bull in the can (canned corn beef), jawbreakers (biscuits), Joe (coffee), pep tires (doughnuts), dog food (corned beef hash), axel grease (butter), and the always delicious looseners (prunes). So, who's hungry?

Actually, for many of the new soldiers, Army chow is the most nutritious and filling meals they have ever had during the tough days of the Depression, no matter how hard Mom struggled to make ends meet—not because the Army was a charitable organization, but because it recognized that soldiers burned thousands of calories a day doing their jobs. So quit your jiving and bellyaching.

CHAPTER TWO

The Old Reliables, Algeria, Tunisia, Sicily, and England

There is an agony in your heart and you almost feel ashamed to look at them. They are just guys from Broadway and Main Street, but you wouldn't remember them. They are too far away now. They are too tired. Their world can never be known to you, but if you could see them just once, just for an instant, you would know that no matter how hard people work back home they are not keeping pace with these infantrymen in Tunisia.[1]

—Ernie Pyle

The convoy drops anchor in Belfast Harbor on October 5, 1942. After finding their land legs, the men rehearse amphibious landings in Wales and Scotland; for the next ten days, the 39th Infantry conducts speed marches. In Scotland, for a week on the rough terrain near Loch Fyne—during torrential downpours of rain—they conduct more marches, fight mock battles against the British army's Black Watch Regiment, and learn combat tactics from the kilted "Ladies from Hell," their bagpipes wailing "Hielan' Laddie."

In Scotland, Al learns another lesson—always have a map. Cooks must participate in the rugged training; during a downpour of rain, Al, hopelessly lost, leads them in the wrong direction. "We were wet and cold that night and the only structure we found for miles around with a roof was an old, abandoned pig pen. So, we slept on the stinking floor bed of that pig pen to keep warm. The company found us at dawn and led us back to the ship, staying at least 25 paces distant from us."[2] At this rate of matriculatin', Al will soon be a professor at the War College.

The regiment sails from England on October 26, 1942, to North Africa, passing through the Straits of Gibraltar. On November 8, the 39th Infantry, as part of Operation Torch, lands just east of Algiers; from the assault ship USS *Samuel Chase*, the First Battalion, under command of Lt. Col. A. H. Rosenfeld, storms ashore at Cap Matifou. The day before, a German torpedo narrowly misses the ship but hits and disables the transport *Thomas Stone*.[3]

Capt. Oscar Thompson commands Company B in the fighting at an airfield outside Maison Blanche, so heavy that Langley Turner later says that he thought he would be killed there. French resistance collapses on November 11; the division then patrols the Spanish Moroccan border. The 9th Infantry advances toward Tunisia in February 1943 and engages in small defensive actions and patrol activity. They find that in the rugged terrain, mules are just the ticket, and they procure so many that even Sgt. DiRisio has several to carry his mess section.[4]

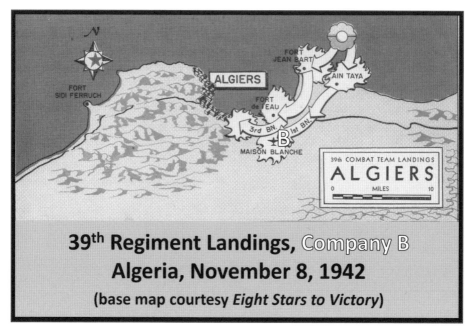

MAP 1: 39th Regiment Landings, Company B, Algeria, November 8, 1942

Lt. Col. Charles H. Cheatham replaces Lt. Col. Rosenfeld. On March 28, the division launches an attack in southern Tunisia and fights its way north. The battalion struggles hard in the hills at El Guettar against elements of the 10th Panzer Division, becoming lost in the confusing melee. Cheatham is wounded. On April 1, the battalion is unsuccessful in capturing Hill 772 near Maknassy. Between March 28 and April 8, 1943, the 39th Infantry suffers 39 killed, 281 wounded, 84 missing, 58 injured, 103 evacuated for exhaustion, and 66 evacuated for disease/illness, including one battalion commander missing in action, and another evacuated for combat exhaustion. Medic Ben Murrell recalls the combat:[5]

> We were advancing an attack up a mountain and came under enemy fire. At a point, a German soldiers threw three concussion grenades at Sergeant Gravino's position. One of the grenades landed approximately eight feet from Sergeant Gravino. He hit the ground hard and was knocked unconscious for a time. Sergeant Gravino sustained a cut on his forehead, a bruise on his nose, and a piece of stone embedded in his right hip. All injuries were caused by the grenade. I pulled him down the hill . . . and sent him to a forward aid station.

After receiving replacements, on April 16 the 39th Infantry moves to the Sedjenane Valley in northern Tunisia. Gen. Eddy relieves Col. J. Trimble Brown, commander of the 39th Infantry, on April 23, after Brown had been captured near Djebel el Garsia, rescued by American troops, but in the process lost a copy of the attack plan. The situation is so dire that in the hours when Brown is missing, Brig. Gen. Donald Stroh, assistant division commander, assumes temporary command of the regiment.[6]

The 39th Infantry attacks Djebel Ainchouna, reaching the summit under heavy fire. Several officers are casualties, and only the leadership of a junior captain, Conrad V. Anderson, saves the battalion from disaster. Shortly afterward, Conrad's jeep flips, seriously injuring him; he later receives the Distinguished Service Cross.[7] The 39th Infantry pushes two battalions to Djebel el Akrat on April 26, as Col. William L. Ritter takes command. The afternoon of April 28, the battalion moves from Djebel Ainchouna to positions on Hill 377, in preparation to advance to Hill 406. On April 30, the 39th Infantry's attack on Hill 406 is successful, and they then occupy Spur 299 and Hill 382. Hawk DiRisio writes to his hometown newspaper about then, describing human-interest stories, forbidden to discuss operations:[8]

Outside of my troubles with cactus plants I'm still able to sit down. I'm in good health, getting tanned up. In fact, I feel better lately. It seems I have more hair, but I guess it's just the tan I'm getting. Since I've been here in North Africa, I've had one "thrill of a lifetime." A colonel walked into my kitchen while I was enjoying my dinner. I really don't like to be bothered when I'm

MAP 2: 39th Infantry Regiment, Company B, Northern Tunisia, April 1943

eating, but he was a colonel, so I saluted him in a military manner. He explained in detail a message for my captain while I stood at attention and my chow was getting cold. "Yes sir! And what is the colonel's name," I asked, "that I may tell the captain?" "Zanuck" was the reply, and he left after returning my salute. Trying to enjoy once again my cold chow and juggling that name "Zanuck" in my mind at the same time, I suddenly dropped my fork and hollered, "Hey, cooks, that was Darryl Zanuck!" Yes, I missed my chance—so long folks.

If only the Hawk had impressed the renowned American film producer, he later might have starred opposite Dorothy McGuire in *Gentleman's Agreement*. But he didn't—so Gregory Peck got that role, but about this time another celebrity becomes interested in the 9th Infantry. With a syndicated column printed in four hundred daily and three hundred weekly newspapers nationwide, thin, gray-haired Ernie Pyle is the most influential American correspondent of the war. Born in Dana, Indiana, he is a master of portraying the little guy, describing his fears and daily strife. In late 1942, Ernie arrives in North Africa. On May 2, 1943, he is in Tunisia near the 9th Infantry and pens the following memorable column.[9]

Now to the infantry—the God-damned infantry, as they like to call themselves.

I love the infantry because they are the underdogs. They are the mud-rain-frost-and-wind boys. They have no comforts, and they even learn to live without the necessities. And in the end, they are the guys that wars can't be won without. I wish you could see just one of the ineradicable pictures I have in my mind today. In this particular picture I am sitting among clumps of sword-grass on a steep and rocky hillside that we have just taken. We are looking out over a vast rolling country to the rear.

A narrow path comes like a ribbon over a hill miles away, down a long slope, across a creek, up a slope and over another hill. All along the length of this ribbon there is now a thin line of men. For four days and nights they have fought hard, eaten little, washed none, and slept hardly at all. Their nights have been violent with attack, fright, butchery, and their days sleepless and miserable with the crash of artillery.

The men are walking. They are fifty feet apart, for dispersal. Their walk is slow, for they are dead weary, as you can tell even when looking at them from behind. Every line and sag of their bodies speaks their inhuman exhaustion. On their shoulders and backs they carry heavy steel tripods, machine-gun barrels, leaden boxes of ammunition. Their feet seem to sink into the ground from the overload they are bearing.

They don't slouch. It is the terrible deliberation of each step that spells out their appalling tiredness. Their faces are black and unshaven. They are young men, but the grime and whiskers and exhaustion make them look middle-aged. In their eyes as they pass is not hatred, not excitement, not despair, not the tonic of their victory—there is just the simple expression of being here as though they had been here doing this forever, and nothing else.

The line moves on, but it never ends. All afternoon men keep coming round the hill and vanishing eventually over the horizon. It is one long tired line of antlike men.

The division rolls into Bizerte on May 7, netting tens of thousands of prisoners of the famed German Africa Corps, although the 9th Infantry temporarily withdraws so that French forces—now on the side of the Allies—may march into the center of the city with appropriate Gallic pride.[10] Between April 11 and May 8, 1943, the 39th Infantry suffers 38 killed, 142 wounded, 4 missing, 54 injured, 89 evacuated for exhaustion, and 118 evacuated for disease/illness.[11]

Losses have a serious morale effect on survivors; thus, when a soldier is killed, his comrades quickly bury him—so the jackals and hyenas cannot get at the corpse—placing the soldier's rifle vertically with bayonet stuck in the ground above the buried man as a marker for graves registration personnel to locate the remains. One soldier sees something different in Africa. "It was an arm. A soldier was buried there. Instead of his rifle, they put his arm there. Maybe they used his rifle for someone that didn't have one. But all I saw was this arm [sticking vertically out of the ground] and yet we still had to do our job."[12] After final combat at Ferryville (Menzel Bourguiba), Tunisia, the regiment deploys inland, described by Lindsey Nelson.[13]

> Other divisions after the end of the Algerian campaign went back to bivouacs near Oran or Algiers, but they sent us to Magenta, 50 kilometers due south of Sidi Bel Abbès in the direction of the Sahara Desert. Sidi Bel Abbès was full of fleas, flies, dogs, and Arabs, and there weren't any souvenirs to buy. All you could do was walk around until you got sunstroke or sit in a café and drink beer that was 99 percent water.

But not for long. War is a maelstrom of emotions and experiences, some horrible—and some humorous. Some events will never be written about in division histories, nor will they be mentioned in veterans' newsletters, such as a little "episode" in late May 1943, when the 39th Infantry and a second lieutenant from Company B establish a you-gotta-be-kiddin'-me bordello at the home of the vaunted French Foreign Legion, in the finest traditions of Beau Geste.[14]

Now, the US Army has always maintained a love-hate relationship with bordellos, termed houses of ill repute, cathouses, and the like. The Army hates them—well, maybe not actually hates—but discourages this activity. Some, if not many, soldiers, on the other hand, love these locales but never discuss them with anyone except their buddies.

In fact, in the over five hundred million letters sent from overseas during the war, "Dear Mom, I visited this charming little cathouse" is probably not a line that a GI ever wrote home.

Bordellos have long been associated with soldiers. During America's western expansion, there were numerous establishments at Bismarck, Dakota Territory, not far from Fort Abraham Lincoln, home of the famed 7th Cavalry Regiment. Back then, these ladies of the evening were termed *nymph du prairie*, and many a nymph undoubtedly shed a tear when a third of "Garryowen" failed to return from the Little Bighorn in 1876. During the Great War, US Army policy on sex was abstinence. The French—as always—scoffed at that concept, and French president Georges Clemenceau wrote Gen. John Pershing, commander of the American Expeditionary Force, offering France's help in establishing special bordellos for American troops. Pershing, knowing this offer was a booby trap if ever he saw one, made no decision on the "proposition," passing the buck up to Secretary of War Newton Baker, who reportedly gasped, "My God, if [President] Wilson sees this he'll stop the war." Needless to say, the war continued.

US military policy in World War II also strictly prohibited the establishment or operation of a brothel. As might be expected, venereal disease rates skyrocket in North Africa. In late May 1943, not wanting his soldiers to become infected by "Dirty Gertie of Bizerte" (a popular Army ballad in North Africa), Col. William Ritter, 39th Infantry commander, calls in 2Lt. Charles "Charlie" Scheffel, who had been a platoon leader in good old Company B.

Entering the colonel's tent, the lieutenant sees an Army doctor, as the colonel immediately cuts to the chase, asking, "Can you stand to look at a naked woman without going crazy?" Scheffel, seeing his possible future military career flash before his eyes, coughs out a reply of "barely," which is good enough for the colonel, and while the doc heads to Algiers to procure as much penicillin that he can carry, Charlie is told to establish a regulated regimental bordello, replete with medical examinations and safety procedures, as well as a transportation system to take the troops to their assignation. The colonel then gets down to brass tacks: "Charlie, I want you to rent us the best whorehouse in town."

With that astonishing guidance, Charlie visits every company commander in the regiment, collecting some $5,000 as operating capital. With a fellow Okie, and medical officer, Lt. James Womble, Charlie then jumps in his jeep and tells his driver, a twenty-eight-year-old from New York, the mission, to which the savvy soldier nonchalantly boasts, "Well, sir, the best whorehouse in Sidi is the French officers' whorehouse." The three amigos then hightail it—before the colonel can come to his senses—to Sidi Bel Abbès, Algeria—home of the famed French Foreign Legion in North Africa. Rolling through the "exotic," flea-ridden city, near the Quartier Viénot they locate a five-story structure formerly "rented" by French officers, whose madam says is "ready for business," as are her one hundred girls. To Scheffel, it looked like a classy Paris hotel, not surprisingly, since Sidi Bel Abbès has a rich history of prostitution with the La Légion Étrangère.

He negotiates a rate, stations some MPs in the lobby to maintain order, and pays the madam in American greenbacks. Then, Charlie requisitions—with Col. Ritter's authority—twenty Army supply trucks to transport interested troops to and from Sidi. Interested? He finds that there are four times as many soldiers "interested" than he has the capacity to transport, so he organizes them into four-man groups to draw straws, long straw winning and thus receiving a coveted red admission ticket. Charles Scheffel becomes known throughout the regiment as "the Strawman," and for almost two months—until the unit moves to the coast—he trucks the lucky ticket holders some 30 miles, from their tents in the desert at Magenta to feather beds in Sidi.

Lt. Womble is tasked to inspect each lady every day. He voices his strongest protest, but the other lieutenants point to their senior date of rank, and "Doc" Womble is stuck with the job. Doc is a big lad, so none of his fellow officers refer to him as the "Chief Pimp"—to his face. But not to worry; Doc will be promoted to captain. And Col. Ritter? Well, he receives a Bronze Star for meritorious service for the period May 5 to June 21, 1943, so his effort to boost soldier morale must have been appreciated by someone. And that someone may well have been his division commander, Matt Eddy, a veteran of good old Leg View High.[15]

The division remains in North Africa near Sidi Bel Abbès at the start of Operation Husky—the invasion of Sicily that began on July 10, 1943. Four days later, the 39th Infantry departs Bizerte; the following day it lands on the Licata-Gela beachhead, on Sicily's southern coast, making contact with the enemy three days later near Agrigento. Hawk sets up his field kitchen when unexpectedly a German mortar barrage targets his location.[16]

I was really ticked off when that happened. It ruined a perfectly good day. To make matters even worse, a mortar shell burst overhead and shrapnel from it pierced holes in some of my best kitchen pots. I was too mad to be scared, thinking about how difficult it would be to replace those big, beautiful pots.

Al will receive the CIB, since, although his skill identifier is 824—mess sergeant, his affiliation is infantry.[17] On July 21, the battalion reaches Castelvetrano, then Campobello di Mazara, and later that evening captures 3,456 Italian prisoners of war. The advance comes with a price when an enemy aircraft strafes Col. Ritter's command car. Ritter jumps out, but another officer then falls on the colonel, breaking Ritter's leg. Lt. Col. John J. Toffey takes command.[18]

Jack Toffey is a hero—son of a major general and grandson of a Civil War Congressional Medal of Honor winner. The perfect battalion commander, during the war he receives two Silver Stars and three Purple Hearts. Now he is the limping regimental executive officer, but still the quickest available man to be acting regimental commander.[19] Under Jack Toffey, the 39th Infantry captures Marsala on July 24, then rolls on trucks 170 miles to Leonforte, advancing to Nicosia and subsequently by foot to Cerami.[20] The next road sign indicates Troina, but it might as well have read "Hell."

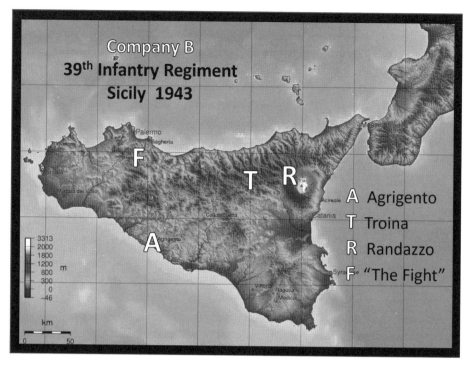

MAP 3: Company B, 39th Infantry Regiment, Sicily 1943

William Ritter did not follow standard operating instructions that during an enemy air attack, one should remain in the vehicle; the break is serious enough to take him out of action for weeks, and the Army doesn't like to wait weeks. Sometimes in Army life, chance plays a role in successful outcomes, and other times it just comes down to seizing an opportunity. For Paddy Flint, both chance and opportunity deal the cards throughout his life, and the irascible but beloved poker player makes the best of every hand. Born on February 12, 1888, in St. Johnsbury, Vermont, Harry Albert Flint takes the road less traveled to become a cavalry officer—he is accepted at the US Naval Academy in 1907, makes it through one year at Annapolis, and . . . resigns.

Unexpectedly, he applies and is admitted to West Point in 1908. His grades are average, but he excels at horsemanship and meets another horseman . . . Cadet George Patton, who will graduate in 1909. When Paddy is a first classman (senior), he is part of the detail that trains new cadets (freshmen) . . . including Dwight Eisenhower and Omar Bradley. Graduating in 1912, he is commissioned in the cavalry.

With the 4th Cavalry Regiment in the Punitive Expedition of 1916–17 to the Mexican border, Paddy is later stationed at Fort Riley, Kansas. He sees the handwriting on the wall in 1917 that the US may enter the Great War, and with minimal use of cavalry, he may miss it. Transferring to the field artillery, Paddy gets to Europe but serves only in various nonfrontline positions. In 1923, Paddy reports to Fort Leavenworth for the one-year Command and General Staff School. In the student body of 249 officers is his friend . . . Maj. George Patton. In 1926, Maj. Flint is selected to attend the prestigious L'Ecole Supérieure de Guerre in Paris, France, where he becomes fluent in French and makes friends with his fencing instructor and infantry tactics teacher Henri Honoré Giraud.

Supposedly, when Paddy returns to Washington in 1928 after this assignment, he "reported to the chief of cavalry, saluted in the French manner, and said with a Gallic accent: 'Sir, I can understand you if you speak English very slowly.'" Maj. Gen. Herbert B. Crosby is a big advocate of modernization and pushes for exercises that include airplanes and tanks as part of the Army's cavalry divisions. In the small office of the chief of cavalry, Paddy is assigned to the Material and Equipment Section. Down the hall, in charge of the Plans Section, is . . . Maj. George Patton.

A decade later, the German blitzkrieg rolls through Poland in 1939 and France and the Low Countries in 1940, with almost no cavalry, panzers having replaced horses. The year 1940 is a good one for Château Margaux bordeaux wine, a bad one for France, and a really bad one for Paddy, since he suffers a stroke. Despite this condition, in August 1941 he secures a position as the division's antitank officer and commandant of trains in the Second US Armored Division at Fort Benning and participates in the 1941 Louisiana Maneuvers. His division commander is . . . Maj. Gen. George Patton. Flint assumes command of the 66th Armored Regiment in the 2nd Armored as Patton departs. Then disaster strikes. Lt. Gen. Leslie J. McNair, Army ground forces commander, implements a policy that men over fifty, unless they are generals, should be prohibited from going overseas in positions of combat command. The oppressively hot and humid Fort Benning is not the place that Paddy wants to ride out the war, so he writes his old compatriots.

A connection works, and on June 29, 1942, Flint receives orders: "The Secretary of War relieves the following named officer from assignment and duty as indicated and assigns him to permanent station outside the continental limits of the United States." Paddy goes to London the following month for an assignment with the commanding general, Services of Supply for the European Theater of Operations (ETO), which is just forming. It is not a combat command—such as an infantry regimental commander—so McNair can shove it. Is it divine intervention? We will never know, although the commander of the Services of Supply, Maj. Gen. John C. H. Lee, is nicknamed "Jesus Christ Himself," because of his initials and apparent ego. Lee, who wears stars on both the front and back of his helmet, has his own private train in Great Britain. Lee is also a West Point classmate of Jake Devers . . . and George Patton.

Paddy finagles an assignment to the G-3 Section that will go ashore at North Africa, and secures a desk in Oran, Algeria, just after the invasion goes in. A month later, fate strikes again, and he becomes the American liaison officer to the French Army of Africa (L'Armée d'Afrique), a Free French organization that after November 1942 becomes allied with the Americans and British. The magnificent mustachioed commander of the unit is General Henri Honoré Giraud . . . Paddy's old friend on the fencing *piste*. In January 1943, Paddy receives a letter from George Patton:

> My dear Paddy, I hope you like the job with Giraud, as I was the one who recommended you for it, remembering well your stories of him when we were together at Benning. Jake Devers [on an inspection tour of the battlefields in North Africa] was here yesterday and told me you were doing a grand job. If you are looking for fighting, it is my advice to keep away from me as I do not seem destined to get in any for the time being, but if things brighten up, we shall certainly get together. Devotedly yours.

In late February 1943, the Afrikakorps slams into the IInd US Corps at Kasserine Pass; Gen. Eisenhower relieves Maj. Gen. Lloyd Fredendall of command. Things brighten up and George Patton assumes command of the corps on March 5. Soon after, Col. Flint is replaced as liaison officer and assigned to . . . IInd Corps Headquarters. Patton remains in command until April 16, when he takes over the 7th Army, but who rolls in to replace him but . . . Maj. Gen. Omar Bradley. Believing he is going nowhere fast, before the end of the month Paddy meets with Brad, saying something that Brad will never forget:[21] "Hell's bells, Brad. I'm wastin' my talents with all those featherbed colonels in the rear." Brad, in turn, meets with Manton Eddy; one of their discussions is the 39th Infantry, and Bradley and Eddy agree that the regiment needs a change. Paddy is on the short list to take command. It took awhile, but Paddy found a way.

On July 27, Col. Harry Flint assumes command of the 39th Infantry, considered a run-of-the-mill outfit that had just fought in Tunisia and is advancing across Sicily with the IInd Corps. The 39th Infantry reacts as if hit by lightning. Does Col. Flint have the soldiers' touch? You bet he does. His first day, as soldiers of First Battalion are returning from the front, they see the 5'5", 155-pound, bow-legged old man wearing a black scarf, standing on a large boulder—looking each man in the eye as they pass, and personally applauding every soldier.[22] He posts a sign at the regimental command post (CP) that reads "Suicide Ranch." He coins the regimental motto of AAAO (Anything, Anytime, Anywhere, Bar Nothing) that the soldiers stencil on their helmets. Down on the line, junior officers add their own interpretation to the motto—that they'll kick the ass of "anybody, anyplace, any time, bar none."

At a meeting about July 30, Manton Eddy shows Paddy's helmet to Omar Bradley, when the colonel is in another tent. Bradley recalled the conversation in his memoir, *A Soldier's Story*, when he was apparently suffering from "Nelson's eye":[23]

> "Brad," Eddy whispered when Paddy ambled off to the G-3 tent for a briefing, "have you seen this?" He held Flint's helmet in his hand. On its side there was boldly stenciled "AAAO." "And just what in hell does that mean?" "Anything, anytime, anywhere, bar nothing—that's what it means. Paddy has had this

thing stenciled on every damned helmet and every damned truck in the whole damned regiment." I grinned. "But haven't you issued some kind of a corps order about special unit markings?" "Manton," I answered, "I can't see a thing today—Nope, not even that helmet of Paddy Flint's."

It is a tough slog. On July 31, temporarily attached to the First US Infantry Division, the 39th Infantry is ordered to seize Troina, a main anchor in the German defensive Etna Line, in a frontal attack, while two other regiments envelop it from the flanks. But at the last moment, the First's commander decides not to commit several other units—the 39th will have to go straight up the 3,000-foot heights at Troina, in the shadow of Mount Etna.[24]

The entrenched and heavily armed 15th Panzer Grenadier Division repels the assault, inflicting heavy casualties. Paddy isn't quitting, attacking again three days later. Lt. Col. William C. Westmoreland is in command of a battalion of 155 mm howitzers in support; the guns are old, and he sends a message to Col. Flint saying that half his cannon are out of action. Flint growls back: "Fire 'em twice as fast!" Troina falls. The unit advances to Randazzo, on the northern slop of Mount Etna, on August 13, 1943. Sicily falls to Allied forces four days later. Paddy is awarded America's second-highest decoration for bravery. The citation reads:[25]

The President of the United States of America, authorized by Act of Congress July 9, 1918, takes pleasure in presenting the Distinguished Service Cross to Colonel (Cavalry) Harry Albert Flint, United States Army, for extraordinary heroism in connection with military operations against an armed enemy while serving as Commanding Officer, 39th Infantry Regiment, 9th Infantry Division, in action against enemy forces in August 1943 near Troina, Sicily. Going forward with the attacking battalions, Colonel Flint spent his entire days moving about the squad and platoon installations to cheer and encourage all ranks. During the attack on August 4, 1943, he personally led the advance through enemy fire, waving to his men to follow him forward. He was often covered and obscured from view by dust and smoke from bursting shells, later to be revealed as standing upright and urging the men forward.

In the assault on August 12–13, 1943, he went forward over a heavily shelled road and established an advance command post with the leading battalion of the Regiment. From this exposed position he personally directed the decisive assault. Colonel Flint's outstanding leadership, personal bravery, and zealous devotion to duty exemplify the highest traditions of the military forces of the United States and reflect great credit upon himself, his unit, and the United States Army.

Lt. Gen. George Patton pins the award on Paddy's uniform. Flint keeps rolling and forms an unauthorized twelve-piece regimental band, calling them the "Black Market Band" because they bought, scrounged, or liberated instruments. He also increases the number of regimental boxing bouts when the troops are off the front—to make sure the men stayed scrappy.[26] The regiment bivouacs at Cefalù, Sicily. On October 25, Patton inspects the troops and later speaks:[27]

> The men of the 9th Division are immortal, even though you die tomorrow you will live forever. Glory and honor are the only things worth living for—any "bastard" can be born and then just die, that just happens to you, but it takes a man to achieve immortality through battle.

Speaking of immortality, back on June 19, 1936, at New York City's Yankee Stadium, German heavyweight boxer Max Schmeling, "the Black Uhlan of the Rhine," knocked out American Joe Louis, "the Brown Bomber," in the twelfth round of their match, as fifty-seven million people listened on radio. Adolf Hitler subsequently proclaimed that the bout was a testament of Nazi racial superiority over the African American Louis, setting up a rematch. In June 1937, Joe Louis won the heavyweight championship of the world but publicly announced after the fight that he refused to recognize himself as world champion until he fought Schmeling again.

That reckoning came on June 22, 1938, at Yankee Stadium. More than seventy thousand fans were in attendance; another seventy million listened on radio in the US, as did a further one hundred million around the world. What they saw and heard was not a boxing match, but a beatdown. In just two minutes and four seconds in the first round, Joe floored Schmeling three times, landing thirty-one power punches and sending Schmeling to the hospital for ten days.

Many of the screaming fans in attendance believed it was the most brutal fight they had ever seen. Had these same spectators been outside Palermo, Sicily, five years later, they might have changed their tune, while watching a bare-knuckles bash between Company B's Joe Gravino and Timber Ridgeway. If the Town Pump was the biggest donnybrook involving 9th Infantry soldiers, then "Gravino versus Ridgeway" takes the cake for two men going toe to toe, one knuckle sandwich after another—and the carnage supposedly lasted almost an hour before anyone ran out of gas.

In those rough and tumble days, when two sergeants got sideways they did not take it to an officer for adjudication but retired behind a barracks or tent, rolled up their sleeves, and went mano a mano for a good old-fashioned slugfest. And after one of these scraps, the protagonists did not run to the division inspector general for redress but followed the path later taken by Sgt. J. J. Sefton in the 1953 motion picture *Stalag 17*. In that film, when Red Cross visitors inspect a German POW camp in which Sefton is held, they see him with multiple facial contusions. One representative asks, "Who beat you?" Sefton answers, "Nobody beat me. We were playing pinochle. It's a rough game."

The exact circumstances leading to the fracas are hazy. Both pugilists had been in the original contingent of Company B; both came from upstate New York. Cpl. Warren Ridgeway fought well in Sicily. Joe Gravino has just been promoted to first sergeant. As the senior sergeant, Gravino must maintain cohesion, while Ridgeway, an excellent combat soldier, marches to the beat of a different drummer in bivouac or training and is frequently in trouble. Despite Gravino and Ridgeway remaining mum, at least three other men held ringside seats—although two later feigned ignorance. Jack Dunlap, then a first lieutenant, wrote a letter in 1994 in support of Joe Gravino to the Veterans Administration concerning wartime injuries:

> As I understand it, Sergeant Gravino is making a claim for an injury he sustained in an unfortunate incident that occurred in Sicily, near Palermo in September 1943. In regard to the incident, I recall that Sergeant Gravino was provoked into a skirmish with a recalcitrant member of the Company whose invective ethnic slurs left him with no alternative but to engage his tormentor into a fist fight. I did not witness the engagement.
>
> But I understand that it took place in an isolated area and lasted the better part of an hour. I did see both participants afterwards and can attest to the ferociousness of the fight evidenced by their dirty and bloody confrontation. I referred to Gravino's tormentor as a recalcitrant, which he was at the time. He was a large well-built specimen of a man who epitomized his civilian pursuits as woodsman and hunting guide in the northern New York forests. He remains nameless because after the fight, he and Gravino became friends, and he was promoted to Squad Leader.

Really, Lieutenant—unfortunate incident, recalcitrant? A second statement came from Edwin Perry, Company B commander at the time of the slugfest. He too remained silent for fifty years.

> [Gravino] is best described as a well-adjusted, no-nonsense, individual but considerate of his troops and sensitive to their needs and capabilities. Also assigned to Company B was a soldier, now deceased, named Ridgeway. This man made an excellent contribution to my command when engaged with the enemy in fire fights. However, during periods of non-combat such as rest areas, training exercises, and battalion reserve he was a constant source of behavior problems. His reluctance to respond to orders and surly attitude were irritants to all whom he came in contact including his platoon leader and first sergeant. At the conclusion of the hostilities in Sicily, the 9th Division was ordered to embark for England. We were at that time in the vicinity of Palermo, Sicily, participating in training exercises. It is during this period, late September/November 1943, that the fight, Gravino vs. Ridgeway, took place.

At this point I must emphasize that I had no knowledge of the fight for many weeks after it took place. I first heard about the conflict from Lieutenant [Ernest] McLaughlin, a platoon leader in Company B. For whatever reason, the incident was not reported to me, perhaps fearing Courts-Martial action might be initiated. I am positive the fight did take place since subsequently a number of men who claim to be eyewitnesses described the action to me. It must have been a hard-fought affair for both men were in excellent physical condition.

Concerning their assertions that they were not present at the skirmish, well, a third witness to the fight, medic Ben Murrell, had no memory "lapses":[28]

We were at a staging area near Palermo, Sicily, on field maneuvers. He [Gravino] was in a fist fight with a well-built man for about an hour. After the fight we went back to our area, and it was there that I gave Sargent Gravino aid. In my opinion Sargent Gravino sustained a broken nose in the fight. I wanted him to go to the hospital, but he refused. He did not want it known that he was beaten bad enough to go to the hospital. I do not believe there are any records of this event.

There sure weren't any records, but every man there undoubtedly remembered the brawl for the rest of his days. And with Paddy Flint's sense of the pulse of his regiment, it is entirely possible that even he became aware of the confrontation. Joe Gravino solidified his position as first sergeant, and Timber Ridgeway continued his rise to squad leader—in the future, no other soldier in the company ever dared challenge the first sergeant's authority again.

Jack Alexander Dunlap, the son of Estelle Breedlove and Leon Dunlap, was born on August 14, 1922, in Charleston, South Carolina. During Prohibition, Leon owns his own restaurant; after that repression is over, the restaurant becomes a beer tavern. Starting his military career at the age of seventeen in the Washington Light Infantry militia, South Carolina National Guard, he enlists in Charleston on September 16, 1940; he is 6'1" and weighs 155 pounds.[29] Selected to attend Officer Candidate School (OCS) at Fort Benning, Jack then heads to North Africa.

On November 10, 1943, George Patton, who probably did not know about the fight or else he might have given both men battlefield commissions as the kind of scrappers he wanted, sends a letter to Gen. Eddy: "My sincerest hope is that when next I have the privilege of going into battle, I shall see the insignia of the 9th Division in the vanguard. With affectionate regards to all of you, I am." The regiment boards the US Army transport *Santa Rosa* for England on November 12, arriving at Swansea, Wales, on November 27.

Capt. Edwin Perry, from New Bedford, Massachusetts, joined the service in 1933 and came up through the enlisted ranks in the infantry before being commissioned as a second lieutenant in August 1942 through the OCS. Perry is awarded the CIB. He would receive the Bronze Star with three Oak Leaf Clusters and a Purple Heart with two Oak Leaf Clusters during the war and serve as an excellent mentor for the lieutenants in the company, since he is a "mustang," a former enlisted soldier.[30]

In January 1944, the 39th Infantry authorizes the award of the CIB for combat in North Africa and Sicily. Paddy receives the award, as do Company B officers Jack Dunlap, Ernest McLaughlin Jr., Stanley Mills, Karl Pratt, John Mingen, and William Wood, and 152 enlisted men, and over a thousand more in the rest of regiment.[31] Included were Cpl. Ridgeway and 1Sgt. Gravino—no strangers to combat of any nature.

Stanley Raymond Mills was born at Potlatch, Idaho, a few miles north of Moscow, on August 8, 1920, the son of George Mills, a farmer from California, and Marie Andersen, a Danish immigrant. By 1930, the family lived in Andrew Springs, Benewah County, in a small home, with three little bedrooms, a tiny kitchen, and a potbellied stove in the teeny living room. No indoor plumbing, no bathroom—but the family has a wooden path to the outhouse.

Stanley attended the University of Idaho in Moscow from 1938 to 1942. Studying was not the only subject on the curriculum; he meets another student, Marie Jakobine "Mere" Havens, and the pair soon go to quite a few dances together. Stanley, a very reserved and reticent young man with dark, wavy hair, could become a scrapper when needed. As Stan's daughter recalled, "Presumably, Mom had a thing for the strong, silent type: Dad actually punched some guy in the face at one of the dances because they were literally fighting over Mom."

Stanley graduated with a degree in agronomy in 1942, marrying Mere on May 31 at Kendrick, Idaho, and entering the Army shortly afterward. Reporting to Camp Robinson, Arkansas, for officer training, Stan wrote Mere: "We went out yesterday morning and just like that teacher says, 'Mills, you be Platoon leader,' so now I have a platoon of officers. Aren't you proud of me, though? (They are more stubborn than a lot of mules and march the same way)." Stan arrived in Company B in North Africa in 1943 and became a rifle platoon leader, before rising to company executive officer.

However, Stan is facing another demon in addition to the Germans. After experiencing weakness in her legs, Mere is diagnosed with multiple sclerosis; the doctor says that she will probably never walk again and that she should not have children. Stan receives the news in England; on March 19, 1944, he sends a telegram home: "Darling, sincerely hope you are better . . . please cable . . . remember, I love you honey . . . just loads hugs and kisses." But with a war on, Stanley can't come home to help her.[32]

The men receive typhoid and typhus shots on February 21, and tetanus shots three days later. The 39th Infantry establishes support relations with the 26th Field Artillery Battalion, 1st Platoon of Company A of the 15th Engineer Battalion, and Company A of the 9th Medical Battalion, which will last the entire war. The division nickname changes. It was originally "the Varsity," in reference to high school and college athletic teams, but someone decides that the name isn't good enough—this being war and not sports. Talented Lindsey Nelson, veteran of the Town Pump, is tasked with developing a new one and discovers a letter from the Vth Corps commander lauding the division's performance and calling the troops "the Old Reliables." Nelson passes the sobriquet to the division chief of staff. It sticks.

On March 22–24, 1944, Gen. Eisenhower, and British prime minister Winston Churchill visit AAAO; Churchill inspects First Battalion in ranks. Maj. Gen. J. Lawton Collins, new VIIth Corps commander, also inspects the regiment. It is a big deal; even Gen. Henry H. "Hap" Arnold, chief of the Army Air Forces, is in attendance, because almost everyone knows Paddy Flint. Later, after a USO show, Col. Flint remarks, "My band can put on a better show than that," and he orders Bennie "the Deacon" Nardone, a thirty-year-old from Columbus, Ohio, and now leader of the "Black Market Band," to rustle up the group, grab a few more men with entertaining skill, and put on a competitive show. While the band assembles, Paddy—understanding the power of a home crowd—orders a battalion to attend the show as spectators.[33] There is no record of who won, other than the soldiers in attendance.

Gray clouds threaten the horizon; talk reignites that older officers should not serve overseas in combat positions. Flint is crestfallen and takes the issue straight to his old plebe, Dwight Eisenhower. Ike is frustrated—not with Paddy but in the policy—and writes back to the old cavalry colonel: "Paddy, your request to stay with your outfit will be fulfilled—no one in my headquarters will deprive you of the right of command-ing the 39th Infantry on the Invasion."[34]

Meanwhile, Langley Turner falls ill with malaria, likely contracted in North Africa or Sicily.

His illness cannot happen at a worse time, because Company B has an imminent date with a place called Normandy. Training continues at Camp Barton Stacey, England, until the morning of May 27, when the 9th Infantry goes on six-hour-alert status. After the first-wave units proceed to English coastal ports, the division begins moving to marshaling areas on the afternoon of June 3. Six officers and 175 enlisted in Company B board the SS *Empire Lance* at Southampton late on June 9 for the voyage across the English Channel. The 7,177-ton vessel approaches within sight of the French coast, where the men transfer to an LCT (landing craft tank) at 1215 hours on June 10, D-plus 4, and in thirty minutes are on Normandy's Utah Beach.

SCHOOL OF THE SOLDIER

YOUR HELMET

The headgear that Gen. Eddy showed Gen. Bradley is perhaps the most iconic battle helmet America has ever had. Less than impressed with the helmet from the Great War, in 1941 the Army rolls out the new M1 helmet. Known as the "Steel Pot," it has a slight brim on its front, to keep rain off a soldier's face, and a slightly lipped rim all the way around, with the sides also trailing down to cover half of the soldier's ears before dropping down to cover the back part of his head. The 2.85-pound manganese steel outer shell cannot stop most close-range bullets or shrapnel hits but offers better coverage of the face and skull than ever before.

Taking the idea for the inside from the liner of Riddell football helmets of the period, the separate helmet liner uses adjustable webbing connected together that can be tightened or loosened, so the helmet conforms to the soldier's head more precisely. It is when the liner is temporarily removed, done with a firm jerk, that the helmet becomes a wondrous household appliance. A soldier can dig with it, pour water into it to shave, or use it as a small portable washing pot for his socks and underwear. He can even heat water in it over a small fire, take a washcloth, and bathe himself. Although the practice is discouraged, because repeated heating could make the metal alloy brittle, the helmet can serve as a cooking pot, since soldiers fill it halfway up with water and make soup, adding whatever they can forage from the countryside. If you get lucky and scrounge up a couple of eggs, you can fire up scrambled eggs in a jiffy.

Now for the chinstrap. Stories abound about troopers, with strap buckled, having a nearby explosion blowing the helmet off their head, causing severe neck injuries. Barracks' gossip even spreads that a soldier had his head ripped off by a nearby blast when his chinstrap was buckled. The chinstrap myth is inaccurate, but the Army develops the T1 Chin Strap Release for the express purpose of allaying soldiers' fears.[35]

As much as any other unit in the Army, the 39th Infantry takes pride in their helmets. While intelligence officers up and down the line get ulcers at the thought of poor operational security, the men delight in stenciling their regimental motto of AAAO on the left side of the helmet. In 1943, then regimental commander Paddy Flint justified the breach in intelligence by stating,[36] "The enemy, who sees our regiment in combat, if they live through the battle, will know to run the next time they see us coming." Whether Paddy's justification was accurate or not, there is no doubt that the men in AAAO stand a little taller wearing it.

PRIVATE SNAFU

On September 20, 1943, the Army releases episode 5 of its *Private Snafu* series of short black-and-white films, the first having premiered the previous June. The cartoons are meant to improve troop morale by instructing soldiers about military subjects such as sanitation, booby traps, and camouflage, demonstrating the negative consequences of doing things incorrectly. Each Warner Brothers Studio four-minute cartoon takes about six weeks to produce. Directed by Frank Capra, most are written by Theodor Geisel, who will later become better known as Dr. Seuss.

None of the twenty-four episodes were to be shown to the general public without the permission of the War Department, so the Production Code Administration does not monitor content, frequently scatological and sexual, which remains uncensored. The five-note musical introduction to each episode is known as "You're a Horse's Ass." The principal character may be the sorriest soldier to ever don a uniform. He is unable to accomplish simple tasks, and his name springs from a military saying of the day: "Situation Normal, All Fouled Up," although many GIs substituted another word for "fouled." Probably no GI ever thought that Private Snafu—goofy, ignorant, and obnoxious—was just like he was, but almost every soldier sure knew a few sergeants and lieutenants who in comparison made Snafu look like Alexander the Great.

"Episode 5—the Infantry Blues" has the intent to inform viewers that every job in the military is important and has its own hardships, but infantrymen especially delight in the episode's introductory poem, narrated by Mel Blanc—perhaps the most recognizable voice in the US for his portrayal of Bugs Bunny and Porky Pig. Mel invented a nasal version of his Bugs Bunny's "Brooklynese" for the part of Snafu, who laments,[37]

> Ah, the Air Force gets the glory. And the Navy gets the cheers. But all the dogface ever gets is mud behind the ears. Yeah, the tank boys ride in comfort. And the sailor takes a sail. But the dogface never gets a chance to sit down on his tail. Poor feet in my shoes. I've got them Infantry Blues.

COMBAT FATIGUE

No one wants to talk about "it." George Patton is once relieved for how he reacts to "it." No one truly knows how many soldiers suffer from "it." But "it" is real. According to one wartime survey, almost 90 percent of GIs had seen a close friend killed or wounded, and 83 percent had seen someone "crack up" in battle, either from an event happening to them or a fellow soldier, or after the GI had killed someone.[38] There is a steady progression to emotional collapse, and one potential sign is a self-inflicted wound or injury, where an inquiry may have to determine what really happened.

Standard treatment at the hospital, upon the arrival of a soldier believed to be suffering from combat fatigue, is to give him sodium amytal so he'll sleep for three days, awaking only to use the latrine, and in many cases he has to be assisted in doing that. If he cannot eat, doctors give him intravenous saline solutions. Docs take him to the showers, where he stands under warm soothing water. Since psychiatrists are scarce at forward hospitals, other medical personnel attempt to explain his condition to him, but because of the shortage of infantrymen, they—and he—know that he will be going back up to the line again.

Because the soldier knows that a diagnosis of "combat fatigue" will not get him tossed into the stockade—unless he does something truly stupid and deserts—this is a way to leave the front, if only for a short time. He's not bucking for a "Section Eight," not wanting this harsh, psychiatric discharge. As a result, combat fatigue casualties may cycle off the front three or four times, or more, before war's end.[39]

MUSTANGS

A "mustang" is an American military slang term for a commissioned officer who first served in the enlisted ranks but later receives a battlefield commission or selection to commissioned officer, on the basis of experience. Mustangs were, in theory, more experienced than their peers who had entered the Army via West Point or the Reserve Officer Training Corps, especially in understanding enlisted soldiers. The term refers to a mustang horse, which might always have a wild streak but can better survive danger, due to its feral instincts, than can a domesticated horse. Infantry divisions needed mustangs, and every other source of lieutenants, since in combat they lose the equivalent of a full complement of second lieutenants every eighty-eight days.[40]

OFFICERS AND SERGEANTS

In American infantry units, officers and sergeants (noncommissioned officers) have different responsibilities in combat. Officers (lieutenants, captains, majors, et al.) plan battles, allocate resources, and maneuver units to get a tactical advantage in the fighting. Planning the fight is pretty obvious: What is our mission? What will the enemy do and in what strength? What assets do we have for the fight?—all these are key questions that officers must answer. Officers then develop a concept of operations, and away we go. Allocated resources may be tank platoons, sometimes temporarily attached, or perhaps combat engineers to help you through a minefield. It can also be supporting artillery, so officers work with the cannon cockers to plan fire missions. In the attack, officers decide which elements will lay down a base of fire to suppress the enemy and which elements will move forward and assault. In the defense, officers try to determine where the enemy will attack, and establish defenses to stop him, including which defensive sector will have priority of artillery support.

Officers, of course, carry their own weapons—often an M1 carbine or a Colt 1911A1 pistol, or even an M1 Garand rifle. Their mission does not depend on using their weapons, except perhaps when a platoon is ambushed, and everyone has to shoot their way out. Officers know that every time they fire their own weapon, they are not doing what they really should be doing, and that is directing the efforts of their soldiers.

Sergeants actually lead the fight. Their basic mantra is "Follow me and do as I do." Sergeants fire their weapons—not so much as to obtain a hit, but to give direction to the squad or platoon to fire at the same target. Sergeants evaluate the best marksman in the squad and then assign that soldier the BAR—since you want your deadliest shot "going to town" with that bad boy. Sergeants often lead patrols, because they often have a better feel for the unknown and can respond quicker than a new lieutenant, who might overanalyze the situation. Overanalyzing anything in combat takes time, and in many life-and-death situations you have to immediately go with your gut instinct. Neither an officer's job nor a sergeant's job in infantry combat is more important than the other; they just do different things that complement one another.

COMBAT INFANTRYMAN BADGE

Of perhaps all the awards that an infantryman could earn, and all the "fruit salad" (slang for medals and ribbons) he could wear—if interviews with veterans are accurate—the Combat Infantryman Badge is that for which he is proudest. The War Department formally establishes the award on October 27, 1943 (eligibility was backdated to December 7, 1941), because[41]

> the present war has demonstrated the importance of highly proficient, tough, hard, and aggressive infantry, which can be obtained only by developing a high degree of individual all-around proficiency on the part of every infantryman. As a means of attaining the high standards desired and to foster esprit de corps in infantry units, the Expert Infantryman and the Combat Infantryman badges are established for infantry personnel.

That is certainly correct, but an ugly truth is that infantrymen operate under the worst conditions, often continuously, suffer the highest casualties, and receive the least public recognition. An uglier truth is that the US Army is having difficulty recruiting infantry volunteers. The criteria state that the recipient of the CIB must be an infantryman at the rank of colonel or below, in a unit of any size but smaller than a brigade, who fought in active ground combat. Perhaps perusing the casualty lists from D-day, the US Congress jumps on board on June 30, 1944, approving an extra ten dollars per month to every enlisted infantryman. Hundreds of soldiers assigned to Company B during the war received the CIB, and all of them earned it.

BOB HOPE

"The European theater was a little like vaudeville," Bob Hope once quips. Of all the Hollywood stars who visit the troops, Bob Hope is the most beloved, not the most popular—that achievement might go to Lana Turner or Rita Hayworth, who, to borrow a line from a popular song of the day, had "the chassis that made Lassie come home," while Bob Hope just had a big schnoz. Bob Hope and the Hollywood Victory Caravan— his "Gypsies"—begin performing for military audiences in May 1941. The organization transforms into United Service Organizations (USOs) and starts touring in September 1942, beginning with bases in Alaska, England, and Northern Ireland. Tweaking senior leaders—to the delight of enlisted soldiers—Hope finds out what the peccadillos are on a base and pokes fun at them.

Bob jokes about women and sex, and the soldiers scream in approval. And then he jokes about sex and women, and the troops cheer some more. With a nickname of "Packy East" from his early boxing days, he never makes fun of the soldiers but always makes light of their situation. GIs who hear him in person will remember the punch lines delivered with perfect timing for the rest of their days: "You remember girls!" or "Isn't it wonderful what you can do with Spam?" More importantly, Bob Hope passes on what he sees to the loved ones of these soldiers—who view his visits overseas as vicarious travels they cannot make: "I was there. I saw your sons and your husbands, your brothers, and your sweethearts. I saw how they worked, played, fought, and lived. I saw some of them die. I saw more courage, more good humor in the face of discomfort, more love in an era of hate and more devotion to duty than could exist under tyranny."[42]

THE ARMY WAY

There's an old saying that every GI has heard a thousand times: "The right way, the wrong way, and the Army way," which refers to how the Army does things. But prior to understanding how the Army operates, you have to understand how the Army is organized, especially the infantry. On March 18, 1944, the Army publishes *Field Manual 7-10, Rifle Company, Rifle Regiment*, defining infantry squad composition as twelve men: a sergeant as squad leader, a corporal—later a sergeant—as assistant squad leader, a three-man automatic-rifle team, two scouts armed with rifles, and five riflemen. Three rifle squads together make a rifle platoon, led by a lieutenant. The platoon has a little headquarters of five soldiers (platoon leader, platoon sergeant, a staff sergeant—sometimes termed the platoon guide, and two messengers, also known as runners). Thus, at full strength a rifle platoon fields forty-one soldiers.

Put together three rifle platoons; add a weapons platoon led by a first lieutenant, with sometimes a junior lieutenant as his assistant, that has a 60 mm mortar section with a total of nineteen men and three M2 60 mm mortars, a light machine gun section with fourteen soldiers and two M1919A4 medium .30-caliber machine guns, and a weapons platoon headquarters of six men (a total of thirty-nine men); and tack on a company headquarters of twenty-one personnel, and you have a rifle company, which at full strength has 184 troops. Seven are commissioned officers, the senior one a captain and company commander. The second in command, known as the executive officer, is usually a first lieutenant: during combat, he controls the company CP and keeps in contact with the battalion.

However, there are other soldiers right alongside, technically assigned to the medical battalion, often three medics and sometimes litter bearers to evacuate casualties. As a line company first sergeant, don't forget your two jeeps with trailers, your single .50-caliber machine gun, and your five 2.36-inch rocket launchers, known as "bazookas." The company also is authorized three M1903 Springfield bolt-action sniper rifles; make sure good marksmen have these.

Somewhere up in the Land of Oz is "First Battalion," usually led by a lieutenant colonel or a major, normally with three rifle companies (A, B, and C) and a heavy-weapons company (Company D) with six 81 mm mortars and four .30-caliber machine guns. It might have an antitank platoon with three 57 mm antitank guns and a few bazookas—good luck if your target is the front slope of a Kraut Tiger or Panther, because you don't have any ruby slippers and you can't just say, "There's no place like home." The battalion also has a headquarters company, doing yeoman's work fixing and replacing weapons, maintaining vehicles, and pushing supplies and food to the line, and all they receive from the troops below is to be called "ash and trash"—unless the line doggies really need something pronto.

WOUNDS

Infantrymen have their own slang for wounds. A slight wound, which a civilian would term a cut, is now called a "teaser," hinting that something else more significant is yet to come. That might be a puncture wound, termed a "ride" because it gets you a ride back to a medical facility for treatment, but within days you're back in your unit. Up the scale is the "million dollar" wound, but despite the scuttlebutt, it only gets you evacuated to England and a few weeks, or even a month, of rehabilitation. At the top of the ladder is the "Big Gal with the Torch," a "Statue of Liberty" wound that obviously suggests that you will be heading back to the States for advanced medical treatment. Likely you will then go to an assignment stateside—perhaps in an administrative job training other soldiers so that they can go out and get their own wounds.[43]

Medics and doctors are expert at wounds, unfortunately because they see so many of them. Artillery and mortar shrapnel wounds are jagged because the fragments are jagged. They have so much force from the explosion of the shells that the shrapnel sometimes goes all the way through your body. Kraut potato-masher grenades, with less explosive powder, produce shrapnel that often does not go completely through an arm or a leg. Sometimes a jagged piece of a tree is sticking out of a bloody hole in a soldier, usually caused by enemy artillery bursting up in the trees, causing the limbs and trunk to splinter. The good news is that these pieces may not be flying quite as fast as the steel shrapnel, which is no comfort when you're hit.

Rifle bullet wounds can be difficult to distinguish from a machine gun, since both weapons fire the same-caliber round. If a soldier has one bullet hole in him, that could have been caused by either; if he has three or four holes, he probably got machine-gunned. Then there are burns, caused sometimes by phosphorus, or a tank on fire, or at times by enemy flamethrowers. You get burned badly and you are going home. Combat fatigue is a mental "wound," but you're never getting a Purple Heart for it. Hospital "wards with shattered and missing arms and legs were bad, but hospitals with vacant and missing minds were worse."[44]

CHAPTER THREE

The Americans Are Coming! Across France and Belgium

The reason the American Army does so well in wartime is that war is chaos, and the American Army practices it on a daily basis.

—A captured German general[1]

The company attacks the village of Saint-Marcouf on June 12 against the German 919th Grenadier Regiment of the 709th Infantry Division. It is a rude awakening; four troopers are killed and another nineteen are wounded crossing an open field—and it's mined! The battalion commander, Lt. Col. Phil Tinley, is hit by a sniper on June 13; two medics put him on a stretcher. During the evacuation, an enemy mortar shell or a mine explodes under them, killing all three men. Maj. Henry P. Tucker assumes command; he will be submitted for a Silver Star five days later and promoted to lieutenant colonel on June 29 by Col. Flint.[2]

Jessie "Doc" Slaughter, a medic for Company B, casts a long shadow from the Lone Star State, because when a buddy calls, "Medic!," Doc runs through hell to get to him. Born in Groveton, Trinity County, on August 16, 1922, the son of Claude Kennedy Slaughter—a farmer—and Cora Bell Hawthorne, he has two younger sisters and two younger brothers. Life is tough in the Depression, and Jessie drops out of school in fourth grade to help his father. But he's just a boy, and if he has a minute to spare, he loves going fishing or hunting. On June 30, 1942, Jessie registers for the draft; he already knows what responsibility means, since he is married to fifteen-year-old Eva Marie Kelley. On November 16, 1942, Jessie enlists at Tyler, Texas; he is 5'9" and weighs 139 pounds, with blue eyes and brown hair. The couple's first child, Jessie W., is born on February 13, 1943, but tragically dies four months later. People who know Doc say he is a man who never wants any praise and will do anything for you—that will save countless lives.[3]

Company B attacks toward the village of Orglandes, defended by the 1058th Grenadier Regiment of the 91st Air Landing Division and five more men are wounded. More ominously, the soldiers make the acquaintance of the 603rd Quartermaster Graves Registration Company—the men who have to bury the dead. Combat is ferocious. The company supply sergeant, Al Baccile, recalled: "The machine gun barrels, and mortar tubes all needed replacing after the fray [they burned out from continuous firing.]"[4]

The battalion withdraws under heavy machine gun fire but retakes the town a day later. Battle often begins at daylight, about 0545 hours, and continues until 2300 hours.

For combat on June 16, Jack Dunlap is recommended for the Silver Star. German troops and tanks counterattack the battalion on June 18 southeast of Bricquebec; the company repels the assault, losing six killed and five wounded. The next day, Bricquebec falls, but another soldier is killed and five more are wounded. Paddy Flint is slightly wounded but remains with the regiment. Ed Perry later recalled morale:[5]

> The morale of the men at this time was not high, nor could it be called particularly low, they had fought a long way since landing on Utah Beach and many of them had fought in Sicily and Africa. To them, war was a deadly game. You ate when you could and slept whenever you were not fighting or eating. The end of one situation usually meant the beginning of another.

Morale may not have been high, but extraordinary heroism certainly was:

CITATION OF 1ST BATTALION, 39th INFANTRY

The 1st Battalion, 39th Infantry, is cited for extraordinary heroism in action on the morning of 18 June 1944 near St. Jacques de Néhou, France. The battalion fought off and later crushed the 1049th Infantry Regiment and other elements of the German 77th Division attempting to break out of the Cotentin Peninsula.

The battalion was in an assembly area when the German forces launched a fierce surprise attack at about 0430 hour. When heavy firing broke out, the troops were quickly alerted by the outposts and placed in position to meet the enemy threat. Bazooka teams went into action and stopped two tank thrusts, despite heavy casualties suffered by the teams. The troops heroically held off two numerically superior and fanatic enemy attempts to surround the battalion's positions by flanking movements; then the battalion commander ordered his men into a new position astride the St. Colombe–St. Jacques de Néhou road. In spite of the intense fire and proximity of the enemy, the battalion moved into the new position in an orderly manner, fighting doggedly and courageously over every inch of the new ground. During this move, communications were cut, isolating the battalion from supporting units.

Braving the intense enemy artillery, mortar, and machine gun fire, the wire section reestablished wire communication with division headquarters. After communications were regained, an artillery concentration was requested to precede a counterattack. With the artillery and all the mortars and heavy weapons of the battalion laying a devastating barrage, the troops eagerly jumped off in the attack, closely following the artillery barrage. The attack gained momentum as the troops aggressively and valiantly fought their way forward, driving the enemy from the high ground and across the Seye River, where they were strafed by Allied aircraft.

This crushing defeat of a German regiment and supporting elements of the 77th Division insured [*sic*] the successful capture by the 9th Infantry Division the following day of the objective at St. Christophe de Foc, 14 kilometers north of Bricquebec, and completely destroyed the striking power of this German division in the Cherbourg Peninsula. This action was the final effort of the 77th Division to break out of the Cherbourg pocket. The relentless drive of the battalion resulted in the death of Major General Stegmann, commanding general of the 77th Division, and over 300 of his men, as compared to 36 casualties suffered by the battalion. This decisive and costly defeat of the enemy was a tribute to the exceptional gallantry, aggressiveness, and determination of each member of the battalion, and exemplifies the highest ideals of military service.

Replacements continue to arrive to replace the fallen. Billie, sometimes called "Willie," Flowers is a scrapper. Born in Lumberton, North Carolina, on March 2, 1924, he is the son of Ophelia "Apie" Atkinson and James Milton Flowers. The family lives in mixed White, Black, and Lumbee and Tuscarora tribal communities of Back Swamp in Robeson County. James and other local farmers form a mutual-aid cooperative and communally farm the land. Billie has ten siblings. In 1940, at age sixteen, he is still in the fifth grade. Leaving school the next year, he has trouble reading and writing. Billie is 5'2" tall and 158 pounds, with blue eyes, brown hair, and a ruddy complexion. Single, he enlists at Fort Bragg on September 23, 1943, arrives in France on June 17, and gets to Company B from the 18th Replacement Depot three days later.[6]

~~AAA~~O rolls north through Quettetot to Octeville, where Company B captures 250 prisoners, when that Cherbourg suburb falls to the regiment.[7] After the 9th captures Cherbourg, Company B moves west to Sainte-Croix-Hague, ending the month at Branville-Hague. For the division, 390 men are killed and 1,851 troops wounded in June 1944.[8] From June 12 to July 1, Company B loses twelve killed, thirty-seven wounded, and three seriously injured. The 39th is pulled off the line for a brief rest; Warren Ridgeway makes staff sergeant on July 3. Hawk DiRisio writes the next day:[9]

We landed shortly after the invasion forces and I, as mess sergeant, along with my cooks, marched with the troops since there was no use for the kitchen when C rations would be more convenient. So they called us "combat cooks" and real soldiers and for two weeks we marched and fought attached to platoons. If you have followed the headlines, you have read about the counterattack by the enemy (the 77th Panzer Division) [actually the 77th Infantry Division] after our 9th Division had them trapped. I was on sentry duty in the early morning and heard tanks in the distance, but like the other sentries we thought them to be "ours" but later that morning I was awakened by my section leader (I was ammunition carrier in the machine gun section) and told the enemy was counterattacking, and within a few minutes we were lined up along the hedges shooting like cowboys.

We were only three companies against a spear-head regiment of Germans. I heard their shouting voices, blowing whistles and what not. We were surprised but they too. They thought the coast was clear. Being veteran soldiers, everybody stood their ground, and our mortars and machine guns held the enemy until our artillery "zeroed" in and what a show! The enemy was slaughtered! All in all, 350 Germans were killed just a couple hundred yards in front of us. Our mortar and machine gun men were heroes, and it can be said that just three companies of our battalion saved a catastrophe.

Funny things happen even in battle. In the middle of the action, a dozen cows moved up in front of our machine gun. My section leader swore at them and attempted to scare them away with empty cartridges but to no avail. So, we mowed them down one after another, until we had a clear "field of fire." The papers and the radio give *boucoup* news on our Ninth Division so keep your eyes and ears open. I, and my cooks, are now back in the kitchen and feeding hot meals to our "B Company Killers," a nickname we're earning.

Company B returns to action on July 10 at Le Dézert. Capt. Perry is seriously wounded; 1Lt. Dunlap takes command. 1Lt. McLaughlin becomes executive officer. Twelve men are wounded as Company B captures the village. But the battalion is in danger on the boundary with the 30th Infantry Division. Early on July 11, a battalion of the 901st Panzer Grenadier Lehr Regiment, of the Panzer Lehr Division, augmented by two companies of antitank guns, attacks along the boundary pushing toward Isigny to strike at the beachheads. After hard fighting all day, the attack is repulsed in an action that will win Distinguished Unit Citations for the Second Battalion of the 39th Infantry and Companies A and C of the 899th Tank Destroyer Battalion. Company B is in the thick of the fighting; eight more men are wounded.

Of all the divisions in the German army, the Panzer Lehr Division is not only one of the most elite, but also one of the most powerful. Formed in 1943, Panzer Lehr is the only unit fully equipped with tanks and half-tracks to transport its infantry—other panzer divisions transport some infantry in trucks. At its core, the division has a large component of expert, highly decorated panzer and infantry instructors from elite training and demonstration units, including the 1st and 2nd Panzer Troops Schools and the 901st Panzer Grenadier Lehr Regiment; many have five years of combat experience. Colonel Georg Scholze, a Knight's Cross of the Iron Cross winner in command of the 901st at Le Dézert, is so hard core that he will shoot himself a week before the end of the war rather than face Germany's defeat.

Panzer Lehr fields two tank battalions, one of Mark IVs, the other with Mark V Panther tanks. It has a handful of Tiger I heavy tanks. The guns on the Panthers and Tigers can bust open any American tank they engage. Commanding Panzer Lehr is Major General Hyacinth Graf Strachwitz von Gross-Zauche und Camminetz, who

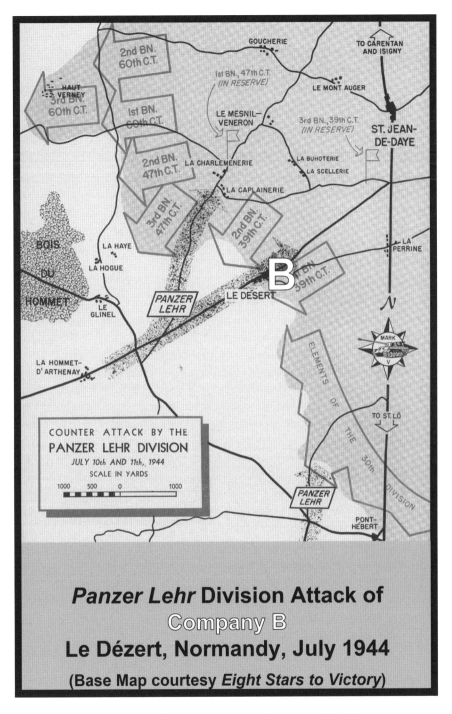

MAP 4: Panzer Lehr Division Attack of Company B, Le Dézert, Normandy, July 1944

has a distinguished combat résumé even longer than his name. With the Knights Cross of the Iron Cross with Oak Leaves, Swords, and Diamonds, he has fought almost continuously since 1939 and been wounded twelve times. Panzer Lehr is the perfect division to push the Allies into the sea.

Nine more men in Company B are wounded on July 12—twenty-nine in three days. Combat near Le Dézert continues; on July 15 three men are killed and five wounded. Over the next three days, the wounded number two, three, and six, respectively, as the company captures high ground near the village of Fief Autin. On July 18, artillery strikes the right flank of Company B, killing several soldiers and wounding many more. It was initially assumed to be enemy fire, but a sergeant finds a fuze plug of a US 155 mm shell in the mess. After several calls to regiment, firing ceases.[10] July 19 is worse: two men are killed and five wounded. On July 20, the company bivouacs 300 yards north of the village of La Cauture; artillery wounds nine more. Pvt. Lionel Martin is reported to be missing in action during an artillery barrage on July 21. He may have deserted.

July 24: First Sergeant Gravino starts seeing double. But all is well; it's just Raymond and Robert Kalvitz, nineteen-year-old twins from Cleveland, Ohio, jumping off the replacements' truck together. Sons of August and Gertrude—who is a native German and a seamstress—they're 5'4" tall, have hazel eyes, and worked for Briggs Manufacturing, which formerly built car bodies but now churns out a billion dollars' worth of aluminum parts for heavy bombers. Company B is a mile east of La Chapelle-en-Juger on July 25; casualties are three killed and six wounded. Jack Dunlap is submitted for an Oak Leaf Cluster to his Silver Star.

For July 24, the regiment loses sixteen killed, fifty-eight wounded, and two missing. All deaths are tragic, but some have seismic effects. At 1700 hours, Col. Harry Flint is mortally wounded in the head near Saint-Lô by a German sniper. A sergeant returns fire, dropping the marksman, perched high in a nearby tree. A litter jeep arrives and carries Flint to the 34th Evacuation Hospital at Carentan. Gen. Eddy directs Lt. Col. Van Bond, the 39th Infantry executive officer, to assume command at 1755 hours.

At 1917 hours, a radio report indicates that the bullet had not penetrated Paddy's skull, but an operation is required to remove a large blood clot, caused when the bullet blew a thumb-size skull fragment into his brain. An Indiana neurosurgeon, Maj. Calvin Basil Fausset, operates, but to no avail. Paddy hangs on to life as long as he can but dies the following day, July 25. He is temporarily interred at the United States Military Cemetery Number 2 at Sainte-Mère-Église in Normandy. George Patton, Lawton Collins, and Manton Eddy attend the burial service.

Manton Eddy, realizing that this is a perilous moment for the regiment, insists that Lt. Col. Bond receive an immediate, as in *tout suite*, battlefield promotion and take permanent—not temporary—command of AAAO. Bond understands how Flint's leadership inspired the regiment and how that leadership can still hold the unit together. Collins and Bradley agree. Van Bond (West Point, 1931) will fill those big boots, a battalion commander in the 39th Infantry later says:[11]

Colonel Van Hugo Bond personified his Alma Mater's duty-honor-country precepts in all our contacts. Most of all he was poised. I saw him under all sorts of pressure, but he never indicated anything but a deep interest in what was going on. He had a great tactical sense, and by this, I mean he could quickly look at the terrain, or its depiction on a map, and properly judge its meaning for both sides. He knew his weapons. He set the example. Bond had a great gift of giving simple, direct, verbal orders.

The move works, and the regiment rolls on, but losses remain heavy. During July, Company B loses eleven killed, seventy-one wounded, five missing, and six seriously injured. For the 9th Infantry, 712 soldiers are killed and 2,989 troops are wounded.

On August 1, mess sergeant DiRisio "procures" another cow for Company B; First Army is now commanded by Lt. Gen. Courtney H. Hodges, who takes over from Omar Bradley. Medics evacuate Warren Ridgeway from the front for illness on August 4. The next day, the battalion attacks toward La Huilliere under a terrific enemy artillery bombardment. 2Lt. and platoon leader Roger Reeves is wounded on August 6 as the battalion defends the village from attacking Germans. One man is killed and seven are wounded. The backblast of a bazooka severely burns Sgt. Michael Szollosy's face. You can't be anywhere behind it when it rips.

Defending just east of the village of Le Reussel, on August 7, Company B tries a new tactic. Using two .50-caliber machine guns (the second one possibly scrounged) on tripods, the company conducts overhead fire, firing the rounds over the heads of friendly troops from their rear. The tracer rounds ignite several enemy-occupied, grass-covered buildings in front of the unit's left flank.[12] The company loses one killed and five wounded. August 9 is rough; again, one soldier is killed and five are wounded, including 1Lt. Ernest McLaughlin, company executive officer. Stanley Mills becomes the new exec. Hoosier SSgt. Julius Kenda is submitted for a Bronze Star for heroic achievement.[13] The First Battalion, 39th Infantry, receives a Distinguished Unit Citation for stopping the German counteroffensive from Mortain between August 6 and 9.

A surprise German rocket attack on August 10 sets fire to buildings occupied by the battalion CP. In the scurry to escape, two trucks carrying mines and ammunition catch fire and explode behind Company B.[14] West Virginian private John Wood and Pfc. Paul Allen, from Illinois, are killed—both are nineteen—and one soldier is wounded as the company attacks and seizes high ground north of Le Mont-Turgon on August 11. On August 12, two men are wounded in the attack on Les Verges, and First Sergeant Gravino is cited for bravery, after he attempts to rescue wounded men under fire; the next day, artillery shrapnel wounds Joe in the wrist.[15] August 14 sees the division advancing north through Couptrain toward the Falaise Gap as 1Lt. Jack Jewell joins the company, and he writes home: "It's a wonderful job that our men are doing here. You can read about it and you may see it in the movies, but you can't realize how enormous and difficult a task it has been. It's no wonder to me that they waited so long for the invasion. It just had to be a success."[16]

Jack Jewell, born on October 5, 1919, in Ottawa, Kansas, will be a rock—a steadying influence—in the company for the rest of the war. Son of Heman "Heam" Everest Jewell—an assistant bank cashier born in Kentucky and raised in Missouri—and Norma Estell Kathrens from Flagstaff, Arizona, who moved to Kansas when she was two, he spends his childhood in Wellsville, Kansas, graduating from Wellsville High School in a class of seventeen students in 1937. Death has already taken a toll on Heam's family by the time Jack is born; Heam's first wife dies four days after giving birth to Jack's oldest half sibling, while Jack's older sister dies at age thirteen months in 1918. After high school, Jack enrolls at the University of Kansas, finishing sophomore year in 1940.

Jack departs school that summer and works at Star Train and Lumber Company, registering for the draft on October 5; he is 6'1" and 150 pounds, with blue eyes and brown hair. He is drafted on July 2, 1941; commissioned a second lieutenant on May 19, 1942; promoted to first lieutenant in June 1943; and assigned to the 417th Infantry Regiment in the 76th Infantry Division at Camp McCoy, Wisconsin, training and testing winter equipment. Jack arrived in France about July 26; now he is the weapons platoon leader.[17]

Cpl. Chester McClurg is winning the race for company bad boy, absent without leave (AWOL) for at least the third time that summer, but the problem is that today, five men go over the hill. Three days later, Company B, losing five wounded, advances into the Falaise Gap and contacts the British near the town of Briouze. Jack Dunlap is promoted to captain on August 18. More replacements arrive. Edward Arnold Pickard is born on November 17, 1922, in Mumford, Tipton County, Tennessee, to Charles Russell Pickard, a farmer and Great War veteran, and Mary Geneva Greggs. Edward, whose parents divorced when he is a toddler, has two brothers and two sisters. He finishes the seventh grade; he marries Martha Nell Perdue in 1942. Registering for the draft on June 30, 1942, he is 5'9", 155 pounds, and unemployed. Edward enlists on August 1, 1943; on September 4, 1943, his son Ronald Edward is born in Missouri.[18]

Maj. Gen. Louis A. Craig assumes command of the 9th Infantry on August 19 from Maj. Gen. Manton Eddy, who is elevated to command the XIIth US Corps. Near Briouze, TSgt. Langley Turner, is wounded by shrapnel in his left knee, back, and head but remains at the front, while Pfc. Henry Rolewski gets a nasty phosphorus burn to his right thumb from an artillery shell. Jack Jewell hints on the action: "We had a little run-in with some of Hitler's boys and we had to get 'em straight on a few things."[19] But at least Company B is eating well, as Jack writes on August 20: "We had good chow today, steak and peas and spuds."[20] The company moves to Bouvillerie on August 22; the division has received the mission to help prevent the retreating German Seventh Army from breaking through. More importantly, the company buys a farmer's cow, so Hawk will be grilling.[21] Military police at the Normandy Base Section place Pvt. Lionel Martin under arrest for desertion on August 23; he had been declared MIA the previous month. Jack sends another letter August 25:[22]

As I told you, this is a good outfit and I'm in a fairly good company. The 9th Division has one of the best records in the Army and has been in some plenty hot places. I have some NCOs in my platoon that were in Africa and Sicily, so you see they are not green by any means. . . . Last week the Company went to one of those portable showers. We all had hot showers and turned in our dirty clothes for clean ones. Our food is fairly good. I have eaten much better, but it is hard to do cooking under these conditions. We buy fresh spuds, carrots, milk, butter, and beef from French farmers. I have been in several towns shortly after their liberation and the people are all out waving at the GI soldiers and giving them cider and wine. There is plenty of wine here but very few of the men get too much.

The division reaches the Seine River southeast of Paris on August 26; at 0742 hours the next day the 39th Infantry crosses at Melun. The next day they "received a very warm welcome from the French People of Coulommiers, as they were celebrating. . . . The streets were packed with civilians."[23] One of the soldiers not marching through Coulommiers is Pfc. Alfred Cusimano from New Orleans—not because he does not want to, but because he cannot. Seventeen days ago, a mortar round hit Al, a veteran of North Africa and Sicily, causing wounds so gruesome that doctors amputate both his legs. He'll be discharged from the Army, never work again, and die in 1956. On August 29, the 9th crosses the Marne River near Chateau Thierry. Capt. Dunlap records the event on the company morning report.

Today history repeated itself to a certain degree as the 39th Infantry found itself in the same area that it had fought so gallantly for in the last war. The company left a bivouac area four miles north of Coulommiers, France, at 0700 hours and using the shuttle system, part walking, part riding, covered 24 miles crossing the historic Marne River and reaching an area in the vicinity of Monthiers, France, at 1800 hours. Instead of the stiff opposition that met Company B in the last war, it was an overjoyous civilian population who were very demonstrative in showing their gratitude for the coming of the Yanks. We are in the vicinity of Belleau Wood and Mount Falcon, where the 39th cracked the German lines and where they gained the name of the "Fighting Falcons." Nearby is the Oise-Marne cemetery where rest our honored dead.

On August 31, the division crosses the Aisne River, racing to Dizy-Le-Gros—an advance of 403 miles for the month. The same day, Warren Ridgeway sends a letter home, mentioning that he was near where Lt. Gen. Leslie McNair, commander of Army ground forces, visiting from Washington, DC, had been killed observing Air Force carpet bombing on July 25. For the division, 376 soldiers are killed and 1,809 troops are wounded during August 1944. The regiment has 84 killed, 10 died of wounds, 49 missing, and 444 wounded. The division buries its dead in temporary cemeteries at Gorron and Solers, France. Among them are the six men killed from Company B, which also had thirty-seven wounded, two missing, and six seriously injured.[24]

On September 1, the 39th Infantry crosses the Belgian border, Company B advancing against fortified positions near Landouzy-la-Ville. One platoon attacks riding on top of tanks—always hazardous—and today that results in three men killed and three wounded. An enemy artillery barrage hits several men. Despite the fire, 1Lt. Jack Jewell administers first aid and carries each man to safer positions. Seeing that the men need more aid, Jack finds a vehicle and rushes all to an aid station, saving their lives; he is recommended for a Silver Star.[25]

The company again rides atop tanks on September 3 but has no casualties. By September 5, elements of the 39th Infantry cross the Meuse River north of Dinant, which is captured by the regiment two days later. Company B quietly crosses the Meuse on September 6; other units are not so lucky, as elements of two Waffen-SS divisions attempt to stem the flooding olive-drab tide.[26] The regiment advances to Villiers le Temple, 10 miles southwest of Liège, and by September 10 reaches Theux, 15 miles southeast of Liège.

On September 9, Lt. Col. Oscar H. Thompson assumes command of the battalion, and Capt. Dunlap discovers what happened to Chester McClurg. Initially posted as missing in action on August 11, the wily corporal actually headed rearward for a little rest and recreation. MPs apprehended him on August 24; he is then admitted to the 298th General Hospital at Cherbourg for gastroenteritis. There are going to be some corporal's stripes available before too long, and Chester won't be wearing them. The company is in reserve on September 11, and the soldiers are able to rest and receive PX rations—candy bars, cigars, and cigarettes.[27]

About this time, there occurs one of hundreds of events that characterize AAAO— for instead of heading away from their unit like Chester, these men are racing to get back to it. Sebastian Andriello of the Second Battalion picks up the story:[28]

We were walking along the road and shells started to come in. The next thing I know, there were five of us and each one of us got hit. I was pretty lucky, I just got wounded in my thigh, two big pieces of shrapnel. One of the fellas the arm, another one in the leg. They couldn't do nothing with us there in the field hospital, and we were shipped to a hospital in England. They operated on me and I was there for about a month. Then they said you can be released. They released us and happened to be that five of the fellas who were with me, we were together, and when they shipped us back from England to France, they went to the repo depot.

This major said: "now we're going to assign you to a division." We said: "Sorry Sir, no way" and he said: "What are you telling me no way?" I said that we want to go back to the 9th Division where we started from in Fort Bragg. He said he didn't know if that was possible. I said that we'll walk wherever the hell they're going until we get to them. He said: "Let me check it out."

About an hour later he comes back and says he has the information about where the 9th Division is. We were happy. "But I'll tell you one thing, you can't walk there, it's not that close," [said the major.] I said, "We'll get there." [The major said,] "Wait a minute. There's a jeep down there. Who drives?" I said I used to drive in the States. He said: "Take that jeep. I'll give you ten gallons of gas, five-gallon tanks, and you follow my map. When you need gas, you go to American gas depots and get more gas." And that's what we did.

When we came back to the outfit, they were all in foxholes because it was as cold as anything. The captain said: "What are you doing here?" I said: "They wanted to transfer us to a different outfit, Captain Pedrico, but we refused." He said: "What about the jeep?" I said: "He gave it to me." [Pedrico said:] "He gave it to you? Oh jeez." It had a big red cross on it. He said: "Go down to Supply and make the fellas paint olive drab over that cross and then just put ours [bumper numbers] underneath. That's your jeep from now on, being that you can't walk too good." I said: "Thank you very much."

Why did Sebastian and his buddies insist on going back to their company? Because it is their home, and their buddies in it are their family. They also go back because Paddy Flint instilled in his soldiers that when they were separated or in an uncertain situation, always march to the sound of the guns. That is where your family is fighting, and they need you. So, you go back.

AAAO cuts the Eupen–Monschau road on September 13, crossing the border into Germany and seizing Rötgen, racing past felled trees, antitank mines, craters, and dragon's teeth (square-base, pyramid-shape blocks of reinforced concrete). Placed in long multiple rows, they slow down and force tanks into killing zones, then to be destroyed by antitank weapons. Rötgen is the first German town to be captured by the Allies on the Western Front. September 14: the regiment advances 4 miles to the east in the rain, reaching the outskirts of Lammersdorf; Company B has one man killed and four men wounded by mortars and small-arms fire as it advances with tanks. Pvt. Frank Pemberton cannot be found. On September 15, the First and Third Battalions flank German units around Lammersdorf; the enemy escapes, but a concrete pillbox with three 20 mm guns is destroyed. Company B is pinned down by heavy mortar and machine gun fire, and one soldier is killed. Sgt. George Rosen performs heroically in action against the enemy and is submitted for a Bronze Star.[29]

On September 16, the company rolls on, knocking out several pillboxes and machine gun nests around Lammersdorf. To the north, the 47th Infantry Regiment pierces the Siegfried Line near the village of Schevenhütte, east of Aachen, on September 17—the first Allied unit to break through this line of defenses. The following day, AAAO destroys eleven more pillboxes, seizing numerous POWs, as the battalion heads north to reinforce the 60th Infantry Regiment near Zweifall, Germany, 8 miles southeast of Aachen. Billie Flowers is wounded in the right arm near Zweifall.[30] On September 19, three men in the company are killed and two wounded southeast of Zweifall during an attack through the woods, capturing several prisoners. 1Lt. Leonard Kane is evacuated for illness.

The following day, the company seizes high ground about 2,500 yards west of the village of Hürtgen, Germany. The cost is high: one killed and five wounded, including Pvt. Manley Fuller, in the unit just two days, hit in the hand by shrapnel, and Pvt. Howard Kaufman—who peeks around a tree trunk just long enough to catch a rifle bullet in the face. Company B has just started running a tab at a joint called the Hürtgen, and the final bill will be brutal. The company continues to slowly push east on September 21.

There is poor, there is dirt poor, and there is Maine poor. Despite his destitute upbringing, however, Manley Fuller will have a leg up on many of the guys in Company B in the winter of 1944–45, because he hails from the Pine Tree State and has been freezing cold more times than he cares to remember. Born on April 21, 1920, in Searsmont, Waldo County, a few miles from West Penobscot Bay, he is the son of Albert B. Fuller and Agnes Geneva Brown. Albert, a farmer, cares for a dozen children, and times are tough; he often must saw wood, making apple crates to sell, and hunt foxes for their pelts when money gets tight. The family has no radio—since they have no electricity. Often, they are hungry and turn to poaching; in one incident his brothers are caught shooting a moose, and Manley, a minor, goes to court, copping a plea that the rifle is his, so that the family will not have the hunting weapon confiscated.

Down the street, an old Civil War veteran pays Manley ten cents a fish to catch a bucket full in nearby brooks and streams. Often on the town's list of the poor, Albert makes toys out of wood for the children at Christmas. Manley's pride and joy is a small sled—which he joyfully rides downhill, when he isn't using it hauling firewood for the cooking stove. After eighth grade, Manley leaves school to become a truck driver, after his parents' divorce.

By fifteen, Manley runs neighborhood errands in a borrowed 1930 Chevy ton-and-a-half truck. He also has a propane delivery route for Consumer Fuels in Belfast, Maine, later nabbing a job delivering coal with Wade & Heard Lumber Company. He shovels 3 tons of pea coal into the truck by hand each day, drives the load to another location, sorts the coal into sixty 100-pound sacks, muscles each sack over his shoulder, and hauls them one at a time up several flights of stairs. Mechanically inclined, when he scrapes together extra money he fixes up old "beaters" and "rolls-rough"—cars he then drives on frozen lakes, spinning doughnuts.[31] Manley works by day in the shipyards, a war-essential job—and takes night classes to learn welding.

It is a miserable existence, since he shares a boardinghouse room with three other men. Their staggered shifts and heavy drinking make sleeping difficult. When the quartet gets ornery, they head to a bar for some really rough action. Manley enlists at Bangor on December 21, 1942, listed as 5'6" and 159 pounds. To assist his family, he makes an allotment for part of his Army monthly pay to be sent home. "I turned down deferrals because joining the Army was better than working another winter as a welder on the Liberty ships in the Maine shipyards."

Manley starts military training at Fort Riley, Kansas, and soon he gets a tattoo as a rite of passage, plunking down a bargain $1.25 for a small, single-color heart on his left forearm with a ribbon reading "Mother." Enjoying practical jokes, one afternoon, noticing a buddy sleeping underneath his bunk to avoid a sergeant's attention, Manley puts "gopher matches" in his friend's shoe sole and ignites them. Feeling the heat, the trooper jumps up, causing their sergeant to notice the victim and put him to work. Manley later confesses that he had been responsible; his buddy replies that it was okay, since it was Manley who had done it.

Manley is at Camp Maxey (north of Paris, Texas) by June 1944, with the 99th US Infantry Division. A few weeks later, he goes by train to Fort Meade, Maryland, and then to Camp Kilmer, New Jersey, and finally to Camp Myles Standish, Massachusetts. Manley and associates go to nearby Boston for vaccine shots and are housed in a converted factory. The night before sailing, Manley attempts one last night on the town but finds that the crafty MPs have locked all doors and windows of their barracks—from the outside. The troops sail on the SS *Brazil* to Gourock, Scotland. Manley heads by train south to Camp Barton Stacey for six weeks, with daily 10-mile marches—rain or shine. Taking a smaller ship across the English Channel, Manley and his compatriots, in full gear, climb down swaying rope ladders into smaller landing craft. Some slip and fall, landing with a sickening thump on the steel decks of the boats below; officers bellow, "Don't look back," as medics handle those with broken bones.

Ashore, the men are instructed not to walk around outside their perimeter at night, since many land mines remain hidden in the ground. Riding through the smoke plumes still rising from St. Lô, he sees burned-out buildings. In Paris, he attends a Bob Hope USO show: "Of course, as he said, he was way at the back of a field full of men, so he couldn't really see what was happening on stage, but he appreciated the show anyways." Then it is on to Company B; with his heavy Maine accent, he may need an interpreter for some of the many West Virginia boys to understand him—and for Manley to understand them.[32]

Almost no one in the infantry is born with a silver spoon in his mouth, including George Holdren. Located in the far south of the state, Mercer County, West Virginia, has massive deposits of the famed "smokeless" Pocahontas No. 3 coal seam, but most people are poor. George Henry Holdren is born at Glen Lyn on September 12, 1914. The son of Bartholomew T. Holdren, a farmer, and Ella Fair Mathena, he has four brothers and two sisters; George finishes fifth grade in grammar school. Bartholomew dies in 1931; Ella Fair, in 1938. Enlisting on March 23, 1942, in Fort Thomas, he works at the F. C. Robinson Sawmill, where in 1939 he earns $200 in total for the twenty-six weeks he works during the year. He is single, is 5'8" tall, weighs 172 pounds, and has brown hair and blue eyes.

"Dale" Lockridge and Israel Reese are two incoming replacements from other families just scraping by. Kermit Dale Lockridge is born April 28, 1924, in Trimble, Highland County, Virginia, son of farmer William "Billie" Henry Lockridge and Elizabeth Mae Terry. He has a younger brother, Harper, and a sister, Martha Jane. He finishes two years of high school, leaving to work on the farm. Because the mountainous terrain has limited tillable land, Dale helps his father raise cattle. Registering for the draft in 1942, Dale stands 5'8" tall, weighs 132 pounds, with blue eyes and blond hair. Times are tough; Billie dies of a gunshot wound on June 11, 1943.[33] Although worried about his mother, Dale enlists on March 24, 1944, at Fort Meade.

Israel Lafayette Reese is born January 19, 1924, in Toombs County, Georgia, son of Claud Reese, a farmer, and Vinnie Dukes—both dropped out of grade school. He has two older brothers and an older sister, and three younger brothers and a younger sister. By 1940, the family has moved to Appling, Georgia, 15 miles west of Augusta. Appling's Mount Carmel Academy educated John C. Calhoun—later vice president of the US. But Israel doesn't have it so good; at seventeen he drops out of high school, after one year, for coastal Brunswick and a job with the Sternberg Dredging Company—it is hot, brutal, backbreaking work. Israel enlists at Fort McPherson, Atlanta, on March 26, 1944, saying he is a farmhand and is single; he is 5'4" and 140 pounds, with blue eyes and red hair.[34]

Perhaps the saddest history belongs to Deloss "Junior" Bradshaw. The southwest corner of Utah has never been confirmed as a hurricane zone, but soon after the area was first settled in 1896, a whirlwind blew the top off a buggy and the startled driver shouted, "Well, that was a hurricane; we'll name this 'Hurricane Hill.'" The name stuck; Deloss Bradshaw is born in Hurricane on June 3, 1909, the son of farmer Benjamin Bruppacher Bradshaw and Drucilla Hartley. Weighing 170 pounds and standing 5'11" tall, he has blue eyes and blond hair. In 1930 he lives at home, working as a common laborer. Benjamin, having lost his farm, is now a fruit peddler.

In the early 1930s, Junior marries Lillian Averett; the couple has several children, including sons Alpine, Grant, and Ottis. They also have twins on May 27, 1936, but one, Murry Dee, dies in childbirth. The other, Gloria Ann, dies at age five after being accidently struck in the head by an ax wielded by eight-year-old Ottis as the two gather wood.[35] By then, Junior and Lillian have divorced. He registers for the draft in Mesa, Arizona, in 1942.[36]

Back on the line, on September 22, the 39th Infantry, minus First Battalion, attacks enemy bunkers at Rollesbroich, Lammersdorf, and Paustenbach north of Simmerath, capturing 125 enemy soldiers. The hamlet of Bicherath is a tougher nut to crack, so US fighter-bombers strafe it. Company B remains north, near Schevenhütte. Six men who were AWOL are reduced to private. Chester McClurg is not one of them, since he has yet to return from the hospital.

On September 24, Jack Jewell writes of entering Germany: "We are eating some German Pork this morning, right good!" But Jack needs some dessert to go with that oinker and requests his folks send four boxes of Fig Newtons, store candy, and a bunch of chocolates.[37] September 26 is another bloody day for Company B. Pfc. Ernie Miguel, of the Quechan tribe from Imperial County, California, is killed by a bullet to the chest, and thirteen men are wounded, including 2Lt. Stephen Kinner, as the company attacks into heavy artillery and smalls-arms fire and is pinned down. Over the next two days, a dozen more men are wounded. Ernie had been overseas since North Africa. The company issues long underwear to the soldiers on September 27, an ominous indicator.[38]

Beginning in 1943, the Army publishes a series of short booklets for soldiers in the ETO titled "Army Talks." These are designed to provide combat tips to junior soldiers, and the September 27 issue is just starting to reach the front; its twenty-eight pages immediately catch the eye when the soldier reads: "Its purpose is to show you how to kill Germans—and stay alive to kill some more."[39] Included is a simple "Soldier's Ten Commandments":

Thou shalt keep thy helmet on. (Your hair is poor protection against fragments.)

Thou shalt keep thy eyes open. (Unless you want Jerry to close them for you, for keeps.)

Thou shalt not bunch-up. (The moment you bunch-up, the Krauts will toss you a foot-locker full of mortars.)

Thou shalt not clink. (Muzzle your dog-tags. Put the quietus on your mess kit.)

Thou shalt not make a light at night. (Or otherwise give away your position with loud talk.)

Thou shalt keep thy canteen filled. (With water or local wine.)

Thou shalt not expose thyself. (Shave with your shirt on, don't hang your mirror on a tree, and don't hang your laundry in the open.)

Thou shalt dig-in. (But not when advancing under fire.)

Thou shalt stay inside mine tapes. (Unless thou wants to meet thy maker.)

Thou shalt keep moving. (So that thou be not pinned down and shot up.)

Pretty decent advice: now, it just remains to be seen who reads and follows it. Three days later, Jack Jewell writes his folks, skipping the Ten Commandments so as not to worry them:[40]

The going has been rather rough and will be even harder in the future.... We were issued another blanket today and it will come in very handy because the nights are cool and it's difficult to sleep well. I have had my bed roll the last two nights and I always sleep warm in that. But I can't always use it because it is kept on the kitchen trucks and sometimes the tactical situation doesn't come up to us. We had three hot meals today and it's good to get away from C and K Rations for a while. We had corn beef hash, rice, jelly, crackers, coffee, and spuds. That's about the way our rations run. ... I washed some socks and shaved—that's something new. I have improved some of my uncultured habits in this remote civilized life, but I guess they won't hurt me any. . . . I wish you could walk through our bivouac area now. It would be a treat and I say a privilege for any American. All the tents are up, and the men have spent the day cleaning their weapons, themselves and getting haircuts. Yes, I got one too. We have several GI barbers in our company, and they do a fairly good job.

For the division, 218 soldiers are killed and 1,551 soldiers are wounded in September.[41] The 39th Infantry suffers six officers and seventy enlisted killed, one officer and eight enlisted died of wounds, one officer and thirty-seven enlisted missing, and twenty-six officers and 354 enlisted wounded, as the regiment submits one officer and seventeen enlisted men for Silver Stars and ten officers and sixty-seven enlisted for Bronze Stars. Company B also suffers grievous losses: twelve killed, fifty-one wounded, and one seriously injured. Since landing in Normandy, forty-one men in the company—the equivalent of one full platoon—have been killed in action or have died of wounds. Hundreds more have been wounded. But morale is high, since the American army is now on the German border. Jack Jewell wrote a letter with his optimistic views on the war: "I'm hoping this will be all over by the time you get this letter."[42]

But it is about to get much worse—much worse than Jack or anyone in Company B can imagine.

More replacements are on their way. Pawnee, Illiopolis, Kincaid, and Bulpitt in rural central Illinois all are one-stoplight towns—minus the stoplight. But these tiny villages are where Leonard LaVerne Pourchot lives and works as a young man. Born on June 17, 1922, in Pawnee, he is the son of James—a power-plant janitor—and Florence. Life is frugal; James, who finished sixth grade, makes $440 a year. During a rough spell, James borrows two silver dollars from Leonard's piggy bank, part of collateral for a loan. By 1930, the family lives in Bulpitt, but Leonard's dreams cannot be confined to the farm. Studying hard in high school in Kincaid, in 1941 he enters Illinois State Normal University to be a teacher. In Kappa Phi Kappa fraternity, Leonard excels in organizing dessert parties. With wire-rimmed glasses, an innocent face, and a dreamy look in his eyes, Leonard cannot wait to teach in his own classroom.

But Uncle Sam has other plans. Leonard registers for the draft; at the time he weighs 160 pounds and stands 5'9" tall. He enlists on March 16, 1943, and trains in Arkansas and Texas, arriving at Fort George C. Meade on August 25, 1944. A few days later, the future social science teacher visits Baltimore and is appalled: "Everything flourishes; drinking, vice, etc. Prostitution is mostly freelance, but not entirely. Nearly nude floor shows are found in the joints. Wiggle-worms perform in abundance and in abandon."[43]

The Galicia area of the Ukraine has cold, miserable winters, so Victor Wasnick and Mary Zehal, Catholic immigrants, feel right at home in Minneapolis. On August 12, 1924, Victor—a freight company laborer—and Mary bring into the world Lloyd Ludwig Wasnick. Mary, John's second wife, already has a son and three daughters. The family speaks Ukrainian. After graduating from high school in 1942, Lloyd finds a job at Rice Brothers Wholesale Florists and Supplies.

Like many young men in Minnesota, he enjoys hunting and boxing. Unlike other guys, Lloyd has genuine movie-star looks and is close to 5'8" if he stands up straight. With his black hair and olive skin, Lloyd has a five o'clock shadow by ten thirty in the morning, and the makings of a good beard in three days. He has only two obstacles against getting to Hollywood. First, he thinks he is all ears and nose, and second, Lloyd can't dance, but neither prevent Lloyd from being inducted into the Army at Fort Snelling, Minnesota, on June 8, 1943, when he lists a trade of fireman and boiler repairman. He weighs 153 pounds and has brown hair and eyes and a ruddy complexion. He volunteers for air cadet training at the 328th College Training Detachment at Duquesne University but is reclassified into the infantry and, after training, arrives in Europe on September 19, 1944.[44]

Born in Omaha, Nebraska, on April 29, 1925, son of Jay Glenn Holman, who makes $672 a year as an advertising agent, and Ruth Speice, Jay Philip "Phil" Holman, later says that he lived a sheltered life, listening to big-band records—his favorites are Glenn Miller and Spike Jones—and going to high school dances and the movies. "The most exciting things to do were to blow up everything in sight on the 4th of July and pulling the electric connection from the streetcar, as it rounded the corner. That prank always got the conductor mad, but he couldn't chase us because of the passengers yelling at him." At Omaha Central High School, Phil weighs 119 pounds—nearsighted with thick glasses. He volunteers for everything: football, bowling, Latin club, orchestra, road show, roller-Skating club, Reserve Officer Training Corps, Spanish club, stage crew, senior play, and National Thespians.

> High school was kind of a pain. Following three very smart sisters was not easy. Every class I went into, the teacher would ooh and aah about this sister or that sister had done so well. So, I did miserably to make up for their efforts. One English teacher liked me so much she invited me back to her class for another semester. And an Algebra teacher could disjoint his thumbs, fascinating the class but not getting the equations through to me. So I took that class over again.

A week before graduating in the spring of 1943, Phil walks into a dark office on Dodge Street. The Marines and Navy take one look at his slight frame and Coke-bottle glasses and send him on to the final desk, belonging to the . . . US Army. The Army sergeant grunts and says, "Welcome." Phil returns to sister Kay's house, since his mother and father had already moved to Los Angeles, where Glenn works for Lockheed Aircraft. Obtaining a delay in induction, in June, Phil follows his parents to Beverly Hills, and enrolls at Santa Monica Junior College, until he opens the mail one morning to find that Uncle Sam has ordered him to report to the Los Angeles courthouse on August 6, 1943, for induction. It was a shock:

There were many men there all kind of lined up looking to the front of the room. I was requested to join them. I did. A kindly-looking burly person in uniform growled some kind of language, then asked us to take one step forward. I did and was amazed at the clanking sound all around me. I found that most of the men in the room were wearing leg irons—had been picked up for draft-dodging, or other indescribable things. (At that time many jails were taking the easy way out and allowing prisoners to enlist in the military service.) Well, I took the oath with a lot of people who were uttering other oaths, and I was in the Army.

Phil hops in a bus for the short ride to San Pedro and Fort MacArthur. He loses most of his hair at the barbershop and discovers that no one cares if his new uniforms fit. Then it's off to the medics, where he is found to be 5'9" tall and still weighing 119 pounds—soaking wet, which he is from sweat. He also gets the opportunity to cough in front of all his new friends. Leaving that bedlam, he hoists his overstuffed duffel bag and staggers to a huge barracks, where he notes that the bunks are stacked three high. Phil learns a valuable lesson: survey your surroundings before you make any rash moves. He plops into the top bunk without looking and, early the next morning, is blasted out of his bunk by a loudspeaker, just above his head, blaring a bugle call and the maniacal scream of a sergeant. Over the next week, Phil and his new pals learn how to wear their uniforms and how to pull kitchen police—the fine art of cleaning pots and pans.

The "misfits" board a train bound for Corvallis, Oregon, and Camp Adair, a sprawl-ing 57,159 acres with 1,800 buildings—of which five hundred are barracks—a hospital, post office, bank, and five movie theaters—where he sees frequent films about the perils of sexually transmitted diseases—and dozens of mess halls, called "slop houses." Over the next year, assigned to the 70th Infantry Division, Phil learns how to curse, how to suffer being cursed, how to march with his rifle, and how to drink 3.2 low-alcohol beer. Then the Army learns that the skinny kid with glasses can shoot; Phil fires Expert and is promoted to corporal. The rifle range is a snap; close-order drill is not: "Orders were given fast, and some minds did not react as quickly as others, and you might, given the order 'to the rear, march,' turn to find a rifle barrel up your nose as the guy behind you tried to remember what to do."

Phil learns it isn't the close-order drill that counts, it's reacting quickly without having to think—and that could keep you alive. On the troopship, seeing no loud-speakers, he grabs the top hammock of a six-tier sleeping arrangement, so no one could "barf" on him during rough seas. The former ocean liner reaches Liverpool in six days. Taking a train to Southampton, he then boards a smaller ship to cross the English Channel to Omaha Beach, where, climbing the steep bluffs, he sees the debris of battle: bunkers, shell holes, and destroyed equipment. The replacements arrive at a train station, where Phil and forty other new friends pack a railcar that appears to have been used for the same purpose in the Great War—and probably not cleaned since. The men disembark at a replacement depot and are fed, medically inspected, issued equipment, and bunked down for a sleepless last night, before heading on trucks to the Ninth Infantry.[45]

James Joseph Rush is born on July 18, 1923, at Scranton, Pennsylvania, the only child of James J. Rush—a Home Life Insurance Company agent—and Edith Honan. By 1940, the family lives with Edith's widowed mother in Chester, Pennsylvania, with his father running the toolroom at an oil refinery down by the Delaware River, making $1,650 a year. Jim, single, enlists in Philly on May 3, 1943, and heads to New Cumberland the same day for induction. Standing 5'10" tall and weighing 140 pounds, he arrives in Europe on September 8, 1944.[46]

Every infantry platoon prays that they do not get a "wet-behind-the-ears" lieutenant, because an inexperienced officer can get them killed with one mistake. They also are leery about a "Pointer" walking through the tent flap, since a West Point officer might be overly concerned with "Mickey Mouse" rules in the "Army Bible" (Army Regulations). Two future platoon leaders are neither.

Francis "Frank" Randall is born on May 15, 1911, in Baltimore, the son of James Louis Randall, an engineer, and Margaret Mary Rheinhardt. He graduates from the Calvert Hall Christian Brothers College and enters military service in 1934 with the prestigious 5th Maryland Infantry of the Maryland National Guard, serving several years. By Pearl Harbor, Frank works a good job as a clerk at a retail store but joins the Army on February 6, 1942. Because of his prior service, he receives a second lieutenant's commission on April 7, 1943; he's 5'8" tall, weighs 178 pounds, and is single. On June 2, 1944, Frank becomes a first lieutenant; he arrives in Europe in late September 1944, where he will join Company B.[47]

Louis Armand Benoist III is born on October 14, 1921, in Natchez, Mississippi, the son of the Benoist Brothers Men's and Boy's Clothing, Men's Furnishings owner, Louis Armand Jr.—who routinely works sixty-six hours a week—and Emma May Harned, a southern belle from Nelson County, Kentucky. Louis's grandfather, "Poppy," had been a Mississippi state senator. A happy youngster—he has a younger brother, Eugene; an older sister, Julia; and a passel of hunting dogs, he plays piano and hopes to become a doctor, although he will study business at the University of Mississippi.

Louis serves as the 1st Platoon leader for Cadet Company B in the "Ole Miss" Reserve Officer Training Corps. On the Dance Committee, Hood's Brigade (an honorary military organization for juniors), the University Greys (an honorary military organization for seniors), and Phi Delta Theta fraternity, Louis enlists as a private at Camp Shelby on February 11, 1943; he is 5'11" tall, weighs 160 pounds, and is commissioned a second lieutenant on May 27, 1943. Louis marries Ann Elizabeth Bahin at Natchez's First Presbyterian Church; they have a young son, Louis, born on September 6, 1944, in Natchez. A few days prior, Louis writes a friend:

> By the time you receive this letter I might be quite some distance from here.
> I got orders last week to go overseas. At the present time it is especially hard

since Anne is so very close to having our child. It is due in only a few days. It is quite a blow on her, and I sincerely wish I could have avoided it at the present time. But I couldn't so we had to make the best of it. Things could be a lot worse! Anne is in good hands and will be well taken care of so I shouldn't worry. Much!!!

Descended from immigrants from Meaux, France, Lieutenant Benoist has the pronunciation of his last name butchered in Company B—from "ben-noyst" to "ben-nwah," which he prefers—especially by soldiers from the less-genteel North, whose concept of French is as a lead-in syllable to -fries or -toast.[48]

Nodell, Seaman, Lavinsky, Pettigrew, and MacLean; although they have never previously met, they will share food, mail, cold, terror, and misery over the next months. They will be part of a group of twenty-four new men all assigned, at roughly the same time, to 3rd Platoon, led by Frank Randall, and later Louis Benoist, who get to know each other better than they know anyone else in the company and have their names appear time and again in letters home and in postwar recollections. An adage of soldiers in combat is not to make real friends with anyone, so if that soldier is killed, it will not crush your morale. It would seem that Noodles, Kenny, Jay, Bob, and Mac—and many others—took that risk and were better for having done so.

The "old man" of 3rd Squad, 3rd Platoon, Company B, will be Robert Shank "Bob" Pettigrew Jr., born in the Bronx on July 22, 1911, son of plumber Robert S. Pettigrew and Margaret T. Snyder. Bob has one older brother and two younger ones. A Protestant, he is baptized on June 24, 1916; he is a devoted fan of the New York Giants baseball team. He is also a scholar, graduating as valedictorian from George Washington High School. Robert marries Mary Sophie Frayler of the Bronx on May 28, 1938. By 1940, Bob, Mary, and six-month-old son Robert live on Hull Avenue in the Bronx, where he works as a clerk and warehouse foreman for Whitehead Metal Company; his annual income is $1,560. He also attends New York University, studying accounting. The family lives in a small apartment five blocks from Fordham University; like many New Yorkers, they have no automobile so travel by bus, streetcar, and subway.

Well past draft age, married, and with a second son, James, born in March 1943, Bob insists on doing his part and is directed to report for a preinduction physical at 367 East 204th Street in the Bronx on February 28, 1944, at 6:30 a.m. He is about to discover that the Army does a whole lot of things at god-awful times in the morning. He takes the physical but is held over an extra day before being accepted, then heads to the Grand Central Palace in New York City to enlist. Bob stands 5'9" tall, weighs 170 pounds, and has red hair and blue eyes.

On March 30, Bob departs for Camp Upton, remaining there for three days. His training starts on April 3, 1944, at Camp Blanding, Florida, where Bob gets all his inoculations on April 15 and qualifies Marksman with the M1 rifle on May 5. Months later, he goes to Camp Kilmer, 22 miles southwest of New York City, and on September 11 boards the troopship *Île de France*. Bob arrives in Glasgow, Scotland, on September

18 and is rushed south on a train. The next day, he departs Southampton on a small ship for the short trip to Omaha Beach.[49]

Kenneth Ray Seaman was born with a ball in his hand—at least that's what his high school friends and infantry buddies probably think. Ken, born August 9, 1921, in Coles County, Illinois, is the son of Henry Seaman and Fern Matherly. In 1930, he lives on a grain farm in North Okaw Township. His 1938 Mattoon High School yearbook shows him on the basketball and baseball teams; he graduates that May. Ken loves baseball statistics and keeps clippings on Chicago Cubs games. Registering for the draft on February 16, 1942, in Mattoon, he is employed at the Hulman Food Company; he is 5'11" and 187 pounds.

Ken travels to Evansville, Indiana, to work at the Republic Aviation factory, which produces P-47 Thunderbolt fighter aircraft. He quickly makes the Republic Thunderbolts baseball team, playing third base in the War Plant League, and meets a coal miner's daughter, Mary Ellen Rickard, from Madisonville, Kentucky. She has also traveled to Evansville for work and is a true "Rosie the Riveter" in the factory, which will build over six thousand P-47s during the war. They marry on May 8, 1943. Ken later enlists and arrives in Europe in late September 1944. He is partial to Canadian Club whiskey.[50] And this baseball stuff isn't just a bunch of malarkey. If you need someone to throw a hand grenade a long, long way, go with Kenny and for the Germans it will be no hits, no runs, and no one left on base.

Harry Charles Nodell, son of Agnes Josephine Bremer and Robert Nodell, a railroad worker, is born in Brooklyn, New York, on March 24, 1914. With five brothers and two sisters, he is a typical city kid, playing street stickball until almost dark, when Agnes yells for him to get home. In 1936, while working at the National Packing Company, Harry meets a young lady who loves his eyes and his great sense of humor. Her name is Mollie. Harry marries Mildred "Mollie" Richman, daughter of Jewish émigrés from Russia, on May 25, 1938, at city hall; they live at 100 Hendrix Street in Brooklyn. Mollie, whose father is a Talmudic scholar, and Harry, who is thoroughly Irish, make for a unique relationship and one that inadvertently prepares him for the Army. Employed as a driver for the Acme Fast Freight Company, Harry has been known to tip a few back on his way home after work. Mollie, having none of it, frequently locks him out of the house, forcing the intoxicated Harry to sleep the night away on the hard, unheated stoop—regardless of the season.

An older brother at Acme devises a bill-of-lading scam, and the two sell purloined merchandise out of the back of Harry's truck. Fortunately for the Nodell boys, no "associates" of Meyer Lansky or Frank Costello ever get wind of the enterprise, but, alas, law enforcement officers do and pinch all involved; it's not a bum rap, and since Harry is at the bottom of the endeavor's totem pole, the judge offers him a choice: go to jail or join the Army. Harry enlists in New York City on November 27, 1943, listing his profession as a commercial driver; he stands 5'6" tall.[51] Harry and Mollie already have a precocious daughter, Barbara June—born in 1940—and are expecting a second child in May 1944. Harry, still in the States, finagles leave, buys a small baseball glove, and heads home. A Brooklyn Dodgers fan, he is convinced that the newborn will be a boy. To his surprise, it's a girl, Susan Leslie. No problem; Harry will teach her to play catch when he returns after the war.[52]

Peoria, Illinois, is a tough river city, a straight-razor-totin' town. Myron Dean "Mac" MacLean, born there on September 4, 1923, is the son of a Nova Scotia–born father, Hector MacLean, who comes to the US about 1910. A coal miner, Hector works in the hardscrabble bituminous mines in Illinois. South of Peoria, his integrated nine-man crew has two Black miners, although by the end of each shift, after swinging a 9-pound sledgehammer all day, everyone is black—covered from head to toe by coal dust. Because Hector's wife also works, sometimes the miner takes the five-year-old minor to the mine and has little Mac sleep next to the canary in a shaft some 130 feet from daylight—there being few occupational safety rules at the time. Neither the canary nor Mac die, so all's well that ends well.

Nobody tells the people of Peoria that they can't drink alcohol. "Roarin' Peoria" has the unofficial motto "Sin Is Here to Stay," cemented for good in September 1925, when three federal agents raid several Peoria "blind tigers"—and a Peoria grand jury, instead of charging the proprietors of the gin joints, indicts the trio of federal marshals for larceny, robbery, and assault to injure. During Prohibition, Hector makes wine in the basement of the house but dies of heart congestion one month before his fiftieth birthday in 1937—black lung disease was not yet widely understood. At fourteen, Mac is now fatherless.

Mac's mother, Grace Saal MacLean, is the daughter of German immigrants Albert Saal and Elizabetha Frey. When Grace is twelve, Albert—a traveling salesman—abandons the family in Peoria and heads to Omaha, Nebraska, never to return. With Hector's death, Grace is a forty-nine-year-old widow with two children: Mac and his older sister, Roberta "Bert." Grace, who calls Mac "Sunny" because he is a cheerful lad, teaches grade school and lives down the block from Bradley Polytechnic Institute. John Gillespie rents an apartment in her basement. Considered almost a member of the family, John fixes things around the house; he is also known to take a nip out of a bottle of single malt every so often and is an inveterate tobacco chewer.

Mac, at fifteen, makes friends easily and enters Peoria High School; a good pal is Robert "Bob" Michel. Mac votes for Bob as class president and Michel wins—foreshadowing his future political career in the US House of Representatives. Along with Bob, Mac is a running back on the football team; he also plays varsity tennis. During the summers, with Prohibition now over, Mac rolls heavy whiskey barrels onto trucks at the Hiram Walker distillery. In his senior year, Mac's life is forever changed by an arrival from Evanston, Illinois. Julie Ann Lane is a brown-haired, blue-eyed whirlwind from the "Windy City."

An only child, she is the daughter of French Lane, a *Chicago Tribune* sports reporter, and Marie Strehlow, a former society editor for the *Peoria Journal-Transcript*, who routinely take her to the Kentucky Derby, where French knows everyone and paid for Julie's birth by winning a daily double at the track on a "good tip." Julie is crushed when her doting father dies on her thirteenth birthday in 1938; she and her mother remain in Evanston until 1940, before moving to Peoria. Julie, a smart girl who is fluent in Latin and French, enrolls at Wheaton College in Norton, Massachusetts, after graduating from Peoria High in 1943.

Meanwhile, Mac, having graduated from Peoria High in 1941, is at Bradley. Mac enlists on September 19, 1942. He is listed as standing 5'7" tall and weighing 164 pounds; the height measurement is generous. Mac remains at Bradley until May 5, 1943, when he reports to Camp Grant, Illinois, for active duty, and then to Camp Croft, South Carolina, for basic infantry training with 3rd Platoon, Company A, 32nd Infantry Training Battalion, with hopes of joining the Army Air Corps. Mac begins to prepare for air cadet training but—more importantly—is hitting his stride mastering the fine art of goldbricking. On New Year's Eve 1943, he attends an all-night party, arriving back at the barracks at dawn for a math test later that day. Getting up at noon some days, he plays basketball once until he is "worn out," thus not studying for a geography test. On February 3, 1944—and many other days—Mac writes in his diary that he "loafed all day." Playing ball, sleeping, and seeing movies; this Army life was OK! On February 12, he goes to the range to fire carbines; that night he sees *Frisco Kid*, with James Cagney. Forced marches follow, with an overseas physical on February 26.[53]

Mac arrives at the 77th College Training Detachment at Austin College in Sherman, Texas, on February 28, when disaster strikes. He starts hearing the dreaded word "infantry"—because nobody, but nobody, wants to be a "dough," "dogface," or "blister-foot." On April 4, Mac writes, "Have to go back to Infantry," and transfers to Company K, 342nd Infantry Regiment, 86th Infantry Division, at Camp Livingston, Louisiana. A unique feature here is the "Snake House," to familiarize solders with dangerous poisonous snakes found in the rolling wasteland and swampy bogs, where mosquitoes, fleas, red ants, and biting flies make life miserable year-round. The worst are chiggers, tiny, red, burrowing parasites causing endless itching.

Mac receives a rifle and starts getting up at 3:45 a.m. for training, falling on his bunk at night "tired as all hell." He fires a 184 at M1 Carbine Qualification on April 24, earning an Expert distinction. A carbine is a lot lighter than a rifle, let alone a BAR, so he hopes for the best. The war continues, as does Mac's march overseas. But first it's time for shots. On July 5, he lines up with dozens of other apprehensive soldiers and receives a smallpox vaccination, a triple-typhoid vaccination, and a tetanus shot. But his shot records will be lost twice, and thus he will end up receiving the immunizations three times—his pleas that he has already had them falling on deaf ears. Mac isn't the only soldier getting poked, as Cpl. John Readey writes at Camp Stoneman, California, in 1942:[54]

They give me shots for tetanus; for typhoid, I get three!
The yellow fever is an excuse; for one more hole in me.
They stick the needle in me dry; they stick it in me wet.

They punch me full of holes, it seems; at every chance they get.

Typhus, measles, housemaid's knee; there's shots for ev'ry thing.

Fallen arches, leprosy; boy, those shots do sting!

Sometimes those vampires stick me good; right in a vein of me.

And then they take a pint of blood; and smile with fiendish glee.

Oh, I haven't been in battle, yet; in war I haven't starred.

But if you saw the holes in me; you'd swear I'm battle scarred!

In August 1944, Mac arrives at Fort Meade, and the Army Ground Forces Replacement Depot #1. During the war, some 1.5 million soldiers pass through here on their way to Europe. They then are transported to Camp Kilmer for final preparations. He gets a pass to go downtown and visits Broadway, where Mac buys a pair of boots. Mac departs New York on September 18, probably on the *Queen Mary*, which has 9,084 troops and 1,110 crew on board, as an individual infantry replacement. The troops sleep in hammocks, layered four and five high. Many form poker groups, but Mac generally sacks out. After arriving in Gourock, Scotland, on September 25, Mac boards a troop train south to Camp Barton Stacey; he gets a one-day pass to London and writes home, ending with "Tell John and Bert to write. Also, Hector soon." John is John Gillespie. He and Mac developed a code for Mac's letters home, since they know the mail must pass censors. "Hector," Mac's deceased father, is part of that code; it means "combat action."

SCHOOL OF THE SOLDIER

MEDICS

Although they are not trained physicians, Bill Mauldin calls medics "the private soldier's family doctor," and these "Docs" are beloved. A medic can provide first aid, apply tourniquets and bandages to stop the bleeding, administer morphine to kill pain, and pour sulpha [sulfa] powder on wounds to delay infection. Medics have the skill identifier of "666—First-Aid Man." It should be #1. A medic has to know how to respond when a gravely wounded man asks, "Don't kid me, Doc; how bad is it?" Most importantly, the medic has to know the art of the possible, in a setting where truly little is available to assist him. Thus, a medic may use his plethora of safety pins to close a wound, because that may be all he has left. But maybe traveling light is a good thing—since medics are expected to evacuate casualties from minefields, and it doesn't take much weight to set off a Kraut land mine.[55]

Stretcher bearers, grimly nicknamed "body snatchers," carry wounded to the rear—from 1,000 yards up to a mile to the battalion aid station—where there is supposed to be a physician, but high casualties to docs means that isn't always the case. Stretcher bearers ideally travel in a jeep. That journey can be the longest in a man's life, and sometimes his last, since the enemy has been known to open fire on litter teams. If it's really bad, litter bearers often work seventy-two-hour shifts.

At the aid station, more-in-depth first aid can be administered, diagnoses made, and seriously wounded stabilized. The chaplain is often located here; it is also where a dead patient is declared "deceased" by the initial physician examining him. Those who die before treatment are termed "killed in action." Those expiring after treatment by a medical officer are categorized "died of wounds." When lots of casualties roll in, doctors often must triage the arrivals, and the lowest priority is that for patients who are expected to die soon. These men are provided with pain medication and as much comfort as possible; the chaplain tries to stay with them, so they are not alone when they die.[56] It is a horror of war, but one that provides the greatest good to the greatest number of soldiers. From here, ambulances—often known as "meat wagons"—transport patients to a collection station, frequently 1 to 3 miles to the rear.[57]

If an inspector general visits an aid station and looks hard, he will find other "medicine" tucked away in a drawer or behind medical textbooks. It doesn't come through the Army supply system, and it's not beer, wine, or champagne. This is "little brown jug" territory; this is the hard stuff—maybe Pennsylvania rye—but it's usually not for patients, because morphine and alcohol don't mix. It's for docs, medics, and padres, who see stuff that makes them puke. But they can't just take the evening off, so they take a belt, or a slug, or whatever Emily Post term you prefer, and they keep on saving lives.

Medics not only save the wounded. They are often the first to gather the dead, and also severed body parts—legs, feet in boots, arms, and heads. The Army understands that the remains of fellow soldiers, lying on the battlefield, lead to poor morale and potential battle fatigue of survivors.[58] You pick up enough body parts and it's time to hit the Pennsylvania rye again.

A typical evacuation scenario follows. A soldier is moving up a draw. The Krauts open up, hitting his company commander in the face and also killing another soldier. A BAR gunner comes forward but is killed before he can set up his weapon. Our trooper is shot in the jaw; he begins to spit out teeth as blood gushes out. The medic gets to his position, gives him a shot of morphine, and bandages the wound, but moments later the medic is killed. Stretcher bearers arrive; seeing the nature of the wounds, they place the kid facedown on a litter, head turned to the side, so he won't choke to death on his own blood.[59]

At the collection station, often near the regimental command post, doctors adjust dressings and administer plasma, the chief weapon to combat shock. Ambulances then take the patients perhaps 8 more miles to the rear to a clearing station, which is authorized twelve physicians and almost a hundred other medical techs, where major surgery can be performed in sanitary conditions. It looks like chaos, but it is organized lifesaving. Transport experts then group patients in ambulances to head back to field and evacuation hospitals, and with each successive destination, the soldier's survival chances increase. But first, it all depends on Doc.

BAZOOKA

What do a piece of chewing gum, an antitank weapon, and a musical instrument have in common? Well, they all are called "bazooka." The musical instrument came first, way back in 1905 in Van Buren, in western Arkansas. Fifteen-year-old Bob Burns had formed his own little string band. Practicing one night in Hayman's Plumbing Shop, Bob spotted a section of gas pipe; blowing through it, he created a unique sound akin to a "wounded moose." Intrigued by the tone, Bob began tinkering—adding an interconnecting pipe here and a slide handle there, along with a whiskey funnel and a trombone-like mouthpiece, until the moose was dead and gone and the creation now produced notes between a trombone and a slide whistle.

Enlisting in the Marines and sailing to France in 1918, he takes his instrument with him, to the 11th Marine Regiment, which later becomes part of the Marine Corps jazz band. Patenting the creation in 1920 as a "bazooka"—possibly derived from a period slang word "bazoo," meaning a "windy fellow," Bob became known as "Bazooka" Burns during a long career in radio. Sanford Kendrick and Noon Johnson also played similar devices—Noon made his device from parts of an old New Orleans brass bed.

Meanwhile, in 1918, American scientist and engineer Dr. Robert Goddard developed a tube-fired rocket for the US Army. With the end of that conflict, the project was shelved until World War II, when Col. Leslie Skinner gave an M10 shaped-charge grenade, capable of stopping some German tanks at close range, to Lt. Edward Uhl, with the mission of creating a parallel delivery system, since the 3.5-pound grenade was too heavy to throw. Ed created a small rocket but needed both to protect the firer from the rocket exhaust and to aim the weapon—finding the solution by chance: "I was walking by this scrap pile, and there was a tube that . . . happened to be the same size as the grenade that we were turning into a rocket. I said, 'That's the answer! Put the tube on a soldier's shoulder with the rocket inside, and away it goes.'"

Test-firing a few rounds into the Potomac River, Skinner and Uhl took the weapon to a competition at the Aberdeen Proving Ground in May 1942. The officers had a problem—the launch tube had no sights, so they fabricated one the morning of the test from a wire coat hanger. The rocket launcher scored several hits on a moving tank, while all other competitors missed. In attendance was the chief of research and engineering in the Ordnance Department, Maj. Gen. Gladeon Barnes, who was delighted by the system—especially after he fired it himself—and exclaimed: "It sure looks like Bob Burns's bazooka." The name stuck.

Bazooka-brand bubble gum, packaged in a red, white, and blue packet, was introduced in 1947 by the Brooklyn, New York, firm Topps Company. Beginning in 1953, Topps changed the packaging to include small comic strips, featuring a character named "Bazooka Joe" with each piece of gum. According to some sources, Bazooka bubble gum owes its ordnance-inspired name to the World War II weapon, which owed its name to the musical instrument. Even more widespread is the attachment of the name "Bazooka" to almost every soldier who accomplishes some feat of marksmanship with the weapon. During the fighting near Arracourt, France, in the summer of 1944, for example, Lt. Col. Charles Carpenter from Edgington, Illinois, piloting a light L-4H observation plane nicknamed "Rosie the Rocketer," straps six bazookas under the wings and reportedly knocks out six enemy tanks from the air, earning him the immortal nickname of "Bazooka Charlie."[60]

HOOCH

It's also called "Al K. Hall, apple jack, white lightning, bathtub gin, bug juice, giggle water, and shaving lotion." Glenn Miller revives a seventy-year-old song about it—"Little Brown Jug," while the Andrews Sisters sing "Rum and Coca-Cola." No one is more creative than American service members at obtaining booze. They drink to celebrate, they drink to reduce stress, they drink to relieve boredom, they drink to avoid facing the images of terror slinking through the dark recesses of their minds, and they drink just to get gassed. So when the Army issues a few beers to soldiers off the line in training areas, it is just bowing to the inevitable. As Lindsey Nelson once said, "I have had field training in Light Scotch, Bourbon, Sour Mash, and Short Beer."

Thank goodness that torpedoes are not part of the Army arsenal, because "torpedo juice" becomes a Navy alcohol beverage made from the 180-proof grain alcohol fuel used in US Navy torpedo motors. When the new Mk. 18 electric-powered torpedo, which did not use ethyl alcohol, is introduced into service, some old salts are observed weeping, because they will no longer be able to slam back a few of the two-parts-ethyl-alcohol and three-parts-pineapple-juice libations. But don't worry; they'll find something else—they always do.

And the Marines? Semper Fi. Marine private first class Vernon Carlson is assigned to the Marine Detachment on the battleship USS *West Virginia* until she is sunk under him at Pearl Harbor on December 7, 1941. Several days after the attack, nineteen-year-old "Oly" is able to send a short telegram home to let them know he is safe, with the message "Japs came by and broke my whiskey. I'm OK."[61]

One problem is that commissioned officers get a monthly alcohol allowance on the basis of rank—the higher your grade, the more booze you get; if you're a general, you get almost enough to open up your own gin joint. Enlisted men do not get an allowance, which causes endless friction. Also troubling: European beer is generally stronger than US beer, and most soldiers know you don't chugalug one. But what sneaks up on them is French calvados—apple or peach brandy in Normandy, which is easier to get than a Coke. The troops call it cider, which sounds benign, but it is strong, as is schnapps in Germany, so don't be too quick to swill it down.

Even George Patton gets into the act. On January 2, 1945, the general writes his wife explaining a new libation, a special old-fashioned cocktail, he had helped create. If he made it with his favorite bourbon, it went as follows: I. W. Harper's Kentucky

Straight Bourbon Whiskey; "melt up a teaspoon of orange marmalade in a glass; add whiskey and stir; then add ice and drink; it is swell. You put a little water in first to melt the marmalade [since] it [doesn't] melt well in whiskey." But avoid wood alcohol like the plague. Some of the troops believe they can make it safe by filtering it through a loaf of bread, but it can make you really sick and even kill you—plus it ruins that bread you just used as a filter, which you now need for that fine Spam sandwich.[62]

SLEEP

For many an infantryman, he is always tired. Really tired; in fact, after the war, a Hürtgen veteran stated, "I saw men die under artillery fire because they were so tired that they were only able to scratch the outline of a foxhole in the dirt."[63] Move here; move there. Carry this; carry that; now carry some more. Dig a foxhole all day; now go out on patrol tonight. Then go back in your foxhole and spend half of the rest of the night awake on security. And tomorrow? Do it all over again.

So, soldiers learn how to sleep in conditions that seem impossible to others. They are ingenious in staying dry enough to fall asleep, when water is dripping from over-hanging trees or oozing up from the wet ground below. Loud noises, causing civilians to wake up startled, are seemingly ignored by soldiers apparently slumbering in infant bliss. Once you get used to a few mortar rounds falling in your general vicinity, you can get used to almost anything. But don't give in to the urge to sleep in captured bunkers; the straw inside is full of fleas and lice.

As to sleeping surfaces, GIs can appear almost to levitate to be comfortable—curling around large rocks, avoiding sharp jutting roots, and steering clear of ground that might appear dry now but will be damp by morning. Louis Benoist wrote about sleep: "You know you have seen pictures of infantrymen sleeping wherever they hit the ground. It can be done—I do it. After so long a time you have to get used to it. Not so bad when you do. After your hips get tough, the ground gets pretty soft." Some soldiers even claim they can slip into a sleeplike trance while walking—trudging one foot ahead of the other in thousands of repetitions—all the while staying the proper distance behind the trooper in front of him.

After the war, former combat soldiers—now fathers and grandfathers—can seem-ingly take a short catnap anywhere: the sofa, the ballgame, outside in the backyard, at the beach, listening to the wife, all while the kids and grandkids are running around screaming, crashing into furniture, playing tag, lighting fireworks, and causing general auditory mayhem.

KRAUTS, JERRIES, HUNS, HEINIES, AND FRITZ

In both world wars, no one was concerned about hurting the feelings of the enemy, so several nicknames for German soldiers came into vogue. Huns, or the Hun, referred to the Dark Ages and the Huns of Atilla, curse of the Roman empire; Hun was used heavily in the Great War. Heinies was a term used by Canadians and some American soldiers, but it does not seem to have been as widespread as some other monikers.

The term "Kraut"—stemming from a stereotype of a sauerkraut-eating German—entered the American lexicon in the mid-nineteenth century. Then, German immigrants flooded the country by the millions, many of whom combined Teutonic efficiency and typical hard work to become quite successful in all walks of life. That term took on a more sinister connotation during the Great War, when Kraut was used in Great Britain and the US as a derogatory term for a German soldier. By World War II, American soldiers continued using the word, while many British troopers preferred the terms Jerry or Fritz. Jerry was possibly derived from the 1916 German helmet, which was said by British soldiers to resemble a chamber pot or Jeroboam. Fritz was short for Friedrich, a popular German name; back in the day in Prussia, people called King Friedrich the Great "Old Fritz" (Der Alte Fritz).

It seems that Jerry and Fritz were more socially acceptable in American military circles—the sort of words that officers would use. Noncommissioned officers, from anecdotal sources, preferred Krauts. As for American junior enlisted infantrymen, the kind who had to fight these German soldiers trying to kill them every day, and in the process see many of their own buddies killed, well, Kraut is a German's last name. His first name starts with God- or Mother-.

IV-FS AND JODY

All military personnel have their own terrors to overcome, on the basis of the environment in which they fight and the character of their enemies. But there is one fear they had already defeated for good, and that was to have been classified as a IV-F by the Selective Service. The goal of most young men is to fall into the category of I-A—available for military service. If you are II-B—deferred in war production, you are contributing to the war effort. Everyone needs to eat, so a category of II-C—deferred in agriculture, is honorable, as are numerous others in the fifty-one classifications. But a IV-F—rejected for military service because of physical, mental, or moral reasons, is often considered a stain on a young man's entire being.

Not only do most soldiers not want to be IV-Fs themselves, they often look down on those who were—for the simple reason that IV-Fs are often believed to be living large at home, while the soldiers are just trying to survive overseas. It became personal, and the IV-Fs became known as "Jodies." While you are in Europe or the Pacific, "Jody" is trying to date your girlfriend back home. And while you are driving an underarmored Sherman tank in France—praying that you do not run into a Tiger tank—"Jody" is motoring around in a Cadillac—with your girlfriend!

GIs cannot just go home and set things straight with "Jody," so they do the next best thing: they sing marching cadences belittling him. "Jody's got your Cadillac" is a popular refrain. And the troops bring these marching songs back home with them. *Battleground*, a 1949 American war film, followed a 3rd Platoon in the 101st US Airborne Division during the Battle of the Bulge. In the final scene, the platoon is seen hobbling in pain and exhaustion down a muddy road, having just been pulled off the front line. Many are wounded; others limp on frostbitten feet. Walking toward them is a fresh unit, perhaps just from the States. Van Johnson, playing wisecracking Pfc. Holley, seeing the fresh troops, calls out to James Whitmore—the hard-nosed, tobacco-chewing platoon sergeant, SSgt. Kinnie:

Holley: Hey, Kinnie; whatever happened to Jody? [gesturing toward fresh troops approaching]

Kinnie: All right, come on! Come on! What do you want these guys to think, you're a bunch of WACs? All right, all right, pick it up now; hut, two, three. Hut, two, three, four. Hut, two, three, four. Hut, two, three, four. Hut, two, three, four. Hut, two, three, four. Hut, two, three, four. You had a good home, but you left.

Platoon: You're right!

Kinnie: Jody was there when you left.

Platoon: You're right!

Kinnie: Your baby was there when you left.

Platoon: You're right!

Kinnie: Sound off!

Platoon: One, two.

Kinnie: Sound off!

Platoon: Three, four.

Kinnie: Cadence count,

Platoon: One, two, three, four. One, two . . . three, four!

Kinnie: Your baby was lonely—as lonely as could be.

Platoon: Till Jody provided company!

Kinnie: Ain't it great to have a pal.

Platoon: Who works so hard to keep up morale!

Kinnie: You ain't got nothing to worry about.

Platoon: He'll keep her happy till I get out!

Kinnie: You won't get out until the end of the war.

Platoon: In nineteen hundred and seventy-four!

Kinnie: Sound off!

Platoon: One, two.

Kinnie: Sound off!

Platoon: Three, four.

Audiences loved it in theaters, and soldiers loved it marching. It was too bad that Pvt. Willie Lee Duckworth, a Black soldier assigned to the Provisional Training Center at Fort Slocum, New York, couldn't copyright it, since he had originated the cadence in May 1944. If only he had the monetary rights to the tune, Willie would now own the US Army!

TIGER TANK

A GI's first response when asked what type of German tank he is facing is inevitably to say that it's a Tiger. And mostly, he would be incorrect, since encounters with Tigers were few and far between. The division may have faced a few Tiger I tanks in North Africa in 1943 and in Normandy in July–August 1944, and the 39th Infantry certainly was 6 or 7 miles north of Tiger II (King Tiger) tanks during the Bulge and would run into *one* dug-in King Tiger in April 1945, but the plain truth is that most armored vehicles they encounter are assault guns with 75 mm cannon—not the Tiger's legendary 88 mm. It was not a GI's fault for the incorrect identity. When the Germans are known—or simply just believed—to have Tiger tanks in the vicinity, British, American, and Soviet troops from private to colonel start sweating. Combat veterans might be seen puking behind a tree before an attack, when "Tiger fever" or "Tiger psychosis" starts to spread. Tigers possess a reputation that few other weapons ever approached, but they are not widespread on the battlefield, except in the imaginations of many an enemy. That's what a great weapon does.

GUARDIAN ANGEL

No soldier in Company B knows his name, but they all have a guardian angel in Elwood "Pete" Quesada. In fact, the commander of the IXth Tactical Air Command is the guardian angel of every infantryman in First Army, which is natural for him; years before, he attended the Wyoming Seminary in Wilkes-Barre, Pennsylvania, before his interest in souls changed to flying the wild blue yonder. IXth TAC has several ground-attack target types, to the delight of American infantrymen: enemy tanks, artillery emplacements, vehicles, troop formations, fixed fortifications; and clearing the skies of the Luftwaffe.

Pete's boys include the 70th Fighter Wing, 84th Fighter Wing, 36th Fighter Group, 48th Fighter Group, 366th Fighter Group, and 404th Fighter Group, and a whole bunch of attached organizations. They fly the P-47 Thunderbolt, the P-38 Lightning, and the P-51 Mustang. The armament on each is impressive. For ground-attack missions, the P-51 has its normal wing-mounted six .50-caliber machine guns and can be fitted to drop a 500-pound bomb or fire three 4.5-inch rockets. The P-38, nicknamed the "fork-tailed" devil by the Germans, has some nasty ground-attack weapons too: one 20 mm cannon, four .50-caliber machine guns, and up to 4,000 pounds in bombs or ten underwing rockets. The P-47, nicknamed the "Jug," carries eight .50-caliber machine guns and 2,500 pounds of bombs, or up to ten 5-inch rockets.

Those eight-fifties put out massive firepower. One observer, watching a P-47 firing, likens the cacophony of the octet, which deliver a combined bullet weight of 13 pounds of lead per second, to "driving a 5-ton truck straight at a wall at 60 miles an hour." As to the 5-inch High Velocity Aircraft Rockets, these 134-pound unguided weapons have 7.5-pound TNT warheads and sizzle off the launch rails at 1,375 feet per second, which, of course, is in addition to the aircraft's speed. Well, they are not nicknamed "Holy Moses" for nothing.[64]

All three planes can butcher a German column of troops and equipment in the open—but it all depends on flying weather, and in this area that's a dicey proposition. But the Germans take no chances and move at night, rather than risk daylight operations under the watchful eyes of the fighter jocks. Sometimes those eyes spot something larger. Legend has it that American pilots have been known to break into "I've Been Working on the Railroad" or "Chattanooga Choo-Choo" in the cockpit when they are fortunate enough to start a strafing run on a German train. Jack Jewell knows how valuable air support is:[65]

Just in case there is any doubt in your mind, I am part of a unit that is considered front line soldiers. All branches of the Service would like to say they are winning the war, I'm sure it takes all branches. But one thing I'm sure we could never do it as fast or effectively if not for the Air Corps. You don't know what a wonderful feeling an infantryman has when he sees his own planes diving and swooping to help him out in a tough job.

Gen. Hap Arnold couldn't have said it better.

CHAPTER FOUR

The Hell of the Hürtgen

I feel like a fugitive from th' law of averages.
— Willie, *Up Front*

Company B is hurtling toward the worst abomination in its long history of bloody combat. Many soldiers quit writing home—so gruesome are their experiences. Months of rapid advances, beautiful weather, and welcoming townspeople are over. Gains here are measured in yards, not miles. For the next 123 days, the company operates in a small area just 25 by 10 miles—almost all grim terrain. Weather is terrible one day and worse the next. The few civilians in the area are often German, not happy to see Americans in their Fatherland. Replacements can arrive in the morning and be dead by dusk—before veterans even learn their names.

The details of day-to-day operations reflect many adages of infantry combat. Rough terrain slows attacks. Artillery kills—them and us. Cold, wet weather causes trench foot, frostbite, and pneumonia. Cloud cover and poor visibility reduce air support.

Much information is derived from the daily Company Morning Report, a type-written card produced every day for every basic unit of the Army—companies, batteries, etc.—by the unit clerk and signed by the commander, before submission to battalion headquarters. It reflects information through 2400 hours (midnight) of the date listed on the report, including troop strength, arriving and departing soldiers, and casualties. The commander often adds comments, but it is not possible to accurately determine if some data are actually a day late, perhaps two, if the unit was heavily engaged. Weather information and daily events also come from regiment and division reports.

OCTOBER 1, 1944: SIEGFRIED LINE

Company B is 1 mile northwest of Lammersdorf, Germany, 15 miles east of Eupen, Belgium.[1] The weather is a high of 63°, a low of 49°, clouds broken to overcast, light drizzle rain, and surface winds 5–8 mph; flying conditions bad till 1000 hours, then fair; cold and rainy. Company combat strength is four officers and 128 enlisted. The company commander is Capt. Jack Dunlap. Pfc. Charles Johnson and Pfc. Joseph Scafaro are evacuated for nonbattle illness; Charles received a Bronze Star on September 15, 1944. The company conducts patrols. The 39th Infantry will be relieved in place by the 4th Cavalry Group, a regimental-size formation of two cavalry (mechanized) squadrons—their horses put out to pasture long ago. Long-range artillery shells the regiment along the entire front, targeting roads and road junctions. The division CP is north, near the Rötgen train station.[2] Jack Jewell writes home. If they actually fill his order for Sunshine Crackers, caramels, and jelly, half the cookies and candy in Kansas will wind up in Company B. The men receive showers and clean clothes.[3]

OCTOBER 2, 1944: SIEGFRIED LINE

Company B remains in position. Weather is a high of 52°, a low of 47°, rain showers about noon, and surface winds 8–15 mph, with flying conditions fair. Company strength is five officers and 132 enlisted. 1Lt. Norman Mickelson arrives from the 92nd Replacement Battalion, which supports the VIIth Corps—located 5 miles from Aachen. Supply sergeant Albert Baccile returns to duty after serious wounds in the thigh and wrist by artillery shrapnel in Normandy on July 19. Pfc. Meyer Metkoff, a married tailor from the Bronx, is evacuated for nonbattle illness. Battalion continues patrolling and planning to be relieved in place. Long-range 170 mm artillery targets Lammersdorf between 1820 and 2400 hours—the high-explosive, 138-pound shells can travel 18 miles.

OCTOBER 3, 1944: SIEGFRIED LINE

Company B location remains unchanged northwest of Lammersdorf. The weather is perfect for catching a cold: a high of 52°, a low of 39°, overcast until 1000 hours, rain showers late, drizzle from 1700 to 2200 hours, and surface winds 8–10 mph, with muddy ground. Strength is five officers and 132 enlisted. Napoleon Daniels, 3rd Platoon, is appointed sergeant and awarded Army occupational specialty 653—assistant squad leader. At 0545 hours, the enemy attacks Second Battalion but is repulsed by artillery fire. The division commander visits AAAO CP at 1105 hours.

The 4th Cavalry Group begins relieving the regiment during the night to hide the activity from enemy observers, which will allow the regiment to attack somewhere else. Five enemy POWs are captured at 2355 hours. Jewell writes home about Hawk DiRisio: "Our mess sergeant is more of a clown than anything else. He sure isn't a cook. He plays an accordion and sings Italian songs. That keeps the boys in good spirits and is just what they need."[4] The young officer is learning that keeping morale high is often more important than anything else. Especially here.

OCTOBER 4, 1944: HÜRTGEN FOREST

Company B, with six officers and 152 enlisted, moves 2⅓ miles southeast of the village of Zweifall, Germany, 8 miles from Aachen.[5] The weather is a high of 50°, a low of 41°, and light scattered rain after noon, with flying conditions good after noon. The morning report reads "The Company left bivouac area 1 mile northwest of Lammersdorf at 0930 hours by foot and marched to an assembly area 2⅓ miles southeast of Zweifall, Germany. Distance marched by foot approximately 8 miles." One enlisted man is evacuated for nonbattle illness. 2Lt. Roger Reeves returns from a wound received in Normandy. Pfc. William Spano and Privates George Holdren and Bert Jones arrive from 3rd Replacement Depot, a "large, bleak, muddy field that housed filthy and worn-out men and equipment."[6] All three riflemen are assigned to 3rd Platoon.

Another new man is Pvt. Richard O'Brian, Army occupational specialty 521-basic, meaning that Richard has completed basic training but requires additional skills to qualify as an infantryman. Instructions for 521s include they be constantly observed and tested to "determine their potentialities." Unfortunately, in the Hürtgen the Germans will cause a few of these men to flunk their final exams. The regiment begins withdrawing at 0400 hours; before daylight, all vehicles must clear Lammersdorf. The 39th will move to southeast of Zweifall to attack the hamlet of Germeter and village of Vossenack in conjunction with the 60th Infantry the following day. The regimental CP is established near a trail junction in the Wenau Woods 2 miles southeast of Zweifall at 0900 hours.[7] The division CP moves to Zweifall.[8] Here, Maj. Gen. Louis Craig pens a letter to Col. Bond, praising the regiment:

> I want to express to you and to the members of your regiment my appreciation for the fine spirit and determination shown in the recent operation in the vicinity of Lammersdorf. Under difficult conditions involving detailed planning and a high grade of small-unit leadership, the 39th Infantry has cleared a great swath in the German fortified line. This has resulted in a large loss of personnel to the enemy and has impressed him with the dogged determination that refuses to be deterred by any obstacle. The spirit of the 39th Infantry in these difficulties has been of the highest, and I hope all members of your command will realize that their accomplishment has been a definite contribution in this period, as in the past, to the final winning of the war.

The company CP is in an abandoned German bunker in a thick woods with a strange name. The men will attack into the Hürtgenwald, the Hürtgen, a 70-square-mile-forest along the German-Belgian border south of Aachen—actually, a combination of several forests: Hürtgen, Rötgen, Monschau, Wenau, and a few smaller ones. It appears on American maps as two words, and the troops just call it Hürtgen, which author Charles B. MacDonald suggests was perfect—"hurt" with some threatening German guttural syllable after it.

The Hürtgen is two steps forward and one step back. The enemy, often just 150 feet away, seems even closer. Some soldiers call it the "Death Factory," and others nickname it "the Hurtin' Forest." Later, the official Army history stated, "Upon entering the forest, you want to drop things behind to mark your path, as Hansel and Gretel did with their breadcrumbs."[9] What the official history did not remind its readers is that those two youngsters were lured deeper into the woods by a bloodthirsty witch, who built a gingerbread house to lure in children, so as to cook and eat them. And while there are no gingerbread houses in the Hürtgen, there are thousands of witches—and they all wear the field gray of the German army.

The forest stands at the northern end of the Ardennes region of Belgium and Luxembourg, and the Eifel region of Germany. Technically a high plateau, it appears as forested mountains, gouged by small, cold streams. To the north is the Aachen Corridor—open attack country; to the south is more rough terrain known as the Hohes Venn. Three bald, exposed ridgelines run through the area from southwest to northeast. The highest elevations lie west of Monschau, at 2,100 feet above sea level; heights fall to 600 feet, where the forest ends just west of the city of Düren. Narrow streams funnel cold, rushing water through steep valleys. Stream width is not the problem in crossing, but the vertical, slippery banks slow men down, causing frequent falls into the water that can lead to hypothermia—because here, in the end, almost everything contributes to hypothermia—temperature, moisture, exhaustion, disease, wounds, injuries and malnutrition:[10]

> The GIs crawled into the forest the way amphibious beasts crawl into the water, with the waves closing around them and never letting go. They crawled through the green darkness of the intertwining branches, and through a jungle of pine needles and muck in a never-ending rain, chilled to the bone day and night, never dry.

Narrow, hard-packed earth and gravel roads, never designed for heavy traffic, become muddy quagmires, with liquid earth the consistency of diarrhea, virtually impassable for all wheeled vehicles; in fact, a few unfortunate soldiers find that some mudholes are knee deep. Deeply wooded ravines make off-road vehicular travel extremely difficult. Foot trails are almost nonexistent, or so twisted and winding that every trail looks the same and can lead to walking in circles—giving an awaiting stationary mine or booby trap multiple opportunities to get you. Gray clouds hang low; rain and cold promote the growth of moss, making German concrete bunkers difficult to see. Eons of forested conifer growth have led the ground between the densely packed trees to be a sponge carpet of pine needles, soaking up cold water. The trees are planted in straight rows some 8 to 12 feet apart, close enough together that the treetops touch one another, creating perpetual darkness underneath.

At regular intervals, foresters have cut 150-to-300-foot-wide strips—called firebreaks—which are devoid of trees, not to augment the defenses but to prevent natural forest fires from burning the whole place down. Firebreaks entice American units to cross them, since they have no downed trees, making movement easier. It is a deadly illusion—because firebreaks create perfect lanes for German machine gun fire. And if you are the target of one of Herr Mauser's machine guns, you are going to get a bellyful of lead. In other areas, trees knocked down by artillery fire make all movement almost impossible, so pick your poison. Famed writer Ernest Hemingway penned an apt description for *Collier's* magazine: "It was cold and raining and blowing vigorously, and before us stretched the dark tree wall of the Snow Eifel where the dragon lived."

Perhaps a bit of artistic license by "Papa" Hemingway, but a dragon's lair precisely captures the foreboding nature of the woods. The Hürtgen is where soldiers walk a few feet from their foxholes and are never seen again—as if a Brothers Grimm dragon swallowed them whole without a trace. Hemingway added, "Whoever survived Hürtgenwald must have had a guardian angel on each of his shoulders." But sometimes not even an angel can help you. Italian writer Dante Alighieri captured the essence of the Hürtgen best—over six hundred years before the battle. In his epic poem *Divine Comedy*, Dante describes his journey through Hell, seeing at the entrance a sign stating "Abandon all hope, ye who enter here."[11]

OCTOBER 5, 1944: HÜRTGEN FOREST

Company B is 2⅓ miles southeast of Zweifall.[12] A thoroughly rotten day: rain showers, surface winds at 8–10 mph, flying conditions fair to moderate, visibility poor for dive-bombers, cold ground, colder air. Company B's strength: six officers and 165 enlisted. Platoon leader Roger Reeves is evacuated for a severe nonbattle injury, as is Sgt. Vallis Alexander of Nashville. Dunlap receives orders to enter the forest, cross the 5-foot-wide Weisser Weh Creek, seize the village of Germeter, and cut the Simmerath–Düren road, as part of the 39th Infantry attack. The advance will occur just north of marshy ground with an ominous name of Todten-Bruch—Deadman's Moor. Overall, the division objective is to seize the crossroads village of Schmidt to the southeast.

The battalion moves forward at 0900 hours to the line of departure. Air attacks scheduled for 0930 hours are delayed thirty minutes. At 0918 hours, division informs regiment that bombing is further delayed to 1100 hours. At 1045 hours, quite frustrated, General Craig informs all units that the attack will be postponed a day. The Luftwaffe has no such delays; nine Messerschmitt Me 109 fighters attack division headquarters that afternoon.[13] Lost in the chaos: today is Jack Jewell's twenty-fifth birthday.

OCTOBER 6, 1944: HÜRTGEN FOREST

Company B is ¾ mile west of Germeter.[14] Another cruddy day: a high of 54°, a low of 42°, cloudy, and light intermittent rain after 0400 hours; flying conditions are poor. Strength: five officers and 158 enlisted. Jack Dunlap writes, "The Company attacked toward Germeter, Germany, and moved forward approximately 2,000 yards; captured several prisoners and two pillboxes." Pfc. Arnold Odette Jr. is killed. TSgt. Lawrence Cherry, Pfc. Joseph Coy, and Privates John Gamble, Louis Montoya, and Shelby Thompson are seriously wounded. Pfc. Ray Goodwin and Pvt. James Scates—the latter a light-truck driver by training but now an ammo carrier—are evacuated for nonbattle illness.

Arnold is from Huntington, West Virginia. Artillery shell fragments strike him in the face and neck, penetrating his occipital bone, killing him instantly. Louis, a 5'3" tall Mexican American trooper from Las Vegas, New Mexico, is in his third day in the company; wounded by artillery shrapnel in the thigh, it is nasty, and Louis spends the next forty-three days in the hospital. Lawrence, from Adaville, Kentucky, enlisted at

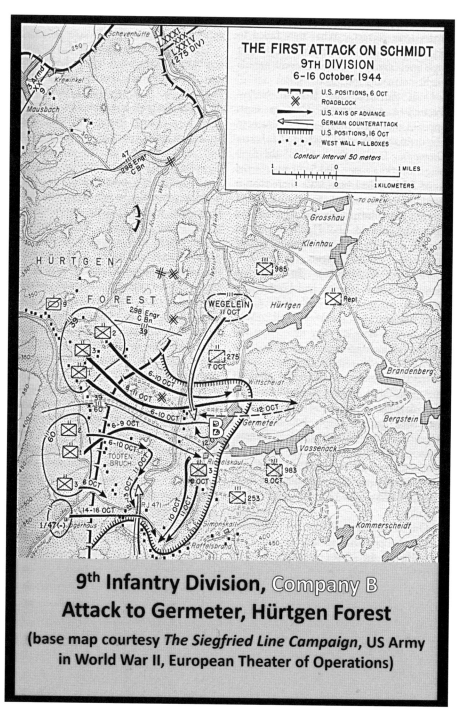

9ᵗʰ Infantry Division, Company B
Attack to Germeter, Hürtgen Forest
(base map courtesy *The Siegfried Line Campaign*, US Army
in World War II, European Theater of Operations)

MAP 5: 9th Infantry Division, Company B, Attack to Germeter, Hürtgen Forest

Fort Knox August 7, 1940, and has been in the company since June 1941; he was wounded twice before, and today an artillery explosion wounds him in the back. He is evacuated to the 188th General Hospital in Cirencester, England, for forty-two days.

Joe Coy, a coal miner from Sewell Mountain, West Virginia, is a light machine gunner; he has been in the company since May 9, 1942. Joe was slightly wounded on November 20, 1942, at Djidjelli, Algeria, and contracted malaria in Sicily. Then he was wounded by an artillery shell in Normandy and evacuated to the 91st Evacuation Hospital and then to the 43rd General Hospital; today he is again wounded by an artillery explosion and will be in the hospital until February 1945. Artillery shrapnel strikes John Gamble's arm; he is treated at the aid station, and back to the company he goes. Shelby Thompson, a widower from Oklahoma, is not so blessed; artillery explodes right next to him, and the blast effects send him to the 136th Station Hospital at Acton Place, Sudbury, England, for forty-nine days of continuous splitting headaches that probably make a brown-bottle-flu hangover seem tame.

To the 39th's left is the 47th Infantry; to the right is the 4th Cavalry Group. AAAO's frontage is 800 yards wide.[15] Its mission: cross Weisser Weh Creek, seize Germeter, cut the Simmerath–Düren road, and capture Vossenack Ridge—which will serve as a launch point for a later attack southeast against Schmidt. The farming village of Vossenack, on a 1.5-mile-long, narrow, windswept ridge, will have to be cleared of the enemy. Meanwhile, the 60th Infantry will seize the high ground (Hill 455) and road junction—commonly called Richelskaul—south of Germeter.

Again, the aerial bombardment plan is a snafu. Original bombardment time is 0730 hours, but at 0645 hours it is delayed until 0800 hours. At 0747 hours, the bombardment is postponed once again—to 0900 hours. But at 0840 hours, the division commander further kicks the can down the road to 0930 hours. It's the weather; if the spotter planes cannot see through the pea soup, the fighter-bombers will not be able to either. And if ordnance is dropped blind, it may accidently fall on friendly troops—because a bomb doesn't care whom it kills.

Fighter-bombers take off at 1010 hours and begin bombing at 1100 hours. At 1130 hours, First Battalion attacks in the south; the Third Battalion attacks in the north, with the Second Battalion following the Third to protect the northern flank of the regiment. Even before the troops, who can see only a few yards ahead in the dense woods, reach their line of departure, enemy small-arms fire begins to pepper them. Fire strikes key roadblocks; worse, advancing soldiers find that they have been booby-trapped—apparent only when the first soldier is wounded or killed by one. The enemy defends stubbornly in sector, using long-range artillery. It is blood-drenched German Great War tactics all over again: "Artillery shapes the battlefield—machine guns defend it."[16]

The first mile is downhill, with streamlets every 400 yards, as the men approach the Weisser Wehe, at an elevation of 285 meters. Across the creek are two pillboxes that Company B captures; three more bunkers guard Germeter. Germeter, their objective, is 1,000 yards east of the creek at an elevation of 448 meters and is defended by units of the 942nd Infantry Regiment of the 353rd Infantry Division. After the creek, the attack will be uphill. Attacking uphill is bad.

At 1240 hours, Company B reaches a trail intersection at elevation 456.[17] Battalion reports receiving mortar and artillery fire at 1325 hours. An hour later, Company B is at the Weisser Wehe and maneuvering against a pillbox.[18] The fighting is confusing in the dark woods. At 1429 hours, Company C reports friendly artillery fire falling on its location. Battalion establishes a forward CP in the woods at 1625 hours[19] and reports at 1955 hours the capture of three pillboxes.[20] All are type R10a bunkers, with 4'11" thick reinforced concrete roofs and walls, are poison-gas proof, and have room for ten to twelve soldiers, with a stepped embrasure facing backward and embrasures at the front and sides for machine guns, and additional portholes for riflemen.

At nightfall, Company B stops 800 yards short of Germeter, having killed or captured thirty men, including one officer. At midnight, AAAO reports that it is facing a well-organized, stubborn defense, supported by heavy artillery and 120 mm mortars. Enemy strength is estimated at eight hundred to nine hundred men.[21] The men will have hot food tonight; they better savor it—they won't have hot chow for the next fourteen days.

OCTOBER 7, 1944: HÜRTGEN FOREST

The company is ⅓ mile west of Germeter.[22] The weather is looking up: a high of 55°, a low of 38°, broken clouds after noon, and early-morning fog: flying conditions are good. Strength: five officers and 155 enlisted. Platoon leader Norm Mickelson is evacuated to a clearing station for nonbattle illness. TSgt. Robert Weber and Sergeants Frederick Naugle and George Rosen are wounded. Previously hit by artillery shrapnel to his left knee on August 19, Robert is severely concussed by an artillery explosion, which also leads to appendicitis; he will spend the next ninety-four days at a station hospital. Shrapnel hits George on the right foot; he was wounded in the ankle by shrapnel in Sicily and wounded again two weeks ago.

An artillery shell blast concusses squad leader Naugle at 1700 hours, his second wound. He is evacuated to the 2nd Evacuation Hospital at Eupen, transferred to the 130th Station Hospital, and then to the 129th General Hospital. Fred arrived in the company on July 8; he was wounded two days later by artillery shrapnel to his left ankle. He is an interesting soldier: born in Roscommon, Ireland, in 1924, he grows up in Grammercy Park, New York City; after he enlists in 1943, he informs the Army that he is an expert horseman and requests a transfer to the cavalry at Fort Riley, Kansas, but Uncle Sam isn't buying that blarney, and off to the infantry Fred goes.

Heavy artillery fire falls during the night, causing the regiment sixty casualties. Enemy mortar fire hits Company B at 0655 and 0749 hours. First and Third Battalions advance at 0800 hours under heavy mortar and artillery fire. By 0903 hours, the two battalions have gained only 100 yards; enemy small-arms fire now is coming from their left rear, indicating a bypassed enemy position that needs to be cleared. Company B's lead platoon reaches another pillbox on a major trail 500 yards from Germeter by

1030 hours.[23] A single tank, protected with thick logs and sandbags on its front slope, of 1st Platoon of Company C in the 746th Tank Battalion attacks the bunker at 1111 hours, raising the ire of Col Bond, who tells Lt. Col. Thompson at 1145 hours not to delay the attack for one pillbox, but to keep up with Third Battalion's advance.

Capt. James R. Shields, commanding Company C, 746th Tank Battalion, later states that while only one tank could fire at a time attacking through woods, a second tank would always follow to protect the lead vehicle. In almost all situations, infantry accompanies tanks, as in the woods, which is essential because of a tank's limited observation. But at night, no one can see:[24]

> The dark of night in the forest was almost beyond description. A man couldn't even step out of his foxhole to relieve himself with any certainty that he would find his way back. Trees less than five feet away were not visible. It was not possible to throw a grenade at night without fear that it would bounce off a tree and come back into the foxhole. Resourceful GIs overcame the problem by placing stones on the edge of the hole in daylight, so they can tell by feel the direction of a safe throwing lane in the dark.

At noon, the regiment reports that it is facing continued defense and is engaged in intense firefights with heavy mortar and artillery barrages. By 1345 hours, Company B has gained only 100 yards.[25] P-47s strafe and bomb Germeter, which has heavy bands of barbed wire strung just west of the village. At 1656 hours, division reports a P-47 with swastika markings flying in the area; four Me 109 fighter planes are sighted twice in sector during the day. Antipersonnel mines halt Third Battalion at 1700 hours. At 1732 hours, Col. Bond informs division of the situation, and that Company B is 250 yards short of Germeter, with most of the opposition being machine gun fire, but that he is moving tanks forward.[26] At 1800 hours, regiment reports artillery and mortar fire on advancing units along the roads to Germeter. "Friendly" bombs strike the First Battalion CP 300 yards west of the Weisser Wehe, severing telephone wires.[27] Enemy field fortifications are well constructed; supporting them is either an enemy tank or self-propelled (SP) gun.

Company B reaches the edge of the woods short of Germeter, 100 yards from the Simmerath–Düren road at 1815 hours, but Lt. Col. Thompson requests tank support before sending his men into the open.[28] The company is receiving artillery fire. At midnight, regiment reports that enemy infantry continues to defend with determination, engaging them in heavy firefights and again firing long-range artillery. Back home, the number one song on the charts is "You Always Hurt the One You Love" by the Mills Brothers, but out here, there is certainly no love lost, since the Hürtgen is trying to hurt everyone.

OCTOBER 8, 1944: HÜRTGEN FOREST

Company B is 440 yards west of Germeter.[29] Weather improving: a high of 60°, a low of 44°, and no rain; flying conditions are good. Strength is six officers and 145 enlisted. Jack Dunlap writes, "Still trying to take Germeter, Germany, and meeting very stiff opposition in the form of heavy artillery barrages and mortar fire." 2Lt. Louis Benoist arrives from the 92nd Replacement Battalion. A bloody day for Company B, with sixteen wounded: 1Lt. Stanley Mills; S/Sgt Timothy Lyons; Privates First Class Michael Carlone, Edward Goodrich, Henry Jones Jr., Robert Kalvitz, Claud Ledford, Alva Moore, Robert Redden, and Clarence Yeakel; and Privates Frank Kryger, John Moore, James Marcinkowski, James Nelson, Paul Taylor, and Warren Young. One enlisted man is evacuated for nonbattle illness.

It is artillery hell in Company B. Lyons, born in Ireland and in the company since the beginning, starting as a young private wearing glasses in June 1941, was wounded by enemy machine gun bullets in the thigh in July 1944 and convalesced for fifty-one days in the 307th Station Hospital—Stoneleigh Park, Kenilworth, England—before returning on September 24. Today, enemy artillery fire smashes his tibia in two places—he will spend the next 901 days in military hospitals. Some luck of the Irish. Shrapnel hits Stanley in the left lower leg; Kalvitz is hit by shrapnel in the left hand but stays on duty—he can shoot fine with one hand. Moore goes down from shrapnel to his right lower leg. Jagged shrapnel penetrates Goodrich's shoulder blade. A hosiery maker from Wallace Pender, North Carolina, automatic rifleman Henry Jones is hit in the back at 1100 hours by shrapnel, and a piece penetrates to within half an inch of his spine; a medic pours sulfa powder on the wound, and Henry is evacuated.

Shrapnel hits Claud in his chest; he will spend the next forty-one days in a hospital. Jim Marcinkowski, in his third day at the front, is hit by shrapnel in the leg. Shrapnel rakes Paul Taylor's eye; he'll be in a hospital for seven months. A jagged piece of shrapnel hits Clarence Yeakel in the right ear, but he remains on duty. A bullet hits James Nelson in the forearm and elbow; another bullet strikes Warren Young in the upper arm. James has been in the company just four days, Frank Kryger and John Moore only three.

At age thirty-seven, Michael Carlone is ancient by infantry standards. Born in Rhode Island, he's a knife maker and tool sharpener when he enlists in Providence on September 28, 1943; he arrives at Company B on August 19, 1944. His days as a knife and tool guy are probably over after artillery shrapnel tears into his foot, forehead, face, and neck—the blast also destroys an eardrum. Over the next six months, doctors remove fragments of Michael's cranium that have been blown into his brain; they worry that he will be permanently disfigured. Nineteen-year-old Claud Ledford is a sheet-metal worker from Little Rock. Ed Goodrich is a welder, all 6'2" of him. Now all they and the other metal man, Michael Carlone, care about are the jagged pieces of Nazi steel in their bodies.

On the basis of German POW information, ~~AAO~~ estimates that it is facing nineteen infantry companies from the German 275th, 347th, and 353rd Infantry Divisions, and that each company fields one hundred men. Enemy artillery falls on the front lines at 0700, an hour before Company B's planned attack. The company is engaged in a small-arms fight at 0800 hours. Battalion reports many casualties in Company B and Company C from artillery fire, but First and Third Battalion commanders believe that the situation is under control by 0825 hours. General Craig visits the 39th CP at 0900 hours. Jack Dunlap is at Company B's CP, in the thick woods, when a German shell hits, throwing a heavy log on top of First Sergeant Gravino and trapping his left leg.[30] Ben Murrell recalled that it took thirty frantic minutes to free Joe, who remained in pain for several days but refused to go to an aid station.

Company L's commander is killed. This loss, and other officer casualties in the regiment, delays the attack until 1100 hours, but it still runs into stubborn resistance, as enemy mortar, artillery, and small-arms fire increases in intensity. At noon, regiment reports long-range artillery began shelling at 0630 hours for thirty minutes and has continued sporadically since. Battalion receives heavy small-arms fire as it approaches Germeter at 1215 hours. At 1350 hours, regiment reports that Company A and Company B are fighting the 2nd Company of the 1412th Fortress Infantry Battalion, recently arrived in sector. At 1545 hours, Gen. Craig tells Col Bond that the VIIth Corps commander, Maj. Gen. J. Lawton Collins—known by the troops as "Lightning Joe"—is anxious to secure the Germeter–Hürtgen road today. "Anxious" means "Move your ass." At 1800 hours, the regiment reports that the enemy continues to shell the battalions that are engaging the enemy; the volume of small-arms fire is heavy. The Company B limit of advance at 2000 hours stretches south of their previous position; two friendly tanks are moving down a firebreak to their rear.

The tanks arrive at 2129 hours, well after dark.[31] Both battalions for the assault the next day request that no artillery prep be fired, so as to gain surprise. At midnight, regiment states that for the day, the enemy shelled the front lines, battalion CPs, and rear areas with artillery batteries and mortars. Barrages have been heavy and effective, particularly mortars, which slow up the advance, especially in the First Battalion attack zone. Firebreaks, road mines, and booby traps prevent cutting the Germeter–Hürtgen road.

Meanwhile, to the north, the First Army encircles and attacks Aachen, the 30th US Infantry Division of the XIXth US Corps from the north and the 1st Infantry Division of VIIth Corps from the south. As they close on the heart of the city, 155 mm self-propelled guns line up in direct-fire mode against German strongpoints a few hundred yards away, and the big guns earn a new nickname—"Doorknockers."[32]

The Germans have artillery too, and it is deadly. Many of the wounded in the Hürtgen are hit by enemy fire that causes trees to virtually explode, as shells burst 80 to 100 feet above the ground—about the same height as the top of tall fir trees. These treetop explosions not only rip the bark off the trees but also send a lethal rain of wood splinters and shrapnel down on the American troops, who instinctively duck down— intuitively but uselessly—at the first sound of explosions.[33] Veteran troops learn to stay standing and "hug a tree" during tree bursts—pressing hard against large trunks to minimize exposed area to just their head and the top of their shoulders. But for "green" troops, their first instinct to run or dive flat on the ground can prove fatal, when "the artillery splinters came down like glowing steel rain." Ernest Hemingway later writes *Across the River and into the Trees*, describing wounds and tree bursts:[34]

> Now every second man in it was dead and the others nearly all were wounded. In the belly, the head, the feet or the hands, the neck, the back, the lucky buttocks, the unfortunate chest, and the other places. Tree burst wounds hit men where they would never be wounded in open country. And all of the wounded were wounded for life.

OCTOBER 9, 1944: HÜRTGEN FOREST

Company B's CP is ¼ mile west of Germeter.[35] The weather is changing: a high of 62°, a low of 46°, cloudy and overcast till 0900 hours, light rain, and surface winds at 3–7 mph; flying conditions are poor until 1100 hours, then moderate. Strength is six officers and 150 enlisted. Capt. Dunlap writes, "The Company attacked outer defenses of the town of Germeter, Germany. Met very stiff resistance, heavy artillery and mortar fire and were forced to withdraw to original position. Remained in defenses."

Pfcs. Walter Frueauf, Donald Gartland, John Gronkiewicz, Ben Lance, John Pawlik, Frank Russo, Gordon Vickers, and Paul Sapp and Privates Clifford Chew and Patrick Yates are wounded. Walt enlisted on April 17, 1943, in Montgomery County, Ohio. He is a machinist; today artillery shrapnel hits his tibia. Don, in the company since June 1941, had been wounded by a bullet in the rear end in Tunisia and in the hand on September 20, 1944, by arty shrapnel, and today he has his kneecap blown off by more shrapnel, a "Statue of Liberty" wound keeping him in hospitals for the next ten months. Gronkiewicz is a big, strong Chicago laborer making auto springs. Both his parents are from Poland; it is his second artillery wound, the first coming in Normandy.

Ben, from Lumpkin, Georgia, was wounded in the neck by artillery shrapnel on August 4; he had just returned on October 2. Today is much worse. Artillery shrapnel causes a compound fracture of his skull, with extensive brain damage; Ben will never marry and will die in 1960—the Hürtgen is still killing sixteen years after the battle. Pawlik, a sheet-metal worker born in Chicago on October 25, 1918, will be discharged from a military hospital and the Army on May 19, 1945.[36] Twenty-eight-year-old New Jersey furrier Frank Russo enlisted on January 23, 1941. Artillery shrapnel hits his spine and shoulder blade. Shrapnel strikes Gordon in the butt and hip. Paul is Regular Army, enlisting at Fort Screven, Georgia, on October 30, 1940. On June 15, 1944, shards from an exploding land mine strike him in the thigh; now shrapnel hits his back. Cliff, from Pennsylvania, arrived earlier today; he is soon hit in the left hand by shrapnel but remains in the fight. Arty fragments hit Patrick in the forearm and neck.

Battalion continues the attack at 0700 hours and immediately makes contact in the small houses along the Germeter–Hürtgen road. At 0750 hours, American tanks set several houses on fire; Company B attacks buildings on the western side of the road with tank support at 1030 hours. One of the houses is actually built over a pillbox, providing perfect camouflage. The company CP locates just outside Germeter at 1040 hours.[37] At 1200 hours, enemy artillery batteries increase their fire as the battalions are engaging enemy infantry units in extremely heavy firefights. The battalion encounters barbed wire protected by enemy machine guns. "Lightning Joe" visits the regimental CP at 1230 hours to urge on the men, as the Germans capture the village of Wittscheidt.

Gen. Craig visits ~~AAA~~O CP at 1550 hours. At 1707 hours, Company C reports that along the Germeter–Hürtgen road its soldiers and the enemy are in the same houses, throwing hand grenades at each other. At 1800 hours, regiment reports that it is still battling for Germeter and still receiving heavy enemy small-arms and moderate artillery and mortar fire, as well as some self-propelled fire, probably from Sturmgeschütz (Assault Gun) Brigade 902 lurking in the area. The company captures one or two buildings east of the road at 1900 hours but withdraws later to the west side of the road. The 39th combat report at 2400 hours summarizes that during the day, the enemy maintained close contact with the advancing battalions, attacking machine gun positions with grenades. As the two battalions near Germeter, the enemy rakes them with extremely heavy machine gun fire. Third Battalion has one constant daylong firefight, as all units experience heavy to moderate artillery fire. Because of the debris caused by the artillery, it is hard to move through the woods.

Back home, the St. Louis Cardinals defeat the St. Louis Browns in game 6, clinching the 1944 World Series four games to two. Meanwhile, the *New York Times*—seemingly oblivious to the savagery of the fighting—reports that "good progress in the Forest of Huertgen has taken our troops to within less than two miles of the village of Huertgen."[38]

OCTOBER 10, 1944: HÜRTGEN FOREST

The company is located at Germeter.[39] No need to worry about enemy aircraft today: a high of 54°, a low of 44°, low broken clouds, overcast, light drizzle rain, fog, poor visibility, flying not possible, wet, and muddy. Six officers and 142 enlisted. Jack Dunlap writes in the morning report: "The Company continued its attack under heavy artillery and mortar fire and captured the town of Germeter, Germany. Set up defensive positions as a counterattack was expected. Received heavy shelling most of the night. Overcoats were issued to all men in the company, and 70 percent of them were thrown away because of the fact that they are too heavy to carry in combat. Suggest that combat suits be issued to front line troops."

SSgt. Gilbert Miller; Pfcs. Leslie Bacon, Ralph Hughes Jr., Charles Mayer, and Walter "Doc" Wilhoite; and Pvts. William Adkins, Charles Carroll, William Farmer, Harry Johnson, Hayden Johnson, Arthur Shockley, and William Spanguolo are wounded. Sgt. Victor Fink is seriously injured. This one, to the wrist, will be the first of three wounds for Gilbert. Artillery shrapnel hits Leslie in the back of the knee; the 35-year-old from Ontario County, New York, was wounded in Normandy by artillery. Shrapnel hits Spanguolo in the leg; he'll be hospitalized till May 1945. Shrapnel hits Ralph's foot; shrapnel also hit his fingers two weeks ago. Charles Mayer is hit by shrapnel in the shoulder and nose.

Artillery shrapnel hits Doc Wilhoite, a twenty-year-old from Kentucky, in the thigh, and by the time he makes it back to the field hospital, the wound is infected; he arrived in the company earlier today. William Adkins, wounded in Normandy by grenade fragments to his hand, just returned yesterday; today several machine gun bullets strike his arm. Charles Carroll, in his second day, is struck by artillery shrapnel in the shoulder. William Farmer's shrapnel wound is in the groin; Harry's is in the thigh. Both arrived five days ago. Shrapnel hits Hayden's knee. Arthur arrived at the company just six days ago; he has the worst wound of the day—shrapnel hits in the leg and the scrotum.

Victor Fink, from Cleveland, is evacuated for his eye injury and is hospitalized until February 1945. 1Lt. Norman Mickelson is evacuated for a nonbattle illness. Many men have wet feet and are sleeping under wet blankets. Warren Ridgeway returns from the hospital and becomes the leader for 3rd Squad, 3rd Platoon. Pvt. Robert Pettigrew, a rifleman, arrives with fourteen other replacements from the 92nd Replacement Battalion and is assigned to Ridgeway. He has sixty minutes before the platoon attacks:[40]

> Had just joined the company and one hour later moved out in attack and was pinned down by small arm's fire. For first time. Pinned down for a short time with small arm's fire. Moved out shortly after as soon as another platoon flanked [the] machine gun holding us out in [the] forest. Finally captured objective [Germeter] after about three hours of fighting.

First Battalion receives artillery and heavy machine gun fire from the right front each time it attempts to advance. Capt. Dunlap moves the CP to the Weisser Weh ravine, due west of Germeter, and sends out a combat patrol that outflanks a machine gun on the southern edge of Germeter, knocking it out.[41] Company B consolidates its positions on both sides of the Germeter–Hürtgen road at 1347 hours as artillery starts again. At 1800 hours, regiment reports that the enemy is continuing to resolutely defend. AAAO has now interrogated fifty-one enemy POWs.

At 2400 hours, the regiment's final daily combat report summarizes that during the day, the enemy defended the main line of resistance with fanatical determination; combat is fierce—just in Company I, thirty men are missing. Germeter is only 31 miles as the crow flies southwest of the massive Cologne Cathedral, Germany's largest—and from vantage points in the Hürtgen, on a good day the church spires can be seen through binoculars. So close, and yet so far. The regiment receives the heaviest artillery barrage and machine gun crossfire yet encountered, suffering heavy casualties, as the enemy brings in a battalion of police and engineers as infantry—disturbing, since German engineers often have *Flammenwerfer*—flamethrowers. But today the Germans have another surprise; they have sown the entire sector with a new and deadly crop—*Schuh* (shoe) mines and *Teller* (plate) mines.

Even the Hürtgen soil is filled with death. Some fiendish devices, known as glass mines, are antipersonnel mines with a glass body to avoid detection by the enemy. The mine's glass bowl, 6 inches in diameter, contains an explosive charge and a detonator. A ¼-inch-thick sheet-glass disk under a thick, molded glass pressure plate covers the top of the device, which detonates under 40 pounds of pressure. Other glass mines use thin wooden sticks or twigs to suspend the glass pressure plate over the detonator fuze, which requires only 7 pounds of pressure to explode. For use in wet forests, each mine comes with a small bit of putty to seal gaps between the parts, making the device waterproof.

Glass mines are not designed to kill victims, but rather to seriously wound them through the loss of toes or feet. Using Teutonic math, German weapons designers feel that it is a bigger loss for one enemy soldier to be seriously wounded, not killed, since it takes two additional soldiers to evacuate that man from the battlefield, and the wounded soldier, whose foot may later be amputated, will never return to combat anyway.

Not so the self-contained antipersonnel mine, named *Schrapnellmine* (shrapnel) or S-mine by the Germans, or "Bouncing Betty" by Americans. These killing mines are buried just underground, with only three small prongs exposed; once a prong is disturbed, the device's propellant charge shoots the mine 3 feet upward, and a second explosive charge detonates it, scattering 360 lethal steel balls outward of 60-plus feet. A nasty variant is found in wooded areas, where the Krauts attach a waist-high trip wire between trees for the mine.[42] Because of the height at which the mine explodes, the Bouncing Betty has a great psychological effect, since it inflicts serious wounds to the groin, a prospect sometimes more feared than an instant death.

Teller (plate) mines are normally antitank, designed to damage a tank track, immobilizing the vehicle so that antitank weapons can finish it off. Sometimes the Germans put two or three *Teller* mines on top of each other. If a tank runs over that baby, the entire crew can be killed. With enough mines, you have a minefield; if it's big enough, it gets its own name, such as the huge German Wilde Sau ("Wild Pig") minefield near Wittscheidt, just north of Germeter.[43]

Back in the States today, Hal Boyle pens "Yank Unit Peeved; Never Hits a City—Ninth Division Gets to See Only Europe's Back Alleys," in the *Deseret News*, Salt Lake City, describing soldiers' frustrations at not hitting a large town to relax in and raise a little whoopee. "'We have never been in a town of any size in French Morocco, Tunisia, Sicily, England, France, Belgium, or Germany,' said Capt. Lindsey Nelson of Columbia, Tennessee, who remarks a little sourly that the boys plan to call the history of their outfit 'Through the back alleys of Europe with the Ninth Division.'"[44] In the Hürtgen, however, nobody is thinking about "whoopee."

OCTOBER 11, 1944: HÜRTGEN FOREST

Company B remains in Germeter.[45] Depressing weather: a high of 49°, a low of 45°, clouds, low overcast, and winds light and variable; flying conditions poor. Jack Dunlap reports six officers and 136 enlisted present; his comments are short: "Remained in defensive positions at Germeter, Germany. Received terrific shelling all day and night." It is a long day for many. The squad leader, SSgt. John "Jack" Gourlay, born in Glasgow, Scotland, who grew up in Niagara Falls, is killed by a massive shrapnel wound; SSgt. Gail Bowman, Pfc. Albert Maresca, and Privates Joseph Montalchi, Henry Rolewski, and Gerson Skinner are wounded. Pvt. Ralph Moore is seriously injured and evacuated, but later the injury is classified as a wound. Pfcs. Carl Baer and Charles Kompanik are evacuated for nonbattle illness. Carl had been wounded in the face in Normandy by a strafing German aircraft. Artillery shrapnel hits Henry's knee; the previous July, shrapnel hit him in the hand, and in August it found his left knee. Gail had just arrived at the front a week ago; now artillery shrapnel breaks his hand.

It is a bad day for the old-timers: Jack was a private in the company in June 1941, as was Albert. Artillery shrapnel smashes Al's foot; he'll need skin grafts in the hospital through June 1945. Gerson, a twenty-two-year-old from Mount Vernon, New York, who enlisted on October 20, 1942, has artillery break a tibia, which will get infected; he will be medically discharged from the Army in February 1946. Joe Montalchi, a truck driver born in Italy, was wounded in Tunisia when an exploding land mine shredded his arm. Today it's the blast of a nearby artillery round; as he is evacuated in the back of a jeep or truck to a medical facility, he is going to feel pain racing throughout his body.

First Battalion's plan is to move east to Vossenack. Gen. Craig visits the 39th CP. At 0930 hours, battalion reports receiving small-arms fire. At 1245 hours, Company A halts after a German *Panzerschreck* (bazooka) knocks out the lead tank of Lt. Robert Sherwood's 1st Platoon, Company C, 746th Tank Battalion, supporting them. One observer believes it's an 88 mm antitank gun; this causes a withdrawal of the other tanks as the drivers slam their transmissions into reverse. The platoon later attacks under cover of smoke, but two more tanks are hit in the melee. At 1321 hours, the battalion reports it is sending Company B south, but at 1410 hours all wire communications are severed. Gen. Craig visits AAAO again at 1510 hours. Battalion reports at 1820 hours that the three tanks knocked out are south of the crossroads.[46] The battalion reaches 100 yards east of the Simmerath–Düren road.[47]

Gen. George C. Marshall, US Army chief of staff, comes to Europe to see operations for himself and visits First Army. Riding in a jeep with a special siren to clear other vehicles off the road, he visits four divisions, including the 9th Infantry at Zweifall— which is a must-stop, since the Ninth commander is Louis Craig, younger brother of Malin Craig, who was Marshall's predecessor as chief of staff. That evening, Marshall returns to Hodges's tactical headquarters at Verviers, Belgium—15 miles from the front—where he, Hodges, and a few other officers have drinks, followed by supper in the three-story château owned by the Count and Countess De Pinto, Belgian nobility of Italian background, who enjoy opening a few bottles of their finest with the general on occasion.[48] Hawk DiRisio cannot match the "four-star" cuisine back at Verviers, so it's C rations or K rations for him.

OCTOBER 12, 1944: HÜRTGEN FOREST

Company B is ¼ mile north of Germeter.[49] Another "Hürtgen Day": a high of 49°, a low of 45°, clouds, low overcast, scattered light rain, and winds light and variable; flying conditions poor. Jack Dunlap reports five officers and 140 enlisted: "The Company withdrew from positions at Germeter and moved over into the Third Battalion sector to fill in a gap. Received very heavy shelling and having a lot of casualties." Sunrise is 0653 hours. Battalion attacks with one company and tanks down the road to Vossenack but reports at 0716 hours of a surprise attack; at 0753 hours it receives artillery fire. The 39th reports at 0853 hours that the enemy has broken through an engineer road-block, heading toward the Second Battalion CP. Two Company C platoons swing north at 0855 hours to respond; the 39th attack is called off at 0930 hours until the situation stabilizes. Company B's reserve platoon moves north at 0958 hours.

An unstable situation attracts a lot of attention. At 1013 hours, General Craig suggests that Colonel Bond move Company B as soon as possible; it turns west on the main supply route to a trail intersection, advances 800 yards north in the thick woods, and moves east to the northern slope of Hill 435, discovering large groups of enemy troops.[50] Capt. Dunlap moves his CP to the western slope of Hill 435, which protects it from flat-trajectory artillery fired from the east.

German Kampfgruppe (Battle Group) Wegelein, of 1,639 officer candidates, led by 161 officers under Colonel Helmuth Wegelein—a German Cross in Gold winner and twenty-three-year army vet—has been trucked north from Dasburg, Germany, during the night, occupies an assembly area near Hürtgen village, and now strikes the northern flank of the 39th. It's organized into three battalions, each of three companies, and is supported by a heavy-weapons company; Wegelein's mission is attack southwest to isolate the Americans at Germeter.[51] A POW states that the physical condition of the unit is excellent, as is morale. Many sergeants in the unit are combat veterans—and motivated to become officers.

Following a short, concentrated artillery preparation before dawn, Wegelein and his men advance along a wooded plateau paralleling the north–south Germeter–Hürtgen road. A platoon of dismounted armor crewmen from the 746th Tank Battalion, securing a roadblock along the left flank of the Second Battalion, is the first American unit to encounter this surprise threat; overwhelmed, the platoon scatters. By 0700 hours, Battle Group Wegelein isolates Third Battalion's rifle companies and slams into First Battalion. Because the woods are dense and communication is spotty, Third Battalion CP is unaware of the extent of this attack.

With no regimental reserve to blunt the thrust, Col Bond requests assistance from Gen. Craig, who directs the divisional reconnaissance troop, with a platoon of light tanks, to assist the beleaguered 39th Infantry. The situation grows more desperate by the hour, so Craig orders the 47th Infantry, located north at Schevenhütte, to send two rifle companies and a company of medium tanks from the Third US Armored Division to reinforce the 39th. From the division rear, individual daily replacements are thrown directly into the front line. At 1355 hours, Third Battalion reports that the

Germans shot up a jeep carrying medics and the wounded. At 1425 hours, Company B's right flank is located in the woods northwest of Germeter,[52] with two platoons heavily engaged at 1735 hours, while one maneuvers.[53] Sunset occurs at 1749 hours. The right flank of Company B at 1845 hours is still northwest of Germeter.[54] The company stretches on a 300-yard front facing north.[55]

Platoon sergeant Patsy Jerome is submitted for the Silver Star for gallantry in action. Pvt. Ralph W. Wallace of Rock County, Wisconsin, is hit in the chest by a bullet and killed; Pfcs. James Vaught and Albert Bittino die of wounds. SSgt. John Kalinowski; Sergeants Napoleon Daniels, William Gladis, and Arnold Olsen; Pfc. James Davis; and Privates Spegiel Burke, Patrick Foley, and Jesus Prado are wounded. James fought in Sicily; now he succumbs to artillery shrapnel to his chest and upper arm. Al, who at age two had lost his father and who joined the company on June 24, 1944, receives massive artillery wounds to his hips; evacuated and receiving plasma, he has lost too much blood and dies. Shrapnel breaks John's finger; appointed SSgt. on October 3, he's been in Company B since 1941. Shrapnel hits Napoleon's hand and fingers and then hits William, another of the old crew, in the shoulder; he'll be gone a month.

Wounded in the leg by artillery shrapnel, Arnold, born in Norway, is not yet a citizen; the deckhand out of New York City enlisted on January 14, 1941. James is hit in the eye with a rifle bullet, but he's lucky and will keep his sight; not so for thirty-seven-year-old Pat Foley: a machine gun bullet destroys one of his eyes—he has been in the company one week; he will be in the hospital for one year, his face will be permanently disfigured, and he will die in five years. A rifle bullet hits Spegiel, from a family of eleven children in tiny Grove Oak, Alabama, in the tibia and fibula, sending him to a hospital for six months. Jesus arrived at the company eight days ago; a rifle bullet hits his knee. The thirty-four-year-old was born in Mexico but moves to Los Angeles before enlisting on March 22, 1944. When men are fighting to stay alive, nobody gives a crap where you were born.

1Lt. Karl Pratt is seriously injured and evacuated to the 2nd Evacuation Hospital, near Eupen. Four enlisted men are evacuated for nonbattle illness, including Billie Flowers; his current illness is pediculosis corpus, severe rashes caused by body lice—he must have gone into a bunker for safety. Privates Kermit Lockridge and Israel Reese become riflemen in Jim Rush's squad. They and twelve other replacements arrive from the 92nd Replacement Depot.

OCTOBER 13, 1944: HÜRTGEN FOREST

Company B is ¼ mile north of Germeter.[56] No air support, since it's a high temperature of 57°, a low of 47°, and overcast; flying conditions are bad. Strength is down to four officers and 129 enlisted men. A grim morning report: "The Company went into the attack at 1715 hours and before they could get very far it grew dark and the men could not keep contact. The Company then came under heavy artillery and mortar fire causing the Company to [be] disorganized. Wounded men were carried out until the early hours of the next day. Most men were evacuated thru different aid stations and therefore it is impossible to know exactly who was wounded in the attack. At the present time, their [*sic*] are approximately 80 men that can't be accounted for. The men are very nervous and tired."

Battle Group Wegelein ambushes two Company L platoons and almost wipes them out; twenty-eight soldiers are missing. But those still alive come back swinging. Four soldiers in Company L are submitted for Silver Stars, and another dozen for Bronze Stars. Company B at 1015 hours reports it is still engaged. At noon, ~~AAAO~~ reports that Battle Group Wegelein, plus a company of the 943rd Infantry Regiment, is attacking in force, supported by artillery and mortars, against the regiment's left flank. Company B's right platoon engages in a firefight at 1250 hours. The same platoon is hit hard again at 1340 hours and loses ground after the enemy captures a .30-caliber machine gun supporting the platoon. The situation is now so desperate that Thompson and Bond discuss sending all new individual replacements in the regiment as a group to plug the line to the right of Company C—a dangerous option for green troops. Artillery is coming in thick and fast; for the next sixty minutes, the fate of the battalion lies on a razor's edge between survival and death.

The enemy tries to outflank Company B at 1420 hours. In twenty minutes, enemy troops are in a wooded gulley, but Capt. Dunlap counterattacks and regains lost ground.[57] Second Battalion captures the adjutant of Battle Group Wegelein. At 1615 hours, five aircraft—flying through bad weather—arrive overhead and drop bombs to good effect. At 1705 hours, Col. Bond, who will receive a Silver Star for "bold and fearless leadership," moves forward and personally directs mortar fire in support of several rifle companies making a dusk attack—"the Old Man" doing it just like Paddy Flint.[58] At 1730 hours, a German with a white flag approaches the company, requesting a cease-fire, while his unit prepares to surrender. Dunlap sends the soldier back to his lines with the message that he will hold fire for only five minutes. Nothing happens; Company B advances—only to run into a hail of small-arms fire. You can't trust the Krauts.

Sunset is at 1749 hours. In the dark, with enemy on all sides, Dunlap orders a withdrawal to a firebreak and digs in at a woods called the Katzenhard, 800 yards west of Wittscheidt.[59] Company B's right flank ties in with Company C, but the left flank is hanging in the wind, as fifty Germans dig in to their west. In addition to Bond, many others save the day. Joe Gravino goes from position to position firing up the troops; Top knows that whether in bare-knuckles fighting or life-and-death combat, you don't always have to be completely braver than your foe—you just have to be a little braver for a little longer. Gravino's own bravery is so significant that he will be submitted for a Silver Star. So will Pfc. Charles Legate, who is hit by a machine gun bullet in the leg:[60]

Charles H. Legate … who distinguished himself by gallantry in action against the enemy on 13 October in the vicinity of Germeter, Germany. As [his] Company was advancing in this area, they suddenly encountered severe artillery, mortar, and small-arms fire from a numerically superior enemy force.

To enable his company to regroup safely . . . [he,] without regard for his personal safety, remained alone in an exposed advanced position, to pin the enemy down with his automatic rifle fire. Although subjected to withering machine gun fire, [he] directed the full firepower of his weapon at vital enemy positions. Besides successfully covering his unit's reorganization, [his] accurate fire eliminated three hostile machine guns and accounted for at least ten enemy casualties. Outstanding gallantry, devotion to duty, and aggressive initiative, were reflected in all of [his] actions.

Pfc. Robert St. Peter is also recommended for this award, while Pfc. Frank Branchfield, in the company just four days, is put in for a Bronze Star.[61] It is a bloody fight. SSgt. Albert Handy, who finished fifth grade in Fries, Grayson County, Virginia, and Privates Paul Bean from Clemons, Montana; Benedict Conrad of Mounds View, Minnesota; Parry Miller from Youngstown, Ohio; and Odie Mitchell from Golden, Oklahoma, are killed. Albert dies of a bullet to the neck; in Tunisia he was wounded by artillery and in Normandy was hit in the leg and head by shrapnel. It is the fourth day in the company for the married thirty-three-year-old Paul, and for Ben, who is killed instantly by shrapnel to his face and forehead. Parry is killed by a bullet wound. Parry and Odie, who dies from an artillery blast in the back, arrived just two days ago.

TSgt. Salvatore Ciccone; SSgt. Perle Buckner; Pfcs. Charles Legate, Benjamin Schoenwald, Arthur Tedeschi, and Waldo Thornton; Privates Walter Bachman, Seymour Berry, Everett Chandler, Lawrence Fleming, John Gamble, Norris Laprairie, David Murphy, and Francis Voltin; and medic Jessie Slaughter are wounded. "Doc" is hit in the face by a machine gun bullet, but it's a grazing shot and he goes right back to doing what he does best—saving lives.[62] Salvatore, from Newark, New Jersey, with a shrapnel wound to his left thigh, joined the company in June 1941; he was wounded in the fingers by shrapnel in Normandy. A Virginian, Perle's tibia is fractured by artillery shrapnel. Benjamin is machine-gunned in the thigh. Arthur Tedeschi, from Passaic, New Jersey, was born in Italy in 1919; his last name is the Italian word for Germans. That doesn't hold any weight with the Wehrmacht, and a German tosses a potato masher grenade that wounds Art in the face.

A machine gun bullet fractures Waldo's lower leg. Walter, from Wilbarger County in North Texas, along the old cattle trail to Dodge City, has been there just four days; now a German machine gun bullet penetrates his skull. Seymour Berry, a Jewish kid and the manager of his DeWitt Clinton High School football team in the Bronx, is hit by rifle bullets in the groin and forearm. Everett, hit by a machine gun bullet in the hand, has been in the company for four days. Lawrence Fleming arrived eight days ago; he is wounded in the liver and forearm by rifle bullets. It is Gamble's second wound in a week, this time a rifle bullet in the head, sending him to the 58th General Hospital at Châlons-sur-Marne, France.

Machine gun fire hits Norris in the face. David Murphy, who arrived on October 11, is hit in the hip by a rifle bullet. Pvt. Lester Rosencrance was wounded in the lower back by artillery on July 13, 1944, in Normandy, and he has been in the medical system since then. But Lester is a rifleman, and every veteran rifleman is urgently needed at the front, so he comes back. Company armorer Morris Mear is evacuated for a non-battle disease; he was awarded a Bronze Star in Normandy. 1Lt. John Mingen, in the company since 1943, is transferred to Company A because of losses there. Up the line, Col. William Westmoreland becomes the 9th Infantry Division chief of staff.

OCTOBER 14, 1944: HÜRTGEN FOREST

Company B is ½ mile west of Germeter. The weather is a high of 57°, a low of 47°, overcast, scattered showers, and surface winds of 20–25 mph; flying conditions are bad till 1000 hours, then fair. Company strength: five officers and 117 enlisted, just 66 percent of authorized. Jack Dunlap reports: "The Company to attack and captured high ground 800 yards north of Germeter, Germany. The Company reached there after cleaning out several machine guns and riflemen. The Company then dug in and set up defensive positions." Today is 2Lt. Louis Benoist's twenty-third birthday, but he isn't celebrating. Pfc. Verdun "Fritz" Fredendall (gunshot: neck) and Privates Jeremiah Ferguson (shrapnel: intestines and thumb) Paul Rouse (shrapnel: fractured femur), and Arthur Wilson (shrapnel: lower leg) are wounded. Paul has been in the company ten days; Jeremiah nine. 1Lt. Francis "Frank" Randall arrives and assumes command of 3rd Platoon, later saying that[63]

> I was well-received by both the officers and men. Practically all of the NCOs, the CO, and Executive Officer were veterans of two campaigns in Africa, then Sicily and the Utah Beach landing, followed by Normandy. But I was accepted and had no problems with the men. I gave them my background to explain that I had no authority on combat and was warned by the NCOs about overexposing myself. I learned that this was a well-disciplined outfit, experienced and battle wise.

Langley Turner is diagnosed with psychoneurosis and leaves for treatment. A veteran sergeant, he has been in combat since 1942 and is platoon sergeant of 3rd Platoon, elevated to this position on July 24, 1944. Sgt. Daniel Douvanis, Greek Orthodox and the son of a small-restaurant owner in Bethlehem, Pennsylvania, is also evacuated for a nonbattle illness. Privates First Class William Lane and Justin Mullaney arrive from the 92nd Replacement Battalion. They are not 745–riflemen, nor are they 746–automatic riflemen. They are 504–ammunition handlers, and they may have thought that they would be loading cases of ammunition on trucks. They will be loading a lot of ammunition in Company B—not onto trucks, but into their M1 Garand rifles or assisting BAR gunners, or machine gunners in weapons platoon.

Severely understrength, Company B evacuates the wounded, but wire communications are severed at 0820 hours. Company B's mission is to attack the nose of the enemy penetration, now southwest of Hürtgen village.[64] Gen. Craig visits ~~AAO~~ CP at 0835 hours. A Company E sniper kills Colonel Wegelein at 0920 hours. No American understands why the colonel is alone. But one man knows. A first lieutenant and former adjutant of Battle Group Wegelein tells an amazing story to his captors. When Wegelein first arrives at the 275th Infantry Division, Major General Hans Schmidt tells him to attack immediately, but the colonel strongly protests, saying he did not have reliable communications with his units. The irate Schmidt says that he will report Wegelein to higher headquarters "for cowardice in the face of the enemy." A charge like that often ends up in front of a firing squad.

Company B arrives online at 1020 hours west of Company K. At 1500 hours, they attack north of Germeter and establish defenses in the Katzenhard.[65] The situation is confusing; Company B's morning report lists the CP at coordinates (028332), but that would put it 500 yards east of Germeter, in the middle of the German defenses! Regiment reports at 1400 hours that enemy activity is now local firefights, a heavy one in Second Battalion. It also reports that Colonel Wegelein was unarmed when found. Sunset occurs at 1744 hours. At 2000 hours, the regimental combat report states that late-day activity is limited to local firefights, with sporadic shelling by medium artillery; enemy mortar fire is lighter than previously encountered. During the previous two days, Battle Group Wegelein suffers five hundred casualties before being withdrawn. Some of the troops hear a distant rumbling to the northeast, caused by 326 B-17s from the First Bomb Division, Eighth US Air Force, unloading 913 tons of bombs on Cologne (Köln).[66]

Ironically, "I'll Walk Alone" by Dinah Shore takes over as the top song in the country. A line from the tune is "If you call, I'll hear you, no matter how far." But "Fanny" Shore has never been in the Hürtgen, where sometimes the noise of the artillery drowns out the screams of the wounded and dying to where you cannot hear them no matter how close they are. Meanwhile, today at First Army headquarters, visiting British king George VI; Generals Dwight Eisenhower, Omar Bradley, William Simpson, and George Patton; and several corps commanders meet with Courtney Hodges. After briefings, the group sips sherry and gathers for lunch, where they are treated to consommé, steak with mushroom sauce, french fried potatoes, salad, pie, and coffee—accompanied, of course, by wine and port.[67] Down in Company B, the men have not had a hot-cooked meal in nine days.

OCTOBER 15, 1944: HÜRTGEN FOREST

Company B is ½ mile north of Germeter (028332). The weather is hopeful: a high of 58°, a low of 45°, clouds broken, and surface winds at 5–8 mph; flying conditions are moderate to good. Strength: five officers and 141 enlisted. Capt. Dunlap reports: "The Company improved their defenses as a counterattack was expected. At 1830 hours, the Company was counterattacked but the enemy was thrown back." Three enlisted men are evacuated for nonbattle illness. Sgt. Jim Rush, who takes over for the wounded Gail Bowman as squad leader, and Cpl. Oliver J. Osbourn, an assistant squad leader, are assigned to the 3rd Platoon from the 92nd Replacement Battalion, as are Pfc. James Millar and Pvt. Jay Lavinsky. A 39th Infantry soldier recalled the conditions:[68]

During the dull damp hours of the day, we gathered in small groups, talking of anything that would get our thoughts away from our unpleasant situation. Frequently we dwelt on rumors that we were to be relieved. The miserable weather and the apparent hopelessness of the situation led to a morbid feeling. After about four days of the dampness in soaking foxholes, we were relieved for a one-nightstand about 800 yards to the rear. It wasn't much better, except that we could put up a pup tent that kept us a bit dryer, and we were able to have small fires during the daylight hours. The little relief was hardly long enough, however, and the next day found us holding down our position on the line. It still continued to rain, and we were so well soaked that we couldn't find a dry match among us.

Jay Harvey Lavinsky is a real scrapper. Born on August 21, 1924, in Philadelphia, he quits high school. At his induction on March 20, 1943, the electrician's helper stands 5'9" tall and weighs 158 pounds; he lives on Hoffman Avenue—a row house near Cobbs Creek Park. The Philly kid has brown hair and eyes and a ruddy complexion. His father, Irving, a second-generation Russian immigrant and antique dealer, completed junior year of high school and is a Great War veteran. His mother, Pauline, a Romanian Jewish immigrant, speaks Yiddish, immigrated in 1906 at age nine, and has completed eighth grade. Jay has an older sister, Claire, and a younger sister, Elaine. Pauline is terrified that the Germans will capture her Jewish son.

A family friend in Philly is like an uncle to Jay—Barney Lebrowitz, who boxes under the name of "Battling Levinsky," former light heavyweight champion of the world. Jay learns as much of the "sweet science" as he can from "Uncle Barney" and departs for England on April 5, 1944. He starts out as a tank driver, but numerous fights with fellow soldiers' help led to a transfer. Then it's on to a paratrooper unit, but fighting and an injured back get him transferred out of that outfit as well. He might have jumped into Normandy with the 82nd Airborne, but nobody dares to ask him! Being Jewish, he has a special hatred for Germans, puts notches in his M1 rifle, and doesn't complain when he's the Browning Automatic Rifle (BAR) gunner.[69]

The sun sets at 1742 hours. A battalion of Regiment Trier attacks in the dark at 1830 hours but is repulsed. POW reports indicate that Trier has 360 men and had been brought from Trier, on the Moselle River, earlier that day. At 1900 hours, an enemy patrol forward of Company B triggers trip flares and booby traps; results were reported as "very effective." At 2025 hours, a Second Battalion half-track strikes a mine, killing one man and wounding two others. The 2000-hours combat report states that during the day, the enemy restricted activity to reorganizing but at 1630 hours attacked, supported by heavy weapons, from east of the Germeter–Hürtgen road against Second Battalion. The report concludes: "enemy wants Reichelskaul crossroads."

OCTOBER 16, 1944: HÜRTGEN FOREST

Company B is ½ mile north of Germeter.[70] Flying conditions are fair; there's a high temperature of 55° and a low of 45°, with scattered clouds, later rain, and surface winds at 5–8 mph; good visibility. 1Sgt. Gravino counts five officers and 148 enlisted. According to Capt. Dunlap, "The Company was attacked by small enemy forces and threw them back without any loss of ground or casualties. The defensive positions were improved during the day." Actually, Pfc. William Karko from Calumet Township, Chicago, is killed when shrapnel penetrates his back.[71] A private first class is listed as having a severe nonbattle injury; this is followed by the abbreviation NYD, "not yet determined," indicative that the injury could be self-inflicted. Clarence Yeakel and Pvt. Walter Skelly are also evacuated for nonbattle disease. Nighttime enemy activity is limited to patrols, but at 0800, an hour after sunrise, the artillery starts up. The 39th Infantry is still facing Regiment Trier. At 1530 hours, the enemy fires a heavy mortar barrage and launches a one-company attack to split Company G.

In continuous fighting, the men have five-day-old beards. Just before dawn, Jack Jewell tears two small sheets of paper from a notebook and begins writing what may be his last letter.[72]

"I'm on my belly in a fox hole and writing by candle. I might add it's raining as usual. It's plenty rough here but as I have always said, I still have plenty to be thankful for as I'm OK in every way . . . just wanted you to hear from me again as I knew you would want to. Don't worry, keep your chin up."

Between October 6 and 16, 1944, the 9th Infantry loses 4,500 casualties and gains 3,000 yards—one man down for every 2 feet of ground. Unaware of these grave losses, Mac MacLean departs Southampton, England, about October 16, 1944, and arrives by a small channel steamer to Normandy. Seeing the destroyed bunkers, that evening he writes his mother, saying that the night is cold and damp, he is sleeping on the ground under a tent, and "The food: the less said the better. I don't like to think about it, and I know the Army doesn't want me to talk about it." If the two nights at Normandy are no picnic, quite soon it will get a lot worse. Mac avoids travel by train in forty-man railcars, where the men in each car are given fifteen cases of C rations, since the ride may take three or four days. Instead, he is trucked 350 miles toward the front.

OCTOBER 17, 1944: HÜRTGEN FOREST

Company B remains ½ mile north of Germeter (028332); strength is five officers and 148 enlisted. The weather is depressing: a high of 58°, a low of 48°, low clouds, erratic light rain showers, surface winds at 5–10 mph, and gusts of 16 mph; flying conditions are mixed. Jack Dunlap is depressed too.

> The Company was attacked by a very small force but again the enemy was thrown back. The new replacements the Company has received aren't worth the space they take up. Never has this organization had so many self-inflicted

wounds as it has in the past few days. The new men don't seem to have what it takes to keep the Company in fighting spirit. And what <u>few</u> <u>old</u> <u>men</u> [underlined in original] that are left isn't enough to carry the load. Some men are assigned to the Company in the morning, and by mid-afternoon they are sent to hospitals with combat exhaustion.

Riflemen Pvt. Kenneth Seaman and Pvt. Lloyd Wasnick report from the 92nd Replacement Battalion to 3rd Platoon. At 1800 hours, a bullet hits Lloyd's index finger on his left hand; the bullet came from his rifle. He states that a bandolier of ammunition caught around the muzzle of the weapon. Medics evacuate him to a hospital; the morning report lists the injury as NYD. Col. Bond selects Maj. James Richardson to conduct a line-of-duty investigation—Richardson rules it had been an accident. A private first class is evacuated for an undisclosed illness, but again the morning report lists it as NYD. Three other enlisted men are also evacuated for nonbattle illness. At 1645 hours, two enemy self-propelled guns and mortars begin firing. After sunset at 1738 hours, the company emplaces mines, booby traps, and flares in the darkness—which is extremely dangerous. In another unit, a sergeant shoots a four-point 150-pound deer, and his company eats venison stew for a couple of days, a good break from the "Corned Willy" (corned beef, potato slices cooked in bacon grease) that is always threatened to be served.[73]

Jack Dunlap can be excused for feeling so frustrated. However, his exasperation probably starts not with the day's problems, but wondering why the hell the US Army is fighting in the Hürtgen in the first place. For crying out loud; in open terrain, American forces hammer the Germans. As shown at Normandy, German panzer and mechanized columns can't move at all during the day, or they'll be shot up from the air. Even Field Marshal Erwin Rommel was seriously injured by strafing aircraft back in Normandy. But here in the thick forest, it is easy for the enemy to remain hidden, and American aircraft can't find them.

The magnificent US speed and accuracy in artillery fire is shown in spades in engagement after engagement through France and Belgium. Horses still pull many German artillery pieces. Horses do not pull American artillery around the battlefield, but horsepower does, mostly in the form of trucks, high-speed tractors, or half-tracks, and the Americans have so many trucks that they can provide hundreds of thousands of US-made wheeled vehicles to the Soviet Union. But here in the forest, well-disguised concrete bunkers of the Siegfried Line protect the enemy from much of the artillery fire, and forward observers often can't even find targets for the guns.

Certainly, the few German Tiger and Panther tanks outclass most American Sherman tanks, although the Firefly model given to the British is pretty deadly. The key to Sherman tanks is to mass them against the German panzers—and the US has nine armored divisions in western Europe, not to mention thirty-eight independent tank battalions! But here in the Hürtgen? You have a tough time employing a company of tanks at one spot, and often, only a tank platoon can slither along the logging trails at a snail's pace—playing follow-the-leader in a little column. A whole tank battalion en masse is out of the question.

So why go into the Hürtgen at all? Because First Army said so. The imminent capture of the city of Aachen, and the breach of the Siegfried Line in the open terrain of the Stolberg Corridor, leaves American forces just 30 miles west of the Rhine River, the last barrier guarding the Ruhr industrial area, which produces so much of Germany's war machine. Crossing the Rhine means the imminent end of World War II and, it's hoped, a ticket home while you are still in one piece. With help from the Ninth US Army to the north, and with the VIIth Corps in the lead armed to the teeth, Hodges can slash 10 miles in the relatively open plain, cross the Roer River, and overrun Düren, all under an umbrella of Pete Quesada's fighter-bombers, which will chew up every German unit in the open terrain.

But Hodges is fixated on clearing the Hürtgen Forest, believing that this will protect the advance from any enemy counterattack that might spring out from the nooks and crannies in the dark woods. This anxiety may have been spawned twenty-five years before in the Great War, when Courtney Hodges was a battalion commander in the 6th Infantry Regiment, 5th Infantry Division. Then, the Germans had used the Argonne Forest as a staging area from which they threatened the flank of the American offensive in France in 1918. As Hodges reflected on the bloody Argonne, he may have been a prisoner of that experience, and unwilling to bypass a potential German stronghold in the Hürtgen twenty-six years later.

Engineers look at aerial photos of the Roer River dams to the south and opine that neither the First Army nor the Ninth Army can safely cross the Roer River until the dams are either captured or destroyed before the crossing. While five of the seven dams lack the capacity to hold water that would substantially affect the river's course if breached, the Schwammenauel and the Urft dams impound lakes that together hold up to 40 billion gallons of water. That water thundering down—a torrent possibly a ½ mile wide—could knock out tactical bridges over the Roer River and isolate all American forces to the east, which might then be destroyed piecemeal by German forces. But Capt. Dunlap does not see anything in his orders or maps about the dams. Nobody sees anything. The dams are ignored. What's going on up there? But back to the original question. There had better be a damn good answer to why attack in the Hürtgen—because over the three months of fighting here, the American army will lose over 33,000 casualties.

OCTOBER 18, 1944: HÜRTGEN FOREST

Company B is ½ mile north of Germeter.[74] It's overcast, with erratic light rain and surface winds of 15–18 mph and gusts to 25 mph. The company has five officers and 146 enlisted: Jack makes no comments on the morning report. Pvt. George Rudd and Pvt. Dewey Allen are evacuated for nonbattle illness. Jim Millar gets his new best friend, a BAR. The night softens under a drizzle of rain; no enemy activity occurs. Gen. Craig visits the 39th CP at 1530 hours and issues an order that the soldiers need to start shaving more often.[75]

OCTOBER 19, 1944: HÜRTGEN FOREST

Company B remains ½ mile north of Germeter.[76] Weather conditions: a high of 53°, a low of 38°, and scattered showers after noon; flying conditions fair. Battle strength is five officers and 144 enlisted. Capt. Dunlap has nothing to write. Cpl. Joe Genaro and Pvt. Grady Roden are evacuated for nonbattle disease. At noon, an enemy four-gun battery fires five volleys into the regimental area. Between 1700 and 1800 hours, the enemy barrages the 47th Infantry. The men test-fire a few illumination flares and white phosphorus artillery rounds in case of an enemy night attack. But there is no enemy activity that night by the 943rd Infantry Regiment, believed to be opposing the regiment. Mac MacLean, carrying his M1, arrives at the 92nd Replacement Battalion. As the *Army Talks* guidebook observes in an indelicate fashion concerning individual replacements, "You're tired of being an unwanted stepchild. Well, Orphan Annie, your freshman days are over. To get right to the point: you're going into combat."[77]

OCTOBER 20, 1944: HÜRTGEN FOREST

The company is dug in ½ mile north of Germeter, with five officers and 162 enlisted.[78] Today's high is 56°, with a low of 44°; it's cloudy and overcast, with intermittent light rain. Tennessean SSgt. William Russell (shrapnel: fractured hand and neck) and Pfc. Ray Goodwin (shrapnel: foot) are evacuated; Ray, a veteran soldier wounded by shrapnel in the arm in March 1943 and on September 4, 1944, will be in a hospital until January. William will be in the hospital until February. Pfc. Donald Pellock and Pvt. Herman Eichel are evacuated for nonbattle illness. Herman, in his fourth day, has a bad hernia and is operated on at the 286th General Hospital.[79] Sgt. Phil Holman, assistant squad leader, and Pvt. Harry Nodell, rifleman, arrive in 3rd Platoon from the 92nd Replacement Battalion, with twenty other replacements. Harry, with two nicknames, "Noodles" and "Brooklyn," becomes the foxhole buddy of Pvt. Jay Lavinsky in 3rd Squad. Aircraft strafe a captured Sherman tank in Vossenack, igniting it at 0935 hours. After dark, a German patrol is driven off. Phil writes about his field pack:[80]

> The field pack, an instrument of torture in which you carried your rations, extra clothing and socks, shovel, mess gear, blanket, tent pegs, and a shelter-half, was another mystery that took getting used to. A full pack weighed some 50 pounds or more and was strapped over your shoulder and hooked to your rifle belt on which you carried extra clips for your rifle, the first-aid pack, and your canteen. When you added your rifle and steel helmet, you had a load. I weighed about 119 pounds and sometimes felt that the stuff I was carrying weighed more than I did.

The previous day, as he was trucked forward, Phil notices bodies stacked like cordwood—grim remnants of a regiment in combat:[81]

A dreary spot where all my comrades were bone tired, wet, and underground in log-covered foxholes. I was welcomed by the squad leader [Jim Rush] (I was his assistant) and given a hole to fall in. My hole buddy [Junior Bradshaw] liked me because I had a dry blanket and a bottle of . . . shaving lotion I think they called it. I was about to look around the place, but something went "boom" quite close, and I decided to seek the shelter of the damp, dank, dark hole.

Phil learns a clear lesson that first day: stay in your foxhole and don't wander around. Jack Jewell also writes home:[82]

I will be very glad when the day comes that I can put Wellsville, Kansas, in that upper right-hand corner instead of Germany. Yes. I have seen, been in, and lived in too darn many pill boxes. That's where I got this paper. Right nice don't you think. . . . It rains almost every day and night, which makes everything very unpleasant. . . . Can't say I enjoy this life but like all GIs we are just trying to make the best of it and hope that it ends very soon. . . . One of my men just brought my dinner over to my hole—menu as follows: hamburgers, mashed dehydrated potatoes, fruit salad, white bread, and hot black coffee. It was good. So, you see everything isn't too bad, but I might add that's the first hot meal that hasn't come from a C-Ration can I've had in 14 days.

OCTOBER 21, 1944: HÜRTGEN FOREST

Company B reports its position as ½ mile north of Germeter.[83] Cloudy weather, with light rain and drizzle and surface winds of 8–10 mph; flying conditions are poor early, then moderate. Six officers and 158 enlisted assigned. Ten men from the 92nd Replacement Battalion arrive. Two enlisted men are evacuated for nonbattle illness. 2Lt. Lucien "Luke" Lucas is assigned from the 3rd Replacement Depot. Jay Lavinsky is promoted to private first class. SSgt. Raymond Olive is recommended for the Silver Star Medal for gallantry in action. The 60th Infantry reports at 1005 hours that a silver aircraft, believed a P-47, strafes their Company G and drops a bomb. At 1305 hours, two enemy tanks, or self-propelled guns, shell the north end of Germeter. At 2115 hours, regiment reports that two American soldiers had escaped from the enemy. During their brief captivity, the men were given one can of sardines a day and were threatened to be shot by their interrogator. Meanwhile, to the north, US troops finally complete the capture of Aachen.

The most played song on jukeboxes back home today is "(There'll Be a) Hot Time in the Town of Berlin (When the Yanks Go Marching In)," performed by Bing Crosby and the Andrews Sisters. The second verse of the song goes "There'll be a hot time in the town of Berlin . . . When the Brooklyn boys begin . . . To take the joint apart and tear it down . . . When they take old Berlin." But with all due respect to Bing, known as "Der Bingle" by his clandestine German listeners, the Hürtgen Forest is a long way from Berlin—an awfully long way. And while we're on Bing, sometimes the old boy really went off the deep end, as Bill Mauldin described:[84]

> When Bing Crosby returned to America after his visit to the French front, he told reporters, according to one news dispatch, that entertainment is needed most by the dispirited troops of the rear echelon rather than by the front-line soldiers. Up there, it seemed to him, "morale is sky-high, clothes are cleaner, and salutes really snap." The dogfaces who read that dispatch in the foxholes didn't know what front Bing was talking about.

Jack Jewell sure didn't: "It's like what Bing Crosby said, 'The further up front you get, the snappier the salute.' Well, that shows he didn't get very far up because we don't even salute up here."[85]

There is another Bing much closer to Company B than the famous crooner is; in fact he arrives at division today. This Bing was not born in the US. This Bing is not a citizen, but he feels a strong obligation to his adopted land. Pvt. Bing San Chin is a thirty-two-year-old rifleman who lives in the Bronx and enlists at Camp Upton on April 2, 1944. Chin has finished one year of high school, is a commercial vehicle driver, and is married. Of all the soldiers in the company, Bing has made the longest journey to the Hürtgen, since he was born in China. The son of Mow Chin, a merchant, and Dong Shee Chin, at age seven he and his family emigrate from Toyshan, Kwangtung, via Hong Kong on the SS *Shinyo Maru* and arrive in San Francisco. Bing's life has been one long march over thousands of miles to make a better life, but these next few yards in the Hürtgen Forest will seem like an eternity.

OCTOBER 22, 1944: HÜRTGEN FOREST

Company B remains ½ mile north of Germeter.[86] A high temperature of 55°, a low of 45°, low clouds, and surface winds at 10–12 mph; flying conditions are fair. Six officers and 167 enlisted are assigned. Pfc. Warren S. Thompson is evacuated for nonbattle illness. Twelve soldiers from the 92nd Replacement Battalion arrive, including Myron MacLean, assigned to 3rd Squad of 3rd Platoon as a rifleman. Upon entering the company rear area, Mac hears several loud voices: "I get his blanket" and "I get his overshoes"—veterans staking their claims to the new equipment of rookie soldiers, whom they believe might be killed soon after arriving.

Mac immediately goes down to the line and is introduced to his foxhole buddy, Ken Seaman, who tells him to "keep his ass down" so the Germans will not see them. At least the pair will have a lot to whisper about, and it's a good thing that both are Chicago Cubs fans. That is important—maybe even lifesaving—because Mac, and every other new soldier, is an individual replacement. The men do not form a separate unit behind the front, train, and develop cohesion, and then that entire replacement unit moves to the front, the way the Germans do. The American system guarantees that new soldiers will be extremely vulnerable until they learn how to survive, as Ernest Hemingway writes:[87]

Well anyway, this regiment was rebuilt as American regiments always are by the replacement system. I won't describe it since you can always read about it in a book by somebody who was a replacement. It boils down, or distills, to the fact you stay in until you are hit badly or killed or go crazy and get section-eighted. But I guess it is logical and as good as any other, given the difficulties of transport. However, it leaves a core of certain un-killed characters who know what the score is, and not one of these characters liked the looks of these woods much.

Leonard Pourchot receives his own rude awakening upon arrival:[88]

In 1944, after several months in the army ground forces in Arkansas and Texas, I arrived in the Hürtgen Forest near Aachen, Germany. I, along with a dozen or so others, was a replacement in an infantry company which had suffered severe casualties in recent fighting. We replacements had passed an impressive number of dead German soldiers upon entering a small clearing in the forest. We were stunned by the horrors and the carnage of war. A sergeant stopped us. A large wooden door opened out of the forest floor. A man with a week's bristle of beard and sharp blue eyes stood up in a foxhole. Captain's bars gleamed. He was handed a clipboard with our names on it. He called one by one, "Private _____," "Private _____," "Private First Class_____." He hesitated a moment and then called, "Corporal Poorshot" (not my name exactly). "Yes sir," I answered. He looked sharply at me and stated, "This is a rifle company. We don't have corporals in this outfit. So, within a week you'll be a sergeant or be dead."

Veterans shun new guys, since rookies make mistakes that can get veterans killed. "New soldiers entering battle sometimes exhibited symptoms like vomiting, shaking, trembling, cold sweat, or loss of bowel or bladder control."[89] After a while, the shunning stops, as the veterans conclude that a new man is fine and will help the platoon. But veterans have their own problems and can suffer from irritability, loss of interest, decreased efficiency, and carelessness—which can also get you killed. New officers get a little better reception. Jack Jewell writes his folks:[90]

Well I'm in the same old hole. But this Sunday hasn't been so bad. I got out of the blankets about 8:30, heated some breakfast, cleaned my carbine, read a letter ... smoked a big cigar, read a *Life* magazine. ... Don't get the wrong idea; I'm still not a rear echelon soldier. We got a new officer in the company today. He is from K.C. so I thought we had something in common. His name is Lucas.

Unknown to Mac, Ken, Bob, or the other men in Company B, the regiment will be relieved in sector by the 109th Infantry Regiment of the Twenty-Eighth US Infantry Division. At 1350 hours, the regimental engineer instructs all units to remove friendly booby traps in front of their positions during the next two nights. Meanwhile, captured Germans tell interrogators that they have been told that the US sends German POWs to Siberia. This rumor is untrue but surely causes a few Wehrmacht troopers to experience a few sleepless nights.

OCTOBER 23, 1944: HÜRTGEN FOREST

Company B is ½ mile north of Germeter.[91] Ugly weather: a high of 50°, a low of 38°, low clouds, overcast, light drizzle, thick ground fog with poor visibility, surface winds light and variable; flying conditions poor. The company is close to full strength, with six officers and 164 enlisted. Pvt. John Longenecker, a rifleman, is seriously wounded in the back by an artillery shell explosion. John, from tiny Annville, Lebanon County, Pennsylvania, will be initially treated in hospitals in Europe and evacuated home on February 3, 1945. Pfcs. Joseph Scafaro and Paul Sullivan are evacuated for nonbattle illness.

Soldiers finish removing all booby traps and flares. Cpl. Leonard Pourchot is improving his covered foxhole—upgrades that include him and Junior Bradshaw carrying three dead Germans away on a stretcher from nearby their hole.[92] Dead bodies turn green, then purple, and finally black and begin to rot with a foul, virtually intolerable odor—and you don't want to try sleeping near any—let alone eating out of your mess kit. At 0300 hours, 3rd Armored Division reports that four 47th Infantry patrols made contact with them, and that all four had the correct password. The 47th is alarmed—they had sent out only three patrols. Chaos erupts for the next hour, until 3rd Armored reports that they miscounted, and that there were indeed only three patrols! By 0915 hours, the battalion is receiving harassing fire, possibly from 105 mm guns. At 1355 hours, some six sections of medium mortars and a battery of artillery are firing on the battalion. At 2000 hours, regiment reports that enemy artillery and mortar fired are increasing. Down on the line, soldiers hear faint swing music played on German amplifiers, an attempt at psychological warfare, but the men enjoy it. Even better, they enjoy a hot cooked meal today.[93]

OCTOBER 24, 1944: HÜRTGEN FOREST

Company B remains ½ mile north of Germeter.[94] More bad weather: a high of 55°, a low of 42°, cloudy, light rain and drizzle, and daylong fog; flying conditions are poor till 1200 hours, then moderate. The company is now overstrength, with six officers and 176 enlisted. Pvt. Frederick McInnis, from Charlottetown, Prince Edward Island, Canada, dies of massive back wounds on his fifth day in the company; Pvt. Verne Mahorney, Milliken, Colorado, is also wounded by artillery shrapnel to his back—it is also his fifth day. Leonard Pourchot believes that both were hit by 88 mm gunfire. Two enlisted, including Dale Lockridge, are evacuated for nonbattle illness. Friendly

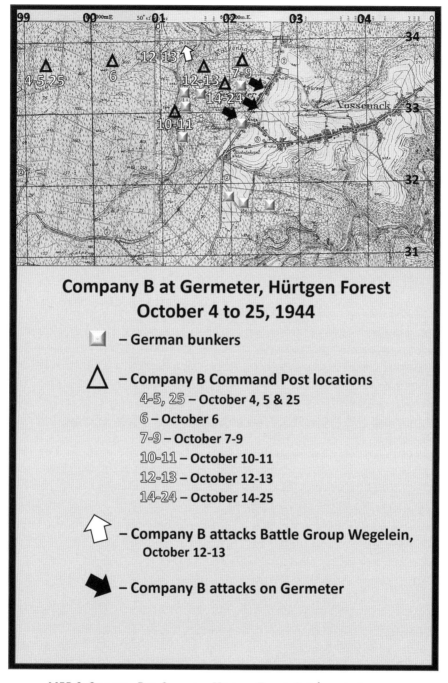

Company B at Germeter, Hürtgen Forest
October 4 to 25, 1944

▨ – German bunkers

△ – Company B Command Post locations
   4-5, 25 – October 4, 5 & 25
   6 – October 6
   7-9 – October 7-9
   10-11 – October 10-11
   12-13 – October 12-13
   14-24 – October 14-25

⬆ – Company B attacks Battle Group Wegelein,
   October 12-13

➡ – Company B attacks on Germeter

MAP 6: Company B at Germeter, Hürtgen Forest, October 4 to 25, 1944

artillery falls near the First Battalion rear CP of at 2200 hours. The company receives one hot cooked meal. Jack Jewell describes leadership in the unit:[95]

> I don't think I have ever mentioned it, but I think I have been most fortunate ever since I joined this company. My job is as good as I could ask for, and our higher officers have the greatest consideration possible for their men. The job is most unpleasant at its best, but it's really something to have confidence and admiration for your leaders.

OCTOBER 25, 1944: HÜRTGEN FOREST

Company B moves to a new location 2½ miles southeast of Zweifall.[96] It's ugly out: a high of 52°, a low of 45°, overcast, low clouds, intermittent light rain, foggy, poor visibility, and surface winds light and variable; flying conditions are poor till late afternoon. Company strength remains the same. Jack Dunlap notes: "The Company was relieved by Company L, 109th Infantry of the 28th Division at 1800 hours. Marched by foot to an assembly area 2½ miles southeast of Zweifall, Germany. Bivouacked for the night. Distance marched approximately 4 miles." Billie Flowers returns. During the day, the battalion gets the jump on a twenty-man German patrol of the 1412th Fortress Infantry Battalion. Armed with one light machine gun and twelve machine pistols, the German patrol's mission was to take two American prisoners "at all costs" from two white houses in Germeter. The Krauts will then fire green flares for artillery support to cover their withdrawal. But this time the Americans are the ones taking the prisoners.

First Army pulls 9th Infantry out of the frontlines in the Hürtgen Forest, and Company B receives orders to move the next day to Camp Elsenborn, in the Hohes Venn area of Belgium. The men are exhausted. Leaving the front, many stumble on the bodies of the fallen.[97] Their replacements are the 28th Infantry Division, a unit that traces its lineage to the Pennsylvania National Guard. Sporting a dark-red keystone division patch (the unit is nicknamed the "Keystone Division"), it soon receives a moniker of "the Bloody Bucket" (Der blutige Eimer) by the Germans, since their patch resembles a bucket of blood. It will not be long before a more ominous reason for the name will be born—endless casualty reports.

SCHOOL OF THE SOLDIER

MAY HOSIERY MILL

Before joining the Army, twenty-three-year-old Vallis Alexander worked for the May Hosiery Mill in Nashville, Tennessee, and if the Germans had ever known about the joint, they would have had a conniption fit. The mill's founder, Jacob May, immigrated to New York City from his native Germany in 1879 with seven bucks in his pocket.

Bouncing around the Northeast for several decades, Jacob headed south after he won a bid to start up a hosiery shop inside the new Tennessee State Penitentiary, located just west of Nashville. Hiring fifty inmate workers, the Jacob May & Company did all right but later lost the contract and moved to several two-story brick buildings in a classier part of town.

The company switched from cotton and wool to synthetic products in the 1920s; business really took off in the 1930s, with contracts from the Boy Scouts and Girl Scouts of America, as well as Montgomery Ward and Sears, Roebuck and Company. In 1936, copresident Mortimer May took the company from the business world to the stuff of legends, returning to his hometown in Germany to rescue local Jews there and help them immigrate to the United States. Between 230 and 280 Jews made it out of Germany with Mort's help and came to Nashville before 1939. A great number of those escapees now work in the mill. During the war, May Hosiery Mill continues to churn out socks. But Mortimer wants to go the extra mile, and the mill joins in the war effort, setting up a machine shop to build mortar ammunition fuses—one tiny company in freedom's Arsenal of Democracy.[98] Skilled Jewish workers employed in the heart of America, churning out millions of pairs of socks that would soon be marching on Germany, and making mortar round fuses to be fired back at their former tormentors—"Ach, du Lieber," the führer would have had a stroke.

NAVIGATING THROUGH THE WOODS

You can't just start singing "Heigh-ho, heigh-ho, it's off to work we go" as you go traipsing through the Hürtgen Forest, or you might run into some Krauts with bad intentions and armed to the teeth. But the engineers have figured out an important key to navigating through the woods.

> In the forest areas along the Siegfried Line it is difficult to determine one's position because of limited observation and lack of prominent objects. However, on the 1:25,000 maps of this area the woods are numbered, and on the ground these numbers can be found on cement survey stones at the corners of firebreaks. These stones rise out of the ground about a foot and are not difficult to find. They are numbered on two or four sides, the numbered sides facing the woods which they identify. Referring to these stones proved to be a reliable method of determining positions.

Still, Doc, Sneezy, Grumpy, Happy, Bashful, Sleepy, and Dopey—don't go out by yourself and don't go out at night if you can help it. Because out here, bad things don't go bump in the night—they go BANG![99]

C RATIONS AND K RATIONS

The C ration is an individual canned, precooked, and prepared wet ration adopted in 1940. Consisting, by 1944, of a 12-ounce meat unit (termed an M unit) and a B-unit bread and dessert can, there are only four variations of the main course: meat and beans, meat and potato hash, meat and spaghetti in tomato sauce, or meat and vegetable stew. Additional meals are developed in late 1944. An individual meal consists of one M unit and one B unit. A daily ration, consisting of enough food for one soldier for one day, contains six 12-ounce cans—three M units and three B units.

Then there are the dreaded three-course K rations. A breakfast unit features canned chopped ham and eggs, biscuits, dried fruit bar, premixed oatmeal cereal, and accessory items such as chewing gum and cigarettes. Dinner units are canned pork luncheon meat, canned processed American cheese, or bacon and cheese, biscuits, and perhaps a powdered beverage packet. So troops have something to anticipate, the supper unit offers one of the following: canned cervelat sausage (mixture of beef, bacon, and pork rind), canned pork luncheon meat with carrot or apple, or canned beef and pork loaf, plus biscuits, a 2-ounce chocolate bar, and a bouillon packet to complete your meal. Watch out for "biscuit blast," though, damage caused to your pearly whites when biting down on the often-rock-hard "dog biscuits" in the K ration.

When the company is on the attack, you'll be getting K rations. In the defense, the two forward platoons mostly have K rations, with C rations every now and then. You can take a chance and light a small candle at the bottom of your foxhole to warm up a C-ration can, but not at night or you'll be spotted by enemy snipers. The platoon to the rear is positioned so that the men can light small fires during the day and not be seen by the enemy. The K-ration box has a wax covering, good fuel for a small cooking fire.

Hot food cooked by the company mess team—soup jockeys—can sometimes be brought forward to the rear platoon and eaten in their mess kits. On good days, it might be pork chops, potatoes, succotash, bread, butter, and crushed pineapple. But for breakfast you know you're in trouble when it's powdered eggs, bacon, and cereal—with the cereal the most edible dish.[100] Platoon leaders try to rotate their men—a few at a time—to the rear to eat and then bring mess kits with hot food forward to their buddies up front. In the Hürtgen, too often this means that the mess kits also have rainwater in them, turning a nice, hot meal into cold, soggy slop. Sometimes you just get loaves of bread and cheese instead.

GERMAN DISCIPLINE

Every day, the 9th Infantry G-2 intelligence officer publishes a newsletter with info about the enemy, upcoming weather, and tactical techniques that work in other units. Although classified "SECRET," the intent for this info is to reach the troops, where it can do the most good. One bulletin has a captured order from Lt. Col. Gerhard Lemcke, commander of the 89th Infantry Regiment, concerning discipline:[101]

After a sergeant and 4 men and weapons were lost on October 6, the same number of men disappeared on the evening of October 11. Since the large number of soldiers involved tends to preclude the possibility of desertion, it must be assumed that they were taken prisoner. From all appearances, no one did anything to prevent this, at any rate no clues were found and none of the neighboring posts noticed anything. This has happened for the last time.... If soldiers disappear again without the sentries noticing it, both the sentries and the soldiers in adjacent posts will be called to account. In the future, all soldiers who are found guilty in connection with these occurrences will be shot by order of the division commander.

The bespectacled Lemcke is a hard-ass, with the German Cross in Gold and the Honor Roll Clasp, and will win the Knight's Cross of the Iron Cross in January 1945. He has served in the 12th Infantry Division since 1939, battled on the Russian front for three years, and survived the encirclement of the Demyansk pocket in the winter of 1942. An expert on machine guns, Herr Oberstleutnant Lemcke will have no qualms about shooting deserters himself.

M1S AND BARS

German infantrymen in the Hürtgen Forest have some advantages over their American foe, but two weapons give GIs an edge. Officially designated the "US Rifle, Caliber .30, M1," to millions of GIs it is just an "M1" and to soldiers fighting the Wehrmacht it is simply a "Kraut-killer." No less an expert than George Patton reportedly once calls the rifle "the greatest battle implement ever devised." What makes the weapon so lethal is its powerful ammo and rate of fire. The .30-06 Springfield cartridge, designed in 1906, can be accurate out to 1,000 yards and has the energy at 200 yards, with its 152-grain spitzer aerodynamic bullet zipping along at 2,805 feet per second, to go completely through the trunk of many trees found in the Hürtgen, and wounding a man hiding behind it.

Its greatest advantage, though, is rate of fire. A German firing a bolt-action Mauser K98k can load five rounds in its internal magazine, fire a round, pull the bolt back to eject the spent cartridge, push the bolt forward to chamber the next round, take aim, and fire again. After the fifth round is fired, the German soldier pulls the bolt to the rear, inserts a new five-round stripper clip to reload the weapon, pushes the bolt forward to load the first round from this clip, takes aim, and fires again. The GI, on the other hand, places the eight-round en bloc clip on top of the follower assembly, places his thumb on the center of the top round in the clip, and presses the clip straight down into the receiver until it latches, then removes his hand, allowing the bolt to travel forward freely. On firing, the rifle—by itself—ejects the spent cartridge and loads the next round in the chamber automatically, the soldier being required only to aim and pull the trigger once for each round until the eighth round is fired and the empty en bloc clip flies out; he then loads another eight-round en bloc clip and repeats the process.

As an extra motivator, an M1 shooter is "penalized" if he does not remove his hand quickly as the bolt goes forward—his thumb is pinched by the bolt, feeling like a hammer has hit it. As rifle instructors used to say back in the States: "There are two types of M1 Garand shooters, those that have received their 'M1 thumb'—and those that are going to."[102]

The second excellent weapon in an American infantry squad is the Browning Automatic Rifle—the venerable BAR. Known as "M1918A2" or Rifle, Caliber .30, Automatic, Browning, M1918A2," the first model, M1918, was used in the Great War. Not only did it serve well in that conflict, but many domestic police departments were later equipped with the weapon. In fact, on a rural Louisiana road on May 23, 1934, six lawmen, armed with at least one BAR, ended the careers of bank robbers Bonnie Parker and Clyde Barrow in a hail of .30-06 bullets.

Many GIs call it "the pig," since it weighs over 19 pounds with a full magazine. A WWII BAR gunner, with the M1918A2, can fire only full automatic but can choose between slow and fast rate of fire; approximately 300–450 or 500–650 rounds per minute. The weapon has detachable twenty-round box magazines. Given that a magazine change is often required, and the weapon kicks like a mule, a BAR gunner can really only cut loose with thirty to sixty rounds in a minute, but that can cause many a Kraut to duck for cover. Effective range is up to 1,500 yards for area targets. But there is a drawback: the barrel can be replaced only by an ordnance depot armorer, and since sustained automatic fire can burn out a barrel, don't let 'er rip all the time. Army doctrine directs that fire and movement tactics center on the riflemen in the squad, while the BAR man, assisted by his team, supports riflemen by providing a base of fire, causing the enemy to hunker down for a few seconds, during which the riflemen can move new locations. When the M1s and the BARs are used correctly, "Everything's jake here, pal."

MORTARS

In this terrain, mortars are worth their weight in gold—on both sides. Often considered small-scale, short-range substitutes for artillery, that view misses qualities that mortars bring to the fight. Above all, mortars are almost always available, since they actually belong to the unit and thus take instructions from their commander. Jack Dunlap controls three 60 mm mortars, and they exclusively fire for Company B. Battalion has six 81 mm mortars, so Lt. Col. Thompson prioritizes which company those 81s will support. Above that, it's hit or miss. Artillery battalions at division might be in direct support of the regiment, in which case Company B might benefit from their fire, but the priority might be given to someone else, and neither Dunlap nor Thompson can do much about it.

The second advantage is a high rate of fire. A mortar is simple, and the way it is set up, the recoil is absorbed through its base plate into the ground. This means that the tube, or barrel if you wish to call it that, does not move. A good gunner can drop round after round down the tube, just as soon as the previous round fires, putting out twenty to thirty rounds a minute, although that might be a waste of ammo, so gunners often fire more slowly. Third is portability. The whole thing weighs just 42 pounds; when it's disassembled into three major components, no soldier has to shoulder the entire load. And it isn't a Rube Goldberg job; it's easy to put back together as well. Rounds weigh about 3 pounds each. The high explosive is close to a hand grenade in effect. Illumination rounds light up the battlefield if an observation post detects enemy out front. White phosphorus rounds produce a small smokescreen on the ground and are often fired against German bunkers to blind their vision. Burns caused by white phosphorus are brutal. Finally, the range and flexibility of the mortar are amazing. The little weapon can fire just over 1 mile, and if elevation is set high, it can fire rounds almost straight up if required for "danger close" missions, where the enemy is almost on top of you. Gunners can adjust the strike of the rounds by their own line of sight, or forward observers can call back with adjustments.

The 81 mm mortar weighs three times as much, can fire almost twice as far, and has shells triple the weight, giving them the bursting radius close to a 105 mm howitzer. Mortars do not have much effect against tanks, but in this terrain, enemy infantry is your target, so mortars fit right in. Now the downside—the Germans have mortars too, and they know how to use them.

MAPS

More than one survivor of the Hürtgen Forest—a battalion commander—accurately grumbled, "If anyone says he knew where he was in the forest, then he's a liar!"[103] In anticipation of lost officers everywhere—and created from a merger of the Engineer Reproduction Plant and the US Army's Geographic Section (USAGS) in 1941—the Army Map Service (AMS) is responsible for the publication and distribution of military topographic maps for US military forces. The AMS does its job well, producing five hundred million topographic maps.

Having said that, though, most soldiers in the Hürtgen have no access to a map. Battalion and regimental commanders and staffs certainly have maps, as do artillery-men—especially forward observers. Anyone associated with aiding airstrikes has a map. An infantry company commander has a map, but the patrol he briefs before it heads forward of the front lines most likely does not have a map. So, the commander can tell the men to go one ridge forward, but sometimes every ridge looks the same, especially if a lot of trees have been knocked down by artillery. And when that patrol returns, they will be hard-pressed to give precise locations for what they have seen. Worse, a litter team that becomes lost without a map can well seal the fate of a wounded man oozing blood from two or three bullet holes.

Company B uses several 1:25,000-scale USAGS/AMS maps (1 inch equals 25,000 inches or 694 yards) during this period. Some might be in color, some in black and white. Each has a superimposed grid system, consisting of thin black horizontal and vertical lines; each line has two digits, such as 90, 91, 92 on the top—the numbers getting larger as you go to the right, until they hit 00, 01, 02, or, on the side, getting larger as you go up. You always read right and then up. In the endnotes, you will find six-digit coordinates: the first two may give the vertical line number, such as 99, and the fourth and fifth show the horizontal line number. The third and sixth digits will be 0–9, because inside a square you can be exactly on the line, or one-tenth of the way to the next line, all the way up to nine-tenths. Thus, a coordinate of 985025 would be halfway between the 98 and 99 vertical lines and halfway between the 02 and 03 horizontal lines. As examples: Germeter is (024333), Merode Castle (050454), Elsenborn Ridge (945083), and Kalterherberg (954135).

PNEUMONIA

A nonbattle illness is often respiratory. The deadly Spanish flu, the influenza pandemic from 1918 to 1920, killed upward of fifty to a hundred million people, almost as deadly as the Black Death of the Middle Ages, and actually reduced the life expectancy in the US by a dozen years during 1919. Luckily, the Spanish flu did not raise its ugly head in World War II, but atypical pneumonia did, causing eight thousand American soldiers in 1944, and another 12,600 in 1945 in Europe, to be evacuated from their units and sent to hospitals. A further 8,655 soldiers were hospitalized for pneumonia other than atypical.[104] Combined, the total was equal to two infantry divisions combat ineffective. You didn't even have to suffer from a disease that had a fancy name such as *Streptococcus pneumoniae*, or whatever it was.

Take the "crud." Highly contagious—oh, that's peachy: we eat, sleep, and share foxholes together—it can be caused by cold-weather snaps, an almost daily occurrence in the Hürtgen and Hohes Venn. And you don't need a doctor to see the telltale signs: runny nose, sinus pressure, sneezing, and a wet cough—lasting a week or more, which typically develops into a throbbing ear infection (made more uncomfortable by nearby artillery explosions), sinus infection, and maybe bronchitis. Crud can also lead to death—not usually by infection, mind you.

A soldier with the crud constantly coughs, a deep, rumbling cough that becomes uncontrollable. Veterans learn that you don't make noise at night, because sounds carry a long way through the forest. When the enemy hears those sounds, he tosses a potato masher in that direction, so a soldier with the crud paints an audio target on his and his buddies' backs—until they convince him he needs to go to the aid station. But many soldiers won't follow instructions. When they report to the medics with all the symptoms of a nasty lung infection, the doc will indicate that they need a visit to a hospital, but not wanting to shirk their duty, they tell him they didn't lose anything at any infirmary, wish they hadn't come to the aid station in the first place, and say that their company needs them up on the line, as they walk away toward their platoon.[105]

SOUNDS

Identifying sources of noise can keep you alive. Since you can't see much in the thick woods or at night, you learn sounds. A GI digging a foxhole with his entrenching tool sounds like crunching; when you hear a metallic ping, he just struck a rock.[106] His BAR has a putt-putt-putt-putt sound to its burst. A German submachine gun or machine gun has a much-faster rate of fire; it sounds like burrrp-burrrp-burrrp, somewhat like a bedsheet being torn in two. That is an awfully bad sound, but at least if you are hearing it; the gunner has not hit you—yet. German rocket launchers make the sound ahoooosh, ahoooosh, ahoooosh—one ahoooosh, which lasts about two seconds, for each rocket fired. Panzers and assault guns are really noisy; you hear the cannon when it fires, you hear the engine, and you hear the clanking and high-pitched squealing of the tracks as they go over the return rollers of the suspension. Panzers have machine guns, so you hear the burrrp-burrrp-burrrp with them too.

When the Germans fire a lot of artillery rounds over your head at some target far to your rear, the noise is described as "freight trains on wings."[107] That is not a good sound, but it is better than the sound of those same rounds impacting near you. Mortars make a krump . . . krump noise as the rounds are fired. Veterans can tell the difference between the impacting explosion of a mortar and that of an artillery round; new soldiers just cower and pray when they hear the explosion, followed by loud ringing in their ears.

Sometimes you want to hear a sound. The German ground-launched, unmanned V1 flying bomb is a rocket-propelled weapon, nicknamed a "buzz bomb." They are set to travel west before diving on large seaports such as Antwerp, where the imprecise weapon may get lucky and hit the dock area or a big, stationary ship. When flying over you, it sounds like a little outboard motor. Jack Jewell explained: "I don't know if I told you or not, but I have seen and heard several flying bombs. They make a lot of noise, reminds you of a Model T Ford in high gear. You can see the sparks fly out the back end and boy they go like heck. They come and go in a zip—I hope they just keep going. I guess they are headed for England."[108] The moment a buzz bomb begins to dive, the rocket engine shuts off and the weapon glides silently to the ground. So as long as you hear the buzzing sound of a V1, which carries a 1,870-pound high-explosive warhead, flying over you, it will be someone else's problem—which will start when the sound stops.

CHAPTER FIVE

The Hohes Venn, Elsenborn Ridge (1), Merode Castle

They don't need pity, because you don't pity brave men—men who are brave because they fight while they are scared to death.

—Bill Mauldin, *Up Front*

The Hohes Venn—High Venn—is a high moor adjacent to the Ardennes, typified by forests, hilly meadows, tall hedges, and scattered villages. The region gradually blends the Eifel hills to the east with the Ardennes. In fact, some ecologists might call the area in which Company B operated, the High Venn-Eifel. The climate is often windy and humid, especially in winter, where clouds, rain, and snow are plentiful—annual rainfall can reach 59 inches. A single snowstorm can deposit 10–12 inches in a twenty-four-hour period. Fog occurs 160 to 177 days per year, when visibility is reduced to 1,000 meters or less, lasting into late morning before it breaks—if it breaks. Hilltops frequently have no trees to block razor-sharp winter winds. There are many ponds and some lakes. Much of the ground is boggy, and the trapped water raises the specter of trench foot and frostbite; the high water table makes it difficult to dig defensive positions in many areas. Wolves have been known to inhabit the thicker woods. Tourist literature describes the area as a "hiker's paradise," with "charming" villages, with a brisk autumn walk "simply a must." But no GI ever says any of that nonsense about the Hohes Venn in 1944.

OCTOBER 26, 1944: HOHES VENN

Company B is 1 mile southwest of Kalterherberg, Germany, a tiny village.[1] Distance from the CP to the German front line is just 3 miles. Bellyaching weather: a high of 52°, a low of 45°, overcast, low clouds, sporadic light rain, foggy with poor visibility, and surface winds light and variable; flying conditions poor until late afternoon. Strength: six officers and 177 enlisted. Capt. Dunlap summarizes the situation: "Moved by truck south 60 miles. Supposed to be in rest area. Last night several rocket bombs flew over the area."

First Army headquarters moves to Spa, Belgium, in the Hotel Brittanique, occupied in the last war by German field marshal Paul von Hindenburg.[2] The division is reassigned to the Vth Corps. Battalion begins moving from Eupen at 1345 hours. The division CP moves to Camp Elsenborn.[3] Battalion CP is located in woods about 3 miles north of Camp Elsenborn; the battalion closes into its new positions by 1700 hours.[4] Whether bivouacking in the woods, or at Camp Elsenborn, the soldiers are well inside enemy artillery range and must stay alert. The 47th CP is shelled at noon. One enlisted man is evacuated for possible trench foot.

OCTOBER 27, 1944: HOHES VENN

Company B is located in the northern portion of the Elsenborner Wald, 1 mile south-west of Kalterherberg.[5] Strength is six officers and 177 enlisted. Sgt. Jim Rush is appointed staff sergeant. Pfc. Edward Pickard makes sergeant and is elevated to assistant squad leader, probably in Timber's squad. The unit conducts maintenance of weapons and equipment. A few men get short furloughs to visit nearby Belgian towns. All regimental officers meet with Col. Bond at the movie tent at 1330 hours. *Babes on Swing Street*, a comedy with Ann Blyth, Peggy Ryan, and Andy Devine, opens in theaters back in the US today, but no movie—known by the troops as "canned morale"—is shown today; Col. Bond congratulates the officers and introduces them to Camp Elsenborn, just a few miles from the German border.

Lager Elsenborn, built at the end of the nineteenth century by the Germans, was found to be an ideal training area by the Prussian army. Originally a tent encampment, it soon evolved to corrugated-metal barracks and some small concrete structures. The area had a succession of owners: first imperial Germany, then the Belgian army after the Great War, then the Germans again in 1940, and, finally, the US Army in the autumn of 1944, but the Germans know the exact coordinates of every building and can fire artillery at any time, so Company B stays outside but goes in to train. To the soldiers, training is secondary—Elsenborn is one of the few places in the Ardennes where you can really get warm. The soldiers don't care that they are not invited to the movie tent, because they get hot showers, clean clothes, and three hot meals today.[6] The word goes out for military courtesy to be improved—the first sign that you are now off the line.

OCTOBER 28, 1944: HOHES VENN

Company B remains in the same location. Bright, clear, and cold. Strength: six officers and 178 enlisted. George Holdren is evacuated to the 4th Convalescent Hospital, at Maastricht, Netherlands, due to illness. The 3rd Platoon shoots a cow and butchers it, and each man cooks his portion over a small fire. This is not a rare occurrence; lots of cows don't know there's a war on. Hawk DiRisio later said, "There were times we'd get so hungry for red meat [that] we'd shoot any stray cow we found." But it gets better, per Jack Jewell:[7]

> Today the Red Cross trucks came to the company. There were three Red Cross girls and they served coffee and doughnuts to the men. They also gave out gum, cigarettes, and writing paper. I sure don't envy such women of their jobs. Our men were like a pack of hungry wolves, and it isn't much wonder. They had a phonograph on the trucks, and it seemed rather unusual to hear good American music again. But if you can imagine hearing Bing Crosby

sing "White Christmas," while you are standing in a pine forest in Germany and especially after being in combat for days, well you're blowin' your top, as the guys say.

OCTOBER 29, 1944: HOHES VENN

Company remains in the same location, with six officers and 181 enlisted. Jack Dunlap reports: "The Company spent the day cleaning up their clothing and equipment. Church services were held, and all the men took advantage of going as it has been several weeks since they have had that opportunity." The company gets its PX rations today, so candy, cigarettes, and cigars are abundant. Jack Jewell lights up a stogie in celebration.[8] "Celebration" is the word of the day, as Gen. Louis Craig presents awards to members of the regiment, including Warren Ridgeway. The commander writes the following letter back to Timber's family:[9]

> On 29 October 1944 I had the pleasure of awarding to Staff Sergeant Warren E. Ridgeway, before an assembly of his comrades in arms, the Bronze Star for heroic achievement. It is a source of deepest satisfaction to me to present this recognition for outstanding service to a soldier who has demonstrated his unselfish devotion to the service of our Country and whose actions have surpassed our high standards of duty. I speak for the entire Division in assuring you that we share the pride you must feel on learning of this award.

Mac MacLean sends a letter to his mother describing the cow that had run into a bullet: "Yesterday I think I ate about half a cow, and it was really fine. The cooks in this outfit when they get the opportunity can really put out some fine food." He also says he has been with Hector lately—code for combat. Later, he added that the cow was "cooked in small pieces over a very small fire we made in a foxhole." Noodles Nodell also finds time to write home:[10]

> I'm sitting in a foxhole somewhere in Germany, and although I'm sweating it out day after day, I'm getting along fine. I had a few close calls the last few weeks and boy I mean close . . . in case you don't already know it, I'm in the First Army, and believe me we saw plenty. It's been over six months since I had a day off to go where I want to. So, you see, kid, I sure could use a couple of weeks at Klein's right now . . . tell Jeffrey the next Kraut I knock off will be for him. I want to thank you for that flashlight you gave my mother for me. It sure will come in handy for me . . . A Pal, Harry.

OCTOBER 30, 1944: HOHES VENN

Company B remains in location, with seven officers and 178 enlisted. Pvt. Milton Montague and Pfc. Sam Sternlicht are evacuated for nonbattle illness. Sam was hit by shrapnel in the left thigh in Tunisia, and again in Sicily. Milt may have an inflamed appendix. All units begin training at 0800 hours. Communication wire is laid and telephone communications are good.

OCTOBER 31, 1944: HOHES VENN

Company B remains in the same location, 1 mile southwest of Kalterherberg. A high of 50°, a low of 36°, scattered light showers, drizzles, and surface winds at 10–20 mph. Strength: six officers and 175 enlisted. 1Lt. Leonard Kane transfers to Company C. Edward Pickard, Pfc. Howard Gasper, and Pvt. Alexander McAfee are evacuated for nonbattle illness: McAfee for trench foot. Canadian, Pfc. James R. Kinrade is evacuated for an injured foot, possibly when a captured pistol discharges. All units continue training, but for obvious reasons no one goes out trick-or-treating this Halloween night, since you're in Germany, the land of the Frankenstein monster, and who wants to run into that guy in a dark forest?

Company B losses for the month are thirteen killed, eighty-four wounded, and four seriously injured. For October 1944, the 39th Infantry suffers three officers and 104 enlisted killed, two officers and twenty-eight enlisted died of wounds, one officer and 104 enlisted missing, twenty-seven officers and 619 enlisted wounded, and one officer and twenty-seven enlisted injured. The Office of the Division Surgeon reports 802 wounded, 59 nonbattle injuries, 319 sickness, and 63 exhaustion casualties treated at regimental and divisional medical installations. Division reports 384 killed for the month (including sixty-two died of wounds), 2,224 wounded (of whom 1,818 are evacuated), 247 missing, 1,684 suffering from disease (of whom 1,014 are evacuated), 474 injured (of whom 343 are evacuated), and 280 cases of exhaustion (of whom 146 are evacuated).

Another indicator of battle ferocity is awards. For the month, ~~AAA~~O submits six officers and forty-seven enlisted (five posthumously) for Silver Stars, and eleven officers (one posthumously) and one hundred enlisted (four posthumously) for Bronze Stars. Back in Washington, senior decision makers finally comprehend the enormity of casualties in the Hürtgen, but their options are limited. The following day, the War Department authorizes the shipment overseas of infantry and armored replacements who are younger than nineteen years old. The "Crusade in Europe" is about to become "the Boys Crusade."[11]

NOVEMBER 1, 1944: HOHES VENN

Company B continues training with six officers and 174 enlisted. A high of 50°, a low of 36°, scattered light showers, drizzles, and surface winds of 10–20 mph. The division CP is located at Camp Elsenborn. Pvt. Curtis Glenn, a rifleman in 3rd Platoon, is evacuated for a nonbattle illness; it's minor, and he's back in three days; Curtis arrived in Europe on September 20. Jack Jewell writes home: "Today we were given some German wax to be used in making candles. Of course, we didn't have any materials, so everyone put his own ideas to work and you should have seen the results. It was a good laugh. I made several and I think they are right good."[12]

NOVEMBER 2, 1944: HOHES VENN

Company B remains 1 mile southwest of Kalterherberg. Typical Hohes Venn weather: a high of 50°, a low of 36°, scattered light showers, drizzles, and surface winds of 10–20 mph. The company has six officers and 173 enlisted. Lang Turner is placed on special duty at division headquarters. Sgt. Thomas Eggleston is evacuated for a nonbattle injury. Late the previous night, a "company patrol" went on a special mission, as Jack Jewell describes:[13]

> Last night some of the men chased a big young bull right up to the kitchen, and this noon I noticed it was hanging in about four pieces (without hide), so I guess there is more beef ahead. These guys don't let anything go by. If there is a potato patch or an orchard anywhere near, they will always find it some way. I sure can't complain about the food situation, except that its rather tiresome eating so many C-rations sometimes. But they are good and clean so that's something.

NOVEMBER 3, 1944: HOHES VENN

Company B remains in the same location, continuing its training. Strength is six officers and 173 enlisted. At 1925 hours, the unit is alerted for movement the following day. Around Camp Elsenborn, where lots of soldiers have passed through, Mac notices much abandoned equipment. One of those items is his gas mask.[14]

NOVEMBER 4, 1944: HOHES VENN

Garbage weather: a high of 49° and a low of 41°, light showers before noon and then heavy rain, and surface winds 8–15 mph, with gusts to 20 mph. The company's six officers and 172 enlisted are moving up to the line again, per Jack Dunlap: "The Company left training area one mile southwest of Kalterherberg, Belgium [Germany,] at 1430 hours by truck, and traveled to an assembly area 1½ miles east of Krinkelt, Belgium, arriving there at 1545 hours. Distance traveled: approximately 25 miles." The regimental CP is in the village of Krinkelt.[15] Company B CP is in the woods of the Büllinger Wald.[16] Pvt. Samuel Armstrong is evacuated for a nonbattle leg infection.

Back in the Hürtgen, antitank crewman John Chernitsky and his crew in the "Bloody Bucket" Division are pinned down by a German sniper, when suddenly he sees the command vehicle of Lt. Gen. Omar Bradley pull up. Chernitsky walks toward the vehicle, meeting the senior officer, who speaks first, asking, "Don't you know who I am?" Chernitsky answers: "Sir, if I salute you, we're both going to be dead." Just then, an enemy bullet strikes a captain standing next to the general, and the potentially unpleasant situation rapidly defuses as Brad—without another word—swiftly retires to his vehicle.[17] "Retires" is a fancy word that applies to the movement of officers toward the rear. For enlisted, they just "skedaddle," "beat a retreat," "run like hell," or "pick 'em up and lay 'em down."

NOVEMBER 5, 1944: HOHES VENN

Company B CP moves west of the Büllinger Wald.[18] More garbage weather: a high of 49°, a low of 41°, light showers before noon, and surface winds 8–15 mph, with gusts to 20 mph. Company strength is six officers and 174 enlisted. The company morning report reads "The Company left assembly area 1½ miles east of Krinkelt, Belgium, at 0800 hours, by foot and marched to a new position one mile east of Krinkelt, Belgium, arriving there at 0900 hours. Relieved Company F of the 22nd Infantry Regiment. Spent the rest of the day improving positions. Distance marched approximately four miles." The division relieves the 4th Infantry Division in sector, completing the operation by noon. The unit continues patrolling and spots enemy patrols. The division CP moves at 1340 hours; Generals Eisenhower and Bradley visit its new location at Bütgenbach, Belgium.[19] Jack Jewell writes:[20]

> Well I'm still enjoying the pleasures of one of those subterranean homes [foxhole.] It's a different one this time, straw lined, but they are all about the same. One nice thing is that it didn't rain today. I guess that's because it rained enough yesterday for two days. . . . Our boys found a big potato patch near our area, and they have been cooking potatoes every which way you can imagine. Our mess sergeant is a funny fellow, and the men have been after him for lard so they could make French fries. This evening I saw a sign on the mess tent, "No Lard," but I know that sign won't stop them. Some way or another a stray cow found its way into our area again. No wonder when about six or eight GIs chasing it. Anyway, I see beef hanging out to cool so we will have more steaks and hamburgers. . . . Well things aren't too bad. I've sure seen them a hell of a lot worse.

Over in the Pacific, Lt. Ray Heiden, Mac MacLean's brother-in-law, is assigned to VB-14 Bomber Squadron on USS *Wasp*. He takes his Curtiss SBW-3 dive-bomber up on a mission, but something happens and the plane crashes into the Philippine Sea. For a time, Ray is missing; Grace only knows that the first carrier *Wasp* was sunk in 1942. It is the second time his plane has gone down; the first was at Guam, when his Curtiss SB2C-1C Helldiver crashes in July 1944. Every day, Grace reads accounts of US military operations around the world, and she is not happy when someone says that one theater of operations is rougher than another one.

NOVEMBER 6, 1944: HOHES VENN

Company B is 1 mile east of Krinkelt.[21] Warmer garbage: a high of 54°, a low of 48°, rained during the night, light to medium showers, and surface winds of 15–20 mph, with gusts of 30–40 mph. Unit strength: six officers and 174 enlisted. Jack Dunlap reports: "Company sent out combat patrols to locate possible infiltration of enemy and did not meet any opposition. Company was paid today." The company CP is just west of the Büllinger Wald. Jack Jewell writes home, as the men continue to improve their positions:[22]

Another day has passed and here I am as usual in a hole writing by candle. It rained last night but my blankets stayed dry until morning, so I didn't make out so bad. I bought a new pair of combat pants yesterday that are really nice. They are warmer than ordinary pants and have zippers on the sides. I see two more hind quarters of beef outside the kitchen tent today, from the same source, no doubt. Don't think that each time I tell you this it's the same animal, it isn't. The officers got their liquor rations today. Among my bottles was a quart of champagne. I just took it in my hole and imagined I was in a fancy place all dressed up—and started in. It came from France. I guess they know how to make it. If I'm any judge, it was good. We have been issued sleeping bags, something like the ones we had in Michigan last winter. The Army is on the job when it comes to supplies. I think the training I had last winter will help me. That's all for now. Keep the home fires burning. I'll be around one of these years.

And the hindquarters of beef? Well, it's just Hawk DiRisio working his magic again. The same day, the War Department has more bad news for Ike, informing him that it is canceling Officer Candidate School programs stateside due to a shortage of qualified candidates. The Army in Europe should now directly appoint lieutenants from experienced enlisted personnel on the Continent.[23] This is bad news because lieutenants are still dying at a high rate.

NOVEMBER 7, 1944: HOHES VENN

Company B is 1 mile east of Krinkelt.[24] Nip in the air: high, 49°; low, 36°; cool and overcast, low clouds; showers beginning evening; visibility generally good; surface winds 10–18 mph; strength the same. Capt. Dunlap writes: "Company again sent out patrols to locate possible infiltration of enemy and did not meet any opposition." The company CP remains west of the Büllinger Wald as the unit continues to improve its positions. At 2000 hours, the regiment reports that it had attacked an enemy outpost and that small-arms fire was received from a firebreak. The terrain has large amounts of barbed wire and is heavily booby-trapped.

Under the attention-grabbing title "Decapitators at Work," Division G-2, Lt. Col. Jack A. Houston disseminates a newsletter featuring three incidents of the Germans intentionally stringing thin, strong metal wire across roads behind the American lines.[25] Often wrapping the wire around trees on the sides of roads to ensure it is taut, Germans place the lines at a height that when an American jeep speeds down the road with its windshield down—as they often do—the exposed necks of the driver and "shotgun seat" passenger strike the wire, decapitating the men. The reports state that these activities are probably done by German civilians, which does nothing to improve the mood of the GIs. US troops quickly assume that piano wire is the culprit, which does not bode well for a fatherland that sired Johann Sebastian Bach and Ludwig van Beethoven.

NOVEMBER 8, 1944: HOHES VENN

Company B is 1 mile east of Krinkelt. Weather deteriorating: high, 48°; low, 34°; intermittent rain and showers; surface winds 12–24 mph, gusts higher. Company strength: six officers and 169 enlisted. Today is a good day per Jack Dunlap: "Today the Company took a shower and received clean clothes and drank some beer." Pfc. John J. Gerbliss and Privates Elvin Landman and James E. Deller are evacuated for nonbattle illness. Sgt. Luther D. Wilson and Pfc. Chris G. Batalaris apparently decide to take a little break from monotony and go AWOL—"going over the hill." Company B continues to improve its positions. At noon, Generals Eisenhower, Bradley, and Leonard T. Gerow, the Vth Corps commander, visit the division artillery, and the division CP at Bütgenbach. Leonard "Porky" Pourchot goes on patrol and then shares a log-covered foxhole with SSgt. James "Candy" Collins and Pfc. Albert "Bulldog" Eckardt in 1st Platoon.[26]

NOVEMBER 9, 1944: HOHES VENN

Company B remains 1 mile east of Krinkelt. For the six officers and 169 enlisted, the weather is depressing: a high of 45°, a low of 37°, cold and overcast, scattered showers, freezing cold drizzle, 1 inch of wet slosh at lower levels, 6 inches of snow at higher elevations (large snow in Company B area), hazy, and surface winds of 4–8 mph; visibility poor, in some areas zero. The company commander reports: "The Company again sent out combat patrols and did not meet any opposition. We experienced our first snowfall of the year this morning." Sgt. James W. Russell is evacuated for nonbattle illness. The men get more PX rations; each soldier receives two or three candy bars, a package of gum, Life-Savers candy, fruit juice, shaving cream, and cookies.[27] The regiment will be relieved the next day by the 393rd Infantry Regiment of the 99th US Infantry Division and return to their former bivouac areas, so it is time to dismantle all booby traps. The 99th Infantry Division, which would receive the nickname "Battle Babies," was indeed inexperienced—arriving in England on October 10 and crossing the Channel to Le Havre, France, on November 3. This will be the men's first trip to the front.

NOVEMBER 10, 1944: HOHES VENN

Crummy weather: a high of 45°, a low of 37°, cold and overcast; scattered showers, snow flurries, hazy, and surface winds at 4–8 mph; visibility poor. Strength is six officers and 169 enlisted. According to Jack Dunlap, "The Company was relieved by Company B, 393rd Infantry Regiment of the 99th Infantry Division at 1600 hours and traveled to an assembly area one mile southwest of Kalterherberg, Belgium [Germany]. Bivouacked for the night. Distance traveled approximately 14 miles." Once relieved, Company B travels by truck to its old position in the woods southwest of Kalterherberg.[28] CP locations are often in heavy woods, making equipment hauling tough: perfect for a weasel.

Its name does not inspire fear and terror in the enemy. It has no weapon. With what is termed "rubber-band" tracks and a 169-cubic-inch, four-stroke, 70-horsepower engine that can run on 72 octane gas, it is a M-29 Cargo Carrier "Weasel," and in the Hohes Venn and Hürtgen it can go about anywhere. Studebaker, who developed a prototype just sixty days after the Army said it needed the capability, will make thousands of Weasels in South Bend, Indiana. With a width of just over 5 feet, a height just over 4 feet, and a length of 10 feet and change, the 3,800-pound Weasel needs only a little trail or the edge of a field or a firebreak to scurry forward with supplies—and, often more importantly, scamper to the rear with a couple of wounded soldiers, through muddy places not even a jeep can go.

A Weasel can make a U-turn in 12 feet, cross a 36-inch ditch, and climb a 24-inch obstacle. It reportedly has ground pressure so low (1.9 pounds per square inch) that it will not detonate German antitank mines, but no one wants to test that theory at the front with such a valuable lifesaver. Company B has no organic Weasels, but medical folks and engineers often do. It is one of those items that Hawk DiRisio is always on the lookout for, should he ever see one parked without its driver.

NOVEMBER 11, 1944: HOHES VENN

On the twenty-sixth anniversary of the end of the Great War, Company B is in its old position 1 mile southwest of Kalterherberg. High, 36°; low, 24°; freezing above 1,000 feet; partly cloudy; drizzling rain, then mixed rain and snow showers; hazy; visibility is so bad that Ike pens a letter to George Marshall:[29]

> I am getting exceedingly tired of weather. Every day we have some report of weather that has broken records existing anywhere from twenty-five to fifty years.... All of us keep hoping that some little spell will come along in which we can have a bit of relief from mud, rain, and fog so that tanks and infantry can operate more easily on the offensive and so that we can use our great air asset.

Capt. Dunlap reports: "A muster of the Company was taken, and all men carried in present-for-duty column were present. Usual camp duties." The muster confirmed six officers and 185 enlisted. Some soldiers, losing appetites, blame dehydrated potatoes; the last fresh milk was six weeks ago. The 39th Infantry establishes a CP on the northwest side of Elsenborn village.[30] The Battalion is placed on a six-hour alert. The division CP moves to Camp Elsenborn.[31]

NOVEMBER 12, 1944: HOHES VENN

Company B remains 1 mile southwest of Kalterherberg. Worsening weather: high, 48°; low, 30°; weather getting colder and colder; overcast; broken periods of light rain and sleet showers, some snow; visibility poor; surface winds 6–12 mph; and gusts 9–18 mph for the six officers and 169 enlisted. Jack Dunlap has little to report: "Usual camp duties." Salvatore Ciccone, one of the old guard, is evacuated for nonbattle illness. The company maintains weapons and equipment. Nights are so cold that soldiers wrap their overcoats over their sleeping bags to keep warm. Some soldiers gang up three men to a foxhole, putting blankets over them. The middle guy is warm but the others can get cold, so they swap positions throughout the night.

Frank Pemberton, who deserted the company the previous September 14 near Lammersdorf, is apprehended near Verviers, Belgium. At Lammersdorf, Company B was attacking German pillboxes when, about 3:30 p.m., Pemberton, heading down a firebreak in the rear area, was stopped by Joe Gravino. Pemberton said that he was lost. The first sergeant returned him to the vicinity of his platoon, but later other witnesses saw him leaving again toward the rear.

NOVEMBER 13, 1944: HOHES VENN

Company B remains 1 mile southwest of Kalterherberg. "The weather is mostly unpleasant, mud, slush, and snow. Beautiful, but bad," writes Jack Jewell.[32] A high of 43°; a low of 34°; cold and overcast; snowed all night; intermittent light rain, slush, and snow; moderate fog and visibility poor; the company strength is unchanged. Jack Dunlap reports: "It snowed again today, and we now have approximately eight inches of snow. A training program was conducted in the Company area today." Area roads require maintenance at the onset of winter; troop details begin repairs. John Gerbliss is evacuated for nonbattle illness. Coughing abounds.

NOVEMBER 14, 1944: HOHES VENN

Company B location and strength remain unchanged. Horrid weather: a high of 38°, a low of 30°, cold, overcast, intermittent light rain and snow flurries, and ground wet and muddy; visibility restricted. The unit conducts road repair and construction. The Red Cross doughnut wagon visits the company, making everyone happy.[33] Many soldiers try to clean their uniforms.

NOVEMBER 15, 1944: HOHES VENN

No change to location; company strength is six officers and 173 enlisted. Worse weather: high, 40°; low, 28°; overcast; intermittent light rain and snow; mud turning to ice; visibility poor. SSgt. Albert Baccile is evacuated for nonbattle illness. Charles Kompanik returns to duty from a nonbattle illness. Bob Pettigrew is presented with his new best friend, a 20-pound BAR that he will carry until April 10, 1945. The troops conduct road repair and construction. The division begins fifteen days in corps reserve. At division headquarters, an awards clerk cuts orders for a Bronze Star for Valor for Jay Lavinsky for earlier actions at Germeter.[34] Mac MacLean and many buddies, who arrived in October, receive CIBs.[35]

Manley Fuller returns to the company after a long truck ride from Paris, where he and Howard Kaufman were in the hospital. Several times during the long trip, the Maine soldier contemplates jumping out of the truck and returning to Paris, a city he will ultimately visit three times.[36] But he knows that he needs to go back to the platoon.

A military hospital is a beautiful place. First, they save your life in there. A close second is that there often are female nurses assigned to the joint. Third, you can get a little shut-eye in peace and quiet. And last, personnel accountability is often not really—shall we say—tight. That's important. You take off from the front for a little stress relieving, and not only will your chain of command find out you're gone pronto, but also they'll assume that you have left your buddies in the lurch and intend never to come back, and that could be desertion, which gets ugly in a hurry. But taking off for a few hours, or a day or two, as a patient at a hospital? They might not even know you're gone, but if they do, when you come back, they'll likely be really lenient, because when they're off duty they often head downtown themselves.

Wounded on September 20, buddies Manley Fuller and Howard Kaufman are getting over their injuries and back to their cheerful selves. Not only is the hospital extremely near Paris, but it also has a set schedule for transportation of recovered soldiers to replacement depots—and the names of the lads are not on the next few rosters. So, Manley and Howard decide to "hit the bricks" and do a little sightseeing in the "City of Light." Being in the infantry, the two think better of just waltzing out the front gate sans pass and decide one evening to climb over a 9-foot-high wall surrounding the hospital area. They pile up a few sturdy pieces of wood, scale the barrier faster than Errol Flynn in one of those adventure movies, drop over, and make a beeline for the shadows of a dark side street.

The boys spend the night barhopping in Paris. But not at Harry's New York Bar in the center of town, supposedly a popular hangout for commissioned officers assigned to the European theater of operation's judge advocate general. These boys run general court-martials, and they might not take kindly drinking with a couple of their enlisted brethren in Paris without a pass—even if you had been wounded. However, all good things must come to an end, and as the exhausted duo approaches the hospital before dawn's early light, they begin to ponder how they will get back inside undetected. Fortunately, an observant French lady has prepared the way for them—and this is not the first time that she has assisted *les Américains* to get back over the wall. Manley finds that prior to their arrival, the *femme élégante* put a ladder at the exact site outside the wall where the boys had previously crossed, and up they go—later the ladder vanishes as mysteriously as it had appeared. *Vive la France!*[37]

NOVEMBER 16, 1944: HOHES VENN

Company B remains 1 mile southwest of Kalterherberg, with six officers and 173 enlisted. The weather is dismal: a high of 39°, a low of 24°, cold and overcast, and scattered light snow showers after noon; visibility is good until 1600 hours, but thereafter poor. Personnel are ordered to remain in their foxholes during a planned massed bombing attack, Operation Queen, forward of the front, in case some bombs fall short. The target: Düren, some 26 miles northeast. In total, 486 B-17s of the Third Bomb Division of the Eighth US Air Force drop 1,688 tons of bombs, destroying upward of 90 percent of the city.[38] Porky Pourchot and Candy Collins listen to the rumble, sitting in a covered foxhole, heating beef-and-noodle C rations, followed by ham and eggs.[39] While none of the bombs fall short, friendly artillery can also hit the wrong targets, as one soldier in the Hürtgen later says:[40] "'Our artillery is better than the Germans.' I know. I caught plenty [near] Kommerscheidt. . . . It has more concussion than the German shells."

On November 16, 1944, the *Newark Courier-Gazette* reports on 1Sgt. Gravino:[41]

Sgt. "Joe" Gravino Twice Wounded, Gets Purple Heart

Twice-wounded-in-action 1st Sgt. Joseph Gravino has been presented the Purple Heart Medal for injuries received in France in August, according to his parents, Mr. and Mrs. Dominic Gravino, Van Buren St., who have just received the medal. Sergeant Gravino was first wounded by shrapnel in the head during the Tunisian campaign early in 1943. After recovering from this injury, he participated in the invasion of France, serving under Lt.-Gen. Courtney Hodges in the First Army, which is now fighting in Germany. He suffered his second injury in France when a shell burst near him—cutting his wrist and throwing him to the ground from the concussion of the explosion.

Closer to the front, Jack Jewell writes home, praising his soldiers:[42]

Well the war goes on. It looks like they are going to stick it out to the end—and if they do there won't be anything left of them. I have a very good bunch of men to work with. Really couldn't ask for any better. They are a crazy bunch and have a lot of fun when the going isn't too tough. This is a song they sing that I think is right good; to the tune of "Wabash Cannonball."

Hear the One-Five-Fives a barking,
Hear the angry shrapnel whine,
The airplanes they will help us,
To saturate the swine,
We'll have our Christmas dinner,
In a big Berlin hotel,
While Hitler and his buddies,
All sweat it out in Hell.

NOVEMBER 17, 1944: HOHES VENN

There is no change to location or strength for Company B. Cool and cloudy, overcast at 2,000 feet, light rain at night, and visibility fair in morning, poor after noon. Company B conducts reconnaissance and forms counterattack plans in the event of an enemy attack. Dale Lockridge returns from a hospital. For the week ending November 17,

AAAO has seven soldiers evacuated for cold injuries.[43] Ed Pickard is one of the lucky ones. Off the front lines, he is able to at least think about his twenty-second birthday today.

NOVEMBER 18, 1944: HOHES VENN

No change to location; strength for Company B is six officers and 181 enlisted. The weather is nasty: a high of 40°, a low of 38°, and intermittent light rain and snow; visibility is borderline. Company B conducts road repair and construction. Lt. Col. Thompson checks counterattack plans. Jack Jewell goes into Camp Elsenborn and has his first encounter with a bathtub since June 20; his other cleanups were showers:[44]

> Again we have fresh cow hanging out by the kitchen. These boys manage somehow. Our food for the most part has always been good. One of our cooks makes pancakes that melt in your mouth, and they make syrup with sugar and cinnamon. Tomorrow is Sunday and I'm going to slip out with the captain about daybreak to hunt deer . . . I guess venison is good eating. We got PX rations again today . . . fruit juice, candy bars, chocolate bars, cigars, and cookies. There isn't enough for every man to get much, but it all helps out some. I just finished censoring and sealing 400 Christmas cards for my platoon. It was some job. But I didn't mind. It was the only kind of present most of the men could send their friends and parents. I know their Christmas spirit will be more in earnest than anyone else's, but it is hard for them to explain it.

NOVEMBER 19, 1944: HOHES VENN

Company B has no change in location; strength is six officers and 179 enlisted. Another ugly day: high, 45°; low, 34°; overcast; intermittent light drizzle and rain; surface winds 5–20 mph. Cpt Dunlap is cheery: "Church services were held for the men. The Company also received three and a half barrels of beer. We all had a swell party." Two enlisted men are evacuated for nonbattle illness. Oliver Osbourn is appointed sergeant, and Leonard Ellsworth is appointed tech sergeant. Frank Terok, a thirty-seven-year-old salesclerk from Trumbull County, Ohio, is appointed technician fifth grade and made a company armorer (511).

Dunlap and Jewell get up before dawn to go deer hunting, after they have a good breakfast of pancakes. During the hunt, the pair recon their counterattack plans, see no deer, but stop at a neighboring company and graciously accept a second pancake breakfast.[45] First Platoon leader Lucien Lucas informs Cpl. Pourchot that he is promoted to sergeant. Porky celebrates with a beer.[46] The 9th Infantry publishes *General Orders* (*GO*) #99, awarding 1Sgt. Joe Gravino the Silver Star for gallantry in action last August 12. Sgt Harold Rogers, with the company since it formed at Fort Bragg, is authorized a furlough home.

NOVEMBER 20, 1944: HOHES VENN

Location and strength remain the same. Mixed weather: high, 52°; low, 36°; visibility good; surface winds 15–30 mph, with gusts to 40 mph. Jack Dunlap reports: "Company reorganized effective November 15, 1944, T/O and E 7-17 dated February 26, 1944, and changes thereto. Authority, *Subject letter "Reorganization" File 320, Headquarters First US Army*, dated November 15, 1944." The new strength specifies one first sergeant, four tech sergeants, sixteen staff sergeants, fifteen sergeants, two technicians fourth grade, one corporal, four technicians fifth grade, 104 privates first class, and forty privates, for a total of six officers and 187 enlisted. For the 39th Infantry, the new strength comes to 153 officers and 3,049 enlisted. Mac MacLean and Bob Pettigrew are promoted to private first class. Pvt. Eugene Leach is evacuated for frostbitten feet. Kentuckian Luther Wilson returns from AWOL, while New Hampshire–born Pvt. Lionel Martin receives an all-expenses-paid trip to the division guardhouse after being a deserter since July 21. Back home, Les Brown and Doris Day record "Sentimental Journey." It won't be a sentimental journey for Lionel.

NOVEMBER 21, 1944: HOHES VENN

Company location and strength remain the same. Fall in the Hohes Venn: high, 50°; low, 47°; overcast; rain early morning and late afternoon; ground very wet, muddy; visibility poor. Luther Wilson is reduced to private; undaunted by likely punishment, Donald Pellock goes over the hill. Company B conducts training, road repair, and construction. SSgt. Asbury Dawkins, 3rd Squad, 1st Platoon, finds a horse and cart, bringing them back to the platoon. Asbury can butcher a cow, and Porky says he does so regularly. Candy Collins finds a bicycle in Kalterherberg. He suggests that Porky write a book after the war titled "14 Mad Men."[47]

Division G-2 publishes tips on patrolling methods gathered from the 60th Infantry. They include not repeating patrol routes and destinations on successive days, and "Don't take the same route on your way back as you took going out." Concerning paths, the best patrol routes were not in draws or bottomlands, but on ridgelines or at least halfway up a ridge. Advice included that the battalion S2 should personally orient the patrols on a map before they depart. As to size and weapons, "We feel that six men is the ideal number for patrols. Four of them should be armed with M1s and the other two with Tommy Guns. A light automatic weapon is vital if you run into trouble. Two Tommy Guns are the answer."[48] Phil Holman recalled patrolling a bit differently: "We had no maps. We had no binoculars. We had no radios. And we had no Thompson submachine guns."

Regimental patrols are almost going out blind; if they spot something significant, they can neither call in artillery fire nor provide accurate enough information for a fire mission later. Without binoculars, they cannot spot stationary Germans more than about 150 yards away. All the soldiers on a patrol carry M1 rifles; a BAR usually just makes the patrol slower than passing a kidney stone. They do have compasses, so they can follow an azimuth on patrol.

NOVEMBER 22, 1944: HOHES VENN

Company strength is six officers and 178 enlisted; location remains the same. Foul, cool weather; intermittent rain; visibility poor. Two enlisted men are evacuated for nonbattle illness. Porky has chicken for dinner in his pup tent. He makes a bucket fireplace to keep warm but later goes into Kalterherberg to scrounge a better stove.[49]

NOVEMBER 23, 1944: HOHES VENN

Company B location remains the same, while strength ticks up to six officers and 182 enlisted. Weather: high, 53°; low, 34°; low clouds, cloudy, overcast; showers and drizzle; foggy. Capt. Dunlap reports: "Today is Thanksgiving, church services were held and most of the Company attended. The men enjoyed a big turkey dinner." Lang Turner returns. Training is suspended. Mac MacLean sends a letter home:[50]

> Today, we all—whether we care to admit it or not—thanked the Lord that we were blessed with the Army's best cooks. It seems like they've done the impossible as far as cooking goes. They get us hot food while other outfits are eating cold "C" rations. Here's what they whipped up today: fried turkey, mashed and sweet potatoes, corn, cranberry sauce, apple cobbler, bread, butter, coffee, and dressing. It looked so good I didn't want to eat it for fear of forgetting what food like that looked like.

NOVEMBER 24, 1944: HOHES VENN

While the company location remains the same, strength increases to six officers and 184 enlisted. Ugly weather: high, 51°; low, 40°; cool and overcast; intermittent scattered showers; morning visibility poor. 1Lt. Stan Mills is placed on quarters for a nonbattle illness, probably pneumonia. Donald Pellock returns from AWOL. Pfc. Wayne Minor returns to the company; he has been a magnet for enemy fire: hit by shrapnel in the neck in Tunisia and Sicily, and in June 1944 an exploding German land mine wounds him in the foot. The battalion is relieved from six-hour alert; however, the entire regiment is placed on six-hour-alert status because the division is still in corps reserve. In another snafu, friendly aircraft strafe elements of the 47th Infantry.[51] For the week ending November 24, the 39th Infantry evacuates two soldiers for cold injuries.[52]

NOVEMBER 25, 1944: HOHES VENN

Company location remains unchanged; strength is six officers and 181 enlisted. Another iffy day: high, 46°; low, 30°; cloudy, later sunny; showers, rain, drizzle; visibility restricted. Jack Dunlap writes: "The Company was alerted to move this morning but for some reason or other we did not move. Continued with the usual training schedule." Pvt. Chester Burd is evacuated; he'll have an appendectomy and return in January. Pellock is busted to private. Chris Batalaris returns from AWOL. Jack Jewell writes home: "Dear Folks . . . We have our radio going this evening and it is quite a pleasure to hear music and be in touch with the outside world again."[53]

NOVEMBER 26, 1944: HOHES VENN

Company location remains unchanged; strength is six officers and 183 enlisted. Poor weather: high, 40°; low, 30°; intermittent light rain; visibility restricted. George Holdren returns from the 4th Convalescent Hospital at Spa, Belgium, as does Salvatore Ciccone. Chris Batalaris is busted to private. The battalion is placed on six-hour alert. *GO #101* announces a Silver Star to "Staff Sergeant Raymond L. Olive, Infantry, United States Army, who distinguished himself by gallantry in action and disregard for personal safety during the period 18 October to 21 October 1944 during the operations in Germany, which reflects highest credit upon himself and the armed forces of the United States." Mac MacLean draws a picture for his mother, writing, "In a spare moment with nothing to do but dream, I concocted this little masterpiece. You can see that my childhood is still with me."

NOVEMBER 27, 1944: HOHES VENN

Location and personnel strength remain the same. High, 48°; low, 26°; low clouds; light drizzle and snow; good visibility; flying weather good. Company B conducts training, road repair, and construction in the bivouac area.

NOVEMBER 28, 1944: HOHES VENN

Company B's location and personnel strength remain the same. Weather to cough by: high, 46°; low, 28°; drizzle and light rain; hazy, light fog; visibility restricted. In the morning report, Cpt Dunlap writes: "Usual camp duty in training area. The Company is alerted to move." Company B conducts training, road repair, and construction. Jack Jewell writes home, discussing his fellow officers: "The officers in this company are a wonderful bunch. They are all about my age and we have a lot of fun together. It's a big help these days to be with a group of men that get along with each other like we do."[54] But not all is wonderful. The 294th Engineer Combat Battalion sends a disturbing letter to all units concerning the dreaded German *Schuh* mine:[55]

> At about 1500 hours, November 27, 1944, one man from the 377th Anti-Aircraft Artillery Battalion went up a hill to cut wood. The area had been marked with "Danger Mines" signs. He stepped on a mine, which shattered his legs. Upon calling for medics, about six men went to his aid. While moving around, another man stepped on a mine, injuring himself and two others. Corporal Arnold F. Benedict, 294th Engineer Combat Battalion, upon hearing the explosion, went up to investigate. When he arrived upon the scene, he worked his way up to the top of the hill in the other men's footsteps.
>
> When reaching the top, he administered morphine and applied tourniquet to the injured. An ambulance driver followed in Corporal Benedict's footsteps with a litter. As he handed Corporal Benedict the litter, he stepped back and on to a mine, blowing off his leg and slightly injuring Corporal Benedict. Upon falling, the ambulance driver fell on another mine, thereby killing

himself. A Captain of the Medical Corps probed his way up to the injured and found one Schuh mine. He then assumed charge of evacuating the wounded. Corporal Benedict, also by probing, found three more Schuh mines in the vicinity of the injured.

NOVEMBER 29, 1944: HOHES VENN

Company B strength and location remains the same. Poor weather: high, 42°; low, 30°; intermittent light rain and drizzle before noon, scattered showers after. Virginian 1Lt. Jesse L. Wheeler is assigned. Company conducts training, road repair, and construction.

AWOL was not rare in World War II; the offense was used to describe a temporary condition, such as trying to sneak back to Paris for a wild weekend. Desertion was different. It implied that you did not intend to ever return to your unit or to military control somewhere else. The Army will just bust you to private for AWOL; for desertion, the Army will crush you. Company B has one of the permanent kind of absentees, and a general court-martial meets at Camp Elsenborn today to try Pvt. Frank Pemberton on the charge of desertion. Pemberton, born in 1920 in Ohio, a high school graduate and married, was inducted on May 12, 1943, at Columbus. He has a track record—never good when a soldier gets into trouble—with one previous conviction by special court-martial for absence on November 18, 1943, right smack at the time of shipment to port of embarkation for overseas duty. He also rode sick call, admitted for minor maladies last January and June.[56] The evidence introduced at trial is compelling. In his defense, Pemberton makes an unsworn statement:[57]

> We were waiting for the attack on these German pillboxes, and the shells were dropping back in there until I couldn't stand it in there any longer. I never could fire a rifle when the shells were falling around me. I was always scared and nervous and excited, and the artillery would make me that way much more so. And that's what happened to me that day.

The court sentences Pemberton to be dishonorably discharged, forfeit all pay and allowances due or to become due, and be confined at hard labor at such place as the reviewing authority may direct, for the term of his natural life. The reviewing authority approves the sentence and designates the US penitentiary at Lewisburg, Pennsylvania, for confinement. "Corner Turner" Pemberton is immediately placed in arrest in quarters. He's lucky. The Army will execute Eddie Slovik for desertion in January 1945.[58] And if you didn't end up at Lewisburg, you were going to spend a lot of years busting rocks back at Uncle Sam's Big House at Leavenworth.

NOVEMBER 30, 1944: HOHES VENN

Company B remains 1 mile southwest of Kalterherberg (915130). Company strength ticks up to seven officers and 188 enlisted. More poor weather: high, 44°; low, 32°;

scattered light morning drizzle, afternoon showers; fog, visibility restricted. Jack Dunlap reports: "In compliance with a Headquarters V Corps letter, dated November 27, 1944, directing an inventory of Medical Department Officers a negative report is submitted herewith"—one more time-consuming Army reporting requirement that never ends.

Technician Fourth Grade Anthony Yannuzzi reports from the 41st Replacement Battalion as a cook (060), making Hawk DiRisio a happy man; Anthony—with Company B since 1941—had been evacuated earlier for an acute sinus infection, because you don't want a guy with a sinus infection cooking your food. He is another "combat cook" who received the CIB. William Spano is evacuated for nonbattle illness. Daniel Douvanis returns to duty from a nonbattle illness. Company B conducts training, road repair, and construction. It is haircut day in the weapons platoon.[59]

For November 1944, the 39th Infantry suffers two enlisted men wounded. AAAO submits two enlisted men for the Distinguished Service Cross, seven officers and twenty-four enlisted men (one posthumously) for Silver Stars, and eleven officers and one hundred enlisted men (one posthumously) for Bronze Stars. Medics reported for November that the division suffered 183 cases of trench foot, caused by a variety of factors, the most important a lack of arctic overshoes by frontline units.[60]

DECEMBER 1, 1944: HOHES VENN

Strength and location of Company B unchanged, while the weather is a high of 48°, a low of 32°, mostly fair with increasing cloudiness, slight drizzle on high ground in the morning, and patches of fog. The division CP is at Camp Elsenborn. For the week ending December 1, the regiment evacuates five soldiers for cold injuries.[61] 1Lt. Stanley Mills returns from sick quarters, still suffering a respiratory infection. Company B conducts training, road repair, and construction. Jack Jewell writes home about what he is reading in newspapers: "I want to tell you right now [that] unless something quite unforeseen happens, this war will last quite a while longer. People had better wise up and quick. These Germans are together, and they are strong. I wouldn't put anything past them, and I wouldn't give them anything but lead."[62]

DECEMBER 2, 1944: HOHES VENN

Location and strength are unchanged, except for one less enlisted. Cliff Chew is evacuated for trench foot and tonsillitis. Slightly warmer: high, 50°; low, 34°; cloudy; light rain. Company B conducts training, construction, and road repair. The platoon huddles around a radio in a tent that evening and listens to the Army-Navy football game. Jack Jewell recalled that the game began at about 2000 hours and that it was raining as usual.[63]

Because Army is ranked number one and Navy number two in the country, the venue is changed to Municipal Stadium in Baltimore, Maryland, which can seat 66,659 fans. Tickets are made available to anyone purchasing war bonds through the Maryland State War Finance Committee. The game sells out within twenty-four hours and raises in excess of $58.6 million for the war effort. Famed sportswriter Grantland Rice predicted that the game would be "one of the best and most important football games ever played."[64]

It was. Millions of soldiers, sailors, and marines listened on ships, air bases, and bivouac areas around the world, while attendees at the game sat through a frigid afternoon—buffeted by a brisk wind that blew through the stadium from kickoff to final whistle. As the boys in 3rd Platoon cheer, Army clings to a precarious 9–7 lead in the fourth quarter, before future Heisman Trophy winners Glenn Davis and Doc Blanchard seal the win for the Army Black Knights with two more touchdowns.

DECEMBER 3, 1944: HOHES VENN

Company B remains 1 mile southwest of Kalterherberg (915130). Seven officers and 187 enlisted experience a high temperature of 42°, a low of 37°, intermittent light rain, and scattered showers. 1Lt. Jesse Wheeler departs for Company L. Training is suspended for Sunday. The men are treated to fried chicken and cake.[65] Often, Jack Jewell just looks at his soldiers and shakes his head in disbelief; this is one of those days. "Today I was walking through my platoon area and what should greet me but a goat. These men collect some of the darndest things I have seen. They also had a tuba and one of the boys was playing a good tune on it."[66]

DECEMBER 4, 1944: HOHES VENN

Company B remains in location with seven officers and 193 enlisted. The weather is worsening: high, 40°; low, 32°; light rain, drizzle, and showers, with occasional snow flurries. "We have had so much rain and snow you can't take a single step without walking in two or three inches of mud."[67] Capt. Dunlap reveals, "The Company is preparing to move." William Spano returns from sick quarters. Sgt. Pourchot, Pfc. John Boyle, and Pfc. Ruben Brady, 1st Platoon, finish constructing their "log cabin" living accommodation.[68] Just after they complete their masterpiece, they hear that AAAO has been alerted to relieve the 1st Infantry Division up north.

DECEMBER 5, 1944: HÜRTGEN FOREST

The company moves 1 mile west of Merode, Germany (035435), with an increased strength of seven officers and 195 enlisted. The weather signals an unease: high, 47°; low, 32°; overcast; slight drizzle; patches of fog. The morning report reveals that "the Company left training area one mile southwest of Kalterherberg by trucks at 0730 hours and traveled to its assembly area near Merode, Germany, arriving there at 1330 hours. Left assembly area by foot and marched to one mile west of Merode, where we relieved Company I, 26th Infantry Regiment. The Company took up defensive positions. Received very little shelling: distance traveled approximately 35 miles."

The division moves to relieve the 1st Infantry Division in the Aachen Corridor. Attached to the "Big Red One" until the division headquarters arrives, the 39th CP moves 600 yards east of the hamlet of Wenau.[69] It's bad. Relieving Company I, the men hear that the 26th Infantry had previously attacked Merode. The attack failed, with 165 men missing in action. After the relief, soldiers go on a "Jerry-hunt" through the woods, ensuring that no Germans are hiding nearby; they find no one.[71] That evening, the division CP moves to Bergrath, southeast of Eschweiler.[70]

Company B is about to become intimately familiar with Merode Castle, but had the soldiers known who owned the joint, they might have just leveled the place. Members of the House of Merode carried the title of "Count" from the fifteenth century, while a branch of the family held the position of "Baron of the Holy Roman Empire" and gained the title of "Prince" in 1759. In 1928, Jean de Merode, grand marshal of the Court of Belgium, received from King Albert I the title of "Prince de Merode." A later family member, Amaury de Merode, served as a grand marshal of the Court of King Leopold III, and president of the Royal Automobile Club of Belgium.

These boys don't marry the girl next door; they marry princesses. These boys don't dine on hot dogs and beer; they guzzle champagne, while complaining about the vichyssoise and the foie gras. These boys didn't give a hoot about how many dogfaces died retaking the castle, and after the war these boys complain that the Americans used excessive force on the place. There were millions of Belgians who got down on their knees every night and thanked God for the American army, but these boys aren't any of them.

DECEMBER 6, 1944: HÜRTGEN FOREST

Company B is located 1 mile west of Merode.[72] The temperatures are recorded as a high of 42° and a low of 35°, with it being cool and overcast; visibility is poor to fair. Capt. Jack Dunlap, lightly wounded by shrapnel in the right leg, remains with the unit, writing, "Remained in defensive positions." Salvatore Ciccone is evacuated for nonbattle illness—gone till February. The company patrols and establishes contact with adjacent units. Mac MacLean goes on patrol to Schloss Laufenburg in the Wenau Forest.[73] Laufenburg Castle, founded in the twelfth century, is partially ruined but is a possible spot for an enemy artillery observer; however, the patrol finds nothing. At 2000 hours, the 39th reports that 150 rounds of artillery struck the unit. The 9th Infantry is assigned to VIIth Corps, where General Hodges visits and approves General Collins's plan for the 9th Infantry to attack in three days.[74]

DECEMBER 7, 1944: HÜRTGEN FOREST

Company B's seven officers and 195 enlisted remain in the same location. The weather is worsening: high, 44°; low, 35°; cold and overcast; rain and snow; visibility poor. Dunlap reports: "Company remained in defensive positions." The division occupies positions west of Schlich, Konzendorf, and Merode in the muddy soil. Enemy lines are as close as 75 yards. Ltc. Thompson receives the attack plan to study. Late in the day, he receives news that the attack has been delayed a day, now expected to start December 10. Jack Jewell departs the company on a five-day pass to Paris. But he can't sleep on the way there, since he's the truck convoy commander. In one foxhole, Lester

Rosencranz, from Ransom, Pennsylvania, is celebrating his thirty-fifth birthday, probably praying he can spend the next one with his wife, Edith. The regiment captures a soldier from 5th Fallschirmjäger Regiment, who tells them that fifty to sixty paratroopers with assault rifles are in the cellars of Merode Castle, precisely where Thompson must attack.

DECEMBER 8, 1944: HÜRTGEN FOREST

Six officers and 194 enlisted in Company B remain in location. There are light rain showers, with a high of 42° and a low of 33°. "Company remained in defensive positions," reports Capt. Dunlap. Joe McQueen is evacuated for nonbattle illness. The 39th reports at 1400 hours that it is receiving artillery and mortar fire. That night, two artillery rounds fall on the CP, while fifty mortar rounds drop on First Battalion. The regiment reverts to control of the 9th Infantry. For the week ending December 8, AAAO loses sixteen soldiers for cold injuries.[75]

Jack Jewell, in the "City of Love," writes home that he attended a burlesque show called "Casino de Paris." Jack doesn't elaborate, but a *Ouh là là* cabaret show in Paris may be a bit different than a tap-dancing skit in Wellsville. Jack and two officers then head to a nightclub, see another floor show, and split a bottle of champagne. Having a grand time, Jack describes the city's fairer sex: "The women are very beautiful and dress exquisitely—hats you should see, smart dresses, fur coats, and they all know how to wear their makeup right."[76] That letter may be causing Mom and Pop to get a tad uneasy back in Kansas, contemplating, "How ya gonna keep 'em down on the farm after they've seen Paree? How ya gonna keep 'em away from Broadway, jazzin' around and paintin' the town?"[77]

DECEMBER 9, 1944: HÜRTGEN FOREST

Location remains the same; strength is six officers and 195 enlisted. Rain and snow showers, overcast, a high of 40° and a low of 32° make the troops miserable. "Company remained in defensive positions." The company conducts final reconnaissance and coordination with adjacent units. Light artillery falls on the sector; mortar fire is rated as medium. Cliff Chew returns after recovering from cold-weather injuries.

The 9th G-2, Ltc. Houston, who assumed his post on August 21, 1944, is a smart guy. He knows that something is up behind German lines, and he wants to ensure that everyone else knows too. In today's *G2 Journal*, he describes a VIIth Corps message, reporting an enemy POW stated that he saw soldiers of 2nd SS Panzer Division Das Reich at Mechernich, 25 miles from the front, and that troops from 1st SS Panzer Division Leibstandarte were at Nörvenich, near Düren. More ominously, a captured enemy soldier reports that there is "talk of counterattack in the next few days; all towns between here and the Rhine River have many troops in them." Later that day, Houston reports that a prisoner from the 991st Infantry Regiment says that his battalion is attached to the 1st SS Panzer Division.[78] Something indeed is up.

Company B is 1 mile west of Merode.[79] Weather worsens: high, 41°; low, 32°; overcast; ground covered by snow at sunrise; scattered rain and snow showers until noon; bitter cold wind; visibility poor. Company strength: seven officers and 197 enlisted. Jack Dunlap writes: "The Company was expecting to attack the town of Merode, but orders were cancelled." Joe McQueen is evacuated for nonbattle illness. Napoleon Daniels returns after recovering from his October 12 wounds. Somebody up the line finally realizes that Wayne Minor has been overseas for two years, has fought in all campaigns, and has been wounded three times, so he receives orders sending him on temporary duty at Fort Meade.

Second Battalion, 39th Infantry, attacks east from Jüngersdorf at 1515 hours to seize the village of D'Horn, just over a mile away. Once that occurs, along with the capture of the villages of Obergeich and Geich by the division's 60th Infantry, the rest of the 39th Infantry—including Company B—will attack to seize Merode and Schlich. The earth is extremely damp; ditches in the fields next to the roads are muddy with standing water. Maj. Gen. Collins arrives to personally observe the attack—actually good news, because when the "Old Man" is watching your attack, you know that you will receive plenty of artillery support.

Company B spends a restless night waiting for next morning's attack. Porky Pourchot hears that there is a medieval castle with a moat. That does not bode well.[80] Company B already knows that two weeks ago, the "Big Red One" attacked Merode, and a lot of them cashed in their chips. Then, behind a strong artillery preparation, the 26th Infantry pushes two companies into the village. The 26th committed a platoon of tanks, but one gets stuck and the others cannot advance; defending paratroopers then surround both companies. Despite several efforts, no reinforcements can get into Merode. About midnight comes a final radio message from the encircled men: "There's a Tiger tank coming down the street now, firing his gun into every house. He's three houses away now . . . here he comes . . . " The radio then goes silent.

Omar Bradley visits First Army headquarters with discouraging news that currently there is no hope in sight for replacements, especially riflemen. When asked, "Would US divisions have to fight decimated and in half-strength like the German *Kampfgruppen* (battle groups)," Bradley replies, "Yes, I am afraid that is so."[81] Bradley isn't the only one worried. Ken Seaman later recalls the night before the attack:[82]

Just one more thing; Millar just asked me did I remember when we were near Merode, where we stayed all night in the castle the following night. And you had got a bunch of letters from Julie, and she asked you if you had read something or other—I don't remember what, a political book or literature or something— anyhow you really blew your top. It was very amusing under the circumstances, what with Jerry planes, mortars, and our own Cannon Company shooting at us—not to mention the weather and us "sweating out" that attack the next morning, knowing the First Division had been kicked out of the same place.

DECEMBER 11, 1944: MERODE, GERMANY

Company B is at Merode, Germany.[83] A high of 40°, a low of 32°, surface winds at 14–18 mph, low clouds and overcast, light continuous rain mixed with snow, with scattered showers in the afternoon; at least the Krauts have bad visibility. Strength: six officers and 197 enlisted. Capt. Dunlap writes: "The Company attacked the town of Merode under a heavy artillery barrage. Captured it at 1000 hours. Captured several prisoners and evacuated several German wounded. Set up defensive positions for the night." Up the line, today's fight will be boiled down to the following antiseptic description in a unit journal: "1st and 2nd Bns succeeded in getting to objective."[84]

The descriptions are inadequate to describe what actually happened. First Battalion attacks just before sunrise at 0800 hours to seize Merode Castle and Merode village; to the north is Second Battalion. German long-range machine gun fire, from over a mile away in Derichsweiler, begins pelting the attackers emerging from the woods. Making matters worse, the windchill is 21°F—low enough to cause frostbite in thirty minutes. Pvt. Eugene Leach's feet are so frostbitten that he is evacuated to a hospital, where he will remain until March.

On the western edge of the village, Merode Castle is surrounded by a moat, measuring 20-plus feet wide and 7 feet deep, actually a rectangular lake with the castle in the center. The stronghold has two towers five stories high, but the black, tapered spires—in which snipers can hide—add another elevation that gives the Germans superb observation. The towers have small, narrow windows that are perfect for snipers. Local tour guides marvel at the castle: "As many windows as days, as many rooms as weeks, as many towers as months in a year."[85]

The castle is not designed as a defensive structure but is more ornate in form—a Renaissance castle with medieval roots. There is one entrance—a narrow bridge 12 feet wide and 80 feet long, facing south over the moat—with neither cover nor concealment. Walls, constructed with thick red bricks, will stop small-arms fire but are no match for artillery. Thick gray granite stones support the entire structure, which has a deep cellar.

Farm fields on three sides give defenders excellent visibility; attackers have no place to hide. The closest concealed positions are 600 yards west in the thick woods. Years in the future, Merode Castle will be considered one of the most beautiful castles of the Rhineland, bathed each December evening with warm light as it hosts the village Christmas market:[86]

All over the property, bonfires will radiate warmth, creating a cozy atmosphere. Feuerzangenbowle, a traditional hot drink, and regional specialty, will be brewed in large caldrons. The delicious aroma of hot wine and fragrance of local foods and sweets wafting through the winter air. Visitors can also warm up in the castle's café and enjoy a cup of coffee or cacao punch with a piece of Christollen, a Christmas cake or other baked goodies.

It truly will be a romantic setting. But not today—today, the castle and town are in the defensive sector of the 5th Fallschirmjäger Regiment of the 3rd Fallschirmjäger Division. These veteran paratroopers are stone-cold killers, some of the toughest soldiers in the Reich. They deploy two battalions forward and one in reserve; three companies are probably in the castle itself. Today, the only objects "wafting through the winter air" are designed to kill. Lieutenant Colonel Karl Heinz Becker commands the regiment: jumped into Poland in 1939, jumped into Holland in May 1940, wins the Knights Cross of the Iron Cross at Crete in May 1941 as his company of the 1st Fallschirmjäger Regiment drops near Iraklion (Heraklion), seizing Hill 491, and later fights in Russia at Velikije-Luki, where he is wounded in January 1943.

Elevated to battalion command, Becker then sees combat in Italy at Abruzzen, Ortona, and Nettuno. In the summer of 1944, he extricates much of his regiment from the Falaise Pocket in Normandy, receiving the German Cross in Gold. Becker will be awarded the Oak Leaves to his Knights Cross in March 1945, one of just 775 men in the entire ten-million-man Wehrmacht to be so decorated. Today his mission is to hold the castle and the village. To make matters worse, 9th Infantry captures a 3rd Fallschirmjäger Division document dated November 30, ending with an ominous note: "Not one more inch is to be lost."

P-47 Thunderbolts from the 368th Fighter Group, out of Chièvres, Belgium, attack Merode and surrounding areas. The ground attack begins; immediately artillery and small-arms fire hits First Battalion, but the men keep advancing, conducting marching fire. The tactic involves a fairly dense skirmish line of infantry, with armored vehicles following closely behind them. As the infantrymen and vehicles advance forward, each man fires two or three times a minute toward the enemy—aimed if he had a target; into a likely defensive position if he did not—shooting a tad low, so that bullets will ricochet off the ground and whistle into enemy positions. Behind the advancing infantry, M10 tank destroyers of Company A, 899th Tank Destroyer Battalion, and Shermans from Company C, 746th Tank Battalion, fire bursts of machine gun fire at likely machine gun nests. By constantly pumping out rounds, the entire formation attempts to keep the enemy's heads down, to reach a point for a quick assault of the castle, since they were—in effect—constantly pinning down the enemy.

Sunrise occurs at 0827 hours. The lead elements reach Merode village at 0835 hours, and for hours the Germans and Americans attack and counterattack each other for control. German machine guns in building cellars can be destroyed only by hand grenades, in a confusing slugfest house to house, with Company B in the thick of it. The paratroopers know the ground well, having repulsed the 1st Infantry attack earlier. At 0915 hours, an enemy artillery observer is reported in the castle. Artillery gouges great holes in the walls, as soldiers of the battalion pepper the castle with rifle, machine gun, and bazooka fire at close range.

Enemy aircraft attack Company B, as do mortars, and even snipers shooting from high in the castle. P-38 Lightning fighter-bombers dive-bomb the village. In the castle, the Germans barricade the portcullis—the entryway into the castle, at the end of the long span—with fallen beams and emplace two MG42 heavy machine guns to mow down any GI trying to cross the bridge. Snipers firing from tower windows ply their deadly craft. Companies A and C charge anyway, pinning down enemy machine gun crews, and prepare to assault the castle. Under covering fire by bazookas and tanks, the infantrymen sprint across the debris-littered bridge over the moat, in a scene resembling the Middle Ages. The first paratroopers in the castle soon begin to surrender, while others leap in the moat to escape. M10 tank destroyers report knocking out one antitank gun and two machine guns.

Sunset occurs at 1629 hours. Focke-Wulf 190 fighter aircraft drop flares over Merode at 1720 hours. By nightfall, the castle—firmly in American hands—hosts some of Company B sleeping inside for a change, although it is filthy, the Germans having defecated in almost every room during the previous several days, rather than risk going outside the walls. The company CP locates in Merode village. The division has taken 520 prisoners in the last two days of fighting. The 2000-hours combat report states that the enemy shelled the advancing battalions heavily and brought machine gun fire from the woods; the enemy also laid heavy mortar barrages on the troops, and the battalion encountered "Bouncing Betty" mines in the fields forward of Merode.[87] That night, Porky Pourchot notes in his small spiral notebook:[88]

> Attack! Village in shambles. No casualties. Castle blasted. Jerries in small woods in hiding. Staff Sergeant Collins and our squad captured about 15. Bull Eckardt, BAR, shot one in leg. I bandaged it and put on a tourniquet. He was an unteroffizier [corporal] and was most grateful. Ray Madison, our first scout, found and gave me a P-38 pistol. Later stood guard in a house.

DECEMBER 12, 1944: HÜRTGEN FOREST

Company B is located ¾ mile southeast of Merode.[89] Strength: six officers and 197 enlisted. Weather remains ugly: a high of 42°, a low of 34°, cloudy and overcast, intermittent rain, and surface winds at 8–12 mph. Jack Dunlap makes a lengthy report:

> The Company continued the attack to clean out the enemy in the southeast part of Merode. After clearing the town, the Company attacked the woods 1200 yards southeast of Merode, cleared the woods, and captured around 80 prisoners, several of them wounded. The Company sent out patrols to contact the 83rd Division on its right. Met patrol of 83rd Division at 1600 hours. The Company was badly in need of food and water, with no roads for our vehicles to travel, we used prisoners to carry the supplies, after completing this we gave the Germans one C-Ration; they seemed pretty happy about the whole thing. They should be: it was the first time they had eaten in three days. The Company is now in a defensive position. The men are well dug in, but they're soaked and wet as it has been raining quite a bit.

New Yorker Leslie Bacon, Pvt. Raymond "Ray" Madison, and Pvt. Carlas Tomes are killed; one man is evacuated for nonbattle illness. Leslie is struck by a gunshot on the right side of his neck.[90] Lumberman Ray, a squad scout killed by submachine gun fire, arrived in the company on October 20, as did Carlas, killed by enemy artillery. Floridian SSgt. Merrill Tindale, who had broken his leg in England in May 1944 and returned to duty in July, is wounded in the right hand by shrapnel.

At 0100 hours, the battalion reports receiving flat-trajectory fire. AAAO attacks east from Merode to seize the villages of Derichsweiler and Rottfeld (on the northern edge of the Hürtgen). At 0800 hours, First Battalion advances through a minefield in the woods southeast of Merode, receiving small-arms and mortar fire from the wooded area to their front, as they move toward Rottfeld and clear the trail intersection at Hill 172.[91] Sunrise occurs at 0828 hours. The M10 tank destroyers report downing an Me 109 fighter. Just before 1100 hours, 1Lt. Frank Randall, 3rd Platoon leader, is out in front of his men—a dangerous place to be, but often necessary.

Frank turns around to signal his men to increase their rate of fire, when a German machine gunner spots and fires at him, hitting Randall with not one, not two, not three, not four, not five, not six, but seven rounds. Later, Frank said, "That gave a Kraut machine gunner time to fix me in his sights."[92] His men rip off a door of a destroyed farmhouse as a makeshift stretcher and put Randall on the hood of a jeep to evacuate him to the 13th Field Hospital at Stolberg. En route, about 1107 hours, two Me 109s strafe the vehicle near the castle, but there are no hits; by now, even the tough Randall is in shock and vomiting blood. His pelvis shattered; he is later evacuated to England for extensive treatment. Years later, Frank, who had been given the last rites at one of the aid stations, filled in the details.[93]

The evacuation process began. The aid man had given me a shot of morphine, and soon I was in the battalion aid station. Because of profuse bleeding, they stripped me. The aid station sergeant removed everything from my pockets, including a letter now soaked with my blood, which was placed with all my worldly goods. At the regimental aid station, they gave me another shot of morphine, one of the chaplains anointed me and gave me a blessing, and I was on my way to the division clearing station, this time on the hood of a jeep.

At 1125 hours, the Germans begin firing heavy artillery against Merode; it is still falling two hours later. Sunset occurs at 1629 hours. Cpt Dunlap moves the company CP to Hill 172. The division captures three hundred prisoners, many from the 942nd Infantry Regiment. The combat report from 2000 hours states that the battalions encountered cleverly laid minefields and faced heavy firefights, but by sheer determination, both units captured all the enemy strongpoints assigned to them.[94] Jack Jewell, back from Paris, sleeps in Merode Castle.[95] Porky Pourchot continues his account:[96]

Pushed into woods across half mile of open ground with close tank and machine gun fire. Huge success. Jerries giving up in droves. They have to be flushed from holes. Lieutenant Lucas surprisingly aggressive with his .45. Lost Madison by a Jerry hole. Dug in after dash through woods. Pushed on through brush, came under sniper fire and failed to contact 83rd except by their patrol. Tonight "A" Company captured 71–75 Jerries in one mob. Bull [Albert "Bulldog" Eckardt] came through splendidly with BAR.

DECEMBER 13, 1944: HÜRTGEN FOREST

Company B is ¾ mile southeast of Merode.[97] Strength is six officers and 196 enlisted. More poor weather: a high of 42°, a low of 34°, cloudy and overcast, scattered rain, and surface winds at 8–12 mph. Capt. Dunlap writes: "The Company remained in the same positions. Patrols were sent out during the day and captured several prisoners, who seem to give up without much fight. Most of them were poorly dressed, and in some cases, they were wearing parts of civilian clothes under their uniforms because they were pretty well worn out."

Shelled during the night by light harassing artillery fire, ~~AAA~~O continues attacking, seizing the rest of Derichsweiler in fierce house-to-house—and room-to-room—fighting; it is shelled by enemy artillery during the attack. Troops in the castle find three more booby traps. Battalion makes contact with the 329th Infantry Regiment, 83rd Infantry Division. One enlisted man is evacuated for nonbattle illness. Artillery shrapnel wounds George Rudd in the foot. Billie Flowers cuts his left thumb with a knife while chipping wood to heat his C rations and gets a penicillin shot. 2Lt. Louis Benoist takes over as 3rd Platoon leader.

Sometimes the brass needs to take a break to relieve stress, and today is no different. Generals Courtney Hodges and Pete Quesada visit Liège and the Auguste Francotte & Cie, makers of fine, limited-edition hunting firearms. Hodges orders a custom piece that will be made to fit him and be ready in a month or so. Not to be outdone, Pete orders two.[98] But as long as Pete's boys are overhead protecting them, the dogfaces can put up with a little officer snobbery.

DECEMBER 14, 1944: HÜRTGEN FOREST

Company B's six officers and 195 enlisted are ¾ mile southeast of Merode.[99] A high of 44°, a low of 38°, overcast, and fog and haze; visibility poor. Jack Dunlap reports: "Remained in defensive positions 1,200 yards southeast of Merode, Germany; receiving some heavy artillery fire." Billie Flowers is evacuated to a medical unit for a look at that finger. The 39th moves the CP to Merode.[100] Artillery falls at about 2000 hours. During the night, enemy medium artillery hits the regiment. Division receives orders to secure the west bank of the Roer River and prepare to attack Düren, gateway to Cologne. Jack Jewell, weapons platoon leader, is now the proud owner of a foxhole formerly belonging to the German army. With a small stove, Jack has no problem staying warm. Still, after Paris, his current location is "noisy, dirty, wet and not too much fun." The silver lining? "We are cleaning out these Germans, and from the looks of the ones taken, Hitler is scraping the bottom for men."[101]

Three soldiers return from the 92nd Replacement Battalion, including Chester McClurg. Porky writes: "Took patrol of six men and contacted 83rd. Met two terrific barrages in woods. . . . Boyle, squad scout, performed with excellence. Got McClurg to complete squad. Improved line of foxholes and 83rd cleared us in front. Got hot chow."[102] Noodles writes:[103]

I'm somewhere in Germany and doing alright. [sic] I've been through England, France, Luxembourg, Belgium, and now Germany. I'm writing this letter from a fox hole and believe me it's no pleasure living in one. Right now, I am trying to keep warm sitting by a fire outside of my foxhole. Well, it looks like I'll be away for another Christmas, so I'll just have to make the best of it. So far, I saw quite a bit and expect to see plenty more before I get home. I saw more dead Germans and slept next to more than you could shake a stick at. . . . I feel as fit as a fiddle and never felt better in my life. It was the good thing that I was used to the cold weather because it sure comes in handy now . . . Harry.

DECEMBER 15, 1944: HÜRTGEN FOREST

Company B is ¾ mile southeast of Merode (058439); strength: six officers and 194 enlisted. A high of 43°, a low of 32°, cloudy, rain late, and surface winds at 8–12 mph. For the week ending December 15, the 39th evacuates twelve soldiers for cold injuries, likely trench foot.[104] Jack Dunlap reports: "Remained in defensive positions." At 0835 hours, the enemy shells the 39th with extremely heavy mortar and artillery fire. AAAO is scheduled to attack east at 1300 hours, but the attack is postponed. Heavy artillery fire falls over the entire sector an hour later, hitting Company B: Pfcs. Elmer Zimmermann (left cheek), Edward Ritter (right hand), Paul Akers (left knee), Charles Nill (left hand), William Lekutis (nose), and Robert Kalvitz (right hand) and Pvt. Robert Decker (right heel). Sgts. Alvin Becker (right hand) and Leonard Pourchot (left hand and shoulder) are also hit by shrapnel. Porky remains in the company, writing, "Got hot breakfast and seconds. Men getting packages. Pfc. Kenneth Temple gave Collins, Becker, Eckardt, and I cookies and candy. Good! We're a bewhiskered, indolent, don't-give-a-damn bunch."[105]

DECEMBER 16, 1944: HÜRTGEN FOREST

Company remains in same position, ¾ mile southeast of Merode. Unit strength: six officers and 195 enlisted. Windy and rainy: a high of 39°, a low of 26°, overcast, intermittent light rain and snow, and surface winds 17 mph; morning visibility poor. Capt. Dunlap again writes, "Remained in defensive positions." At 0800 hours, heavy enemy artillery fire falls between Derichsweiler and Gürzenich. Pfc. Lawrence Dotson, a West Virginia farmhand, is evacuated for a nonbattle illness. The regiment will attack east at 0800 hours, but that's delayed six hours and later rescheduled for the next day;

something must be up. At 2000 hours, the enemy shells Derichsweiler with artillery and mortars. Leonard Pourchot, still suffering from his wound, stays in an abandoned hotel but is feeling bad: "Fell out on a hike with hemorrhage. Had GIs and was in damn poor condition."[106] It looks like dysentery.

To the south, temperatures drop to 10°F in a raging snowstorm, as at 0530 hours the Germans launch a last-ditch Ardennes Offensive, known to history as the "Battle of the Bulge." The Germans may not be as lethal as they once were, but they are as desperate as they ever were. And desperate men are dangerous men. They have rolled through these Ardennes before; in 1940, they smashed through terrain deemed impenetrable to tanks, on their way to crushing their historical nemesis—France—in six weeks. Now they are back for a return engagement—over 1,200 tanks, tank destroyers, and assault guns. It will be blitzkrieg all over again.

They are the last of the old guard: Panzer Lehr, 2nd Panzer, 116th Panzer, and the Waffen-SS: Leibstandarte, Hitlerjugend, Hohenstaufen, and Das Reich, and with Russian front veterans, the 3rd Panzergrenadier, and the new Führer Escort Brigade. Now their goal is to blow through the Americans, capture the vital supply port of Antwerp, isolate the British from the Americans, and gain a stalemate in the west. But first, they must pulverize a thin olive-drab line of freezing young Americans in the path of their main effort, which runs smack dab through Elsenborn Ridge.

Their best commanders are back together for what may be the panzers' last ride. Gerd von Rundstedt—the grand old man of the German army, which he entered when Hitler was three years old—commanded an army group in the 1939 invasion of Poland, another army group in the 1940 invasion of France, and another army group in the 1941 invasion of Russia. Sacked twice, rehired twice, now commander in chief in the West. Walter Model—hard-driving, monocle-wearing "führer's fireman"—sent to salvage the most-desperate situations on the Eastern Front; maybe the Third Reich's best tactical commander, he led the 9th Army at the Battle of Kursk and later simultaneously commanded Army Groups Center and North Ukraine. Now he's leading Army Group B. Brutal in his command style, reportedly Model even intimidates Adolf Hitler.

Josef "Sepp" Dietrich: the old SS man, started as Hitler's chauffeur and bodyguard and reportedly is unable to understand a battle map, but he doesn't have to—he just points his troops in the right direction, and the asphalt soldiers are nearly unstoppable. Sepp commanded the Leibstandarte SS Adolf Hitler Waffen-SS Division, 1st SS Panzer Corps, and now Sixth SS Panzer Army, which will make the main attack in the Ardennes. Finally, Hasso von Manteuffel, standing 5'3" tall, casts a giant shadow in whatever distinguished unit he commands: 7th Panzer, "Grossdeutschland," and now Fifth Panzer Army, which attacks just south of the Sixth SS Panzer Army. The Krauts are going down swinging.

DECEMBER 17, 1944: AACHEN CORRIDOR

Company B is at Langerwehe, Germany.[107] Strength: six officers and 196 enlisted. Weather: a high of 43°, a low of 34°, overcast, rain showers, and surface winds of 10–14 mph. Capt. Dunlap writes: "The Company withdrew from positions 1,200 yards southeast of Merode, Germany, by foot at 1600 hours and marched to the town of Langerwehe, arriving there at 1900 hours. The Company moved into buildings. We are now in Division Reserve and are ready to move when called. Distance marched, approximately four miles." Enemy aircraft drop antipersonnel bombs on the regiment at 0100 hours, which begins the attack at 0750 hours, receiving heavy small-arms and artillery fire. Sunrise occurs at 0832 hours. The regiment receives heavy small-arms fire from the Gürzenich Sports Platz at 0930 hours.[108]

Company K clears out resistance in the northern end of Gürzenich by late afternoon, but a strongpoint is resisting fiercely. Fierce house-to-house fighting occurs near the Sports Platz.[109] Company K reaches the railroad embankment.[110] Louis Montoya is wounded.[111] The regimental S2 "foresees trouble in taking the sports platz."[112] Meanwhile, First Battalion is detached from the regiment at 1230 hours and begins marching to the rear to Langerwehe to serve as the Division Reserve. Dunlap sets up his headquarters at Stütgerlach, next to Langerwehe.

DECEMBER 18, 1944: AACHEN CORRIDOR

Company B's six officers and 195 enlisted are located at Langerwehe, Germany (040475). A high temperature of 47°, a low of 38°, broken clouds, scattered showers, and surface winds light. Jack Dunlap reports: "The Company is still in Division Reserve and billeted in houses." Pvt. Saul Kessler is evacuated for acute respiratory infection. The division, now assigned to the Vth Corps, is to move south to stop the German offensive; the 104th US Infantry Division will relieve it. Word of the German offensive to the south spreads like wildfire—especially concerning a massacre of Americans. Jack Jewell hears the latrine gossip on the Kraut attack: "Just in case anyone asks you, you can tell them for me this war is a long way from over—unless a miracle happens. These Germans are fighting and hard too. The newspapers make things look too favorable. I can't see any way out but the end, and I hope it comes sooner than I think it will."[113]

Jack's going to see that hard fighting up close and personal; the division is being sent south to plug the line against the German offensive, code-named Wacht am Rhein (Watch on the Rhine). If the troopers did not shave today, they will remain unshaven until January 5, per Phil Holman, getting a dig in on rear echelon troops: "We didn't shave once the fighting started—except in battalion, regiment, and division headquarters. So, we (me) were pretty ugly looking."[114]

SCHOOL OF THE SOLDIER

TRENCH FOOT

First documented in Napoleon's army in Russia in 1812, trench foot consists of injury to the skin, nerves, and blood vessels of the feet due to lengthy exposure to cold/wet conditions, falling under the category of immersion foot. It does not require freezing temperatures and can occur in temps up to 60°F; damage can begin within thirteen hours: a change in color of the feet to either red or blue, numbness, and progressing to swelling of the feet, blisters, and open sores. Untreated, trench foot usually results in gangrene, which may require amputation of the toes, portions of the foot, and in the worst cases your entire foot.

The winter of 1944–45 in Europe is the coldest and wettest of the last thirty years; this, combined with the tactical situation of relatively static lines, precisely creates conditions most favorable for trench foot and frostbite. Veterans keep an extra pair of socks under their uniform shirt, close to their chests, so they can change into warm, dry socks just before sleeping. Another trick is to submerge a full-metal canteen in hot water, wrap it in a sock, and slip it into your sleeping bag, where it serves as a bed warmer.

But if you are without the ability to dry your feet, when the pain becomes too great you'll stumble out of your foxhole and try to crawl back to the platoon CP, where you hope a medic will be. Because if your feet are too swollen, Doc may have to cut your boots off and then—as your feet swell some more—reassure you that he's seen worse and not to worry about amputation—psychological first aid that you may or may not believe. You'll know you have trench foot when your feet hurt like hell and are as white as snow.[115]

UNIT CALL SIGNS

The Army in Europe uses a simple system of unit call signs when talking with each other on landline (wire) telephones and by radio. The 9th Infantry is known as "Notorious": Notorious 6 is the division commander, Notorious 1 is the G-1 personnel officer, Notorious 2 is the G-2 intelligence officer, Notorious 3 is the G-3 operations officer, and Notorious 4 is the G-4 logistics officer. Infantry units subordinate to the division are designated as follows: 39th Infantry Regiment: Nudge, 47th Infantry Regiment: Nostril, and 60th Infantry Regiment: Nutmeg. Similar to the division staff, the regimental staffs also use numbers: Nudge 6 is the regimental commander and Nudge 3 is the S-3 operations officer for 39th Infantry.

Each infantry regiment fields three battalions: First Battalion is known as Red, Second Battalion is White, and Third Battalion is Blue. Within First Battalion, Company A is Able, Company B is Baker, Company C is Charlie, and Company D is Dog. Second Battalion generally has assigned to it Company E (Easy), Company F (Fox), Company G (George), and Company H (How). Within the Third Battalion, Company I is Item,

Company K is King, Company L is Love, and Company M is Mike. Therefore, good old Company B of the 39th Infantry Regiment is known as Nudge Red Baker.

Within the division artillery, Noisy, are 26th Field Artillery Battalion: Nudist, 34th Field Artillery Battalion: Normal, 60th Field Artillery Battalion: Nuptial, and 84th Field Artillery Battalion: Notary. Division organic support units include 9th Medical Battalion: Nostrum, 9th Infantry Reconnaissance Troop: Nomad, 9th Infantry Signal Company: Nora, 9th Quartermaster Company: Nougat, and 15th Engineer Battalion: Noxema. Units that are not organic but that are often attached to the division include 746th Tank Battalion: Campus–Blue, 899th Tank Destroyer Battalion: Jersey, and 376th Antiaircraft Artillery Automatic Weapons Battalion (Mobile): Noble.

Some call signs put everyone in a near panic. Vth Corps is called Victor, VIIth Corps is Jayhawk. First Army is Master and Supreme Headquarters Allied Expeditionary Forces Headquarters is Liberty. So, when Jayhawk 6 is on the horn, you have the honor to speak with Gen. J. Lawton Collins, but just call him "Sir," not "Lightning Joe"; if Master 6 is on the phone, Gen. Courtney Hodges wants to speak with your commander—immediately. As for Liberty 6, it is either Ike or maybe mess sergeant DiRisio just pulling your leg.

LATRINES

Whether you are in the Hohes Venn or the Hürtgen, relieving yourself can be a dicey proposition. Soldiers quickly discover two things about US Army latrines. You don't go in to read the newspaper, and nothing wakes you up faster than a frigid seat early in the morning. Back home, if you're lucky, you have flushing toilets. If not, it's the outhouse and the Sears catalog. In a bivouac area, such as Camp Elsenborn, engineers—or a company detail selected by 1Sgt. Gravino—dig narrow ditches, often known as "slit trenches," about 1 foot wide and 18 to 24 inches deep. For a company, Top Gravino calculates he needs 30 feet of trench—so when you are visiting, you get a luxurious 2 feet all to yourself. No seats are provided; you straddle the trench, drop your trousers, and squat. Earth from the trench is piled at one end, and after using *les toilettes*, you cover your deposit with dirt from the pile.

Privacy? Fuhgeddaboudit, as New Yorker Vito Spano might say. In the Hürtgen, Top Gravino outdoes himself, and behind the company CP is a "three-holer" latrine, constructed so patrons can actually sit down. However, before you write home about it—there are no sides or roof. They'd just get destroyed by artillery or mortar fire anyway.[116] Often, you have nothing. When you are advancing, the sergeants will tell you—during brief halts—to scrape a hole with your entrenching tool or a stick, do your business, and cover the hole with dirt. In the defense, you do anything to avoid soiling your foxhole. So very carefully get out of your defensive position—while your buddy keeps a lookout for the enemy—and scratch a hole behind a large tree trunk, so you don't get shot. In wooded areas, tree roots are underground almost everywhere, making that difficult. The best result is a messy experience; the worst, a German sniper getting a bead on you—or at night, if you can't find your way back to your foxhole in the pitch-black dark.

The Town Pump, Fayetteville, 1942. The fights, brawls, and near riots here involving soldiers of the 9th Infantry and 82nd Airborne proved that the US Army had found its "hard core of scrappers." Note 9th Infantry patch on bottom center soldier. Fayetteville Observer, *November 14, 2021*

Col. Harry "Paddy" Flint outside his headquarters, England, in 1944. The 39th Infantry took on his fighting spirit and trademark A̶A̶A̶O. The black handkerchief? Paddy explained, "It's the pirate in me!" *NARA, file 309-Inf (39)-.01, box 6478*

"Men of Company B, 39th Infantry," checking a demolished Siegfried Line pill-box for any remaining Jerries." September or early October 1944. NARA, file 309-Inf (39) .01, box 6478

39th Infantry Regiment .30-caliber machine gun, Hürtgen Forest, October 1944; note AAAO on helmets; one source shows the unit as Company D. NARA, US Army Signal Corps

39th Infantry bazooka team in woods.
Note AAAO on loader's helmet. *NARA,
US Army Signal Corps*

Maj. Gen. Joseph Lawton "Lightning Joe" Collins
during Merode attack. When the corps commander is
watching your attack, you know you'll get plenty of
supporting artillery. *NARA, US Army Signal Corps*

Front gate of Merode Castle. Bouncing Betty land mines, barbed wire, machine guns, and snipers could not prevent First Battalion from storming the castle. *NARA, US Army Signal Corps*

39th Infantry combat patrol, Elsenborn Ridge, January 1945; with no snow suits, soldiers stuck out like sore thumbs. *NARA, file 309-Inf (39)-0.2, box 6478*

39th Infantry 60 mm mortar squad, Elsenborn Ridge, January 1945. The company commander owned three, and they fired for him. *NARA, file 309-Inf (39)-0.2, box 6478*

Tall trees in the Hürtgen. Artillery rounds exploding in the treetops showered the troops with lethal rain. *NARA, photo 334958, box 705*

39th Infantry Intel & Recon Platoon breaking trail in deep snow near Höfen, January 31, 1945. *NARA, photo 199690, box 248*

39th Infantry reconnaissance patrol on Elsenborn Ridge in January 1945. In these situations, your life can be snuffed out in a second. *NARA, file 309-Inf (39)-0.2, box 6478*

9th Infantry Division soldiers cross barbed wire in deep snow near Fuhrtsbachtal, January 30, 1945. *NARA, file 309-Inf (39)-0.2, box 6478*

39th Infantry advancing south of Höfen on January 31, 1945. Combat in the Siegfried Line and Hürtgen was reminiscent of World War I. *NARA, photo 270825, box 502, T/4 William I. Spangle*

39th Infantry medics transfer wounded from sled to jeep and Weasel near Höfen, January 31, 1945. *NARA, file 309-Inf (39) .02, box 6478*

Company B sprinted across the Remagen bridge under heavy fire on March 10, 1945. "When we got to the end we found a captain and his driver in a jeep burning like an inferno, a direct hit." *NARA, US Army Signal Corps*

First photo of American forces liberating Stalag VI G, April 13, 1945. Unit chaplains organize a religious service for the prisoners. *Courtesy of Klaus-Dieter Gernert and Helmut Wolff, Das Geheimnis der Versöhnung heißt Erinnerung*

Down on the line, 9th Infantry soldiers dine on fried chicken, January 13, 1945. *NARA, photo 329121, box 691*

Company I, 39th Regiment; soldiers Pfc. Edward E. Gladsford (Chicago) and Pfc. Oscar L. Lombardi (Los Angeles) dine on C rations, February 27, 1945. *NARA, photo 201466, box 254*

4 HOURS SEPARATE SON'S LETTER AND DEATH NOTICE

City Soldier Wrote That He Expected War To End Soon

Mr. and Mrs. Joseph Reiser, 12 South Hancock street, city, received a letter from their soldier son in Germany yesterday afternoon, saying the war was almost over and that soon he would be home to wear his medals gained overseas.

Four hours later they received an official government telegram informing them that he had been killed in action.

Their son who lost his life on the German battle front, appearing in today's casualties, was Staff Sergeant John E. Reiser. His wife, the former Margaret Spear, Jones street, also received announcement of his death which occurred March 17.

The letter to his parents, written March 2, arrived yesterday afternoon. "This war will be over soon and I will be home to wear my medals so have them ready for me," it stated. Last evening the notice from the War Department said he was killed in action two weeks after his letter was written.

The citation which the young soldier earned while with the Ninth Division, 39th Infantry, First Army, in Africa, Sicily, invasion of France on D-Day and only recently the invasion of Germany, includes two presidential citations, two Oak Leaf Clusters, Purple Heart, Silver Star, and Good Conduct Medal.

3 SOLDIERS GIVE LIVES FOR COUNTRY

Two City Men Make Supreme Sacrifice—Third Was From West Side

S/Sgt. John E. Reiser

Pvt. Michael Ferris

John Reiser, killed in action March 17, 1945. The news crushed his parents. Times Leader *(Wilkes-Barre), March 18, 1945, and* Wilkes-Barre Record, *April 6, 1945*

Company B had several Black soldiers assigned in the spring of 1945. 3rd Squad, 3rd Platoon: Lang Turner (*center front*); *first row, left to right*: Joe McGarvey, James Millar, Seben Gore, Willie White, Phil Holman; *second row, left to right*: Gail Bowman, Lorenzo Vargas, Robert McClanahan, Andy Jenyk, Gleason Long, Andy Glenn. *Courtesy of Phil Holman*

Soldiers often thought about food, family, and holidays, hoping they would see their families again. Mac drew and sent this small sketch to his mother on November 26, 1944. *Author*

When the Army issued a few beers to soldiers off the line, such as to the 9th Infantry in November 1944, it was just bowing to the inevitable, because no one is more creative than American service members at obtaining booze. *NARA, photo 196601, US Army Signal Corps*

Private Snafu—goofy, ignorant, and obnoxious; star of twenty-five episodes of short US War Department black-and-white films instructing soldiers what not to do. One of the best was "Episode 5—the Infantry Blues." Most were written by Theodor Geisel, later author of children's books under the pen name of Dr. Seuss. *Warner Brothers Studio, now public domain*

YANK magazine printed two million small cards of the odds for craps gambling, so that soldiers could paste them inside their helmets! *Tichnor Bros Inc. period postcard*

9th Infantry Division soldiers producing snowsuits from sheets; even a simple improvement could save lives. *NARA, photo 329124, box 691*

Company B. Names in black are soldiers who didn't survive.
Author; collage of individual photographs from various sources

3rd Platoon. *Author; collage of individual photographs from various sources*

Eighty-eight Company B soldiers died in action from June 1944 to May 1945.
Author; collage of individual photographs from various sources

The Army used mattress covers to inter the dead in temporary cemeteries. This is a fragment of the one used for Staff Sergeant (and squad leader) John "Jack" Gourlay, killed in action on October 11, 1944, at Germeter, Hürtgen Forest, and first buried at temporary cemetery Henri-Chapelle #1 in Belgium. Dark-brown-red spots are dried blood. *NARA, St. Louis, IDPF John Gourlay*

Harry "Paddy" Flint grave, Normandy. *NARA, US Army Signal Corps*

Henri-Chapelle Military Cemetery; Belgian children put flags on American soldier graves after the war. *NARA, photo 286356, box 557*

Gen. Patton awarding a Silver Star to the commander of the 39th Infantry. The scrappy 39th was one of his favorites. *NARA, US Army Signal Corps*

Company B soldier decorations on a piece of artillery shrapnel. *Left to right*: Combat Infantryman Badge; Purple Heart; Silver Star, Bronze Star for Valor with Oakleaf. *Author photo*

GAS MASKS

There will be a reason, after the war, why Army-Navy Surplus stores are packed with gas mask pouches, but the masks themselves are often nowhere to be found—because, despite threats of dire consequences from officers and noncommissioned officers, American soldiers continue to "lose" their masks at an alarming rate. For some strange reason, though, they seem able to keep their canvas gas mask containers, which make wonderful haversacks after the mask "disappears." Hung over their shoulder, these sacks are water resistant and perfect for extra ammunition, mess kit, food, rare roll of toilet paper, or storage space for a souvenir—maybe a bottle of wine—if you ever are fortunate enough to liberate a town.

DEUCE AND A HALF

Fortunately, Company B often gets a lift to their new location. The Army refers to it as a 2½-ton, 6×6, medium-duty truck, but the troops call it a "Deuce and a half," a "Jimmy," or simply a "Deuce." It can haul about 5,000 pounds of cargo, or an infantry squad, in all weather conditions and over most terrain, but in the winter, troops in the unheated rear cargo compartment are going to freeze their tails off, and if it then gets stuck in the mud, and the driver asks for help, you are going to hear curses that would embarrass even a long-haul teamster.

For the supply-starved infantry, deuces in the Red Ball Express, at its peak, number 5,958 vehicles, organized into 140 truck companies, and daily carry 12,500 tons supplies to the front. Colonel Loren Ayers, a 1931 West Point graduate, organizes the effort, putting two men in each truck so they can spell each other, training drivers in long-haul missions and kicking butt so often that he is known by his soldiers as "Little Patton."[117] Drivers are instructed to stay under 25 miles per hour. But commanders know that the men will frequently, against orders, disable engine governors to go faster. Add in pure adrenaline; some 75 percent of the drivers are Black, and they want to live up to their growing reputation among combat units, not to mention war reporters, who send home stories about their moxie.

Trucks can move lots of infantrymen in a hurry to threatened areas of the front. Most American infantry are termed "straight leg." To move anywhere, it is "shoe leather express"—they walk, which takes a long time (for 25 miles, almost all day), and the soldiers are bushed at its conclusion. So, when needed, a truck company unfolds the troop seats in the sideboards of the trucks, moves to a pickup point, and hauls an infantry battalion those 25 miles in a snap—and that infantry is ready to dig in, string barbed wire, and lay mines immediately on arrival. The venerable "Deuce and a half": to the British it is scary because the Americans drive the beasts on the wrong side of the road. But to tens of millions of civilians in France, Belgium, Italy, Luxembourg, and the Netherlands, the "Deuce" is a dream come true—because it means that the Americans are coming.

FOXHOLES

The term "foxhole" originated in 1918 in a US Army report that described some German soldiers not defending in trenches—the norm in the Great War—but rather building "a hole in the ground sufficient to give shelter . . . to one or two soldiers." To the uninitiated, a foxhole looks like a crude pit in the ground, maybe man-made, but nothing special. But foxholes are art forms, and while few are memorialized in the Louvre, they are venerated in many men's memories—men who survived combat thanks to that little, dirty, muddy, cold hole. Constructing a foxhole really is determined by two variables: the type of digging tools available, and the type of soil in which the hole is to be built. The word "built" is intentional, since a foxhole often consists of much more than just a hole.

The first artist to look at the canvas is often your squad leader, who ensures that all the foxholes in the squad are mutually supporting one another and that the end foxholes support adjacent squads in the platoon; if his squad is the flank squad of the platoon, he has to know where the next unit has their foxholes located, so that there are no gaps in the defenses for the Germans to sneak through. Gaps are bad. "Mutually supporting" means that if the enemy attacks, everyone protects everyone else. In fact, some tacticians lay out foxholes, so you never shoot directly to your own front, but to the front of your buddies' foxholes to your left or right.

After you know where to dig, you . . . well . . . dig.

Sometimes both foxhole buddies dig at the same time; in other situations, one digs while the other provides security, looking for the enemy. Many of the foxholes in the Hürtgen and Hohes Venn are prone shelters, not deep, but long enough in which to lie down flat. Once the dirt is scraped out, the men cover the position with a low roof of logs, dirt and finally limbs from nearby trees. Doing both effectively gives you two things: cover and concealment. Cover means actual protection from enemy fire, but no matter how well you build your protection, the Germans have some bigger weapon that can kill you. Your roof may be thick enough so that if a potato-masher grenade explodes on it, all you get is temporary deafness, but if a German 150 mm howitzer round scores a direct hit, you're a goner. Rather than resign yourself to that fact, just keep improving your foxhole and the roof, so that fewer and fewer enemy weapons can hurt you.

When digging, you hope that you do not run into shale, which, sadly, is present throughout the area. Shale tells you that your foxhole is soon going to resemble an artesian well, with water seeping in through the sides, regardless of whether or not it is raining. Nobody wants in artesian well in his living room, and as one 9th Infantry foxhole expert says, "They just haven't gotten around to equipping foxholes with anything but dripping cold water."[118] Concealment is the art of becoming invisible to aimed enemy fire. The enemy may know your general vicinity, but if he can't see you or your position, he likely won't waste ammunition—at least that's the theory. When the enemy does start shooting for no apparent reason, veterans say, "the Gestapo is 'Court-Martialing' again."[119] The key to concealment is to blend in with your surroundings. You never want to look different in combat; looking different gets you in trouble.

A prone position usually has a small opening in the rear to crawl through head first, naturally on cold, wet ground. The positive side is that it is low to the ground; the negative is that you are lying on cold, damp earth all night long, the cold sinking to your bones, making you miserable the entire night and most of the next day. If you can get straw or pine needles, you put those on the floor as insulation. If you can dig deep, you dig deep, since not only will that protect you from direct-fire weapons such as machine guns, but it will also reduce the angle that exploding artillery shrapnel can fly into the hole, since artillery may be the biggest killer.

When you get the foxhole deep, you may try to build a roof, but you do not want your position to be higher than the ground around it. Many soldiers just put their half of the shelter flat over the top of the hole after getting inside, but invariably a pool of cold rainwater will collect right in the center of the shelter half, causing it to collapse on you—about two in the morning. Despite their best efforts, soldiers can do only so much, and in many instances they go to sleep with cold feet and wake up with cold feet.

Don't forget that, in most instances, there will be two men per foxhole, so they can rotate security at night in two-hour shifts: awake two hours, asleep two hours. When you are the one awake, take your shelter half off the top of your side of the hole so you can hear and maybe see the enemy. If you don't, and just stay down in the hole while you're on guard, the next words you might hear are *Hände hoch!* Since your foxhole will need to accommodate two, invariably your buddy will be a big guy who needs a lot of room. Foxholes aren't just for enlisted men: lieutenants have to prepare positions, as Jack Jewell writes: "I'm glad I know how to dig ditches because sometimes that's the safest place here."[120] There is an economic impact as well, as Phil Holman later said: "If I had a dime for every hole I dug in Germany I would be a rich man."[121]

After a few days in position, some foxholes have grenade sumps, where if an enemy grenade is thrown in the hole, you can kick it into the sump and the blast is directed away from you; they tell you that in training. And don't forget to run some commo wire to nearby foxholes. At night, if you have to crawl over to the next hole, grab the wire and let it guide you to your buddy's position, so you don't get lost. And don't get mad, because invariably, about the time you get your own fighting position the way you want it, your sergeant will tell you the unit is moving out for a new area—and you can't take your foxhole with you.

BOOBY TRAPS

The American infantryman has two exceptional qualities: adapting to changing situations and improvising in the absence of orders or lack of resources. That is shown in spades concerning booby traps. In the absence of mines, infantrymen create small homemade explosive devices to deter enemy patrols from approaching at night. Known colloquially by the troops as "de-nutters," each device consists of a ½-inch piece of wood through which is driven a nail until the point of the nail is about a ½ inch through the other side. The wood is placed in a small hole, with the exposed nail sticking upward. The GI then places a short 2-inch metal pipe, open at both ends, over the nail and places a shotgun shell—just smaller in diameter than the inside of the pipe and slightly greater in length—with the primer end gingerly sitting on top of the pointed nail. For practical reasons, 12-gauge shotgun rounds are used, since military police often carry riot shotguns and are often willing to donate a few rounds to the cause. Then you cover the whole contraption with small, light sticks, and finally pine needles.

An enemy soldier stepping on the device causes the shotgun shell to press down hard on the point of the nail, which sets off the primer, detonating the round, with the lead pellets going upward into a Kraut where he doesn't want to be hit. If you don't have any shotgun shells, use a hand grenade, tied to a tree trunk. Fix some wire to the safety pin and stretch it pretty tight about 2 or 3 feet above the ground to another tree. Then v-e-r-y gently straighten the safety pin on the grenade so it will slide out easily when a Kraut runs into that wire. And make sure you tell your buddies where you put it.

Germans make booby traps too. A grenade under a German helmet can go off when an unsuspecting GI picks it up. Abandoned vehicles can have grenades affixed to hatches. Opening a door or switching on a light in a room might just be the last thing you ever do.[122] A rumor floats around that Germans will booby-trap the right-side door of a double door, since Germans usually go in the left side and Americans the right—but do you really want to trust your life to a rumor?

THE UNIFORM

The American infantryman wore a fairly efficient combat uniform, if you receive one that actually fit, of course. Starting with an infantryman's most important piece of attire—footwear—Sgt. Phil Holman recalled the clothes that helped him survive:[123]

Footwear. Basic leather boots. When I got to the company, I remember going back to an open area where there was a large pile of overshoes. We had to dive in and find a pair that would fit. These were not galoshes, but rubber boots with a wick material inside the bottom to collect moisture from your feet and socks. Every night in your foxhole you had to dry the wick out. *Dry socks,* etc. I had plenty of socks and underwear. But on the front lines you carried very few since they took up space in your combat pack. Most were back in your duffle [*sic*] bag with the company supply sergeant.

Leggings. They were canvas, and we wore these during basic training. If you got them on the wrong legs, you could trip and fall because the hooks would catch each other. We did not wear them in combat. Trousers were stuffed in top of your boots (bloused) to keep them from getting soaked and dirty. Later, we built up our combat boots by getting some German cobbler to sew a 4-inch flap that closed with straps on the boots.

Uniform. You wore one; the others were in the duffle [*sic*] bag in the rear. In combat, most guys wore underwear, a t-shirt, a uniform shirt, a sweater, and a field jacket. I guess we smelled pretty raunchy—just like the Germans. I don't remember changing clothes until we were taken back for a bath and clean clothes—which was very seldom. We (or I) wore no rank insignia on our uniforms.

Field jacket. Looks like everyone had an M1943 cotton sateen one that was sort of wind proof and MAYBE water resistant but certainly not waterproof. Gloves. Most guys probably had gloves, but remember, if you wore them in combat you could have trouble getting your trigger finger in the trigger housing to push off the safety and pull the trigger. May have cut a slit in trigger finger of glove to take care of that problem. *Overcoat*. I do not remember being issued one—if I did, it was in the duffle [*sic*] bag in the rear, since it was too cumbersome to wear on the front lines.

Helmet. We did have ~~AAA~~O on the helmet. But it soon wore off, as we used the helmet for more than head cover. On the front lines we wore the helmet, clothing as mentioned earlier, and a combat pack, large enough to carry a mess kit, extra socks, underwear, and a day's worth of K-rations. Besides that, we had our ammo belt, first-aid pack, canteen, shovel or pick, bayonet, and compass. On top of the pack was our shelter-half with poles and pegs, and blanket roll (fart sack, if you will). A poncho was hanging from the back of the ammo belt. Besides all that, we had a gas mask, rifle, and at least two hand grenades fastened to the front of the pack. We had no room for anything else. In fact, the gas mask was the first thing to go when we were tired, foot sore, and slogging through the snow or mud."

A lieutenant recalled that he and most of the men wear one set of underwear and uniform continuously for ten days before having an opportunity to change. And Manley Fuller recalled seeing men walking around wearing their sleeping bags for extra warmth. They'd cut holes in the bottom and wore them like ponchos.[124] Jack Jewell recalled:[125]

I guess I told you I am wearing long handles [long underwear] and they feel very good. I have a silk bandana made from a camouflaged parachute. It keeps my neck warm and also keeps some of the dirt off my shirt. I had a new field jacket . . . but it is beginning to look plenty dirty and worn. Our clothes take a beating when we jump in and out of foxholes. Mud and water doesn't make much difference when lead is flying around in our direction.

FORAGING, SCROUNGING, AND LOOTING

Ever since humans began fighting each other, they have "obtained" items, not originally their own, from other than approved supply sources, in other than approved methods—"approved" being defined by their commanders. Some chiefs—Atilla the Hun comes to mind—appear to have had a lenient view of what the lads could take as they rolled through Europe. Of course, in Atilla's case, it seems that he was getting first dibs of the loot. Other commanders were negative regarding these practices, and a few even had some of their own soldiers executed for looting. Other military leaders professed that such conduct never happened in their own units—and they were flat wrong. If terms such as "foraging," "scrounging," "moonlight requisitioning," or "looting" offend you, just call it all "liberating."

Foraging came first and involved living off the land for food. In Napoleon's time, entire cavalry units rode ahead of the army to search for provisions—both for themselves and their horses. Napoleon knew that "an army marches on its stomach," and the farther that army was from Paris, the more it depended on foraging. Of course, the local farmers didn't much care for their hard work ending up in the soldiers' stomachs, but usually they weren't French farmers, so who really cared? Certainly not "the Little Corporal." Foraging works best in summer, when crops and fruits ripen. North Africa was slim pickings; Sicily a little better; better still in Normandy, where soldiers grab a chicken here and an apple there but generally understand that the French people suffered greatly under Nazi occupation and so pay for victuals, especially alcohol. In Germany, GIs often trade Army chow for local chow, angering some of the locals, who later probably thanked God that the Americans occupied their village—and not the Soviet Red Army.

Scrounging is not appropriating civilian property so much as American military items belonging to other units, and, if caught, a soldier can be court-martialed for theft of Army property. That is—if they are caught—and very few Army junior commanders in combat are going to punish their own solders for obtaining something from which the entire unit benefits. Vehicle parts, complete vehicles themselves, extra cases of rations, uniform items—anything that isn't nailed down—might turn up missing, and even if it is nailed down, such as plywood, it might get "unnailed" in a hurry one night. "Midnight requisitioning" is just scrounging at night.

Looting is defined by many academics as the indiscriminate taking of goods by force as part of a military in a war. Which shows you how much academics really know—most infantrymen don't want indiscriminate items; they want specific stuff, such as Lugers, perhaps some high-quality Zeiss binoculars, maybe an SS dagger, or a Luftwaffe peaked hat. Most GIs don't want gold artifacts from churches, or fancy oil paintings, and trying to bring home an intact Mercedes is out of the question. Besides, the previous owners of pistols, daggers, or binoculars had been the German military, and that outfit is about to file for bankruptcy, so all you have to do is get a lieutenant to sign off on your new Luger as a "war trophy," and that baby is all yours.

But what about taking personal items off Germans? Many GIs don't think twice about grabbing an Iron Cross, as decorations have swastikas on them, which is a symbol of the regime. That's called "de-souveniring."[126] But souvenirs can be dangerous. Manley Fuller sometimes picks up potential keepsakes. Once, he sees a watch on a dead German, who had died holding a potato masher. Manley is worried it could be booby-trapped. Finding a length of wire, he carefully hooks it to the German's belt and pulls the corpse over. The grenade moves; for an instant Manley thinks he's a goner, but the potato masher just lies there. Manley tiptoes over to the watch, but he cannot forget the feel of the dead man's cold arm and feels so guilty that he never takes a souvenir off a dead German again.[127]

That is probably the view of most GIs with respect to taking items off the dead. But what about real "grave robbing"—such as taking gold wedding bands off dead bodies? In some units, it is rumored that one guy has a bag of German wedding rings, and Company B is no exception, but the practice does not seem to be widespread, for a practical reason if not an altruistic one—if a GI is captured by the Germans and found to have German wedding bands on his person, he is probably not going to be sent back to a German POW camp.[128]

RADIOS

Radio communication in the infantry is in its infancy. Although in close quarters, the lieutenant platoon leader can use a whistle, yell, or give hand and arm signals; if bullets are flying or the line of sight is blocked, communications are tough. Telephones, hooked together by wire passing through a switchboard, are decent, until enemy artillery cuts the lines. Telephones in the offense can be used from rear headquarters but can be difficult up front.

Early military radios are bulky and heavy, taking mobility out of the equation. Later, in a perfect situation, an infantry company will have a Motorola SCR-536 "walkie talkie," known as a "chatterbox," for the company commander and platoon leaders. The size of a quart of milk in a paper carton, it weighs 5 pounds with the battery. But the range of the unit is based on line of sight and varies with terrain, from a few hundred feet to approximately 1 mile, and since the terrain in the Hürtgen and the Hohes Venn is rotten, that 1 mile is almost unattainable. Even thick stands of trees interfere with the signal. Forward observers frequently use SCR-300 radios to report the fall of artillery rounds and radio back aiming corrections. At battalion, they have the SCR-694, a portable two-way radio set, weighing almost 20 pounds. Voice communications can reach to 15 miles, with Morse code a bit farther.

Tanks have SCR-506 radios and have a small external telephone in the rear so that dismounted infantrymen can talk to the tank crew and help direct their fire at enemy targets. The problem is, however, that most infantrymen do not even know that the telephone is there.[129] You can always stand on the tank's rear deck and yell through the open commander's hatch, but when you are an infantryman riding on top of a tank racing into combat, you usually forget the chatter and just try to hang on for dear life.

INFANTRY TACTICS

Two up and one back; understand this ratio and you are halfway home to comprehending small-unit infantry tactics. In the attack, a platoon often advances with two of its three squads forward, heading in the direction of the immediate objective of the attack—a hill, a farm, a road junction, or a pillbox and so forth. Each squad has a BAR team, sometimes under the assistant squad leader, which covers the squad leader moving forward with the M1 riflemen—sometimes walking online upright and sometimes scampering from tree to tree, or anything that affords some protection from fire.

Once the squad leader feels he is about to get out of range of the supporting BAR, he halts the riflemen and the BAR team moves forward to his position, or a supporting position nearby, and the procedure is repeated. Shoot and move to another covered position. Sometimes, the squad deploys two riflemen forward as squad scouts. Squad formations include the "squad wedge" (which looks like an upside-down V) or on line. The third squad in the platoon often follows in the rear, a reserve in case something bad happens; it often moves in a loose column, spread out so a single mortar round exploding nearby will not kill everyone.

The platoon leader, with the medic and a couple of riflemen, moves around—sometimes behind the two lead squads, sometimes between them, and once in a while in front of them, wherever he can get the best "feel" of the situation. Communication with squads is usually by hand and arm signals or verbal commands. Lieutenants who go too far in front of the platoon often get killed. The platoon might have special attachments for specific missions: a mortar observer from the company's weapons platoon or the battalion's heavy-mortar platoon, one or both of the company's two light-machine-gun teams, or a heavy-machine-gun section from the battalion's heavy-weapons company, or a two- or three-man antitank rocket ("bazooka") team might become part of the platoon. Commo with company headquarters is usually messenger.

The same principle—two up and one back—is in play at the company, which in the attack deploys two platoons up front and one in reserve. The company commander and his small command team often follow a lead platoon. One platoon may stop, laying down a base of fire, while another platoon moves forward. In the attack, communication between the battalion CP and the rifle companies is by messenger. "When sufficient means are available," battalion may allocate sound-powered telephone equipment or portable radiotelephones to frontline companies for communication, but they are often unavailable. Stuff always happens that you didn't foresee, so always have some type of reserve "just in case."

No matter what the tactic, the key to survival in the infantry is to follow the principal of KISS—Keep It Simple, Stupid. That rule of thumb is especially true over here in this neck of the woods, since a long time ago lived the Brothers Grimm of German fairy-tale fame. Their fable "The Fox and the Cat" has the two animals meeting in the woods, discussing how many escape strategies each of them knows. The fox boasts that he has a hundred tricks and "a whole sackful of cunning." Dismayed, the cat confesses that he has only one. Suddenly, hunters arrive with their dogs; the cat quickly safely climbs a tree—that being his sole strategy. The fox, however, begins to ponder which of his many schemes to employ but does not immediately act on any, which causes him to be caught by the hounds. KISS.

PENICILLIN

Sir Alexander Fleming first discovers the bacteria-killing properties of penicillin during his research in 1928 in London's St. Mary's Hospital. The find is accidental; Alexander leaves a petri dish uncovered in his disorganized laboratory. Over the next dozen years, he tinkers with his find but has difficulty isolating and mass-producing the substance. Australian scientists Howard Florey, Ernst Chain, and Norman Heatley improve on Fleming's work from 1938 to 1940, but because British facilities are making other drugs for the British war effort, Florey and Heatley travel to Peoria, Illinois, to collaborate with researchers, who have perfected the fermentation necessary to grow penicillin by using corn, not sugar, as the nutrient source.

Over the next three years, twenty-one US companies produce 2.3 million doses of penicillin, possibly saving hundreds of thousands of lives during the war. Meanwhile, Germany and its allies can produce only small amounts of penicillin and must rely on less effective sulfonamides. Axis troops will die in the tens of thousands because of a lack of the miracle drug, while American medics give penicillin to soldiers with even trivial injuries, such as cutting a finger with a pocket knife.[130]

MALMEDY

On December 17, 1944, elements of Battle Group Peiper of the 1st SS Panzer Division Leibstandarte SS Adolf Hitler transport eighty-four American POWs to a snowy field near the Baugnez crossroads outside the village of Malmedy, Belgium, and machine-gun them. They will kill more captured US soldiers at other locations. Joachim Peiper, leader of the perpetrators, has a ruthless track record; on the Eastern Front, his unit was called the "Blowtorch Battalion," burning Russian villages to the ground and massacring the inhabitants.[131] Hitler wants the offensive to be brutally executed to frighten American troops, who he believes are racially inferior. A POW from the 12th SS Panzer Division Hitlerjugend tells that his division commander made the following statement to the troops prior to the start of the offensive: "I ask you and expect of you not to take any prisoners with the possible exception of officers, who might be kept alive for the purpose of questioning."[132] The actual effect is not to intimidate the Americans, who will remember Malmedy and fight even harder.

CHAPTER SIX

Battle of the Bulge, Elsenborn Ridge (2), Kalterherberg

This is undoubtedly the greatest American battle of the war.

—Winston Churchill

DECEMBER 19, 1944: ELSENBORN RIDGE

Company B is 1¼ miles northeast of Elsenborn, Belgium,[1] with six officers and 195 enlisted. The weather: a high of 52°, a low of 41°, and broken clouds; visibility good. Capt. Dunlap writes: "The Company left Langerwehe, Germany, where we were in Division Reserve at 0800 hours and traveled by trucks to an area 2,000 yards northeast of Elsenborn, Belgium. Set up defensive position as a counterattack was ordered. Distance traveled approximately 45 miles." AAAO moves by truck through Gressenich, Stolberg, and Aachen to Eupen. It "de-trucks" at Sourbrodt, 5 miles west of Elsenborn, and foot-marches east to the Schwalmbach (also known as the Perlenbach) River along Elsenborn Ridge, occupying former positions of the 99th US Infantry, so the "Battle Babies" can shorten its lines, having been hit hard by the Krauts.

Wallace Wade is the commander of the 272nd Field Artillery Battalion, one of the units the 9th Infantry is relieving. He is not a career Army officer; no, he is far more important than that. From 1923 to 1930, Wallace was the head football coach for the University of Alabama "Crimson Tide," winning three national championships. Wade then stuns the college football world by leaving Alabama for Duke University, coaching the "Blue Devils" until 1941, when, after Pearl Harbor, Wallace enlists, later becoming a senior field-grade officer. When Ltc. Wade sees "the Old Reliables" moving into the line, the old ball coach tells his men: "Stop worrying. Everything is going to be all right now. They've sent in the first team."[2]

Behind Company B, AAAO establishes a CP 1½ miles north of Camp Elsenborn at 1340 hours.[3] The companies form a defensive line extending from the north slope of Hill 580 southeast to Hill 557, facing east.[4] The division CP moves west of Sourbrodt.[5] Sgt Pourchot noted: "En-trucked and headed for 'Perry Hill' area to stop Nazis from slaughtering the 99th."[6]

DECEMBER 20, 1944: ELSENBORN RIDGE

Company B is 1¼ miles north of Elsenborn; strength unchanged.[7] Weather: a high of 46°, a low of 32°, and cloudy; visibility poor. Capt. Dunlap summarizes: "Company remained in defensive position; received heavy artillery fire." The company improves its positions and ties-in with flank units; the CP is in the low ground at the bottom of the western slope of Hill 597, known to locals as the Büschelberg, a treeless, windswept ridge 2,500 yards east-northeast of Elsenborn. Porky Pourchot receives a treat today—he gets to talk with a real, live assistant division commander. "Talked with Brigadier General [Hugh T.] Mayberry of the 99th. Regular Joe, he. He was so glad to see friendly faces that he almost kissed me."[8] The men must dig new, deeper foxholes, but the ground is frozen too hard for picks and shovels, so they obtain dynamite, probably from combat engineers, to blow holes in the frozen earth. At 1535 hours, the enemy shells the battalion CP. Lawrence Cherry is recommended for the Bronze Star for heroism this day.

DECEMBER 21, 1944: ELSENBORN RIDGE

Company B remains in position with six officers and 189 enlisted; the weather is a high of 52°, a low of 42°, cloudy, and rain and snow. Jack Dunlap writes: "The Company remained in defensive position. We were shelled most of the day and night by artillery fire." The unit improves defensive positions, ties in with flank units, and establishes listening posts. Battalion receives harassing fire at 0013 hours. Regiment reports fifty enemy troops in a draw 300 yards in front of friendly positions, and an unknown number 200 yards out, with enemy movement a mile to the northeast.[9] The division CP moves northwest.[10] Gen. Leonard T. Gerow orders that the Red Cross flag will not be observed when displayed by the enemy, since German units have been infiltrating forward while their medics are taking care of the wounded, a violation of Red Cross conventions.

Enemy artillery fire wounds Candy Collins; Pfcs. Harold Slack, Stephen Smetana, and Carl Stock; and Pvt. Lafayette Timmons—Harold in the thigh and knee, Carl in the foot, Lafayette in the leg, and Candy in the hand. Harold and Carl arrived on October 9. It is Timmons's second wound. For Stephen, son of Polish immigrants in Chicago's 15th Ward, shrapnel badly damages his arm's radial nerve, and he will remain in a hospital for ten months. Merrill Tindale is evacuated for a nonbattle illness. Soldiers move to new duties. Collins, son of a Massachusetts railroad brakeman, was the squad leader; now Porky Pourchot steps up: "Candy . . . left me in charge. Becker is assisting me. We strung [barbed] wire in front of our lines. Received packages from Mom yesterday, cake, cookies, white handkerchiefs, tobacco pouch, and gum. Boy, oh boy!"[11]

It will be "boy, oh boy," all right. The harassing fire is about to become a deliberate enemy assault, since after relieving the 12th SS Panzer Division, the 3rd Panzergrenadier Division, with even some veterans of the brutal fighting at Stalingrad, begins to attack west—right toward the 9th Infantry. The 3rd Panzergrenadier began life in the Wehrmacht in 1934 as the 3rd Infantry Division, although one of its regiments traces its lineage to the Prussian army in the time of Napoleon. After fighting in the 1939 invasion of Poland and the 1940 invasion of France, the unit is upgraded to a fully motorized division for Operation Barbarossa against the Soviet Union. As the 3rd Motorized Infantry Division, it fights in the advance on Leningrad, before transferring to Army Group Center for the push toward Moscow in December 1941. That operation fails in the bitter cold, but the worst is yet to come, since the unit is reassigned to the German Sixth Army to attack Stalingrad, where it is encircled in November 1942, and destroyed with the rest of Friedrich Paulus's army. Re-formed—in part with wounded veterans, who had been air-evacuated from Stalingrad before its fall—as the 3rd Panzergrenadier Division in March 1943, by mid-1944 the unit is commanded by Major General Walter Denkert, a Knights Cross winner and veteran commander who had previously led the 6th Panzer Division and the 19th Panzer Division in Russia. The division's infantry is in the 8th and 29th Panzer Grenadier Regiments. The division also fields the 103rd Panzer Detachment. However, instead of tanks, the detachment has forty-two turretless 75 mm assault guns, often deadlier infantry killers than the panzers. The division is familiar with the American army, having fought at Anzio and Nettuno in Italy. Now it is assigned to the Sixth SS Panzer Army.

As if the men need any reminder about the "Malmedy Massacre," at 2132 hours, Vth Corps transmits the following message:[12]

> General Gerow desires all commanders to notify men of the following incident: On December 17, 1944, at 1500 hours, near Malmedy, German panzer troops, after capturing nearly 200 American soldiers, lined them up in a field, disarmed and robbed them, and then mowed them down with MGs firing from tanks passing by at a distance of from 50–100 yards. The few men who escaped fell to the ground and played dead.

The message provided numerous details of what had occurred at Malmedy. But Americans far and wide in the Ardennes had already heard the grisly story. And they are out for blood.

DECEMBER 22, 1944: ELSENBORN RIDGE

Company B is located 1¼ miles northeast of Elsenborn.[13] The six officers and 195 enlisted are experiencing changing weather: a high of 45°, a low of 34°, cold, windy, cloudy, low overcast, light drizzle before noon, snow, and fog. Capt. Dunlap reports: "The Company remained in the same position; received heavy shelling all day and night." Pfc. Lloyd Vunk, from Clinton, New York, dies of wounds. SSgts. Julius Kenda and Michael Szollosy are wounded, as is Paul Sapp—Sapp's third wound and Kenda's second. Mike was one of the first Company B men wounded in North Africa on November 20, 1942. Joe McQueen is evacuated for nonbattle illness.

The 3rd Panzergrenadier Division smashes westward, surrounding two platoons of the 99th Infantry Division's Reconnaissance Troop, 1 mile southeast of Kalterherberg. About 3 miles north of Elsenborn, the ghosts of Stalingrad cross the small, frozen Drosbach Creek and slam into Company E, 47th Infantry, which reports twelve soldiers missing near Hill 603, to the northeast.[14] General Denkert orders his division artillery to fire a smokescreen, through which he can crush the Americans on Elsenborn Ridge once and for all. The 29th Panzer Grenadier Regiment advances through the smoke, coming for the throat of the First Battalion, ~~AAAO~~. Phil Holman later recalled what happened after midnight:

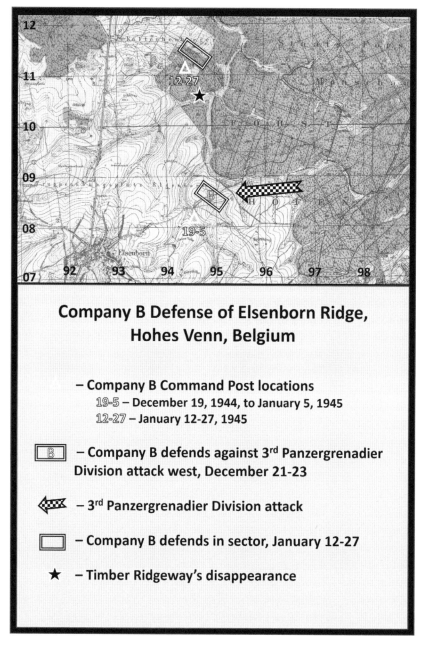

MAP 7: Company B Defense of Elsenborn Ridge, Hohes Venn, Belgium

A star shell lit up the quiet, white battlefield. They came out of the mists of the morning snow, tank tracks screeching, engines rumbling, guns firing. Tanks, along with infantry, came out of the woods on frozen trails, across the small icy creek and up the hill toward our positions. The noise was terrific—artillery shells falling near our lines; tank fire drumming on our positions; the crackle of small-arms fire. Some of the shells blew up the barbed wire we had put in front of our positions, sending up clouds of dirt, snow, and shards of wire. Our own artillery answered, adding to the ear-shattering sound of battle.

Occasionally you could hear the cries of the wounded, both theirs and ours. As daylight came, we could see the havoc created by war—burning tanks, wounded and dead German infantry, some festooned on parts of the barbed wire to our front—but more were coming. Finally, the Germans fall back down the hill and across the creek, into the hills from whence they had come. They left behind the burning hulks of their armor and many wounded and dead men.

As they attack, the Germans are about to experience what is known in the 9th Infantry as a "Zombie"—when all available artillery is ordered to fire on a single enemy unit. The ensuing bombardment is a fierce barrage—a "Give it everything you've got, boys" effort. Gunners, sweating from exertion in the freezing air, slam round after round into the scorching-hot breeches of every available gun. Gun sergeants scream, "Fire!" at the top of their lungs, their crews almost deaf from the continuous cannonades. Artillery in support of the division fire Zombies of 11,000 rounds of high-explosive hell at the advancing Germans. Dazed POWs say that the First and Third Battalions of the 29th Panzer Grenadier suffered heavy losses. Captain Karl-Heinz Weise, commander of 3rd Battalion and German Cross in Gold winner, is killed; he will posthumously be awarded the Honor Roll Clasp of the German army. Major Gerhard Türke, commander of 1st Battalion and Knight's Cross winner at Stalingrad, survives.[15]

Of course the 3rd Panzergrenadier experienced awful artillery bombardments in Russia, but this one is insidiously unique. There, the Russians targeted terrain that the Germans were expected to occupy. But a Zombie bombardment slow-dances you around the battlefield, a fiend contemplating how to kill its prey: if you advance, it advances with you, apparently knowing where you will go before you do; if you withdraw, it follows you—its explosions inhuman cackling at the fatal misfortune of exposing your back. Every frozen field, every wood line, every road intersection, where you tried to hide, that the Zombie touches is first left with a deafening silence of the dead—followed by a rising, sickening chorus of the wounded.

Sunrise occurs at 0836 hours. The enemy probes forward again and again. Artillery disperses another attack by the 8th Panzer Grenadier and 29th Panzer Grenadier Regiments about 1030 hours. Enemy artillery barrages are constant and heavy in return. Sunset is at 1632 hours. An enemy infantry battalion, preceded by an artillery barrage, attacks Second Battalion about 1715 hours and gets halfway up the ridge but is repulsed in heavy fighting. Later, historians will credit the defense of the Elsenborn Ridge to be comparable to Gettysburg's "Little Round Top," from American Civil War fame. For the week ending December 22, AAAO has four soldiers evacuated for cold injuries.[16] But not Pfcs. Jay Lavinsky and Fred Liberman; they earn the Bronze Star with V for Valor on this day.

DECEMBER 23, 1944: ELSENBORN RIDGE

Company B remains dug in 2,200 yards northeast of Elsenborn.[17] Cloudy weather; a heavy fog and a "Russian high"—a cold northeasterly wind—freezes the ground. Icy wind and snow whips the Büschelberg, freezing canteen water. In open areas, where Company B is defending, snow is 2 feet deep, and it's knee to waist in gullies. Company strength: six officers and 181 enlisted. Jack Dunlap reports: "Remained in the same defensive positions; still receiving some heavy shelling." SSgt. Floyd Redmond and Sgt. Carl Baer are wounded. Shrapnel hits Floyd's cheek. For Carl, who arrived on October 4, shrapnel to the face is his second wound. Bing Chin heads to the 45th Evacuation Hospital at Eupen for a nonbattle illness. Pvt. Joe Wienhoff is evacuated for frostbitten feet; for William Gladis, a fellow soldier's bullet may have accidentally hit him—his tibia is smashed, and he will be in a hospital until September. Chester McClurg is busted to private.

The 103rd Panzer Detachment makes one last lunge west but is hit in the flank by AAAO from their positions on the Büschelberg, 800 yards south of the Schwalmbach; First Battalion fires machine guns and BARs until the barrels are scorching, and again calls in massed artillery fire, driving the Germans back east; the air is filled with the stench of blood and smoke. It will be the final attempt by the Sixth SS Panzer Army on its northern flank during the Ardennes Offensive, dooming Hitler's plan to split American and British forces. The failure of the offensive, in turn, heralds the imminent defeat in the west for the Third Reich. During the fighting, TSgt. Peter Dalessandro of Company E earns the Congressional Medal of Honor, but all the soldiers in AAAO fight above and beyond the call of duty on this day.

DECEMBER 24, 1944: ELSENBORN RIDGE

Company B location unchanged; strength is six officers and 183 enlisted. A high temperature of 45°, a low of 30°, low clouds, increasing afternoon cloudiness, and light fog; visibility is good. Jack Dunlap writes: "Company remained in defensive position; received heavy artillery fire." Bomb fragments hit Sgt. John Spaan, an original member of Company B, in the leg and hand, when two P-47s mistakenly attack about 1440 hours.[18] Charles Mayer returns from convalescence after being wounded on October 10; Shelby Thompson also returns—he was wounded October 6. Pvt. William Harris is apprehended by military police; his life is about to go into the crapper, since he has been absent over three months. A Regular Army soldier, William enlisted in February 1940 and is the company bugler—known as the "company windjammer"—and can serve as a signalman, and a foot or motor messenger. He drives one of the company headquarters ¼-ton trucks, so when he is missing, people notice.

A V1 "Buzz Bomb" crashes intact 1½ miles north of regimental headquarters.[19] At 1740 hours, the enemy attacks First Battalion but is dispersed by artillery fire. Five minutes later, division G-2 notifies all units that they can expect a large attack of five hundred aircraft in sector.[20] At 2110 hours, a patrol finds a German tracked vehicle just south of the Schwalmbach River.[21]

DECEMBER 25, 1944: ELSENBORN RIDGE

Company B is 1¼ miles northeast of Elsenborn.[22] Low clouds, light fog, and 2 mph surface winds; company strength is six officers and 184 enlisted. Jack Dunlap muses: "Merry Xmas to all except Company B. We are having a heck of a time trying to keep warm, and still duck shells. 'C'est la guerre.'" One soldier, just in from the 3rd Replacement Depot, takes a peek around and goes AWOL; what did he expect, Santa Claus? Company B, still defending on the open Büschelberg, conducts patrolling; light artillery falls during the day. Ice forms on the sides of the foxholes. Units rotate companies off the front so men can get a chance to get warm. At the front, it's canned C rations—hash, minced meat, and Spam, and a few K rations, although a few hamburgers find their way to the line. Phil Holman's holiday dinner features a frozen can of hash, half heated over a candle in the bottom of his foxhole. In another foxhole, Jack Jewell has hot coffee and a can of meat and beans.[23]

At 0955 hours, G-2 notifies all units that any Germans found in American uniforms will be sent to First Army headquarters, tried as spies, and—if convicted—returned to the area where found and executed.[24] Seventeen Germans will be shot by firing squad, sixteen by First Army.[25] At 1230 hours, ack-ack weapons near the AAAO CP shoot down three enemy aircraft; pilots are observed to bail out of two. The aircraft are likely Focke Wulf 190 A-8s from the Luftwaffe's 54th Fighter Wing, "Green Hearts."

DECEMBER 26, 1944: ELSENBORN RIDGE

Jack Dunlap reports: "In defensive positions northeast of Elsenborn, Belgium. Receiving enemy shelling as usual." Company strength is six officers and 184 enlisted. The weather is a high of 40°, a low of 20°, light rain, and drizzle; visibility is restricted. Company B reports medium artillery shelling at 1900 hours. Battalion reports forty rounds of airburst artillery shells. Ohioan Pvt. Willard D. Frase, assigned to 3rd Squad of 1st Platoon on October 22, is killed when an artillery round rips opens his stomach.[26] Shrapnel hits 2Lt. Merl Benton from Beebe, Arkansas, in the right leg, but he stays in the company. Battalion fires at an enemy observation aircraft about 1940 hours. Pvts. Wira Jones and Henry Rolewski return from the 3rd Replacement Depot. Company patrols skirmish with enemy patrols in the limited visibility, after suddenly running into each other. Sgt. Pourchot, under sniper fire, sprints with rations and heat tablets to an outpost blockhouse and three of his men, worried that Chester McClurg will be lost to the squad for previously being AWOL.[27]

DECEMBER 27, 1944: ELSENBORN RIDGE

Company B strength: six officers and 185 enlisted. "Remained in same positions, receiving the usual shelling." Only the weather changes: fair, cloudless, early fog and haze, surface winds at 2–6 mph. At 1110 hours, regiment reports knocking down three aircraft, one a Focke-Wulf 190 A-8 southeast of Kalterherberg. George Rosen is submitted for the Silver Star. SSgt. John Reiser arrives from 3rd Replacement Depot and takes over Collins's old squad in 1st Platoon, allowing Porky Pourchot to return to assistant squad leader. Jack Jewell describes the cold:[28] "It is quite cold here. I'm sleeping in a hole with my wireman. I sleep in my sleeping bag [in uniform] and have four blankets under me. That keeps us warm but any less wouldn't. We get a plentiful supply of C-rations and ammunition and that's about all that is required in this life."

DECEMBER 28, 1944: ELSENBORN RIDGE

The company remains in position, patrolling; strength is six officers and 184 enlisted. Weather is a high of 43°, a low of 26°, and low overcast clouds; visibility is good. Dunlap writes:

> The Company was alerted as a counterattack was expected. The enemy shelled our positions most of the night, but no casualties were suffered. At 0530 hours, the enemy launched an attack on our right flank. Artillery was immediately fired on them, and the attack was broken up. They must have suffered *beaucoup* casualties. The men at the present time are having quite a time trying to keep warm. It is very cold up here on the hill, and it is impossible to get up and walk around in order to warm up because our positions are under direct enemy observation.

First Battalion CP is shelled at 0852 hours. At 1008 hours, fire lands in Company B. More artillery hits First Battalion at 1050 hours. The company receives artillery fire at 2130 hours. Ohioan Pfc. Newton Yount dies of artillery shrapnel wounds, after doctors try to save him with a blood transfusion; he had arrived October 20. Shrapnel wounds Pfc. Edward Matulevich in the right thumb, but he remains in the unit. One enlisted man is evacuated for nonbattle illness. Capt. James Flowers Jr., the battalion liaison officer from the 26th Field Artillery Battalion, is killed by artillery fire. It is a grievous loss, since the officer, who was awarded two Purple Hearts and a Bronze Star in combat, is the key link to receiving timely and accurate artillery support. Lt. Col. Thompson requests a replacement; Capt. Gordon Ryder arrives and picks up the baton, and the guns keep firing.[29]

DECEMBER 29, 1944: ELSENBORN RIDGE

Today is musical-chairs day. "The Company is relieved by Company A, 39th Infantry at 1800 hours. Company B then moves into Company A's old positions. Sat at defensive positions. Still receiving heavy shelling," writes Capt. Dunlap. Company strength is six officers and 185 enlisted; the weather is a high of 38°, a low of 25°, low clouds, light snow at higher elevations, and surface winds at 2–8 mph; visibility is restricted. Lloyd, nicknamed "Russian," Wasnick returns from the 3rd Replacement Depot—the direct support replacement depot for First Army—and becomes foxhole buddy to Bert Jones from California. An SP gun fires into the battalion area at 1400 hours, making seventy-five rounds of enemy artillery fire for the day. For the week ending December 29, ~~AAA~~O loses seven soldiers for cold injuries—expected, since windchill is 16°F.[30]

DECEMBER 30, 1944: ELSENBORN RIDGE

"In defensive position northeast of Elsenborn, Belgium." The six officers and 184 enlisted occupy the old positions of Company A; they are slightly off the front line in battalion reserve but still receive enemy long-range artillery fire. Weather is cold, with a high of 36°, a low of 22°, light snow, fog, and haze. Nineteen-year-old private Ambrosio Solano is wounded in the fingers by shrapnel—his second wound; shrapnel wounds Pfc. William Gordon in the left wrist. Some men in the company headquarters and weapons platoon get a chance to wash up and get a field haircut. Jack Jewell writes home: "It's like a band of gypsies. We go from the woods to the plains, from cellars to mud holes to shelled buildings and so on."[31] Company G of the 47th Infantry hits the jackpot today, stumbling upon a distillery.[32]

DECEMBER 31, 1944: ELSENBORN RIDGE

"In defensive position northeast of Elsenborn, Belgium." Six officers and 185 enlisted remain in current positions, while the weather is a high of 40°, a low of 22°, cold and windy, overcast, and fog. Sgt. James Russell, Pvt. Noel Waters, and Pvt. Charles Carroll arrive from the 3rd Replacement Depot. James had been evacuated on November 9 for a nonbattle disease. Noel, from Santa Paula, California, is a combat veteran as well. Charles promptly becomes a nonbattle casualty and is evacuated; he had been wounded back in October.

For December, ~~AAA~~O reports forty-two enlisted men killed, one officer and four enlisted men died of wounds, zero officer and seventeen enlisted men missing, and ten officers and 243 enlisted men wounded. The division surgeon reports 329 wounded, 21 nonbattle injuries, and 269 sickness and 7 exhaustion casualties in the regiment, treated at divisional medical installations.[33] The regiment submits one enlisted man for a Distinguished Service Cross, five officers (one posthumously) and twenty-two enlisted men (two posthumously) for Silver Stars, five officers and seventy-five enlisted men for Bronze Stars, and one enlisted man for a Legion of Merit.

There are no unit records describing any special celebrations this New Year's Eve. But considering that it is Hawk DiRisio's twenty-ninth birthday, it is likely that at the CP, a special bottle is passed around in salute. And Hawk's silent wish is undoubtedly that next New Year's Eve, everyone will be back home celebrating in style.

JANUARY 1, 1945: ELSENBORN RIDGE

New Year's Day: Company B still northeast of Elsenborn, Belgium.[34] Six officers and 185 enlisted present; the weather is a high of 35°, a low of 25°, low clouds, snow showers, surface winds of 5–10 mph, and a windchill of 15°F—"beastly cold," described by one.[35] Jack Dunlap reports: "The Company had turkey for dinner. It was rather difficult getting it to the men, but we managed. Received the usual shelling." In some places, the snow is up to the men's belts. At 0310 hours, the battalion reports heavy artillery fire, and by 0850 hours enemy mortars are also firing. At 0916 hours, Third Battalion shoots down an enemy aircraft near its CP, and two minutes later, First Battalion shoots down another, capturing the pilot and plane intact, a Focke-Wulf 190 A-8 fighter—probably near Company B. At 1000 hours, thirteen enemy fighters fly over the lines, strafing artillery positions and roads.[36] Later that morning, the enemy knocks out a Sherman tank supporting Third Battalion with a *Panzerschreck* shot through the turret.

A four-gun artillery battery begins firing at the battalion at 1415 hours; six enemy infantrymen, probably a patrol, try sneaking up a draw. An enemy 105 mm battery bombards the battalion at 2010 hours. An observation post reports an enemy tracked vehicle 300 yards out, and battalion fires artillery on it. Company L reports three killed, eleven wounded, and three soldiers with frozen feet. The division CP is located at (825245).[37] Mac MacLean writes home, thinking of food: "I received a package from John yesterday, and it was swell. Peanut butter, chopped ham (don't send any more) and cigarettes and candy. They all hit the spot, but the ham, and I don't have much of a chance to heat it or otherwise it might have been better."[38] Jack Jewell also writes home, musing on the meaning of life:[39]

> This is a funny life. Your morale goes up and down like a cork on rough water. Some seconds seem like hours, and you wish they would end, and then you wish some hours would never end. You want to spend the duration, or even life, doing just what you are doing at the moment . . . the Germans are tricky, but lots of things happen in the excitement of battle through fear, misunderstanding, and because few men can speak or understand the enemy's language. You just have to take all things with the idea that it's kind of a game that has no rules and all is fair.

JANUARY 2, 1945: ELSENBORN RIDGE

The company's six officers and 182 enlisted "remained in defensive position. Receiving the usual shelling." They are cold: a high of 38°, a low of 22°, increased cloudiness, several inches of snow during the night, intermittent rain and snow, and surface winds of 5–18 mph. Gen. Craig visits the regimental CP at 0900 hours. Col. Bond visits Company B, undoubtedly pleased that for the previous two days the men have had two hot meals per day: pancakes and cereal for breakfast and meat, potatoes, and vegetables for supper.[40] The battalion receives enemy mortar fire, and Company B spots mortars in a draw at 0947 hours; artillery fire hits a patrol at 1040 hours.

Charles Mayer and Pvt. Chris Batalaris are wounded. It is the third for Charles—again hit in the shoulder by shrapnel—and the second for Chris, in the company since 1941.

Pfc. Robert St. Peter and Pfc. William Maxwell are evacuated for nonbattle illness; Bob will be sent to the States. Robert will remain in a hospital for four months and then be discharged. It may be frostbite, since at its lowest today the windchill is a frigid 8°F. The regiment measures the base of a shell that exploded in its area and finds that it is 30.3 centimeters in diameter.[41] That caliber can only be a railroad gun, rumored to be in Düren, the projectile from which can kill you 100 yards from impact point.[42] Noodles Nodell finds time to write:[43]

I'm sitting in a foxhole somewhere in Germany and am getting along alright [*sic*] . . . spent many of cold days when I was with Acme, but none of them were anything like I'm spending now. . . . Just to give you an idea of just how I spent my Xmas & New Years. On Xmas day I got up out of my foxhole around six in the morning and the whole inside was covered with ice. I made myself a cup of coffee and heated up a can of beans. For my Xmas dinner I had another cup of coffee and a couple of cheese sandwiches and crackers. [They got] a hamburger sandwich to us and I made another cup of coffee. It was no fault of our kitchen, because if it were any possible way they could get to us, they would go through hell trying.

Well, New Year's dinner was better because they managed to get a turkey dinner to us.

Anytime you think an Infantryman can't take it, let me know. I saw us sleep in a foxhole with no fire, and it was way below zero and for us it was just another day although we were cold. . . . You better write now that the [Christmas] rush is over, because if you don't, I'll knock your block off when I come home. Don't forget that I'm getting good practice over here with all the Krauts. Ha. Ha. . . . If these damn Krauts would only give up I would. . . . Larry, the reason I'm writing so small is that we have a hard time getting envelopes and paper, so I got to make it last.

JANUARY 3, 1945: ELSENBORN RIDGE

Strength increases to six officers and 183 enlisted; unit remains northeast of Elsenborn.[44] A high of 37°, a low of 25°, overcast, intermittent light snow and rain, fog, and surface winds of 8–12 mph. The sector is generally quiet during the night. Gen. Craig visits the regimental CP at 0835 hours, and Col. Bond begins visiting battalions at 0945 hours. Windchill drops to 14°F.

JANUARY 4, 1945: ELSENBORN RIDGE

Company strength inches up to six officers and 184 enlisted; a high of 39°, a low of 20°, snow showers, and surface winds of 8–12 mph; icy roads. All units report a quiet night. Gen. Craig again visits the regimental CP at 0930 hours. Windchill plummets to 8°F. Louis Benoist writes a letter to the sister of a fraternity brother at "Ole Miss."[45]

> I hope I can keep on dodging the 88s tho. They say people can get hurt with these things.... Doesn't look like this war will ever be over. We are sweating it out over here. Kind of cold too. Had 8 inches of snow last night. I tried to get out of my foxhole this morning and had to call for help. I was snowbound. Good thing a Jerry didn't take a notion to beat one of my men to it.... Letters from home are all we look forward to.... War is so very horrible and ugly that it gets you down. Letters are the only thing ... which helps to obliterate its horrors.

JANUARY 5, 1945: HOHES VENN

Company B moves to 1 mile southwest of Kalterherberg.[46] Company strength drops to six officers and 184 enlisted. The temperature drops too: a high of 32°, a low of 20°, windchill remains the same as the previous day at 8°F, overcast, heavy snowfall during the night, surface winds of 4–12 mph, and in open areas, average snow depth is 18 inches, but high winds cause snow drifts of up to 4 feet.[47] Capt. Dunlap reports: "The Company moved out of its defensive position near Elsenborn, Belgium, and was relieved by Company E of the 395th Infantry Regiment. The Company started moving out of the defense area at 2130 hours and traveled by foot approximately three miles, arriving at new area near Kalterherberg, Belgium at 0130 hours. We are now in Regimental Reserve and are occupying the same area we occupied in November."

At 0200 hours, before moving, the battalion observes enemy activity 1,000 yards to the front. A battalion outpost receives twenty rounds of 88 fire at 1415 hours. At 1545 hours, two enemy aircraft strafe the Elsenborn–Kalterherberg road and Elsenborn Ridge. Sunset is at 1645 hours. Pfc. George Holdren is evacuated for nonbattle illness. For the week ending January 5, the regiment evacuates nineteen soldiers for cold injuries.[48] The 9th Infantry publishes GO #2, awarding Joe Gravino an Oak Leaf Cluster to the Silver Star for action on October 13.

JANUARY 6, 1945: HOHES VENN

Company is located 1 mile southwest of Kalterherberg; strength is seven officers and 185 enlisted. It is quite cold: a high of 36°; a low of 20°; overcast; low clouds on hills; slight drizzle, rain, and snow mixed, then 6 inches of snow; haze; surface winds of 4–12 mph; deep snow with frozen crust. "The Company improved its foxholes during the day. We are still in Regimental Reserve," writes Capt. Dunlap in the morning report. Col. Bond visits the battalions at 1100 hours. The rest of First Battalion takes over defensive positions of Third Battalion near high ground just west of the Schwalmbach, 2 miles south-southwest of the village of Alzen, Germany. William Maxwell and Bing Chin are evacuated for nonbattle illness. Lucien Lucas is promoted to first lieutenant. 1Lt. Robert Russ transfers to the unit from Company D. Billie Flowers returns from the 3rd Replacement Depot. Chester McClurg and Lionel Martin head to the Division Stockade for confinement, while William Harris goes into quarters' arrest.

JANUARY 7, 1945: HOHES VENN

Company B location and strength remain unchanged. Weather is similar to yesterday: a high of 33°; a low of 24°; overcast, low clouds on hills; 8 inches of new snow during the night, then mixed rain and snow; light fog, haze. One enlisted man is evacuated for nonbattle illness. The enemy attacks a Company C outpost at 0730 hours in response to a US patrol capturing three Germans. At 0900 hours, 60th Infantry reports that an enemy patrol captured four men. Col Bond visits battalions at 1000 hours, as Gen. Craig visits the regimental CP. Facing ~~AAA~~O for much of January is the 277th Volksgrenadier Division's 990th Volksgrenadier Regiment. In command is Lt. Col. Josef Benedikt Bremm, who has been in almost continuous combat since 1940 and wounded six times, once in Russia in the throat. Bremm has the Knights Cross with Oak Leaves; his actions in 1945, especially at Elsenborn Ridge, will earn him the Swords to his Oak Leaves—one of only 157 men in the ten-million-man Wehrmacht to be so awarded.

JANUARY 8, 1945: HOHES VENN

Company B location remains unchanged; strength is six officers and 183 enlisted. A high of 32°, a low of 22°, overcast, cloudy, scattered light snow showers all day, light fog, haze, limited visibility, and "6 or 8 inches of snow on the ground and still snow-ing."[49] Jack Dunlap added: "The Company was paid today. It is still snowing out, and we now have over a foot of snow." Stanley Mills receives orders for temporary duty at Fort Douglas, Utah. Jack Jewell becomes company executive officer. Joe Gravino departs on a 30-day furlough, bound for Fort Dix due to his distinguished time overseas since 1942. Keith Lewis becomes the first sergeant. Gen. Craig visits the regimental CP at 1400 hours. Division engineers put snowplows on trucks to clear the supply roads, until they can bring bulldozers forward. Numerous enemy prisoners over the last few days say they are afraid of the lavish US use of tracer rounds. Other POWs say they fear the painful burns of US phosphorus shells.

JANUARY 9, 1945: HOHES VENN

Company B, remaining in current locations, has six officers and 182 enlisted. A high of 32°, a low of 22°, overcast, light snow at night, scattered snow all day; visibility is limited, sometimes down to zero, and some snowdrifts are now 12–15 feet high. One enlisted man is evacuated for nonbattle illness. All regiment commanders meet at the division headquarters at 1330 hours. Gen. Craig then visits the battalions.

JANUARY 10, 1945: HOHES VENN

Strength is six officers and 181 enlisted; company location remains the same. A high of 30°, a low of 9°, overcast, showery conditions, light snow at night, haze, and surface winds at 6–12 mph. The morning report: "The Company waiting for orders to move to new positions." Two enlisted men are evacuated for nonbattle illness. Windchill temperature plummets to new depths of misery at −6°F. Men exposed to the vicious wind can suffer frostbite in just minutes. Sometimes you fear the weather as much as the enemy.

JANUARY 11, 1945: HOHES VENN

Strength is six officers and 180 enlisted; location remains the same. Weather: a high of 30°, a low of 9°, hazy, surface winds of 4–9 mph, and windchill −4°F. Capt. Dunlap writes: "Company preparing to move to new position." Oliver Osbourn is promoted to SSgt. in 3rd Platoon and takes over as a squad leader for Timber Ridgeway, who goes to 1st Platoon. Pvt. James Carter is evacuated for frostbitten feet. Gen. Craig visits the regimental CP at 1545 hours.

JANUARY 12, 1945: ELSENBORN RIDGE

Company B moves 1½ miles northeast of Elsenborn.[50] Strength: six officers and 181 enlisted. A high of 27°, a low of 5°, overcast, snow flurries, and surface winds of 4–8 mph. Capt. Dunlap comments: "The Company moved from position near Kalterherberg, Germany, and relieved Company B, 60th Infantry Regiment. We are now in a defensive position about 3,000 yards northeast of Elsenborn, Belgium. The Company moved by platoons, leaving old area at 1000 hours, and traveling by foot, arriving in new area at 1100 hours. The occupation of the defensive position was completed at 1800 hours." Carl Stock returns from his December 21 wound but is evacuated for a nonbattle illness. First Battalion relieves First Battalion of the 60th Infantry and begins patrolling. Capt. Dunlap locates the CP in a tiny clearing on a wooded slope 700 yards southwest from Hill 604—called the Hohe Mark by locals.

For the week ending January 12, AAAO has one soldier evacuated for cold injuries.[51] Windchill temperatures dive to −8°F. Frank Pemberton is transferred from the First Army Stockade to the Loire Disciplinary Training Center at Le Mans, France.

JANUARY 13, 1945: ELSENBORN RIDGE

Company B is 1½ miles northeast of Elsenborn; strength is six officers and 181 enlisted.[52] Weather: a high of 32°, a low of 22°, low overcast, fog, and haze. One enlisted man is evacuated for nonbattle illness. Mortar and long-range artillery fire hit Company A at 0430 hours. Lt. Col. Thompson returns to the CP at 1135 hours after checking the companies; a Company B patrol discovers an enemy listening post in a small clearing in the Kalterherberger Wald (Kalterherberg Woods) at 1150 hours.[53] At 1630 hours, Second Battalion is hit by fire from some of the big boys—150 mm—one round every twenty seconds for a half hour.[54]

Jack Jewell writes home.[55] He now shares a foxhole with 1Sgt. Keith Lewis and company clerk T/5 William Kelley. It is no ordinary foxhole—deluxe is more apt: clean straw on the ground, built-in shelves made of ration boxes, and a small stove for warmth, which can accommodate a coffeepot. It has two small lights made from empty C-ration cans, wire, nails, and discarded radio batteries that have a little juice left. Hawk DiRisio provides three cans of grapefruit juice, and Jack has fresh fried eggs for breakfast. In the infantry, this is called living high on the hog.

However, snafus can happen, and one night the guys occupy the foxhole about 2100 hours. It's quite dark, and the men can't see their hands in front of them. Jack crawls into the hole, takes off his boots, and feels something large and hairy beside him. Striking a match, in the flickering light he sees a large nanny goat—obviously, the goat has heard about the plush digs and wants a room. Jack boots the goat in the rear and out she goes. It could have been worse—it could have been a wolf. But the goat has left them a parting gift. Jack had received hard candy and gum in a Christmas box from home. During the visit, the goat smelled and ate these treats and deposited the remains in the form of "little black marbles" in Bill Kelley's sleeping bag. Mail call the next day must have been a riot.

JANUARY 14, 1945: HOHES VENN

Company B location and strength are unchanged. Weather: a high of 34°, a low of 7°, cold, fair and then steady snowfall, and surface winds moderate. Capt. Dunlap reports: "Company still in defensive position. Several patrols were sent out today." John Gronkiewicz is evacuated for nonbattle illness. After noon, Pete Quesada's boys drop eleven bombs on suspected enemy positions. At 2155 hours, a Focke-Wulf 190 A-8 strafes a Company F outpost with 20 mm cannon fire.

JANUARY 15, 1945: ELSENBORN RIDGE

Company B occupies the same position; strength is six officers and 179 enlisted. The weather is still poor: a high of 31°, a low of 22°, clear and cool, low clouds later afternoon, and light fog. Capt. Dunlap writes: "Still in defensive position." Shrapnel wounds New Yorker Pvt. Stephen Buscemi in the face; he'll be in the hospital two months. Pvt. George "Greek" Maliongas, from East Peoria, Illinois—a scout in John Reiser's squad—is evacuated for a nonbattle burn, while Pfc. Clarence Kinney departs with a nonbattle illness. Another enemy aircraft strafes Second Battalion at 0430 hours. Company B reports small-arms fire from the edge of a wood line about 0710 hours.[56] A battalion patrol engages a German patrol near a destroyed American tank and really opens up on the Germans. Jack Jewell, who is "munching on some dehydrated rice and beef," writes: "The snow is still with us and it's rather cold but not too bad. I still have the warm foxhole to sleep in and plenty of rations to eat. The mess sergeant sent me another can of tomato juice, and I'm enjoying that. Everything is going fairly well, but I sure wish this war would end soon."[57]

JANUARY 16, 1945: ELSENBORN RIDGE

Company B in same position and strength. The weather worsens: a high of 31°, a low of 15°, broken overcast, light snow, surface winds of 8–12 mph, and snow 12 inches deep. Jack Dunlap writes: "Company still in defensive position. Several patrols were sent out during the day and night." *GO #9* awards the departed Detroit native Robert St. Peter the Silver Star for gallantry in action last October 13. Artillery shrapnel wounds Kentuckian Pfc. Joe McQueen's hand; Joe had previously been wounded last July 25. Pfc. Charles Kreager is evacuated for nonbattle illness. At 1000 hours, Col Bond visits the battalions. At 1450 hours, Gen. Craig visits the 39th CP. Twenty mortar rounds fall on Company B at 1650 hours. Sunset occurs at 1700 hours. AAAO patrols, in 1.4°F windchill, attempt to destroy the knocked-out tank, hitting it with a bazooka round at 1808 hours. Jack Jewell writes home: "I just finished supper: a can of hot coffee, peach jam sandwich, and a Breakfast K-ration. Not bad eating, but I could stand a change . . . well, I'm just looking forward to the day I can smell the Russians coming my way."[58]

JANUARY 17, 1945: ELSENBORN RIDGE

Company B's location and strength remain the same. A high of 32°, a low of 18°, overcast, light rain in the morning, light snow flurries and then snow showers in the afternoon, fog, and haze. "Still in defensive position," reports Jack Dunlap. Nudge Red Baker continues patrolling. At 0300 hours, a patrol returns with a negative report.[59] Col. Bond departs to visit the battalions at 0930 hours. Gen. Craig arrives at the AAAO CP at 1500 hours. The battalion emplaces forty rolls of concertina wire and twenty spools of regular barbed wire to improve defensive positions.

JANUARY 18, 1945: ELSENBORN RIDGE

"Still in defensive position," Capt. Dunlap reports, and a company strength of six officers and 179 enlisted. The weather is a killer: a high of 40°, a low of 22°, overcast, rain, a later blizzard with high wind and snow, large drifts, and significant tree breakage. One enlisted man is evacuated for nonbattle illness. Col. Bond visits the battalions beginning 0930 hours. At 2220 hours, the company reports twelve rounds of 105 mm howitzer falling on 1st Platoon and its outpost, but no one is wounded. The company sends out four patrols, but all report negative contact.[60] Jack Jewell has a problem: "Dear Folks . . . I would like to know how to make coffee in a can and make the grounds settle so they wouldn't be in the coffee you pour out to drink."[61]

All Jack has to do is ask the company mess sergeant; so how does Hawk DiRisio brew up coffee? Well, it isn't in fine Limoges china, and it isn't small amounts. Hawk uses big containers because the soldiers drink gallons of Joe. First, the cooks make sure the vessel is clean—with no soap residue in it. Then they place the container over a heat source, a campfire or gas burner. Water is heavy; a 5-gallon container is almost 42 pounds, so the larger the kettle, the more cooks are needed to move it. Put the can on the heat source first, then quickly add water; when it's done, use big ladles to distribute the coffee to smaller insulated containers for transport.

Now the details; first, bring the water to a rolling boil, then remove the container from the heat, either by turning down the gas or physically moving the can, and then let it cool for a minute or so before stirring in the coffee grounds and then returning the container to the heat. Then bring the coffee to a simmer, which is about 195°F. How do they know when it hits that? If they have a cooking thermometer, fine, but a trained Army cook is one step below a hydrologist and can look at the water's surface and know precisely when it's ready.

A coffee barista would then talk about steeping the coffee. "Barista" is likely a word that has never rolled off Hawk's tongue, so he just removes the coffee from the heat and lets it sit still for a couple of minutes. Then he removes the lid for good to allow fresh colder air in that cools the coffee grounds, which then sink to the bottom of the kettle, or if he has some really cold water, he will gently pour that water in with a ladle around the top inside rim of the pot. If the grounds don't sink, well your coffee is going to be a little chewy this morning. Highbrow ways of making coffee do not leave any oil on the surface—caused by oils in the grounds. But the way Hawk makes coffee, you're going to see more oil than during a Deuce oil-filter change.

Bad coffee is called "battery acid." Hawk has some tricks for getting rid of any bitterness. Hawk adds crushed eggshells to settle the last grounds, or he can add just the right amount of salt to reduce the bitterness, but the exact quantity is shrouded in such mystery that it puts the secrecy surrounding the plans for the Normandy invasion to shame.[62] Then, cooks slowly pour the coffee into small containers so as not to stir up the grounds, and never pouring in the last few ounces that have the grounds in them—throwing the dregs away, unless Hawk wants to scrub pots and pans with them. Stay away from the little packets of coffee powder—instant coffee. It's called "predigested coffee" for a reason. Jack Jewell described the troops' fondness for the beverage: "You mentioned several times how the boys in France wanted coffee sent to them. That's because all soldiers are great coffee drinkers. Our men drink it three times a day and more often if they can get it."[63]

Coffee with Hawk; it ain't "Puttin' On the Ritz." But when you're standing in the wet snow in your foxhole, your hands are freezing, your nose is running, and your eyes are tearing up—because your heart is aching for home—that cup of hot coffee just might be worth a million bucks to you about now.

JANUARY 19, 1945: ELSENBORN RIDGE

Company strength and location are unchanged. The weather: a high of 38°, a low of 29°, cold, overcast, snow blizzard, and surface winds of 12–18 mph; deep, heavy snow remains in drifts in draws, presenting an obstacle to patrolling; "All the snow, or ice, is frozen to the trees, and when the wind whips the tops, it acts as an oversize pendulum." Jack Dunlap writes: "Still in defensive position. Several patrols were sent out during the day and night. It has been awfully cold out and the wind has knocked down several trees." A huge blizzard hits the division area, as windchill approaches 16°F. Two enemy mortar rounds strike Company B at 0430 hours, as does machine gun fire from a draw out front that hits a 3rd Platoon outpost but wounds no one. Gen. Craig visits the regimental CP at 1045 hours. That evening, the company sends out four patrols; all return without making enemy contact. For the week ending January 19, the regiment has two soldiers evacuated for cold injuries.

Billie Flowers and Mac MacLean are frequently paired together—with Billie, nicknamed "the Eye" for his excellent eyesight, and Mac, "the Ear," due to exceptional hearing—often forward of the platoon at night, serving as early warning of enemy action. Billie has a hard time reading and writing, so Mac reads him letters from home and then writes letters for Billie to return—but not in an outpost.[64] OPs are tough duty, since winter darkness in the Hohes Venn can last fifteen hours a day. Israel Reese celebrates his twentieth birthday. Jack Jewell writes home: "What a storm we are having, snow and wind. Last night it blew so hard that the pine trees were falling all night long. This morning you could hardly walk around because of the fallen trees. I'm still in a warm hole so just sleep through it all, or try to."[65]

JANUARY 20, 1945: ELSENBORN RIDGE

Company strength is six officers and 180 enlisted; same location. Weather: a high of 34°, a low of 21°, overcast, scattered snow showers, and surface winds moderate. "Company still in defensive position. Patrols were sent out at intervals during the day and night," writes Capt. Dunlap. Bing Chin is evacuated for nonbattle illness. Company B observes enemy flares to the front at 0230 hours, which wake a whole lot of folks up. Col. Bond departs at 0930 hours to visit the battalions. At 0940 hours, Company A reports that on its patrol #1, one soldier has been accidentally killed.[66] Frontline units report the enemy withdrawing eastward, so patrolling increases; sometimes an entire squad goes on patrol together. That morning, Company B sends out three patrols and, late in the afternoon, sends two more, but none spot the enemy.[67]

JANUARY 21, 1945: ELSENBORN RIDGE

Company B's location and strength unchanged; weather is miserable: a high of 37°, a low of 21°, overcast, rain/snow showers, and morning visibility restricted. Jack Dunlap writes: "Still in defensive position. A combat patrol was sent out today." Sunrise is 0826 hours. The company sends out three patrols. Timber Ridgeway, now in 1st Platoon, is posted missing in action on one. It's a tough loss; Hawk DiRisio—a good buddy of Timber—later said, "We kept asking ourselves, Why me? Why do we have to keep on until we all get killed? It seemed we just went on and on."[68] Donald Pellock and William Farmer are evacuated for nonbattle illness. At 1000 hours, Col. Bond visits the battalions. Doc Slaughter becomes a father; his son Billie Joe is born today back in Trinity. It is also Patsy Jerome's birthday, but he's known Timber a long time.

JANUARY 22, 1945: ELSENBORN RIDGE

Company B's location unchanged; strength is six officers and 179 enlisted. Weather: a high of 30°, a low of 19°, fair, and light fog. Jack Dunlap writes: "Still in defensive position." The unit continues patrolling. Col. Bond visits the battalions at 0910 hours.

A dozen artillery rounds hit, beginning at 1420 hours. Patsy Jerome receives his Silver Star earned the previous October.

JANUARY 23, 1945: ELSENBORN RIDGE

Company B's location unchanged; strength is six officers and 180 enlisted. Weather worsening: a high of 34°, a low of 20°, overcast, light to moderate rain and snow, and surface winds of 10–15 mph. Dunlap writes: "Still in defensive position." Patrols in windchill of 7°F try to capture prisoners for information. At 0805 hours, enemy mortars hit Company B with ten to twenty rounds. At 0900 hours, Company B's patrol #2 is fired on by enemy machine gun from the base of Hill 580.[69] Col Bond visits the battalions at 0935 hours. Gen. Craig visits the AAAO CP at 1020 hours. At 2130 hours, one enemy artillery round falls on Company B, causing no casualties; more mortar fire arrives at 2350 hours.[70] They cannot locate the enemy observer calling in the fire, but they feel certain he is hidden nearby.

JANUARY 24, 1945: ELSENBORN RIDGE

Company location remains the same, but strength drops to six officers and 179 enlisted. Weather: a high of 38°, a low of 24°, overcast, low clouds, and snow showers. Capt. Dunlap notes: "Still in defensive position." William Maxwell is evacuated for nonbattle illness. Howard Gasper returns after being AWOL and is placed in confinement. Combat patrols meet strong enemy resistance. Intelligence indicates that the 689th Volksgrenadier Regiment is in the sector. Weapons platoon takes up residence in a Belgian home, so they can sleep warm and dry for a change. Hawk DiRisio and his cooks shoot three deer, so venison is now on the menu. Jack Jewell notices the shrapnel has damaged hundreds of trees and limbs, so whenever a hard snow falls, lots of wood does too.[71]

JANUARY 25, 1945: ELSENBORN RIDGE

Company location remains the same; strength is six officers and 180 enlisted. Temps drop: a high of 31°, a low of 15°, cold, overcast, and scattered light snow. Jack Dunlap writes: "Still in defensive position. Several patrols were sent out during the day and night. Three German soldiers walked up to the 2nd Platoon outpost and surrendered this morning. This was quite unexpected, as the missions of most of these patrols was to bring back prisoners and were unsuccessful." Mortars hit Company B with eight rounds at 1100 hours. The POWs are from the 2nd Company, 990th Infantry Regiment— in the woods on Hill 603.[72] Nudge 6 returns to the CP at 1720 hours to plan a recon near Kalterherberg. Jack Jewell hears that his Silver Star is approved. At 2340 hours, Company B outposts report movement. Mac and Billie detect something.

JANUARY 26, 1945: HOHES VENN

Company B's six officers and 179 enlisted are 1½ miles northeast of Elsenborn.[73] Bitter weather: a high of 32°, a low of 10°, overcast, light snow in the morning, a snowstorm at sunset, fog and haze early in the morning, and freezing winds. Capt. Dunlap reports: "Company still in defensive position." Sgt. James Russell and Ruben Brady are wounded. Russell arrived October 4 as a corporal. Shrapnel hits Ruben's hand; at the aid station a doctor finds that he also has trench foot. An enemy patrol captures a Second Battalion outpost. Gen. Craig visits the 39th CP at 1615 hours. At 1710 hours, twenty-five mortar rounds hit First Battalion.

At 2230 hours, a company trip flares goes off, and bullets fly. Over the last two weeks, Porky Pourchot goes on six patrols, the fifth a combat one. For the week ending January 26, the regiment evacuates two soldiers for cold injuries. Jack Jewell writes, "I washed and shaved in my helmet today and feel much better. We are getting two meals of C-rations and one meal (Supper) of a meat sandwich. It is usually hamburger, ham, pork chop, Spam or some such stuff."[74]

JANUARY 27, 1945: KALTERHERBERG, GERMANY

Company B is in the village of Kalterherberg.[75] Company strength: six officers and 180 enlisted. A high temperature of 35°, a low of 10°, clouds, light snow, fog early, and light surface winds. Small-arms fire strikes a company outpost at 0210 hours; no one is wounded. Col. Bond visits the battalions at 0910 hours. Capt. Dunlap recaps: "The Company was relieved from defensive position 1½ miles northeast of Elsenborn, Belgium, by Company F of the 393rd Infantry Regiment. The Company was relieved by platoon starting at 1030 hours and completed by 1700 hours. The Company traveled by foot approximately 1½ miles to new positions in Kalterherberg. We are now in Battalion Reserve and are billeted in houses." The company CP is just west of the main north–south road in Kalterherberg. At 1540 hours, First Battalion reports: "One platoon 'B' completely out, one platoon on way back, and one platoon in process of coming out," as the unit departs old positions. In Kalterherberg, Mac MacLean writes his mother:

> It seems that about every other day now someone in the squad gets one of the Xmas packages, so we get a lot of candy and fruit cake and it really hits the spot. My packages go just as fast, but they have been so good that it doesn't matter. It's still pretty cold over here, but I can stand the cold if the Russians keep going as fast as reported. That really builds up the morale and takes some of the pressure off.

JANUARY 28, 1945: KALTERHERBERG, GERMANY

Company B in Kalterherberg with six officers and 180 enlisted; a high of 31°, a low of 20°, a fair day, 6 inches of snow during the night, scattered light snow evening, and a damp snowy mist.[76] Capt. Dunlap reports: "Company still billeted in houses. The day was spent issuing new winter equipment to the men. The men also took showers and cleaned up today." Soldiers receive special gear, including shoe packs, mittens, water-repellent pants, and scarves. Most important are the shoes, rubber bottoms with a laced top well up the calf, of waterproof leather. They are intended to be worn with felt insoles and one or two pairs of wool socks and are good in snow, slush, and mud. It will be Mac's last hot shower for a very long time.

Meanwhile, ~~AAA~~O begins planning for an upcoming offensive. Pfc. John A. Moore is evacuated for nonbattle illness. The 39th CP is on the eastern edge of Kalterherberg.[77] Company B is nearby, and the men can attend services in a church in the middle of town; Capt. Dunlap moves the CP 300 yards north, still inside Kalterherberg. The division CP moves to the Reichenstein Monastery, a few miles southwest of Monschau.[78] Nestled against the scenic Roer River, the monastery is good digs—if you can get it.

JANUARY 29, 1945: KALTERHERBERG, GERMANY

Company B remains in Kalterherberg; strength is six officers and 181 enlisted. Weather: a high of 25°, a low of 10°, overcast, intermittent snow, wind/cold, and heavy morning fog; "Snow is belt deep in the open ground and knee deep everywhere"[79] Dunlap reports what's on everyone's mind: "Company getting prepared to move into attack." George Holdren, evacuated January 5 for nonbattle illness, returns. Herman Eichel is evacuated for frozen feet, and he heads to the 77th Convalescent Hospital.[80] It's a tough loss, since Herman often has the M1903 Springfield rifle for duty as a sniper.[81] MPs haul William Harris to the division stockade.

Third Battalion will lead the attack tomorrow. Then, one of those unpredictable events in war happens. Company L reports a large outbreak of food poisoning at 1205 hours and will not be able to attack. So, Company B is designated to take their place and is attached to Third Battalion; the two elements have not worked together for a long time. Battalion commanders meet at 1430 hours to discuss the upcoming attack. At 1558 hours, Company B closes into an attack assembly area. Third Battalion CP is in Kalterherberg.[82] Gen. Craig visits the 39th CP at 1930 hours. Company B stays in several abandoned houses in Kalterherberg, as Mac writes to his mother telling her not to buy a pair of new boots for him.

Tomorrow, the soldiers will face fortifications known as the Westwall, or Siegfried Line as it is called by the Allies, which they had a taste of last September. In 1939, British troops marching off to France happily thought that the Siegfried Line was a joke, singing, "We're Going to Hang Out the Washing on the Siegfried Line." Actually, near Aachen and the Hürtgen Forest there are two defensive lines—the Scharnhorst Line in the west and the Schill Line a few miles east. In front of the Scharnhorst line are bands of "dragon's teeth" antitank obstacles—named after General Gerhard Johann David von Scharnhorst, first chief of the Prussian General Staff, noted for his reforms of the Prussian army. The Schill Line is named for Major Ferdinand Baptista von Schill, who led an unsuccessful revolt against Napoleon; he was executed for that transgression in May 1809.

While fixed fortifications prove to have limited effectiveness at the strategic level during the war, down at the platoon they are no joke. Around the small village of Alzen, the objectives for the attack are fifteen concrete bunkers. South of Alzen is

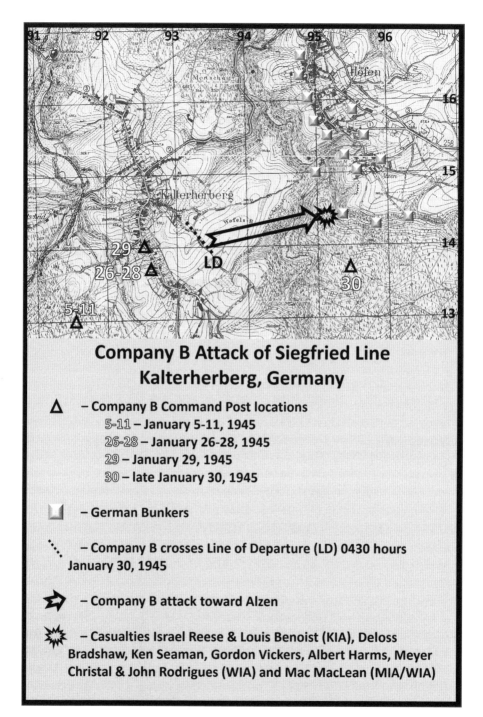

Company B Attack of Siegfried Line
Kalterherberg, Germany

△ – Company B Command Post locations
  5-11 – January 5-11, 1945
  26-28 – January 26-28, 1945
  29 – January 29, 1945
  30 – late January 30, 1945

▨ – German Bunkers

⋰ – Company B crosses Line of Departure (LD) 0430 hours
January 30, 1945

➤ – Company B attack toward Alzen

✸ – Casualties Israel Reese & Louis Benoist (KIA), Deloss
Bradshaw, Ken Seaman, Gordon Vickers, Albert Harms, Meyer
Christal & John Rodrigues (WIA) and Mac MacLean (MIA/WIA)

MAP 8: Company B Attack of Siegfried Line Kalterherberg

Bunker 101a, typical in the area, a double machine gun position, in that it has openings for one machine gun firing to the northwest and another firing to the southeast—at the same time. Pillboxes can be 25 feet wide, 20 feet high, and 45 feet deep; walls and roof can be 3–8 feet thick. In a worst-case scenario, the Germans will have in this bunker two MG42s (Maschinengewehr 42) 7.92 mm caliber machine guns that have a cyclic rate of fire of 1,200 rounds per minute—three times that of a BAR. A good gunner will fire only about 160 rounds per minute because rate of fire is not the best attribute of the MG42; effective range is. With a tripod, the weapon can engage a group of enemy troops at 3,800 yards.

Known as "Hitler's buzz saw" or the chilling nickname "bone-saw," the MG42 does not fit in some of the smaller bunkers, so there might be only an MG34, not quite as capable—but if you are hit by either, you'll still wind up dead or badly wounded. Bunker 101a is large enough to hold a dozen men, protected by 762 cubic meters of reinforced concrete. Many bunkers are in mutually supporting positions, meaning that GIs attacking one bunker can be effectively engaged by one to four other bunkers at the same time. To some top First Army staff, the Siegfried Line looks like a waste of concrete—but most of these staff officers never had to charge a pillbox, protected by barbed wire and tanglefoot, ringed by a minefield of Bouncing Betties, and covered by one or two bone saws fired by gunners with murder in their hearts.

JANUARY 30, 1945: SIEGFRIED LINE, KALTERHERBERG, GERMANY

Company B will end up 1½ miles southeast of Kalterherberg, but it has some fighting to do to get there.[83] Although the accounting strength is six officers and 190 enlisted, only 181 are in the attack. The weather will make attacking difficult: a high of 32°, a low of 10°, fair, overcast by dark, high wind, and deep snow. Capt. Dunlap writes: "Went into attack attached to 3rd Battalion." "Hitler's buzz saws" are working overtime. Machine guns kill both Louis Benoist and Israel Reese, Israel struck in the head by a bullet.[84] Kenny Seaman, Deloss Bradshaw, Gordon Vickers, Pfcs. Albert Harms, Meyer Christal, and Pvt. John Rodrigues are wounded. Machine gun bullets break John's wrist and penetrate his chest; he'll be hospitalized until July 1945. A machine gun bullet hits Albert in the face, while another causes a compound fracture of Meyer's leg. Shrapnel hits Gordon's hand. Pfc. Warren Whitcombe Jr. is injured. Mac MacLean is wounded in the head and reported missing in action.

Vth Corps begins a major attack eastward to seize the key towns of Gemünd and Schleiden. The 9th Infantry advances against the 164th Volksgrenadier Regiment of the 62nd Volksgrenadier Division. At 0415 hours under a bright moon, Third Battalion crosses the line of departure to gain surprise to reduce friendly casualties. ~~AAAO~~ is to seize the Wahlerscheid road junction, moving slowly through deep snow, crunching with each step. First, they must take Alzen, 2 miles east of Kalterherberg. It will be brutal: "The extreme cold and snow causes numerous cases of frostbite and exposure; fatigue and chilling perspiration from moving through the deep snow added to the discomfort of the troops. Routes and methods of supply and evacuation are most difficult to establish and maintain."[85]

Company B advances, but exactly what happens is confusing, and why determining what actually occurs at platoons and companies is so difficult. The men probably have a last warm meal about 0200 hours. The attack starts at 0415 hours. By 0800 hours, the going is slow through the deep snow and steep slopes; sweating from exertion, they have yet to contact the enemy. Sunrise occurs at 0815 hours. At 0840 hours, Company I, on the left, makes enemy contact, as Company B comes under close-range small-arms fire from log bunkers 400 yards southwest of Alzen.[86] At 0901 hours, the Third Battalion commander, Lt. Col. Robert H. Stumpf, reports the terrain is very difficult, and resistance is mostly from small arms. A Third Battalion soldier recalled:[87]

By daylight, we were deep in the Monschau Forest and deep in the snow also. It took us several hours to climb a very steep and wooded hill. The snow was about waist deep. Several of our men were hurt by booby traps at the top of the hill, and the entire company was pinned down by German fire for over an hour, during which time the snow melted on us and soaked our clothing. When we finally got our path cleared and started moving ahead, our clothes froze and cracked with each step we took. Throughout the day, we ran into scattered pockets of resistance.

At 0910 hours, Ltc. Stumpf reports that he is maneuvering against bunkers in forested low ground adjacent to the Fuhrtsbach, a small stream. The area is noted for the daffodils that bloom in the spring from late March to mid-May—but today, the only things blooming are explosions. By 1033 hours, Third Battalion reports contact with the enemy main line of defense and is maneuvering against it, bringing the rest of Company B forward, but Company B is still held up by small arms from its front and right at 1200 hours. During this time, Mac is wounded in the head by a large explosion that knocks him out. When he comes to, a German soldier is standing over him with a rifle pointed at his face. The location is likely on the steep slope going up Hill 556, just southwest of Alzen.[88] Decades later, Ken Seaman states that he saw Mac go down and that Lt. Louis Benoist, seeing one of his men in peril, jumps up from his position and yells: "Charge!"

Kenny sees a "bone-saw" instantly kill the lieutenant with a burst of bullets, which also strike Seaman, finishing his role as a witness.[89] A letter during the war from the unit chaplain to the Benoist family says that Louis was instantly killed by enemy artillery fire (not machine gun fire). After the war, Louis's widow, Anne, receives another letter from a platoon member, relaying its contents to relatives.[90] "He was leading his men through a wooded area up a hill where the Germans had dug in and planted their machine guns. He was shot in the hip, chest, and shoulder. One of his men who wrote us said he didn't suffer, and I don't see how he could with such severe wounds."

Years later, Phil Holman still remembered January 30. He, Israel Reese, and Junior Bradshaw are advancing together through the deep snow. Moving to the left of Lt. Benoist, they run into tanglefoot and are fired on by the enemy. Israel has the BAR and tries to fire, but in the cold, he is exposed too long and is killed by a burst of fire to the head.[91] Hand grenade shrapnel wounds Deloss in the face, as Phil slides down the hill in the deep snow toward Benoist, who has just been hit. It is brutal for the wounded, as a soldier later describes:[92]

> The dense woods, the deep snow, and the extremely high hills made travel by Army vehicles impossible and there were no regular roads. Any wounded had to be taken back on sleds to the rear aid station, a process that took almost half a day and accounted for the death of many of our wounded before they could get back.

Later, Jay Lavinsky writes to Mac's mother: "Our lieutenant was hit on one attack and although his rifle was not working, your son went up to cover him until an aid man could be brought up. But the Jerrys snuck up and took him prisoner." In another letter, Bob Pettigrew wrote: "Lieutenant Benoist died up there as we couldn't get up to him." Finally, the Army had its own official view of events expressed in a Silver Star award citation:

> At this time Pfc. MacLean's platoon was forced to reorganize and redeploy after a bitter enemy counterattack. In diverting enemy fire, two members of Pfc MacLean's automatic rifle team were wounded . . . Pfc. MacLean employed automatic rifle fire incessantly against the enemy, and by so doing drew the hostile machine gun and rifle fire to his own position. . . . Pfc. MacLean moved from place to place, drawing the enemy's fire until his platoon had safely regrouped.

The 39th Infantry identifies the 2nd Alarm Company, estimated to be some four hundred men strong, of the 190th Grenadier Regiment, in the 62nd Volksgrenadier Division, to be defending stubbornly from strongpoints along a line 950148 southeast to 954142, just south of Alzen; heavy small-arms firefights are ongoing. At 1415 hours, Company I and Company B still have not established contact with each other. Lt. Col. Stumpf reports at 1507 hours that he is moving Company I to the right to outflank the enemy in front of Company B.

Third Battalion captures prisoners and reports at 1630 hours that it is sending a dozen of them to the rear. Companies B and I establish contact with one another at 1655 hours. Sunset occurs at 1753 hours. Third Battalion's line is (951148—500 yards west of Alzen) to (952144—700 yards southwest of Alzen) to (951141—1,000 yards southwest of Alzen) to (947141—1,200 yards southwest of Alzen). At 2000 hours, regiment reports that the enemy, including an element of the German Combat Engineer School, is defending in dug-in, log-covered positions and that weather and terrain are extremely difficult.

Gen. Craig visits the 39th CP at 2225 hours. Command post tents are equipped with M1941 US Army Tent Stoves for warmth. The simple but effective steel potbelly stoves burn wood or coal and turn orange when they are really humming. Given that American soldiers consume 32.5 pounds of coffee per trooper per year, and the Army Quartermaster Corps is in the coffee-production and transportation business, numerous coffeepots sit on top of the stoves for a hot "cup o' Joe" on a cold evening.[93] But where Mac MacLean is on this frigid night, there won't be any hot *Kaffee* in a warm tent.

SCHOOL OF THE SOLDIER

GLENN MILLER

The day before the Battle of the Bulge is a day the music dies, when a Noorduyn single-engine UC-64A Norseman—bound from Twinwood airfield in Bedfordshire, England, to France—goes missing over the English Channel. Aboard the aircraft is Major (and famed big-band leader) Glenn Miller, who has just delivered a hangar concert at RAF Kings Cliffe, England, and is scheduled to fly to Paris for a series of shows for those lucky frontline troops there for a few days on "R&R" (rest and recreation).

In 1942, desiring to contribute to the war effort, Miller petitioned the Navy for a position in the reserves. For some inexplicable reason, the Navy turned him down and Miller tried the Army, writing to Gen. Charles Young in Washington, DC, in August 1942: "I should like to go into the Army if I could be placed in charge of a modernized army band. I feel that I could really do a job for the Army in the field of modern music."[94] In the easiest decision of the war, the Army sends a telegram to the most famous musician in America (a small detail the Navy had apparently overlooked)—accepting his offer. For many GIs overseas, and millions of Americans back home, Glenn Miller's music—especially his famous hit "In the Mood"—is the sound of World War II. His influence crosses oceans; as the biggest star of the Big Band era, he is the greatest recording artist in the world, now mourned throughout the country.

The wreckage of the aircraft is never found. German intelligence agents spread lies that Miller died of a heart attack in a Paris brothel. Theories of the disappearance run rampant until 2014, when a plausible fate surfaces that because of the altitude at which the aircraft was flying, the fuel intakes froze, causing the engine to swiftly die and the plane to plummet into the Channel 30 miles south of Portland Bill, Dorset, before any "Mayday" signal (the internationally recognized SOS to indicate distress) could be sent.

HEY, JOE. WHADDYA KNOW?

Before the start of the German Ardennes offensive, a rough Waffen-SS officer, Otto Skorzeny, assembles a group of English-speaking commandos who will wear American uniforms, infiltrate US lines, and cause general mayhem and destruction in the rear area. Skorzeny is a tough man. Austrian, he sports cruel scars on his cheeks, resulting from fifteen bouts of university fraternity saber-dueling matches, in which the objective is not to avoid getting struck, but rather not to show pain or fear after getting your face slashed—by a very sharp saber.[95] Fluent in English, Skorzeny rescued deposed Italian dictator Benito Mussolini from his captors in 1943 on the rugged Gran Sasso mountain plateau in Italy.

Key to infiltrating is to use American passwords to fool checkpoints and outposts. And if American soldiers had stuck with official challenge and response passwords, Skorzeny might have pulled it off. The challenge and password come down from higher headquarters, changing every day. The intent is for the challenge—the word you first say to an approaching person—to have nothing to do with the correct response—the password that the approaching soldier replies. Thus, if "banana" is the challenge, "split" will not be the response, since an English-speaking German might be able to guess that.

The challenge and response cannot be complicated, because every American soldier must memorize them. Not every company, battalion, and regiment can have its own password, or there would be too many to memorize, so the Germans need find only a few, and these will work. But the Germans go further. They will ask American POWs what the password and challenge are, and if the Germans get rough, they may find out. Some soldiers—never thinking they will be captured—write the challenge and password on a small piece of paper put in their wallet, just in case they forget. And of course, the Germans will find that small scrap of paper. And since the front has been static, the Germans often put concealed listening posts close to American outposts so they may be able to eavesdrop and overhear passwords.

So almost at the same critical time, across a 60-mile-wide front, without being ordered to do so, GIs take the initiative and start asking questions at checkpoints—above and beyond the challenge and password. When an unfamiliar soldier approaches their position, a GI might yell: "Hey, Joe. Whaddya know?" And since they know Les Brown's 1941 hit song "Joltin' Joe DiMaggio," they are expecting the approaching soldier to reply with that song name—unless you're from Texas and you refer to Tex Beneke's song "Whatcha Know Joe." Or they might ask: "What pro football team plays in Chicago?" And the correct reply would be either the Bears or the Cardinals. Who plays "One O'Clock Jump"? Count Basie is your answer.

During a postwar interview with the *Washington Post*, Omar Bradley recalled his own experiences with these questions:[96] "The first time by identifying Springfield as the capital of Illinois; the second by locating the guard between the center and the tackle on a line of scrimmage; the third time by naming the then-current spouse of a blonde named Betty Grable." So, if a stranger starts giving the wrong answers to questions—well, itchy fingers start slowly moving toward triggers or lightly touch the pin on a hand grenade—just in case.

SPAM

What Mac didn't say was that John's chopped ham was probably a little too close to Spam for comfort, and that culinary "delicacy" probably deserves its own introduction about now. The Hormel Company introduces Spam canned meat on July 5, 1937, to increase the sale of pork shoulder, not considered by the public to be a choice cut of meat. Popular belief has it that the name was an abbreviation of spiced ham, but GIs aren't buying that baloney. Instead, they refer to the never-popular food as "ham that didn't pass its physical," or "Special Army Meat," and the ever-popular "meatloaf without basic training." But these insulting terms do not hinder the US military from procuring 75,000 tons of Spam by war's end. Prorated for every service member, that amounts to over 12 pounds per trooper, a truly nauseating thought. Spam's chief advantages are affordability, accessibility, and extended shelf life; it needs no refrigeration.

And in all honesty, Spam assists many foreign countries afflicted with natural disasters. Canned Vienna sausages also occasionally appear on the *menu du jour*. But as one soldier writes home: "Never mention them to me when I get back!"[97]

CONTINENTAL STOCKADE

Frank Pemberton arrives at the Loire Disciplinary Training Center (DTC) at Le Mans, France, just in time to see Army master sergeant John C. Woods hang general prisoner James W. Twiggs for the crime of murder. Pemberton is lucky he isn't executed for desertion, but life is going to get really difficult nonetheless. Known to many GIs as the "Continental Stockade," the Loire DTC is a rough place because it has rough inmates, some 1,600 by the time Pemberton shuffles through the gate in handcuffs and leg irons. The Army believes that anything easier might lead many soldiers to ride out the war in the safety of the rear, rather than face the rigors of combat.

Stockade administration ensures that each prisoner works eight hours per weekday, three hours of which consists of hard labor. These jailbirds also participate in thirty minutes of physical training and thirty more minutes of close-order drill every weekday. Soldiers live in two-man pup tents; the center administration works in red-brick buildings. During fights, military police tear-gas the warring parties. Often unable to determine who hit whom first, guards employ mass punishment to discourage bad behavior, including exposure to freezing weather on a windy hill, or squeezing up to fifteen men in a 6-by-10-foot "hole"—until everyone gets the message.

In one instance, inmates burn their army blankets—so they sleep in their uniforms without blankets, outside, until the supply system gets around to issuing new ones, which ain't that high a priority on anyone's list, pal.[98] Finally, many of the MPs assigned at the DTC are "big city" cops—guys you wish you had never met. They carry 22-inch-long, lead-weighted, hard ash wood batons, and these MP sergeants are more than willing to beat a version of "Drum Boogie" on your noggin that would make jazz drummer Gene Krupa proud.

BARBED WIRE

Sometimes the simplest weapons are the most effective, and barbed wire is certainly both. It will not kill you—not even seriously wound you. But if emplaced thick enough, it can delay, and sometimes stop, advancing enemy troops. Barbed-wire obstacles can be made by stretching lengths of barbed wire between stakes of wood or iron. Termed a single-apron fence, it can be breached with wire cutters, satchel charges, or Bangalore torpedoes. A double-apron barbed-wire fence is composed of a line of pickets with wires running diagonally to stakes on the ground on either side of the fence. Horizontal wires are attached to these diagonals; this type of fence is harder to breach but takes more time to emplace.

By the Great War, soldiers also had barbed wire in loose concertinas. The beauty of concertina is that it can be employed quickly; the rolls of wire are packed flat for ease of transport and then can be deployed as an obstacle pretty quickly; a platoon of experienced soldiers can deploy a single concertina barrier at a rate of hundreds of yards per hour. Naturally, the Germans take barbed wire a step further. In the 1930s, Horst Dannert produces oil-tempered concertina wire from high-grade steel, which makes it able to stand upright without support stakes. With Dannert wire, one soldier can deploy a 15-meter barrier by himself. Germans often stretch two rolls of concertina on the ground next to each other, with a third roll on top.[99]

A nasty obstacle is tanglefoot—consisting of metal engineer stakes driven into the ground in a grid pattern 4 to 6 feet apart, with 12 inches of each stake sticking above ground. The defenders then wind barbed wire around the stakes and crisscross the strands. An attacker facing tanglefoot must slow and start high-stepping or his feet will get tangled in the wire, causing him to fall down—hence the name "tanglefoot." In winter, snow often hides tanglefoot, and your first indication of it is when you trip and fall down face first. American soldiers often affix empty C-ration cans to their own barbed wire, then putting a few small stones in the cans. When an enemy soldier touches the wire, the cans bounce, creating a rattle—an easy form of early warning. Regardless of barbed-wire type, effective defensive fire must cover the obstacle, or the enemy will quickly clear the barrier. With defensive cover fire, barbed wire can trap men who are machine-gunned before they can escape.

FRUITCAKE

The immortal fruitcake. Every mother believes that her son loves her recipe, and every son is more than happy to share the dessert not only with his foxhole buddy, but with anyone else in the platoon who cares for a piece—leaving very little for him, but allowing him to fib with a straight face in his next letter: "The guys loved it, Mom." The Germans are amazed that the Americans will devote precious fuel and transportation resources to send the brick-heavy desserts halfway around the world.

There are midwestern-style fruitcakes, and southern fruitcakes, and hundreds of others simply called "Grandma's fruitcake." All last for ages and are the butt of endless jokes. The soldier may not relish Mom's fruitcake, but he knows his buddies are not going to say anything bad about it. And if nothing else, the arrival of a fruitcake is proof positive that someone back home loves you and cares about you enough to skimp together rationed items and take many hours to turn that into some little treasure she hopes you will enjoy.

VICTORY MAIL

Victory mail, popularly called "V-mail," is a valuable tool for the US military to reduce space required for mail on valuable cargo ships, increasing space for war materials. By microfilming specially designed letter sheets, instead of using whole letters, for example, a single V-mail sack can replace thirty-seven mail bags required to carry 150,000 one-page traditional letters—a move that reduces the weight of that same amount of mail from 2,575 pounds to only 45.

These V-mails are based on special letter sheets, a combination of letter and envelope, and the author writes the message in a limited space on the sheets, constructed and gummed so as to fold into a distinctively marked envelope. The sender then adds the name and address of the recipient, folds the form, affixes postage if necessary (usually not), and mails the letter. At special postal centers, V-mail correspondence is photographed to thumbnail size on microfilm. The rolls of microfilm are sent to prescribed destinations for development near the addressee. At these locations, the images of the letter sheets are reproduced about one-quarter original size, and the miniature mail is delivered.

Between June 15, 1942, and April 1, 1945, some 556,513,795 pieces of V-mail are sent from the US to military post offices, and more than 510 million pieces are received back home from military personnel abroad. The huge amount of letters home comes, in part, because so many troopers—who on the outside portray themselves as Romeos in uniform—are actually desperate not to join the "Brush-Off Club" (also called the "Ex-Darling Club") of guys dumped by their girlfriends. Regular mail continues, but V-mail lessons transportation requirements.[100] Now, if V-mail can only miniaturize a fruitcake.

CHAPTER SEVEN

Mac's War Stalag VI G

The first time you quit, it's hard. The second time, it gets easier. The third time, you don't even have to think about it.
—Paul "Bear" Bryant, Alabama head football coach

Mac regains consciousness and sees a German soldier pointing a rifle down at his face. His head hurts and is wet with blood. Although painful, the wound doesn't appear to be serious, probably from German potato-masher shrapnel. Enemy troopers march him a few miles east through the snow to the German rear. Exhausted, cold, and hungry, he is led into a dugout; a German major enters. Mac knows little, hoping at least that Jay Lavinsky has not been captured with him, because it probably would not go well for the Jewish soldier. He knows that a month ago, the Nazis murdered almost a hundred American prisoners of war at Malmedy, Belgium, just a few miles away. Rumors say that the Krauts may have killed a few hundred more. Those guys were Waffen-SS, and these guys are army, but they are German.

Prior to asking him a few basic interrogation questions—the Germans are well aware that privates know little of value—the major examines Mac's dog tag; the German now knows he is Protestant and had a tetanus shot in both 1943 and 1944. MacLean's shot records must have been lost—dumb Americans—and he got an extra double load of the injections. The major also knows the address of Mac's next of kin from the tag and can assume that is Mac's address as well. The major speaks excellent English and informs Mac that he visited Peoria in 1936 as a businessman and tells him that the address, St. James Street, is quite close to Bradley.

Mac shudders; his mom's house is less than 100 yards from campus. The officer then asks the scared American if there is still a house of ill repute in Peoria on Adams Street. Quaking inside, Mac does not think that cathouses are national secrets, but does not answer; he now believes that the Germans know everything about Peoria. Mac also decides not to tell the German that two grandparents were German. Who knows how the Krauts would react to that, and better not to find out. But Mac does know that if he can just hang on one day at a time, survive, and not quit, he can make it to the end of the war, no matter how long that takes.

The interview ends. When the major departs, a German soldier indicates that he wants Mac's new waterproof boots. With nothing to be gained but a rifle butt to the teeth, or a bullet to the head, Mac surrenders the boots. In return, he receives a pair of Dutch wooden shoes. The clogs are said to maintain warmth during winter, but Mac quickly finds they do not. Stuffing dirty straw into his new footwear, hoping for insulation, he soon develops frostbite.

With their latest charge sporting his brand-new size nines, the Krauts have Mac and other American prisoners unload supplies from trains and carry food from field kitchens forward. Mac assesses his predicament. He is alive. His wound has stopped bleeding and is not life threatening. Minus his boots and helmet, which probably flew off when he was hit, his rifle and bayonet are long gone. Mac sees no opportunity to escape. He does not know the other American prisoners, who are forbidden to talk with one another.

Mac does not know where he is, but had he seen a German railway map, he would see he is now in the small town of Hellenthal. He hears the rumbling of artillery to the west; he is only 6 miles from American forces in the dense Schleiden Forest. Mac does not speak German; he took Spanish in high school and might barely be able to order a meal in a Mexican restaurant. On February 2, 1945, the Germans truck the Americans to Euskirchen—a large village about 20 miles east of Nideggen—where he is held with a few other POWs in the city jail. This is not the first time that Euskirchen has held prisoners; in 1942 the Nazis operated a collection site for Jews here, who were then sent to the Theresienstadt concentration camp.

During the ride, there is no opportunity for Mac to escape, and the people of Euskirchen are not going out of their way to be charitable to their American guests. They couldn't really be blamed. Ninth US Air Force B-26 Marauders struck a bridge at Euskirchen on December 9, 1944; a dozen B-17s of the Eighth US Air Force hit the village on December 11; two days later the B-26s were back; sixty-two B-24 Liberators bombed Euskirchen on Christmas Eve; seventy-two B-17s struck the railroad marshaling yards on December 27; and on New Year's Eve, thirty B-24s hit the rail bridge over the Erft River on the town's east side.

After five days, the Germans march the Americans by foot from Euskirchen 8 miles southeast to the Flamersheim Work Camp, outside that small village of two thousand inhabitants. About 160 Americans are already here. The next day, German ack-ack brings down an American aircraft. Two crewmen bail out of the plane, which subsequently explodes in the air; they are severely burned, but there are no German medical personnel in the camp to give first aid. American prisoners do what they can for the men, but they all will later have to walk to their POW camp. Unknown to Mac, on February 21, 1945, an officer in the Office of the Adjutant General of the War Department sends his mother a telegram: "The Secretary of War desires me to express his deep regret that your son Private First Class Myron D. MacLean has been reported Missing in Action since thirty January in Germany. If further details or other information are received, you will be promptly notified."

The next day, the War Department Adjutant General sends her a letter:

Dear Mrs. MacLean, this letter is to confirm my recent telegram in which you were regretfully informed that your son, Private First Class Myron D. MacLean, 16122373, has been reported missing in action in Germany since 30 January 1945. I know that added distress is caused by failure to receive more information or details. Therefore, I wish to assure you that at any time additional information is received, it will be transmitted to you without delay, and, if in the meantime no additional information is received, I will again communicate with you at the expiration of three months.

The term "missing in action" is used only to indicate that the whereabouts or status of an individual is not immediately known. It is not intended to convey the impression that the case is closed. I wish to emphasize that every effort is exerted continuously to clear up the status of our personnel. Under war conditions this is a difficult task as you must readily realize.

Experience has shown that many persons reported missing in action are subsequently reported as prisoners of war, but as this information is furnished by countries with which we are at war, the War Department is helpless to expedite such reports. The personal effects of an individual missing overseas are held by his unit for a period of time and are then sent to the Effects Quartermaster, Kansas City, Missouri, for disposition as designated by the soldier. Permit me to extend to you my heartfelt sympathy during this period of uncertainty.

Sincerely yours,

J. A. Ulio, Major General, The Adjutant General

Back in Germany, as the Allies advance toward the Rhine River, on February 24, 1945, the Germans transfer Mac and other soldiers from the Flamersheim Work Camp across the Rhine at Bonn to Stalag VI G at Hoffnungsthal (Rösrath)—some 32 miles. Established April 17, 1941, this POW camp initially holds only Polish enlisted men; many are officer candidates. Although the young Poles have a difficult time in the camp, they are more fortunate than the 22,000 Polish officers whom the Russians murdered in the Katyn Forest near Smolensk, Russia, in 1940. The Poles remain the camp's only prisoners until September 17, 1944, when other nationalities arrive. During its early history, the camp is named Arbeitskommando Nr. 281—Work Commando Number 281.[1] Located in the Königsforst (King's Forest) east of the Rhine, 8 miles southeast of Cologne, the camp is formed in a rectangle; the Wahn Luftwaffe base is 2 miles west of the camp. Mac observes German Messerschmitt Me 262 jet aircraft overhead but does not know exactly what they are—since they sound unlike any plane he has ever heard.

It is a crazy time in Cologne during the final death throes of the Reich, where the Nazis execute some 1,800 accused resistance fighters from January to March 1945, as firing squads and *Scharfrichter* (executioners) work overtime. Some officials, knowing that the fatherland will lose the war, believe their survival depends on their leniency to fellow Germans and imprisoned foreigners. Others want to take every enemy of the Reich, maybe even POWs, with them when they plunge to their own *Götterdämmerung* (catastrophic collapse), and it is impossible to know which way these officials will come down until it may be too late.

By 1945, 1,500 prisoners of various nationalities are in the camp; 177 are Americans. Air Corps first lieutenant Wallace "Wally" Boyes (0826086), from Mobile, Alabama, captured on January 28, 1945, is one of the senior American POWs; he keeps the men's morale up and looks after the injured. Wally piloted a B-17G (tail number 42-97164; nicknamed "Rebel Queen") in the 749th Bombardment Squadron, of the 457th Bombardment Group, that was hit by flak at 1430 hours that afternoon, about 24,000 feet up during a bombing mission on the Cologne rail yards; the plane crashes near the village of Weibern, west of Koblenz. Wally and his crew bail out just before. He sees the copilot, 2Lt. Elmer Felgenhauer, and bombardier, 2Lt. Merritt Turner, floating downward and hears shots from where he believes both have landed, near the village of Kempenich. Both men are declared missing and later listed as killed—possibly by civilians or local military.[2] Wally is lucky. He survives and heads to Stalag VI G.

Each one-story barrack contains prisoners of a single nationality. Some of the Poles have been here for almost six years. After the war, the Germans will convert the camp into the "Pestalozzi Children's Village" for parentless and homeless children, of which there will be many. Surrounding it is a nature preserve called the Wahner Heide, delightfully tranquil in the promotional material:

> A walk through the Wahner Heide promises an encounter with extraordinary nature and regional history. On a six-kilometer circuit, visitors can gather a variety of impressions and, at the end, also take a break in the "Bambi" beer garden.... The Wahner Heide offers bogs, ponds, sand dunes and heath areas, pine forests, and swampy terrain with birch trees. It is a nature reserve that provides a habitat for a large number of animals and plants.

But not in 1945. In 1945, there are no beer gardens, and Bambi was killed and eaten long ago, but there are, indeed, a large number of animals—called body lice. Inside the barracks are hard wooden bunk beds, but no mattresses; two or three prisoners crowd together in bunks made for one man. It is a tight squeeze at the start of confinement, but in a wicked way, as prisoners shed weight during captivity, they actually gain more room. The bottom bunk is about 18 inches off the ground, and 22 inches above that is the top bunk; thus, the prisoners on the bottom cannot sit upright. There is at least one woodburning heater per building; every 5 feet is a window. Unsanitary latrines are in separate buildings. Locked in the barracks at night, the men can visit latrines only during daylight—causing obvious problems, especially with the rampant dysentery. At night, the men use a communal bucket. Sometimes there is toilet paper.

There can be 160 prisoners per barracks; each barracks has a senior prisoner whom the Germans refer to as the company leader. A large, white, multistory building—the camp headquarters—is outside a barbed-wire fence; inside the wire are eighteen structures—prisoner barracks and security buildings. In the center of the compound, an aboveground, open-top cistern 5 feet deep holds water for firefighting. In 1942–43, the Royal Air Force accidentally dropped firebombs on the camp. That could happen again.

Multiple 20-foot-high watchtowers, each with two to three guards armed with a machine gun, ring the perimeter. Guard dogs, big and well fed, snarl and snap at nearby POWs. Each morning, German sergeants enter the barracks, screaming, "Raus, Raus" (Out! Out!) to wake the men for morning roll-call formation, held adjacent to the water cistern—rain or shine—in an open square the Krauts call the Appellplatz (Roll-Call Place). While the prisoners stand *Appell* formation twice a day, guards check the barracks for contraband and signs of an escape attempt. Through early 1944, guards came from the 9th Land Protection Battalion; by 1945, they have been replaced by fifty to sixty men from an army light-truck column.

Prisoners work outside the camp in vegetable gardens, others cut wood in the forest, and still others march to civilian farms to assist in the planting of crops, since it is turning spring. Prisoners try to smuggle an occasional sugar beet, potato, or turnip if they can hide it. This late in the war, the guards are getting nervous about the outcome and will not shoot men bringing a turnip in; they will, however, shoot anyone trying to escape. Other prisoner details use horse-drawn carts to transport garbage and latrine waste outside the camp. The carts are called "honey wagons," a joke concerning their noxious odor.[3]

The prisoners, too weak from hunger and disease to try to escape, know they are in Germany but have no info about what lies outside the wire. If you decide to blow the place, you might get shot or have to outrun a big dog for a really long way—and you'll have no disguise, no compass, no money, and no map. Moreover, a story circulates that one night back in January, the Krauts caught a fleeing prisoner, poured water over him, and tied him to a post outside his barracks—where he froze to death.

Deadly disease is rampant, including tuberculosis, dysentery, and typhus. Just over 30 percent of the prisoners are sick. Almost all constantly itch from lice. If you see small bands of white anywhere on your clothes, those are hundreds of lice eggs.[4] In 1943, the camp faces an epidemic of jaundice; in early 1945, diarrhea is rampant. Food is meager. But there is something even worse. Many non-American POWs just give up and lose their will to live, despite the fact that American GIs, fluent in Polish or Russian, try to convince them that the war will be over soon, and the Nazis will be defeated. Mac tries to communicate by showing his wristwatch to a Russian prisoner, who had pointed to it, since the Russian does not know what it is.

Some sit outside in the cold near the fences, staring straight ahead, oblivious to dogs that snarl and lunge at them. Refusing to eat the meager scraps of food, they are silent; no noise, no complaining, no crying—just sitting and waiting to die. Guards don't shoot them; why waste a bullet? Soon, their weak bodies cannot sit upright, and in their own filth of diarrhea, they roll over on the cold ground and die. Work details place the emaciated corpses on horse-drawn wagons, taking them outside the camp for burial; no markers with a man's name, no keepsake to send to his family—he just disappears off the face of the earth. Because he quit.

Mac believes that there is a chance the Russians will get to the camp and liberate it. He finds a small pencil and scrap of paper and asks his Russian-speaking friends in the barracks the Russian words for various foodstuffs. He is not wild when discovering that borscht may be a staple on the menu, but he is not going to quit like the men sitting silently near the fences. On March 2, 1945, the British, in a rare daylight raid, launch 858 aircraft—including 531 heavy Avro Lancaster bombers—against Cologne. Pathfinders mark the target, and observers in de Havilland Mosquito aircraft conclude that the raid was "highly destructive."[5] Because it's a daylight raid, the prisoners cannot see the explosions, but they hear the rumble.

While Mac is in Stalag VI G, on March 22, from "Somewhere in Germany," Bob Pettigrew writes a letter to Mac's mom in Peoria. Technically, the men are not allowed to write to the families of soldiers, who become casualties, until after the War Department conducts official notifications. However, the guys in your squad know a lot more about your family than Washington ever will, and countless soldiers make verbal agreements with their buddies to "let Mom know what happened":

> Dear Mrs. MacLean, I really don't know how to start this letter or introduce myself to you. I was with your son Myron for a while; at least we were buddies and slept, ate, and stuck pretty much to one another. I don't know if you were advised of his whereabouts, but since the beginning of February, he is a prisoner of war somewhere in Germany. I was one of the last to see him right before he was captured, and I am sure when I last saw him, he was alright [sic]. I know this must be quite a shock to you, but I just had to tell you and get it off my mind. Bob Pettigrew. PS. Received all of Mac's packages and distributed them to the rest of the boys.

Unbeknown to Mac or his mother, help is on the way, and the modern-day cavalry is coming. In a billeting area near the village of Beaunay, Normandy, the 46th Tank Battalion, of the Thirteenth US Armored Division, receives orders on March 15 to move 300 miles east to Avricourt, France, and wait in reserve as units of Seventh US Army cross the Rhine. Task Force (TF) Delnore—named for Lt. Col. Victor Delnore, commander of the 46th Tank Battalion, a thirty-two-year-old officer born in Kingston, Jamaica, to Lebanese parents who later immigrated to the United States—is about to saddle up and ride.[6]

The TF receives Company C of the 67th Armored Infantry Battalion; in return, Companies A, B, and D depart to other units. With the addition of the infantry, the task force should be able to defeat any array of enemy forces it might encounter. On April 1, Lt. Col. Delnore is ordered to move to Kirchberg-Simmern, 20 miles west of the Rhine, to help control displaced-persons camps filled with Poles and Russians.[7] On April 5, the provost marshal general of the US Army sends Grace MacLean a telegram confirming Bob Pettigrew's information:[8]

Following enemy propaganda broadcast from Germany has been intercepted, "Safe and well in a German prisoner of war camp SGT Myron D. MacLean 16122373." Pending further confirmation this report does not establish his status as a prisoner of war. Additional information received will be furnished.

Meanwhile, on April 6, TF Delnore begins a move that will not only burn daylight but darn near consume a regiment's worth of gas. Now assigned to the Third Army, the task force races from Simmern, crosses the Rhine, continues to Alsfeld, and advances northeast to the village of Beiseförth—some 174 miles. Deep in Germany, Lt. Col. Delnore now is ordered to turn around and head west to Altenkirchen—adding another 130 miles to their tanks' odometers—where he will report to the First Army.[9]

The gasoline cowboys are in a race against time. Disease and starvation at Stalag VI G kill two French prisoners on March 28, while the Russians are dropping like flies. Another Frenchman dies on April 4, and still another expires on April 6. Whatever the illness is—and it looks like typhus—it is killing guys quickly. Mac is certain that he received a typhus shot back in the States but recalls something about a booster every six months, and that book is way overdue. And because the men sleep in the same bunks, when one man becomes ill, all will get sick. Almost as bad, Mac sees that his louse-ridden uniform is drooping on him, since he is dropping weight every day—a lot of weight. But he's still alive, and that's what counts.

Early in the war, the German military running the camps for Western prisoners devises a ration system that will keep Allied prisoners alive on the cheap. To that end, each Anglo-American POW receives 9 pounds of potatoes per week, augmented by 5 pounds of bread and 2½ pounds of cabbage. Supplemental rations include 7 ounces of sausage and small amounts of sugar and salt. That was then.

Now, POWs do not remember receiving that much, primarily because they didn't receive that much. Russian prisoners don't count—they are considered subhuman ideological enemies and starve by the tens of thousands, since they receive mere scraps—over three million Russian POWs die during the war. By 1945, the Germans can no longer prevent the prisoners from slowly starving, since they now receive just two meals a day—thin soup with some cabbage, and black bread, which seems fortified with sawdust—and sometimes have a thin fake coffee that tastes like it was made from charred acorns—which it is.

Although Red Cross parcels arrived in German POW camps early in the war, by 1945 these have stopped. The prisoners add dandelions to the soup; while the plant can enhance digestion and can serve as a mild laxative, it has almost no calories, and that is what the men desperately need. Everybody seems to have dysentery. Mac recalls never having a hot shower at Stalag VI G, which perhaps could have killed the rampant body lice. The Germans did, albeit infrequently, have the prisoners stand naked outside in the open, where they are hosed down with frigid water from fire hoses. The men cower in the cold; of course, there is no soap. Even worse, afterward they must put on their same dirty, flea-ridden uniforms. Fleas bite, causing intense itching. Because the men are always dirty, their scratching causes the bites to blister and fill with pus, which then itches some more; day after day—night after night.

Task Force Delnore rolls into Altenkirchen late on April 9, having driven the past two days and nights without sleep. The unit is ordered to move 10 miles north to cross the Sieg River at Hennef, receiving additional combat elements including the 1st Platoon of Company A of the 124th Armored Engineer Battalion, and a platoon of 90 mm M36 tank destroyers from the 630th Tank Destroyer Battalion—just in case they run into German King Tiger tanks.[10] They attack north on April 10. Near the village of Diessem, German 88 mm antitank and 20 mm antiaircraft guns hammer the task force, knocking out several tanks, but worse—killing two soldiers and wounding another twenty-five. The attack stalls and a field artillery battalion moves into position. After a thorough artillery preparation, the next morning, the task force breaks through, continuing the attack north, seizing Diessem as well as the villages of Birk, Inger, Algert, and Breidt by nightfall. On April 12, TF Delnore advances west and seizes the village of Lohmar. Stalag VI G is now only 6 miles away.[11]

No German doctors are in the camp, only a few medics to change dressings. Their bandages now are paper, not cloth. For extremity wounds, the Germans take a small board, place it next to the injured arm or leg, and wrap a bandage around both, almost ensuring that infection sets in. The wounds suppurate; every ten days the medics change the dressings. But the pus has dried, and removing the bandages often rips off a layer of skin as well.

TF Delnore liberates Mac MacLean and hundreds of other prisoners at Stalag VI G on April 13, 1945. Prisoners will recall the exact date for years, as they hear that President Franklin Roosevelt has just died. Mac is malnourished, losing 42 pounds during captivity, and now weighs under 100. As the men eat their first real meal, one prisoner, consuming too many doughnuts, falls unconscious and dies—the shock of the sugar may have been too much for his system. The camp's liberation is later recorded:[12]

As Korf and his men made their way north toward Düsseldorf, they liberated POW Camp Hoffnungsthal. They found close to 800 prisoners, 177 of whom were Americans captured during the Battle of the Bulge. Though Americans had been generally treated well at German POW camps, Hoffnungsthal marked an exception to the rule. Korf was prepared for the fact that wartime shortages could account for the poor condition of the inmates. But what he saw went beyond shortages. He described conditions as "gruesome." He learned that prisoners had been wantonly abused. An American pilot who had shattered both legs parachuting from his plane was forced to walk to the camp and denied medical treatment. They also found thirty-three cases of dysentery. The prisoners were evacuated immediately.

The next day, Mac writes a letter to his mother from somewhere in Germany:

My Dearest Mother, I'm alive and well and eating again. I prayed for strength for you often. Please do not worry about me as I am receiving wonderful treatment. . . . I will let you know when to write and what address to use. Please call Julie and let her know the news. And do not worry about me as I am in whole. God bless you and take care of you so that we may spend many moments together soon. Tell John and friends hello. Your Loving Son, Mac PS. I <u>was</u> a Prisoner of War.

On April 15, Mac begins traveling from Germany to France. The next day, he is in an Army hospital in Paris and writes another letter to his mother:

My Dearest Mother, Here I am, writing from France. My last letter written from Germany was yesterday. As you can see by my address, I'm in the hospital but I'm feeling fine. After being a prisoner for so long this chow is wonderful. The treatment by the nurses and fellows is something I'll have reason to remember forever. We have so very much to be thankful for. I know now that faith in God helped me to be here today. Faith is a very wonderful thing. I pray that you have been well, and please notify Julie that I have been recaptured. . . . Your Loving Son, Mac

Cranking out yet another letter two days later, Mac isn't waiting for the War Department but does not go into details of being wounded:

Dearest Mother, This is my fourth letter to you since my recapture. I expect that one of these days the War Department will send you the notice of my recapture but I'm writing so that you'll know ahead of time. You'll also receive my Purple Heart but don't worry about it as it was just a scratch and I'm completely healed. I'm eating once again—anything and everything that is put before me. Guess being hungry for so long makes you appreciate good food. . . . Hope these past months haven't been too hard on you. Your loving son, Mac

The following day, another letter to Mom, probably from Normandy:

My Dearest Mother, I hope you've recovered from the pleasant shock by this time. I've been eating like a horse trying to get my weight back. I lost only 42 pounds so I'm one of the lucky ones. I'll be in top shape soon so don't worry about anything. The treatment at the hospitals all the way back has been wonderful. If I didn't know better, I'd say I was in heaven. But tain't so . . . Save some beer. Your loving son, Mac

On April 20, the 195th General Hospital Center reassigns Mac and twelve other liberated prisoners from Hospital Plant #4364 to a staging area in Normandy, where more than twenty staging camps are located, in what the Army labels the "Red Horse Staging Area," while the troops call them the "Cigarette Camps." Known as "Philip Morris," "Lucky Strike," "Pall Mall," and "Old Gold," among others, thousands of tents and wooden huts house soldiers who are about to leave Europe. Lucky Strike (St. Valery, France; 45 miles from Le Havre), specializing in care of former POWs, feeds no fewer than 100,000 troops daily. On April 24, Mac receives a typhus vaccination. He and the other former prisoners receive another physical examination, and if the doctor has any doubt, the patient receives additional inoculations. A fellow 9th Infantry soldier, and a POW for several years, may hold the record for inoculations at Lucky Strike at fourteen.[13]

Nearby is a small factory that produced 50 gallons of ice cream per day. That ain't going to cut it, so US Army logistics cranks into high gear, because nothing is too good for these former prisoners. The camp becomes a veritable US town with a post exchange, movie theaters, hospitals, and gift shops, and over 12,000 tents. On arrival, the men receive hot showers and are deloused again for any little critters that still might be living rent free. After that, the men continue on a soft diet: boneless chicken, noodles, asparagus, white bread, canned peaches, and peach jam. Their instructions go something like this: "You ain't payin' for this grub so grab another helping." The itinerary might seem dull to some: eat, read, and sleep, but after their experiences over the preceding months—and sometimes years—boring peace and quiet is a welcome relief.[14]

On April 26, Jay Lavinsky writes from Hospital Plant #4178 in southwest England, where he is recuperating from his own wounds:

Dear Mrs. MacLean, I don't know quite how to start this letter as we have never met—but I am a good friend of your son. The reason I am writing this letter is to find out whether you have gotten any recent news about the whereabouts of Mac. You see I'm in the hospital now and have been corresponding with the fellows back in the company, and they asked me to write with hopes of hearing that he has been liberated in this last drive. As you must know, your son was very happy-go-lucky, and most of the fellows used to say Mac didn't realize there was a war on. When the chips were down, he was always at his best—and really was a swell soldier. Our Lieutenant was hit on one attack, and although his rifle was not working, your son went up to cover him until an aid man could be brought up.

But the Jerries snuck up and took him prisoner. But Mrs. MacLean, you do have a son to praise and be proud of. When we were on guard, he used to talk about you all and also his girl Julie and he was really proud too. Well, this is about all and I do hope you get some good news about Mac soon. If you happen to have a few spare moments I would sure appreciate it if you would drop me a line and let me know if you have gotten news of him, Best of Luck, Sincerely, Jay Lavinsky

On April 28, the adjutant general of the US Army sends Grace MacLean this telegram:

The Secretary of War desires me to inform you that your son Pfc. MacLean, Myron D. has been returned to military control on 18 April 1945. Report further states, however, that he is hospitalized, due to enemy action. New address and further information follow direct from hospital.

On May 6, Mac departs Le Havre, France—probably on USNS *John Ericsson*, carrying soldiers back to the United States. Two days later is Victory in Europe Day. Mac misses the celebration in Paris but is happy to be leaving. He didn't quit, and he survived. For the rest of his life, however, he feels that he was one of the lucky ones— given what happened to the rest of the guys in Company B from January 30, 1945, to the end of the war, when the Grim Reaper was their constant companion.

SCHOOL OF THE SOLDIER

DOG TAGS

You may not be able to teach an old dog new tricks, but you can tell a lot about that hound by his dog tag, such as his Army serial number: if it starts with a **1**, he is Regular Army, and if so the second digit indicates the Corps Area / Service Command number in the States that issued the tag (e.g., a **6** would indicate Illinois, Michigan, Wisconsin); if it starts with **20**, he is from the National Guard, and the third digit again indicates the Corps Area / Service Command number; if our pooch has a tag starting with a **3** or a **4**, he is a draftee. An officer's tag starts with the prefix **0**. Blood type (**A, B, AB,** or **O**) is on every dog tag, as is year of last tetanus shot and religion. Jewish soldiers in the European theater of operations could opt out of having an **H** for Hebrew and instead have a **P** (Protestant); Catholic soldiers have a **C**. If a German trooper ever captures an American officer with an Army serial number on his dog tag of 03822, 03807, 02686, or 02605, it will be his lucky day, and he might even get to meet the führer; the soldiers who own these dog tags are Dwight Eisenhower, Omar Bradley, Courtney Hodges, and George Patton, respectively.

MISSING IN ACTION

Missing in action (MIA) may be the most misunderstood casualty classification because it can mean several different things. A soldier initially listed MIA may have been killed, or captured by the enemy, or deserted. If captured, the soldier could also be wounded. It can be a transitory term; a soldier may initially be declared MIA, and later the enemy announces that they have the soldier as their POW. That announcement could come within a few weeks or never come. It can even occur when a gravely wounded, unconscious soldier who has lost his dog tags is evacuated to an American medical facility. If his identity is not known in the hospital, and his unit does not know what happened to him, they might list him as missing in action, even though he really isn't.

At the end of World War II, some 79,000 Americans remain unaccounted for; the bulk of them are missing in action. Many MIA have, in fact, been killed, but their remains have not been recovered. Understanding that each family must come to closure, after the war the US military waits one year after the soldier is first declared missing in action, and at that one-year mark, if no remains have been found, the War Department declares that he is deceased, in part because both Germany and Japan are occupied and thus their POW camps no longer exist. Many families do not agree with that procedure and spend decades after hostilities hoping that their loved one will one day walk through the door.

TYPHUS

One word is dreaded above all others in a German POW or concentration camp, and that word is . . . typhus. Known as epidemic typhus, or typhus fever, typhus is a lethal bacterial infection spread by lice, chiggers, and fleas. During the French army's retreat from Moscow in 1812, more of Napoleon's soldiers may have died of typhus than were killed by Russians. Typhus killed hundreds of thousands in the Great War. Fear of typus is not irrational, since perhaps 60 percent of those with epidemic typhus may perish. Areas where people are crowded together in filthy conditions are ripe for outbreaks. Typhus has already occurred at Auschwitz, Bergen-Belsen, and Majdanek concentration camps; now typhus, *Fleckfieber* in German, is raging through Stalag VI G. The bad news is that symptoms include joint and muscle pain, headaches, body-wide rashes, and a fever that can reach 106°F. Worse news is that you can suffer from low blood pressure, abdominal pain, nausea, vomiting, chills, coughing, sensitivity to light, delirium, and bleeding into the skin. And the worst news? If it gets bad enough, you die.

CHAPTER EIGHT

Dying a Man at a Time

Tell your friend that in his death, a part of you dies and goes with him. Wherever he goes, you also go. He will not be alone.

—Jiddu Krishnamurti, philosopher

On January 31, 1945, Company B is 2½ miles east-southeast of Kalterherberg. The weather is bad: a high of 25°, a low of 14°, overcast, cloudy, stormy, intermediate light snow and sleet, scattered showers later, and blowing snow. Capt. Dunlap records: "Company in 3rd Battalion Reserve during attack. Survived heavy shelling; rained all day." Caught in the steel rain, Verdun Fredendall, Hayden Johnson, Paul Akers, Pfc. Phil Frankel, Medic John Bulaski, and Pfc. John Hall are wounded as Company B remains attached to Third Battalion, which in turn is attached to the 47th Infantry to continue the attack east. One enlisted man is evacuated for nonbattle illness.

It is Verdun's second wound; shrapnel causes compound fractures in both bones of his lower arm, and over the next twelve months, doctors use bone grafts to treat him, but he will have a limited range of motion. Shrapnel hits Paul and Phil in the chest. Phil remains on duty, a long way from being at City College of New York. Shrapnel hits John Hall in the rear end and hip. Hayden has compound fractures of a tibia, fibula, and big toe smashed by artillery. He will remain in the hospital an awfully long time—until April 1946. A machine gun bullet smashes Doc Bulaski's knee; the soldier from Rhode Island will later receive a Bronze Star for heroism on this day.

The 47th Infantry reports that they are in Alzen at 0035 hours. At 0115 hours, the 15th Engineer Battalion radios that the road between Kalterherberg and the village of Höfen should be cleared of mines by morning. Second Battalion begins moving to an assembly area at 0730 hours. ~~AAA~~O establishes a new CP in Höfen at 0930 hours. At 0945 hours, Col. Bond visits the Second Battalion CP; the battalion is ready to go. Battalion relocates its CP to the eastern edge of Höfen at 1025 hours. The regiment attacks. By 1400 hours, First Battalion is 1 mile east of Alzen.[1] Victor, Vth Corps, suggests using flame-throwing tanks to increase the speed of the attack, and the scramble is on to find the nearest ones.

Second Battalion reports at 1545 hours that three attached tanks are damaged by mines; infantry have reached a line of advance in the middle of the Monschau Forest by 1620 hours. The advance slows down; at 1915 hours, Col. Bond orders First and Second Battalions to resume the attack the following morning at 0400 hours. His platoon leader dead, Langley Turner displays extraordinary gallantry rallying the platoon; he will be submitted for a Silver Star. Division *GO* #19 awards the Silver Star to Sgt. George Rosen for gallantry in action on December 27. Between December 19, 1944, and January 31, 1945, the average maximum temperature at the front is 33.5°F; the average minimum temperature is 22.6°F.[2]

After repelling enemy counterattacks lasting until 0300 hours on February 1, the regiment attacks at 0430 hours in difficult weather and seizes the key road junction of Wahlerscheid.[3] Ed Matulevich is hit in the cheek by shrapnel, his second wound. After the regiment sweeps several roads for mines, the attack continues and seizes twelve pillboxes and twenty log bunkers; shrapnel wounds Pfc. Robert Shew in the neck. Pfc. John B. Nielsen is evacuated for trench foot; Leonard Pourchot is also evacuated.[4] The weather is terrible on February 3, when the 39th receives orders to move to the vicinity of Dreiborn; it begins moving at 1530 hours. First Battalion moves into Dreiborn by truck and departs Dreiborn at 2205 hours to continue the attack into Herhahn, finding that the road between Dreiborn and Herhahn is mined. It meets stiff resistance from defenders in the houses, elements of the 277th Infantry Division, but captures eighty-seven POWs; shrapnel wounds Gilbert Miller in the right hand, but he remains at the front. Luther Wilson is recommended for the Silver Star for gallantry in action at Herhahn. 1Lt. Eugene Taylor is awarded the Oak Leaf Cluster to the Bronze Star.

At 0020 hours on February 4, enemy panzers lunge toward AAAO from the southeast; two enter Herhahn. During the night fighting, two American tank destroyers hit mines while maneuvering, as engineers try to clear lanes in the minefields. A low-flying enemy aircraft bombs and strafes the road southeast of Dreiborn. The attack then captures Morsbach, just northeast. Shrapnel tears into Pvt. Calvin Adams's right shoulder, but he remains in his platoon. George Rosen, recipient of both the Silver Star and the Bronze Star, gets his third wound, a horrible double-compound fracture with a tibia sticking through his skin, caused by artillery shrapnel. But it is worse; another piece of shrapnel perforates his colon. He is evacuated quickly, but surgeons must divert a piece of his colon to an opening in the abdominal wall; George will remain in the hospital until April—April 1946.[5] Even worse, SSgt. Ray Olive, a squad leader and Silver Star recipient, in the company since May 1943, who had contracted malaria in the Mediterranean, is hit in the chest by a German sniper's bullet and dies of his wounds.[6]

AAAO attacks at 0730 hours on February 5, with First Battalion on the right; their mission is to clear the area to the Urft River, 2 miles eastward. Battalion encounters log bunkers and scattered small-arms and artillery fire. SSgt. Sergeant Pedro Gonzalez is killed, as is Pvt. Walter S. Burke. The massive concussion of a German artillery shell kills Walter, who is posthumously awarded the Silver Star.[7] Pedro had received the CIB for combat in Sicily and had been wounded in the arm by a bullet the previous July; a nearby artillery shell kills him also.[8]

Fred Liberman; Patrick Yates; Pfcs. David Moyer, Robert Dzierga, Melvin Rutledge, Donald Stine, Raymond Rose, and Berry Honea; and Pvt. Arthur Hyman are wounded. David is a twenty-three-year-old farmhand from Duncansville, Pennsylvania, who loves to hunt and fish and maybe become a carpenter. Shrapnel wounds nineteen-year-old Robert in the mouth and arm. Hit by artillery shrapnel in the hand, Melvin is a nineteen-year-old farmhand from Toppenish, Washington; he has five brothers and arrived in the company on June 24. It is the second wound for Pat, from Memphis; a piece of artillery shrapnel causes a compound fracture of a big toe, and he'll be in a hospital till June.

Fred, a twenty-six-year-old Jewish carpenter born in Warsaw, Poland, has the CIB and Bronze Star; artillery struck his arm on September 26, and this shrapnel wound is to his fingers. Don is a twenty-two-year-old carpenter born in North Dakota; a bullet fractures his shoulder blade. A rifle bullet hits Ray in the shoulder. "Bud" Honea, a 6'1" farmhand born in Waco, Texas, has the bad luck to have artillery fragments penetrate his elbow and thigh. He will remain in the hospital for two months, as will Rose. Company B reaches their objective with one platoon at 2150 hours and halts to plan for moving across the open ground defended by elements of the 272nd Infantry and the 62nd Volksgrenadier Divisions. Patsy Jerome departs Europe on a furlough home.[9]

Still near Herhahn, on February 6, Warren Whitcombe, Carl Stock, and Pfcs. John Halpin, Howard Mosley, and Claude "Buck" Atkins are wounded. Artillery shrapnel hits Carl in the knee; it is his second wound. Buck, a tough lumberman from Shannon County, Missouri, is hit in the left hand by shrapnel but stays at the front. "Shorty" Halpin, born in the Irish Free State, arrived on October 14; today a bullet smashes his forearm. Artillery shrapnel hits nineteen-year-old Howard, from Georgia, in the heel; he arrived on October 4. Warren, injured a week ago, has artillery smash his leg, and the compound fracture will send him to the hospital through the end of the war. "Dee" Dietrich, BAR gunner in John Reiser's squad, performs gallantly and will later receive a Silver Star:[10] a BAR team often draws enemy fire and is thus frequently called a "suicide squad":

Private First Class Robert J. Dietrich . . . distinguished himself by gallantry in action against the enemy on 6 February 1945 in the vicinity of Herhahn, Germany. While his unit was in a defensive position, it was suddenly attacked by a strong enemy force. While other members of the company were hastily deploying to meet the sudden thrust, Pfc Dietrich, with total disregard for personal safety, ran ahead to an exposed position less than thirty yards from the enemy. With an automatic weapon, he fired continuously until his ammunition was exhausted, and then started hurling hand grenades. His gallant actions disrupted the enemy assault long enough for his company to organize and successfully repulse the savage attack. Devotion to duty, aggressive initiative, and the intrepidity, were reflected in all of Pfc. Dietrich's actions.

Shrapnel hits Pfc. Lewis Montague's left thigh on February 7; he stays at the front. Shrapnel hits John Reiser in the right wrist on February 8; he stays—and keeps fighting.

But the offensive stalls, and ~~AAAO~~, attached to the Second US Infantry Division from February 8 to 12, halts on high ground west of the Urft River through February 17. Chester McClurg returns to duty from his "break" at the division stockade. Every able-bodied man needs to pick up a rifle, even a jailbird.

Casualties do not stop but actually get worse. On February 9, Pfcs. John Boyle, Warren Lorio, and Harold Rinebolt are killed: Warren, when artillery shrapnel tears into his stomach; the same happens to Harold. According to Manley Fuller, the foxhole buddy of John Boyle, near Schleiden someone in the platoon shot a deer, and the word passed around for anyone who could help butcher it. John, a meat cutter in civilian life, gets out of his foxhole, promising to bring back a share of the meat, but makes it only a few feet before shrapnel hits him in the stomach—"gut-shot" in the grim parlance of the front.

Another piece of shrapnel just misses Manley's leg, as he and several other men run to Boyle. Manley says, "You'll be okay, Boyle; you'll be okay." But he and the others are lying to spare their friend, and John dies quickly. The scene descends into *Dante's Inferno*. With snow so deep that vehicles cannot get up the hill, Manley and several others attempt to use a stretcher to take Boyle's body back to the company CP. It is rough footing on the hillside, and in the struggle the body repeatedly falls off the stretcher and begins sliding downhill. The men grab the corpse, put it back on the stretcher, and continue their morbid journey.[11] The night before his death, John had received a package from home, containing Christmas cards from his two small children.

The faucet of blood, never quite drowning the unit, now averages over a casualty per day. Shrapnel wounds Pvt. Glenn Schell, from Union County, Pennsylvania, in the thigh on February 10; Manley Fuller, who watched his friend die the day before, is evacuated for a 101° fever and cough. Wounded in the hand in September by artillery fragments, today Manley is suffering something far worse. In addition to pneumonia, it is clear that Manley has battle fatigue, with the death of his foxhole buddy pushing him over the edge. At the hospital, Manley remains silent for a week, feeling that no one knows what he has experienced. They don't know about Boyle, and they don't know that near Manley's foxhole were six dead Germans that he had to step over each night. They also don't know that near him are several other Germans, killed behind a stone wall, their eyes frozen open—staring at him in death.

While at the hospital, Manley visits Paris, wandering alone down narrow streets, finally arriving at a "beer parlor with a little something else goin' on upstairs." One of the ladies gives him a knowing look and announces that she will freely sleep with him all night, but, still shaken from combat, Manley declines and spends the rest of the night by himself, lost in his thoughts, near the Eiffel Tower. Meanwhile, the Army loses track of his status and sends a telegram to his mother, Agnes, that Manley is missing in action. That snafu lasts for about a week before it's corrected, but now Agnes is depressed too.[12]

On February 11, chow in the company is good, as Jack Jewell writes: "We are having a light snow again today and it is a little colder. We have had fried chicken the last two days, and one of the boys found some flour, so we had white gravy. I hear that some are even making biscuits."[13] Pvt. Herbert Russell, from Massachusetts, is wounded. A spider bit him the previous July, but this is no arachnid gnawing on his arm. Three shell fragments penetrate his colon, as well as hitting a lumbar vertebra; Herbert will be in the hospital until December 1946.

Artillery shrapnel hits Pvt. Leo "Gus" Kossives, of Muscatine, Iowa, on February 13, penetrating his knee, thigh, and foot. Medics evacuate the son of Greek immigrants to a hospital, and although he is promptly treated, the wounds become infected, with the abscesses required to be drained for the next six months; he now faces reduced movement of his leg. St. Valentine's Day is a happy one, as five veterans return to the company from hospitals. However, Julius Kenda must be evacuated for illness, as is Herman Eichel. Artillery fragments wound Sgt. George Mavis in the hip and buttocks on February 19.[14]

The 9th Infantry is assigned to the IIIrd US Corps on February 17; AAAO is again attached to the 2nd Infantry Division and remains in positions, as shrapnel hits 1Lt. Luke Lucas in the right knee. He remains with the 1st Platoon as it is pummeled by heavy enemy artillery. The Germans aren't going down easy. Back home, Mary Seaman receives a letter from Lt. Col. Marvin Larson, commander of Hospital Plant #4272, 176th General Hospital in Normandy, that her husband, Ken, is making normal improvement in his wounded left hand.[15] AWOL Pvt. Clyde Carl is apprehended. The 3rd "Repple Depot" scours the walking wounded and sends eleven men up to the line in Company B, including Leonard Pourchot, now recovered from his wound. The company catches a break and spends the night at Dreiborn Castle, just outside Dreiborn. Out of the cold, there is one more treat—hot showers. On February 20, AAAO begins planning to be relieved in position by the 23rd Infantry of the 2nd Infantry Division. Medics evacuate Pvt. Joseph Miller for illness the next day.

The 39th begins moving at 0800 hours on February 22 by truck off the front line to assembly areas near Germeter-Vossenack, with the AAAO CP located at its old stomping ground of Germeter. It is not recorded how many men relived nightmares of the fighting from the previous October that night, but up the road at the village at Hürtgen it is a bad visage, with a field hospital and a Graves Registration section. Jack Jewell fights his own demons: dysentery. Medics treat him as best they can, and he stays with the company. Company B rests and refits, cleaning weapons and recovering abandoned equipment. Cpt Dunlap is told that the men will start receiving two Coca Colas per week; another offensive must be about to start.

On February 24, division informs regiment that it will make the initial crossing of the Roer River; the same day, Pfc. George Johnston is seriously injured and evacuated. At mail call, Luke Lucas receives a fresh apple sauce cake from his aunt and shares it with the other officers.[16] At 1850 hours on February 26, the company moves in trucks to the village of Winden, near Kreuzau, and then marches by foot to concealed assembly areas, closing at 0240 hours. The 39th launches the attack at two hours later, with First Battalion in reserve. Second Battalion in the north crosses the Roer River and advances on the farming village of Thum (about 300 inhabitants, located just northeast of Nideggen), from which it is receiving mortar fire; during the fight, Mac MacLean's high school buddy Bob Michel, in Company F, is wounded. In the south, Third Battalion crosses the Roer River and clears Nideggen by 1405 hours.

Meanwhile, First Battalion clears the woods just west of Nideggen, during which Oliver Osbourn, 3rd Squad leader in 3rd Platoon, suffers a lacerated ureter. T/5 John Schultz Jr. (land mine; foot); Pfcs. George Wolfe (shrapnel; forearm), Sidney Ewalt (shrapnel; thigh, back, pelvis, and abdomen), and Howard Miller (shrapnel; thorax); and Pvts. John Kacmar (shrapnel; toes, and abdomen), Clarence Kinney (shrapnel; leg and head), and James Shields (machine gun bullet; hip) are wounded. Schultz, Miller, Kacmar, and Shields are from Pennsylvania; James worked in a slaughterhouse in Allegheny County. Sidney and Howard will be in a hospital until November. The division's *GO #32* awards the Oak Leaf Cluster to the Silver Star to Capt. Jack Dunlap for the previous July 25.

Before the dawn's early light on February 28, the battalion advances against small-arms fire, mines, and self-propelled gunfire at the western edge of Berg, 2 miles southeast of Nideggen. Of a former population of a thousand inhabitants in Berg, just two hundred remain; 80 percent of the houses are damaged. In support is 1st Platoon, Company C, 746th Tank Battalion. Jay Lavinsky and Harry Nodell, whom Jay calls "Brooklyn," are involved in street-clearing operations. In the dark night, Jay cautiously leads part of the squad, supported by a bazooka team, down the left side of a street, when he hears German floating from a basement window and tosses a hand grenade through it. On the right side of the street, Nodell spots a German half-track and approaches it, despite a cry of alarm from Lavinsky. The vehicle machine-guns Brooklyn with a lethal burst to the neck. As other soldiers engage the enemy, Jay runs to his fallen comrade and holds him in his arms, screaming, "Listen, you son of a bitch; you better not die on me!" Harry looks Jay in the face, winks, smiles, and dies in his arms. Jay will go several days before a change of clothes is available to swap for his blood-soaked uniform—drenched with the blood of his closest friend in the world.

Meanwhile, a fellow soldier checks out the basement room and reports to Lavinsky that his grenade killed five Germans—a father and mother and their three children—forever scarring the tough Philly kid. Texan Noel Waters is also killed at Berg. William Lekutis (rifle bullet; face/forehead), Phil Frankel (shrapnel; stomach), Claud Ledford (shrapnel; cheek), and Paul Akers (hand grenade; face and eye) are wounded. It is Paul's third wound; he will be in a hospital until September. William is the son of a Lithuanian steelworker in Cleveland, Ohio; it is his second wound. Phil and William are recommended for Silver Stars:[17]

> Private First Class Phil Frankel ... distinguished himself by gallantry in action against the enemy on 28 February 1945 in the vicinity of Berg, Germany.

Although wounded while protecting his Platoon's flank, Pfc Frankel voluntarily exposed himself to enemy fire to obtain aid for a wounded companion. Upon returning to the position and finding it abandoned, he directed the Medical Aid man to go back for reinforcements. Threatened by a numerically superior force, Pfc Frankel remained at the strategic point, delivering a heavy volume of fire at the enemy until relieved by the arrival of the supporting riflemen. His devotion to duty, aggressive initiative, and courageous actions insured [sic] the security of the platoon's flank, contributing materially to the success of the operations.

Private First Class William T. Lekutis . . . distinguished himself by gallantry in action against the enemy on 28 February 1945 in the vicinity of Berg, Germany. While protecting his platoon's flank, Pfc Lekutis's position was subjected to intense enemy fire and attacked by a numerically superior enemy force. Although seriously wounded, he continued to direct a heavy volume of fire against the hostile force. With complete disregard for his personal safety, he stayed in the exposed position, firing his BAR until captured by several Germans who had managed to creep up behind his position. His devotion to duty, aggressive initiative, and courageous actions were instrumental in securing his platoon's flank, contributing materially to the success of the defensive operations.

William does not remain a prisoner and is evacuated to a hospital. February turns to March, and back home, newspapers trumpet that the war will be over soon. But in Germany, the devil's meat grinder continues to slice and dice Company B. On March 1, First Battalion launches a 0600-hour attack and captures Thuir, 1 mile north of Berg, by 0625 hours. Edward Matulevich is evacuated for frostbitten feet. The company heads northeast toward the villages of Müddersheim, Disternich, and Sievernich, arriving at Disternich at 1800 hours.

On March 2, the battalion rolls into Niederberg, 4 miles east of Disternich, but the attack is bloody. Merl Benton, Buck Atkins, Pfc. Richard Rapuano, and Walter Frueauf, as well as Privates James Ballard, William Brady, and Walter Shafron, are wounded. Shrapnel hits Merl in the right forearm, his second wound, but he remains with the company. Buck is evacuated for shrapnel to his face. Shrapnel hits Richard in the leg; he will be in a hospital until October. This is the second wound for Walter; today, artillery shrapnel causes a compound fracture of his forearm, almost snapping it in two. Shrapnel strikes Ballard and Brady in the face, and Shafron in the hand. Vallis Alexander, Frank Branchfield, and Billie Flowers are evacuated for nonbattle disease, Billie with trench foot.

March 3 in Lommersum is even worse. A bullet wound to the head kills T/5 Bill Kelley, former president of his high school class and now company clerk.[18] Shrapnel strikes TSgt. Leonard Ellsworth in the face, but he stays in the unit; he had been wounded in the back and neck by artillery shrapnel last August 9. Sgt. Robert Mathies (artillery shell explosion; concussion), John Gerbliss (blast effects; skull and vertebrae), Calvin Adams (artillery shrapnel; stomach, groin, hip, and butt), John Kalinowski (artillery shrapnel; hip and butt), and William Gordon (artillery shrapnel; thigh), as well as Pfcs. Albert McCamey (artillery shrapnel; thigh), Henry Ambrose (artillery shrapnel; face and mouth), and George Reber, are casualties. Calvin remains in the hospital until February 1946.

A tank platoon, Company C, 746th Tank Battalion, knocks out two 88s near the Swist River.[19] James Millar is injured and Robert Shew is evacuated for shrapnel wounds; it is his first day back at the front from a previous wound. It is also the second wound for Gerbliss, Kalinowski, and Gordon. George Reber, wounded last August 4 in the neck by artillery shrapnel, today has artillery shrapnel break his fibula, causing a compound fracture and sending him to the hospital for over six months; despite several skin grafts, his leg will remain scarred and disfigured.

It is raining, with light snow and clouds, and visibility is poor on March 4. Company C crosses a stream at 0110 hours with little opposition; Company A moves down the main road toward Derkum, receiving machine gun fire at 0255 hours. Company B crosses the Erft canal and captures the railroad station at Ottenheim (352346). By 0650 hours, they have eliminated all resistance, but long-range artillery fire begins falling at 0924 hours. Two enemy tanks approach Company B but then withdraw. Jay Lavinsky's luck runs out near Derkum, as machine gun rounds strike him in the stomach, lower back, groin, and pelvis; both legs; and a foot. A medic considers giving Jay enough morphine to put him out of his misery, since he obviously is dying, but instead Jay is evacuated to hospitals in the Netherlands, England, and finally to the US. It is a true "Statue of Liberty" wound.[20]

Kansan Pfc. Alan Bauer is killed; Pfc. Raymond Wahlstrom dies of wounds in the same fight. Alan arrived in the company October 17, Raymond three days later. Sgt. John Hill, Cpl. Marvin Smith, Pfc. Joseph Koziol, and Ralph Hughes are wounded, the third for Ralph, hit by artillery shrapnel in the fingers; Joseph arrived in the company on January 3. He is another 521–basic and has completed basic training but little more. Shrapnel hits Marvin in the shoulder; he'll be in the hospital for two months. Artillery shrapnel hits John's hip; he'll stay in the hospital through June. Wira Jones, who had arrived in the company on August 16, is injured. West Virginian Pfc. Basil "Buster" Chamberlain and Pfc. Johan Tanem are evacuated for nonbattle illnesses. Johan, a 675–messenger, had been awarded a Bronze Star on August 12, 1944.

The company returns to Lommersum on March 5. Edward Pickard, Charles Mayer, and Paul Sullivan are evacuated for nonbattle disease. Paul arrived at the company on October 11. By March 6, the regiment captures the villages of Strassfeld and Ollheim and fifty-two POWs, as cool, rainy weather continues. 2Lt. Charles Wieland hurts his back but remains on the line. Division slams fourteen men from 3rd Replacement Depot into the company to try to stem the bleeding, including Pvt. Vasilios Mantos, a thirty-one-year-old born in Kastoria, Greece, who until a year ago had been a furrier on Sixth Avenue in New York City.

March 7 is rainy; First Battalion—including the fourteen rookies—as regimental reserve, jumps on half-tracks and tank destroyers and moves at 1500 hours toward Ippendorf, a suburb of Bonn, where 3rd Platoon seizes the village at midnight. Pvt. Charles Finerd is evacuated for a nonbattle illness. It's still raining on March 8, and Second Battalion attacks into Bad Godesberg, capturing Lieutenant General Richard Schimpf, commander of the 3rd Fallschirmjäger Division, and most of his staff. The battalion captures 263 POWs and two 88 mm guns. On March 9, Bull Eckardt is evacuated for a nonbattle illness.

On March 10, Capt. Jack Dunlap is diagnosed with pityriasis versicolor, a fungal skin infection, and evacuated; Capt. Leroy Floriano, from the battalion headquarters company, assumes command, as AAAO moves out from Villip to rejoin the division.[21] Lee had won the Silver Star the year before in the Forty-Fifth US Infantry Division. Leonard Ellsworth is sent on furlough to Fort Dix; the twenty-nine-year-old-soldier from New York entered the Army on May 16, 1942, and had been wounded twice. Crossing the Ludendorff Bridge over the Rhine River on March 10 at Remagen, Company B goes into hasty assembly areas. On the perilous crossing, the attached tank platoon reports that "enemy artillery fire was heavy on the bridge." Hawk DiRisio added:

When crossing the bridge, enemy shells ripped over and under our kitchen truck. When a shell hit the girders, it was like lightning had struck. The driver had to be careful he didn't run the wheels into the open holes in the bridge's floor. When we got to the end, we found a captain and his driver in a jeep burning like an inferno, a direct hit. Death was instant for them. The driver had to squeeze the truck between the girders and that burning jeep.

With consummate understatement, Capt. Floriano notes on the morning report that "the bridge was under shell fire and being bombed while crossing it." 3rd Platoon has no vehicles and must hoof it as fast as possible across the 1,306-foot-long span, avoiding 30-inch shell holes on the bridge's surface. Bodies of dead Germans have been squashed flat by American tanks racing across. It was no time for lollygagging, as Phil Holman recalled:

The thought running through my head as we took off across the bridge, dodging shell holes and seeing the water through the gaps in the timbers, had to do with, wow, here I go and who is going to come and help me on the other side. We knew that the Germans would mount large counter attacks since they had to keep us from breaking through their lines. They had to destroy the bridge. Well, that dash was probably the bravest thing I did during the war, knowing that I probably would not make it back. The shells were falling, and the aircraft were trying to bomb the bridge. We reached the other side, and the carnage was terrible. I can remember seeing a burning jeep with the driver still in it as we turned south after crossing the bridge.

For nine days, 367 Luftwaffe soties, including Messerschmitt Me 262 jets and Arado Ar 234B-2 turbojet bombers, try to destroy the bridge—followed by underwater frogmen with explosives, but these too fail. The Wehrmacht then brings out the really big guns—a 600 mm Karl siege howitzer and 380 mm railroad guns—and even fires V2 missiles at the bridge. But enough American troops cross before the bridge finally collapses on March 17. Battalion occupies Bruchhausen, northeast of the bridge, by 2152 hours. Casualties are light. Al DiRisio describes the town:[22] "I was instructed to set up the kitchen, of all places, dead center in a glass bottle factory. There were hundreds of crates of glass bottles stacked high all around my kitchen. If a bomb hits that building, forget it! By this time, I was a nervous wreck, and the food probably tasted like it."

~~AAA~~O is attached to the Seventy-Eighth US Infantry Division on March 11. First Battalion moves from Bruchhausen at 1330 hours to a new assembly area, where it is attacked by artillery and small-arms fire. Shrapnel strikes James Lombardi in the face; evacuated for nonbattle illness are Herman Eichel and Pvt. Marshall Taylor. Once you have frostbitten feet, it returns again and again like a bad in-law. On March 12 at 0445 hours, the enemy attacks First Battalion, and soon small-arms fire pins down Company A, along with artillery and mortar fire. Company B attempts to move around to the right; Pfc. William Uveges, a welder from Elizabeth, Pennsylvania, and Junior Bradshaw are killed; artillery shrapnel wounds Bert Jones in the thigh, while the flying metal hits Spanish-born Pfc. Charles Rojo in the wrist. Shrapnel also wounds Pvt. Rex Duvall, a North Carolina farmer, causing a compound fracture of a femur so devastating he will remain in a hospital for twelve months. Phil Holman saw Junior fall:[23]

We had just come up out of a ravine, to a plateau and saw that we were in trouble, hitting the ground about the same time a direct-fire weapon, I think it was an 88 mm, hit on Bradshaw's right, killing him, and sending me back into the ravine. When the shell exploded, it sounded like a giant hammer hitting a flat rock.

The 88's fragments rip into Junior's shoulder and chest, instantly killing him.[24] Pvt. Glenn Smith is evacuated for a bruised knee, and Pfc. Alfred Vito is evacuated for a nonbattle injury. Charles had been wounded on July 25 and had returned to duty on October 29. Company C moves to the left, but Company A is unable to advance due to enemy self-propelled artillery fire, failing to take Himberg and Rederscheid. On March 13, the battalion attacks at 0705 hours over difficult terrain. Patrols get lost; a large firefight develops short of Kalenborn. Casualties are reported as "medium." Tell that to SSgt. Frank Falbo; Pfcs. Acie Lockwood, Melvin Myers, and Clifton Reed; and Pvts. Francis Martin and Ralph Moore.

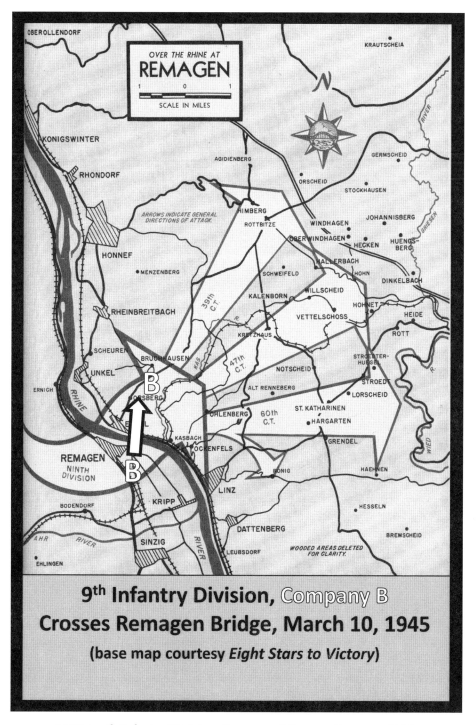

MAP 9: 9th Infantry Division, Company B Crosses Remagen Bridge, March 10, 1945

Frank, in the company since June 1941, was wounded by artillery shrapnel in Tunisia and was promoted to sergeant on June 18. Now artillery fractures his leg and rips open a shoulder. Shrapnel strikes Francis in the knee, Clifton, in the arm—it is his third wound. Ralph, hit in the hand by shrapnel, had arrived on October 4, as had Melvin; shrapnel gashes his thigh. Acie arrived on October 11. The twenty-eight-year-old from Fort Worth is an aspiring musician in Los Angeles, where he enlists in February 1944. Today, artillery shrapnel and debris smash the fiddler's face—making for a dirty wound at risk of infection. Elmer Zimmerman is evacuated for a nonbattle illness.

~~AAA~~O pushes forward with Third Battalion in the lead, but intense small-arms and self-propelled gunfire stops the attack at the line of departure. The attack resumes at 1845 hours but again encounters bitter resistance. Floyd Redmond is wounded in the hip by shrapnel, his second. Pfc. Walter Wlodarczyk, from Niagara County, New York, is evacuated after being accidentally shot in the leg. Jack Jewell writes home; he can't give details but says, "Well, I'll let you guess which side of the Rhine I'm on—you shouldn't have much trouble."[25]

On March 15, Ken Seaman returns. In clear weather, Company B advances between the Second and Third Battalions near Schweifeld under heavy fire; ~~AAA~~O suffers heavy casualties but gains 1,000 yards. Sgt. James Russell, wounded on January 26, is killed, while artillery shrapnel wounds Pfc. Frank Grofford in the leg. Henry Jones has dirt blown into his eyes, temporarily blinding him at 1400 hours, but he keeps fighting. March 16 finds the battalion in regimental reserve; the 39th takes fifty-four POWs, and casualties are "light," but new officer 2Lt. Charles Wieland is wounded.

On March 17, First Battalion, supported by 1st Platoon of Company C, 746th Tank Battalion, attacks at 0500 hours, receiving 20 mm antiaircraft fire and tank fire from three panzers, entering Hallerbach at 0615 hours. Enemy fire increases at 0800 hours, but the battalion clears Hallerbach by 1110 hours, except for a schoolhouse, the source of heavy resistance, but 1st Platoon, probably with a bazooka team in support, will soon take care of that. A night combat patrol finds an enemy infantry company and two self-propelled guns and calls in artillery fire. Eight more replacements arrive from 3rd Replacement Depot.

Near the schoolhouse, John Reiser is killed; later, SSgt. John McPherson dies of his wounds. Jim Rush is separated from his squad in another building. As Jim readies to sprint 60 feet to their location, an enemy rifleman gets a bead on him and fires a round—ricocheting off the door and passing through Jim's thigh. The squad frantically stops the bleeding, finds a truck, and rushes their sergeant and other wounded men to the rear. Jim is evacuated to the 48th General Hospital. Phil Holman takes charge of Rush's squad; Leonard Pourchot takes over Reiser's squad. T/5 Herbert Swan and Pvt. Edward Blanchard are wounded. Shrapnel wounds Paul Sapp in the left leg—his fourth wound. Pvt James Arnold, from Washington, wounded in the hip by artillery on September 17, is now wounded again in the chest. Shrapnel strikes Pfc. Walter Gabriel in the foot. James Davis is evacuated for a nonbattle illness; he had been wounded in October.

John Reiser has been in the unit since 1943, promoted to SSgt. on June 15, 1944. The steelworker from Wilkes-Barre, Pennsylvania, received the CIB for combat in Sicily and was hit by rifle fire in the wrist in Normandy. John McPherson just arrived, having previously served for two years in Trinidad. Wounded by a bullet in the chest, he makes it to a station hospital and a blood transfusion, but doctors cannot save him. Herb Swan arrived that morning; shrapnel breaks his hand, a compound fracture, sending him to a hospital until October.

Eddie Blanchard, from New Orleans, Louisiana, born on February 23, 1926, has just turned nineteen. His parents run a small neighborhood grocery; he delivers groceries on his bicycle before and after school. But his father dies of a rare blood disease, putting the family in dire straits. Living near Clay Square, Eddie graduates from the Redemptorist Boys and Girls High School, located in the "Irish Channel" area of New Orleans, and promptly enlists at Camp Beauregard, Louisiana, on June 20, 1944. In his fourth day at the front, running across a street in Hallerbach, Eddie hears the whine of incoming artillery and feels the pain in his knee, knocking him down. Believing he will be killed by the next volley, he is amazed to see two medics with a litter emerge through the smoke to rescue him. He will spend the next three months in military hospitals and must learn how to walk again; Eddie will have pieces of shrapnel in his knee for the rest of his life.[26] Sgt. Alvin "Beck" Becker, 1st Platoon from New Jersey, later receives a Silver Star at Hallerbach, as does Porky Pourchot:[27]

Leonard L. Pourchot, 39th Infantry, who distinguished himself by gallantry in action against the enemy on March 17, 1945, at Hallerbach, Germany. Advancing against strongly fortified enemy positions, the leading elements of the infantry encountered a numerically superior enemy force supported by several tanks and guns. When his squad leader became a casualty, Sergeant Pourchot assumed command and immediately reorganized his men for an assault on the enemy emplacements. During the action which followed he single-handedly captured five of the enemy and led his squad in taking ten more prisoners. After the town was cleared, with the exception of one house [schoolhouse] overlooking the village, he deployed his men to attack this strongpoint. Leading his squad, he charged into the house and captured twenty-five of the enemy. Sergeant Pourchot's courageous actions and aggressive leadership were an inspiration to himself and to the armed forces of the United States.

On March 18, the battalion advances just after midnight for Frohnen. In a firefight, they take the village by 0405 hours and continue the attack, seizing the village of Hohn by 0720 hours. The 39th captures 216 POWs and knocks out four enemy armored vehicles. Artillery shrapnel wounds Langley Turner in the fingers; he is evacuated. T/5 William Widdis has a compound fracture of the hand, also from shrapnel. Pfc. Michael Kelly is injured. Shrapnel hit him in the ribs on June 12 at Normandy; today it breaks his nose. Robert Decker is evacuated for a nonbattle illness.

About this time, ~~AAA~~O introduces a new tactical wrinkle against the Germans.[28] "They started capturing towns by artificial moonlight. Beams of giant searchlights were projected through the solid blackness of the forests. The effect was like that of a full moon behind clouds. The whole battle area was covered with a weird white light in which the soldier could see dimly 100 feet ahead." The key to success for the new technique is counterintuitive. Instead of directly shining the searchlights at enemy positions, operators aim upward and "bounce" the beams off the bottoms of low clouds, so it reflects downward as indirect light.

The battalion attacks on March 19 at 2000 hours against light resistance. Twenty new soldiers arrive, including Pfc. Nieves Castañon Jr., a 521–basic soldier, listed as a Mexican, born in Laredo, Texas. Another soldier of Mexican decent, Pvt. Lee Lopez, rolls in—born February 9, 1926, in Weston, Colorado, who had worked in the Ordnance Depot in Pueblo. Two 607–light mortar crewmen also arrive. Alva Moore, in the unit since North Africa, goes on temporary duty to Normandy, and a seven-day furlough to Great Britain. Joe Tanem returns from 3rd Replacement Depot on March 20, as does Robert Shew. Gordon Vickers is evacuated for nonbattle illness on March 21.

Amid the losses, the soldiers can find humor. Jack Jewell describes a comic incident: "I'm holding my sides with laughter. Two of our boys are just trying to get a large skillet from a German woman to fry her chickens for himself. He's trying to tell her that the Lend-Lease Bill will pay her. Some of these guys are pretty funny."[29]

Joe Tanem, with the unit since North Africa, is evacuated on March 22 for another nonbattle illness, as is Pfc. Herman Gellman. Thirteen soldiers are promoted to private first class, including Chester McClurg and Russian Wasnick. 1Lt. Jewell reports home: "Speaking of junk, that's all that will be left of Germany when we get through. Boy, you should see the place. Everything has been hit. But still the crazy people fight on."[30] On March 23, Billie Flowers returns to the company from the 3rd Replacement Depot, as do Henry Ambrose and Elmer Zimmerman.

Napoleon Daniels is promoted to SSgt. on March 24; Gus Douvanis, with the unit since November 1943, has shrapnel fracture his hand—his fighting days are over, since he'll be in the hospital until May. Langley Turner returns after treatment for his wounded fingers. Manley Fuller returns from the hospital too. The luckiest man in Company B on March 26 is Michael Szollosy, who receives a seven-day furlough to the US Riviera Recreation Area in southern France; he has "paid" for the trip by being wounded three times.

Artillery shrapnel wounds Sgt. James Thurston in the left hand in the late afternoon of March 27. On March 28, Pfc. Leroy Monte and Henry Rolewski are diagnosed with nonbattle illnesses and evacuated. Salvatore Ciccone, 1st Platoon sergeant and an original soldier at Fort Bragg, receives orders for temporary duty at Fort Dix. March's last casualty is Lewis Montague, evacuated for a nonbattle illness on March 30. The division is assigned to the VIIth Corps on March 31. The 39th reports eighty-three killed for March, fourteen soldiers die of wounds, 395 are wounded, and fifteen are missing.[31]

On April 1, Pvt. John McIntyre, of Simpson County, Mississippi, is killed, as the company attacks Winterberg at 0130 hours; after little resistance during the darkness, the unit gains 6 miles against significant resistance that began at dawn, and panzer fire hits the company that evening. The attack ends at 2145 hours, due to poor visibility. James Millar returns from 3rd Replacement Depot. A land mine explodes; shrapnel hits Pvt. Soon Shin Lee's face and Pvt. Joseph Lim's leg. Soon is a twenty-two-year-old from Hawaii. His parents had emigrated from Korea; his father is a gardener for a wealthy family in Honolulu, and Soon followed him into this work, before he enlists on September 15, 1944.[32] Joseph Lim, a carpenter, is also from Hawaii and is also a Korean American; his father is also a carpenter. They both have been in the company since March 19 and probably are in the same squad. On the basis of their consecutive service numbers, they enlisted on the same day—and on the same day they are wounded, by the same land mine, in the same location, halfway around the world from the Aloha State.

It gets really confusing for the first sergeant, however, since jumping off the truck with them on March 19 is Pvt. George C. M. Lee. He is also Korean American, is also from Hawaii, and also enlisted on September 15, 1944—his service number is only a few hundred from the other two men. Fortunately, he does not join a "Purple Heart trifecta" and is not wounded.

On April 2, First Battalion conducts another night attack at 0200 hours and enters the town of Winterberg at daylight, clearing the eastern portion, before being tied down in the western half. Opposing them are elements of Panzer Lehr, their old nemesis from Normandy. Multiple artillery shrapnel pieces strike Pfc. Henry Ambrose, an ammo bearer, in the back, killing him; the soldier from Pittsburgh had the CIB and previously had been wounded on March 3 but returned to duty to keep fighting.[33]

1Lt. Lucien Lucas, 1st Platoon leader, is seriously wounded, as are Pfc. Irving Wahl and Pfc. Bernard Jacobs. Artillery fragments hit Irving in the leg—resulting in a compound fracture—and the stomach, seriously damaging his intestines. Bernard, an ammo bearer, is a nineteen-year-old Jewish kid from Syracuse, New York; his father, Max, emigrated from Manchester, England; his mother, Kate, from Poland. Now, Bernie has a compound fracture of the upper arm caused by artillery fragments. It is a "Statue of Liberty" wound; Bernie will be invalided home and remain in hospitals for nine months. Pfc. Dominic Buongermino, born in Elizabeth, New Jersey, and enlisted in January 1943, is hit by artillery shrapnel, causing a compound fracture of his heel and numerous wounds to his chest; he will remain in the hospital until October 4, 1945, when he is discharged. Robert Kalvitz injures his ankle.[34]

On April 3, the battalion remains in Winterberg, sending out strong combat patrols and firing on targets in the vicinity of Hill 720. AAAO captures one self-propelled gun, eight 150 mm artillery pieces, and 150 POWs. In an after-action report, the 746th Tank Battalion reports that "Winterberg was mopped up by Company C and the 39th."[35] Had the average dogface read the report, he would have pleasantly informed its author that the phrase "mopping up" is one of the most despised expressions in the infantry, since it minimizes the effort involved to clear every nook, cranny, and cellar in close combat, where—unlike a tank—a dogface's armor is exactly as thick as his wool shirt. Or maybe the dogface just would have punched the staff officer in the kisser.

On April 4, the battalion attacks at 0800 hours; Company B reaches Hill 720 by 0930 hours, encountering self-propelled and artillery fire but taking ninety-three POWs. Sgt. Mitchell Branham; Pfcs. Leon Weiner, Claud Ledford, and Luther Little; and Pvt. Harold Marti are wounded. One other soldier is evacuated for a nonbattle disease. Mortar shrapnel wounds Russian Wasnick in the hand; it will earn him a Purple Heart. Born in Kentucky, Mitchell is a twenty-six-year-old married farmer. Harold, a nineteen-year-old farmer from Lamar, Missouri, has been in the Army only since October 11 and now sports a shrapnel wound to the hip. It is the third wound for Claud, hit in the face by artillery shrapnel, and he is treated at an aid station and sent right back to the line. Luther is an ammo bearer. Leon has the dubious distinction of the worst wounds of the day, when shrapnel breaks his shoulder blade and slices into his abdomen, destroying parts of his intestines. Doctors save him, but Leo gets a seven-month stay in a general hospital.

The attack is rolling, and on April 5 ~~AAA~~O takes 330 POWs. Company B is relieved from Hill 720 as the battalion advances slowly, sweeping the woods, moving north and west. Patrols move forward, and at 1825 hours the battalion attacks toward Siedlinghausen. Heavy rocket fire west of town forces the attack to halt at 2100 hours. During the day, the 39th knocks out two Panther tanks from Panzer Lehr. Later Phil Holman writes a short story on events:[36]

The wakeup whisper came at 3:45 a.m. A lukewarm cup of coffee, an indigestible something for breakfast, nobody talking—probably like the last meal before an execution. A last-minute check of the rifle to make sure the safety is on; tightening of the combat pack straps; grenades ready; quick jump to make sure nothing rattled; one last drag on a hastily lit, well-hidden, cigarette and off we go in the dark of night.

Destination? The assembly area and then the line of departure from which when morning twilight begins, we will jump off to attack something we could not see—a town, a hill, a river, or whatever stood in our way in Germany. Morning twilight is the time between dark and day when you can see about 100 feet ahead, far enough so you won't run off a cliff or into a tree. It is also the time when the enemy is supposed to be most alert. So, alive, scared, fed, well-equipped, we move quietly to the line of departure and wait for the signal. Normally, an attack comes after a barrage of either mortar fire or big gun shells, supposed to soften up the enemy.

This time the plan was to attack without the shell fire, hoping to take the enemy by surprise. Sometimes it works. Our line of departure was the last line of trees and brush on a hill overlooking a small town nestled in a valley.

No matter how many times you do this, the start is always the same, adrenaline boiling over—fear always present. The signal came and off we went. Pouring out of the trees and brush we rushed down the hill toward the town. Now, all you want to do is get to the shelter of the houses, gather your squad, and begin the house-to-house fighting. Getting to the house is another thing.

As I ran down the hill, my foot caught in a rut and down I went (One of the squad members later told me he thought that there goes Sergeant Holman). He was wrong. I got up, ran on, jumped a fence, and reached the house that was my goal. There was sporadic small-arms fire coming from the town, but nothing serious. One of the men had a bullet pierce his canteen and feeling the wetness of the water thought he had been shot. In the attack, and especially when you fall down on the way, you lose contact with your friends—at least I did this time. I found myself alone in a street, no friends in sight, so I stormed the front door of the house ahead of me. The door was locked so of course I shot out the lock with my M1.

Unfortunately, as I found out when entering the house, one of my bullets or a piece of the door had wounded a woman, hiding inside, in the hand. I couldn't stop to give first aid. I cleared the rest of the house, then moved on to find my buddies. The usual way to clear a house is to throw a grenade upstairs, go up and make sure it is clear, then move downstairs to the basement. I didn't grenade the basement this time because the woman was shouting "Kinder," and I knew enough German to realize she was saying "children." With a hand motion to her, she yelled something else, and the children came up—three of them as I remember. They ran to the shelter of mama—I left for the next house.

This town was built in a square, with a park in the middle. A nice grassy place with benches and a few statues—a great gathering place. One side of the town backed up to the hill I had just charged down. The other side backed on a small valley, a paved road, and a gently rising, tree-studded, hill. Our company quickly took the town. I found the rest of the squad, who had not only fought their way through the houses but had been able, on the way, to find eggs, chickens, and blood sausage.

I even found a blood sausage in my pocket—anything was better than the K-rations we were issued. As I moved through the town, I noticed a German woman run outside her house, grab a wounded German soldier, and drag him inside her home. A brave woman on her part. The noise of a motor turned our attention to the road. Down it came a German truck rolling along as if there were no American soldiers nearby. Our machine gun put an end to that journey.

That day I learned a lesson. It nearly cost me my life. Basic training taught me many things. Advanced training taught me more, particularly that you never, never go up close to a window to look out. I forgot. I can still see the slope across the valley and the road, and the rifle swing up and over towards me. I froze. The bullet came through the window, passed by my head by about an inch and whacked into the wall behind me. To this day, some 70 years later, if I find myself in front of a window I back away.

I'm not too fond of balconies, either. Alive but shaking, I ran into the kitchen of the house, stood back from the window there, and fired a clip of ammo, eight rounds, at the spot where I saw the rifle. I don't know if I hit anything but perhaps, I scared someone as he had scared me. You seldom live after making a mistake like that. To make two mistakes in one day and survive is miraculous. I had made the second mistake soon after the first, when I "volunteered" for a task. They don't teach you that, but you learn quickly to look away when someone—usually of higher rank—asks who would like to do this or that. The platoon sergeant looked directly at me. So away I went, my job to investigate a small structure a few yards from the back of the house and facing the valley and road.

Rifle at the ready, I ran out to the structure where I found three German soldiers outside what was a potato dugout. They had evidently been in the dugout, got caught by the attack, and were now signaling their friends across the road. When I arrived, they surrendered. One indicated there was one other in the dugout. I did not draw fire from the enemy because they were afraid, they would hit their own men. So, in I went. The poor guy was asleep in the potatoes. Quite a reaction when I poked him with my rifle. I took the four back to the house and turned them over to the platoon sergeant. Another escape. So endeth another ugly day on the front during World War II. Nothing outstanding, just a warning that life can be snuffed out in a second if you make a mistake.

On April 6, the battalion attacks at 0530 hours in rainy, hazy weather toward Siedlinghausen, coming under fire from a dug-in King Tiger heavy tank. The behemoth withdraws, and the battalion advances into town by 1310 hours, capturing 262 POWs. With overwhelming injuries and shock, Pfc. Irving Wahl, from Everett, Washington, dies of wounds received on April 2; Irving arrived in the company on October 20. Jack Jewell writes home: "Sometimes I think this war gets worse as time goes on. The people may think the war is over but there is plenty of fighting here—and it's rough, believe me."[37]

April 7. Battalion moves to Brunskappel and attacks from there at 0800 hours. Company B receives small-arms fire, and later artillery and *Nebelwerfer* (rocket) fire. Making slow progress, in part because of booby traps, the unit takes a rugged trail north around Hill 675, flanking Elpe, which it moves through from the least expected northern side against small-arms fire. At 2005 hours, the battalion moves toward Heinrichsdorf, occupying it at 2218 hours. Pfc. Carl Erickson is killed by gunshot wounds to the chest and shoulder. James Marcinkowski and Pfc. David Moore are wounded. Exploding booby trap shrapnel hits Eugene Ervin's knee; George Ledford's neck and thigh; William Richardson's nose; Jerome Magluilo's upper arm, chest, and abdomen; James Thurston's head; and Walter Shafron's foot.[38] It looks bad for Jerome.

It is the second wound for Jim Marcinkowski, in the company since October 5, the second for James Thurston, and the second for Walter, a twenty-nine-year-old Jewish soldier from Philly. It is at least the third for Eugene Ervin, who had been seriously wounded on June 15 by a land mine; Eugene fought in Sicily and is a good friend of Lang Turner. Artillery hammers Dave Moore in the thigh; invalided home, he is discharged from a general hospital in October 1945. George Ledford has been in the company nineteen days. Nineteen-year-old sergeant John W. Hudson sprains his ankle taking evasive action during an artillery barrage. Victor Fink (acute bronchitis and enteritis) and Pvt. Thomas Tome are evacuated for nonbattle disease. 1Sgt. Keith Lewis is formally assigned from Company H. Born on October 2, 1918, in Peytona Boon, West Virginia, Lewis is Regular Army, enlisting in the mid-1930s. ~~AAAO~~ destroys two Hunting Panther tank destroyers (Jagdpanther) probably belonging to Panzer Lehr and takes 235 POWs.

Back in December 1944, a combination of events led to the formation of Black infantry platoons that would be integrated one per infantry regiment. While the Army already fielded the Ninety-Second US Infantry Division in Italy, a mostly Black unit with many white officers, this was the first integration of the infantry of the Army in Eisenhower's command. Black soldiers, to be sure, had served in a multitude of logistical units, and in combat with the 614th Tank Destroyer Battalion and the 761st Tank Battalion. The latter, in George Patton's Third Army, is reviewed by old "Blood and Guts," who then gathers the men around him:

> Men, you're the first Negro tankers to ever fight in the American Army. I would never have asked for you if you weren't good. I have nothing but the best in my Army. I don't care what color you are as long as you go up there and kill those Kraut sonsofbitches. Everyone has their eyes on you and is expecting great things from you. Most of all your race is looking forward to your success. Don't let them down and, damn you, don't let me down! They say it is patriotic to die for your country. Well, let's see how many patriots we can make out of those German sonsofbitches.

As the infantry run out of replacements and as more and more Black soldiers volunteer for infantry duty, the 9th Infantry now receives three platoons. ~~AAAO~~ assigns forty-one men who had arrived on March 14, 1945, as a Fifth Platoon for Company G, and as Lindsey Nelson might say, "The rest is history." On April 7, Fifth Platoon, Company G, encounters heavy machine gun fire near Siedlinghausen. Up jumps twenty-one-year-old Pfc. Edgar Zeno, a former Transportation Corps soldier from New Orleans, and sprays the enemy with BAR fire as he charges their positions. When he gets within 25 yards, the wounded Edgar throws a hand grenade, killing seven enemy soldiers and wounding another three. That is good enough for Gen. Louis Craig, who awards Pfc. Zeno the Silver Star.[39]

Company B gets in a scrapper as well—twenty-year-old Pvt. Willie Scott White. Born on February 27, 1925, in Dallas to James White, a chauffeur, and Anna Dee Scott, a cook, Willie enlists on November 10, 1943, and joins the 555th Port Company in the Transportation Corps. While the unit performs a valuable duty, it isn't enough for Pvt. White, and he volunteers to go into the infantry in December 1944. Maybe it was pure patriotism, maybe he wanted to fight at the front, or maybe Willie, who is Black, heard comments such as "colored" and worse, and it was about time to put up or shut up, and Willie is a put-up guy. Arriving in Belgium on January 16, 1945, he receives accelerated infantry training before joining Company G, of AAAO, and then to 3rd Platoon, Company B.[40]

On April 8, Company B moves through Company A at 0820 hours and begins receiving tank and small-arms fire at 0902 hours. The company runs into a roadblock and more enemy fire. A panzer guarding the obstacle withdraws, as American artillery fire falls around it, but the company continues to receive panzer and small-arms fire at 1225 hours. In steep terrain, the company consolidates its position west of the village of Werden. For the day, the 39th seizes 348 POWs. SSgt. Lawrence Carter, an original soldier in Company B, wounded the previous September by shrapnel, and Pvt. Lawrence Mariano are wounded.

Carter, who won the Silver Star on August 7, 1944, at Bulloyer, France, has a machine gun bullet smash his jaw, which doctors will have to wire shut. He enlisted on November 27, 1940, at age seventeen. Mariano is Filipino American, Hawaiian-born after his parents emigrated from the Philippines. His father works in a pineapple cannery, and his mother toils as a laundry presser operator. First Battalion attacks out of Ramsbeck at 0800 hours on April 9 and advances northwest toward the tiny village of Berlar, where it receives small-arms fire. It clears the area by 1203 hours, when Company B advances toward Blüggelscheidt, clearing it by 1530 hours. Bull Eckardt is evacuated for a nonbattle disease. The 39th seizes 198 prisoners. Their luck ends the next day; eighteen-year-old Jerome Magluilo dies of wounds received three days earlier. Russian Wasnick is evacuated to the 96th Evacuation Hospital for hypertension. Jack Jewell writes: "Well, more hard days have passed, and I hope we are that much nearer the end."[41]

On April 11, Company B receives hot showers and clean uniforms; at a formation, Jack Jewell finally receives his Silver Star. Lloyd Wasnick returns from the 662nd Medical Clearing Company but is evacuated again for a nonbattle illness, as is Pfc. Rufus Morman. 1Sgt. Lewis departs on furlough to Camp Atterbury, Indiana; he has been in the company just four days. Company B receives a dozen replacements, including Pvt. Chester Demery, part Lakota from the Standing Rock Reservation, and Pvt. Ramon Bojorquez-Montijo, a Mexican born in Arizona; Ramon joined the Army on July 20, 1944; married his girlfriend, Concepcion, in December; is a farmhand; and turned nineteen twenty-four days ago; now he's an ammo bearer.

Chester's white grandfather was a corporal in the 6th US Infantry Regiment in 1876 at Fort Abraham Lincoln, Dakota Territory. On his mother's side, a great-grandfather, Sitting Crow (*Kangi Iyotanke*), was a noted Blackfoot Lakota chief. Chester has always appeared on US Indian Census rolls; now he's on the morning report—just like every other soldier in the outfit. Chester and Ramon will be fine; some of the other replacements may not be. Already dipping to take eighteen-year-olds, the Army is now converting soldiers from other specialties to the infantry at an alarming rate.

Sgt. Roy Hess was a light-truck driver; now he's walking to work. Cpl. Carmine Eannace, an embalmer in civilian life, was a supply clerk; now he's counting bullets, not blankets. Cpl. Francis Szymanik is a former welder who, after enlisting as a clerk, packs up his typewriter and now is unpacking storage tubes of Mark II "Pineapple" hand grenades, saving a few for himself. And former mechanic Pvt. Elwyn Dolan, who had been building B-24 bombers in San Diego, won't be riveting aircraft panels; he'll be changing en bloc clips in his M1—and changing them fast.

Jack Jewell wonders of the future: "Well, I guess this war will continue until the last German is taken prisoner or killed."[42] The company is in a rest area at Blüggelscheidt on April 12; Alvin Becker and Buck Atkins are evacuated for nonbattle illnesses. Pvt. Willie White is promoted to private first class. The next day, Company B loads trucks and travels 170 miles to Rottleberode in the Harz area of Saxony, and to VIIth Corps.

On April 13, ~~AAA~~O attacks toward Stolberg/Hesse, seizing the villages of Rotha, Dankerode, Breitenbach, and Horla. A tank company tries to keep up but runs out of fuel at the village of Holungen. It rejoins the battalion the next day. A pistol bullet wounds Pfc. Jack Poole, a light machine gunner, in the hand on April 15, after the company, riding in half-tracks and on tanks, rolls through Wippra, Friesdorf, and Mohrungen. Pfc. Willie White is promoted to Sgt. just three days after his last promotion.[43] Nieves Castañon, Gilbert Miller, Carmine Eannace, and Louis Montoya are wounded and evacuated on April 17 fighting Waffen-SS troops and an assault gun deployed in a cemetery at Ulzigerode, as the unit also captures Stangerode and Alterode, along with 140 prisoners. Pfc. Robert Shew receives the Bronze Star.

Nieves arrived on March 20; now he has a bullet in the chest. It is Gilbert's third wound, a machine gun bullet to the thigh that puts him in a hospital until November. It is also Louis's third, as he is again hit by artillery shrapnel. One of the penetrating shrapnel wounds to his upper thigh is severe, and multiple shrapnel wounds to his chest and neck are considered moderate; finally, a piece of shrapnel also penetrated his back just to the left of vertebra C-5, so close to the spine that doctors cannot remove it. Over the next 204 days in various military hospitals, Louis will have a hard time counting all the pieces of German steel now in his body.

Early on April 19 at Rieder—southeast of Quedlinburg—the company captures over a thousand POWs; Lee Floriano remarks that "by the way the prisoners are coming in, it really looks like the war is almost over." However, the Grim Reaper connects with one final horrendous haymaker on Company B's chin, when they attack toward the village of Stecklenberg, under continuous self-propelled artillery shelling, and Chester

McClurg and George Mavis are killed; George arrived in the company on October 11, and Chester was the free spirit the Army could never contain. Pvt. Michael Sim, son of an immigrant coal miner from Galicia, Austria, sprains an ankle. Cpl. Edward Helmer, company clerk, is evacuated for a nonbattle injury.

The next day, Pfc. Thomas Naud is wounded when a nearby artillery shell explosion ruptures an eardrum. Thomas, born June 26, 1926, may be the youngest soldier in the unit. He has been in the company eight days. The son of a racehorse-track cashier, he lived on West 180th Street in Manhattan; the eighteen-year-old will now call a hospital home for the next four months. On April 21, the 9th Infantry relieves the 3rd Armored Division along the Mulde River, near Dessau.

The next day, Pfc. Jim Collins is evacuated for a nonbattle illness; he has been in the company since October 9, joining the Regular Army in 1939. Pvt. William Brady is hit in the wrist by shrapnel but remains on duty. Everyone in the rear is looking to get some frontline time now: the division sends 1Lts. Melvin Freedman and John Henry to the company as platoon leaders. The company clears the woods west of Stecklenberg, capturing forty prisoners on April 23. On April 24, veteran Sgt. John Schopper secures a seven-day furlough to England. The next day, the company is trucked to Reppichau, 40 miles northwest of Leipzig. About this time, Pfc. Manley Fuller and four buddies decide to sleep inside a German house.

> So the German family moved upstairs, and we slept on the floor downstairs. We left our rifles there and went for something to eat, and we decided to steal a car and we stole a German Opel and took off with it. We were riding around hills; the war was still on, and we shouldn't have been doing it. You're not supposed to go anywhere without your rifle.

Manley later found a red/maroon American Buick, but it was on the fritz. The boys walked up to a big house to find someone who could help them crank up the car.[44]

> We knocked on the door and three women came to the door. And they nodded behind them and said, "Offizieren, Offizieren." We didn't know if the officers would be American or German, but we figured they'd probably be Germans. So, she showed us the door downstairs and we opened the door quick, and they all put their hands up. They all had pistols, but they weren't loaded. One of them could speak English, and he gave me his pistol and showed me how to load it. And the German said: "Now you're going to shoot us." So I said, "I'm not going to shoot you; I don't think anyone is going to shoot you," so they gave up.

Now Manley has a problem. The Opel holds five passengers, so two troopers go with two German officers to scrounge a vehicle for all ten people. They get lucky—an operational Kraut half-track.

> The other soldiers got in the front and the Germans were in the back. I drove behind them in the Opel. The soldiers waved their helmets out the side windows to show they were American so no one would shoot us. So, we took them back to the prisoner stockade and left them and the half-track there. And then we took the Opel back to the house.

The incident never makes it into the morning report. On April 26, Pfc. Seben Gore, a boiler room operator from Gonzalez, Louisiana, is evacuated for a nonbattle illness. The following day, Capt. Floriano departs Company B, assigned to battalion headquarters. 1Lt. Eugene Taylor assumes command. Lang Turner, an original trooper in Company B since 1941, departs on furlough to Camp Atterbury, Indiana. On April 28, Edward Pickard returns from the 3rd Replacement Depot. A great sign that the end of the conflict is near occurs on the evening of April 29, when the company shows movies in camp.

Sometime during the month, artillery shrapnel hits George Ledford in the tailbone and pelvis, wounding him for the second time, and strikes William Harris in the foot. The 9th Infantry publishes *GO #57* on April 30, awarding Langley Turner the Silver Star on January 31, 1945, and Luther Wilson for gallantry on February 3, 1945. It also awards John Rodrigues, a bobbin machine operator from Massachusetts, a Silver Star near Alzen on January 30, 1945. Then the dying in Company B just stops. The regiment reports forty-eight killed for April; seven soldiers die of wounds, 196 are wounded, and four are missing.[45] The last of the division's dead are buried at temporary First Army cemeteries at Ittenbach and Eisenach, Germany. On May 8, 1945, 1Lt. Eugene Taylor notes on the Company B morning report: "Company went on a ten-mile hike this morning and won a game of softball with Dog Company by a score of 4 to 3. The war with Germany ended today at 1500 hours."

The guns go silent.

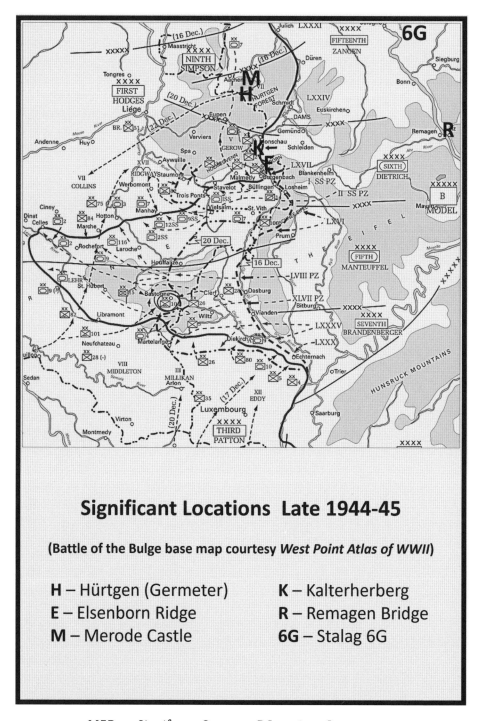

Significant Locations Late 1944-45

(Battle of the Bulge base map courtesy *West Point Atlas of WWII*)

H – Hürtgen (Germeter)   **K** – Kalterherberg
E – Elsenborn Ridge   **R** – Remagen Bridge
M – Merode Castle   **6G** – Stalag 6G

MAP 10: Significant Company B Locations, Late 1944-45

SCHOOL OF THE SOLDIER

REPPLE DEPOTS

Military slang for replacement depots; also applies to replacement battalions. Out of perceived necessity, they handle replacements in an impersonal, assembly-line manner by permanent depot staffs. Replacement battalions generally are located well forward in the corps sector, so the divisions have a minimum distance to send trucks to pick up the new men. The 41st Replacement Battalion provides replacements when the division is part of Vth Corps, and the 92nd Replacement Battalion does the same when the division is with VIIth Corps. Two other replacement battalions, the 48th and the 86th, support the VIIIth Corps and the XIXth Corps, respectively. The rated capacity of a replacement battalion is 1,200 soldiers, but the 92nd Replacement Battalion once reaches 7,000.

Timely replacements are dependent on timely submissions by units for replacements. Normally, requisitions are filled within forty-eight hours from the time they arrive in the replacement headquarters. Concerning military occupational specialties, most are not difficult to process, with one exception—rifle-trained infantry. Eisenhower's problem boils down to finding enough physically qualified men in theater to meet combat losses of infantry. He has three options: (1) retrain overstrength occupational noninfantry specialties and send them to infantry units, (2) find men in duty positions classified as theater overstrength and transfer them, and (3) "shanghai" general-assignment men in the supply services of the Communications Zone, who can be converted to a combat arm and replaced by men no longer physically qualified for combat.

What the entire replacement system—from the informal grabbing of mechanics, clerks, and cooks; handing them rifles; and telling them they are now in the infantry, to processing replacements from the States through replacement depots—has to avoid is the "You want it bad, you get it bad" syndrome. While it is easy to tell someone they are converting to be an infantryman, you have to provide them with rudimentary skills, so they will survive in the most dangerous new occupation imaginable.

SILVER STAR

Also known as the Silver Star Medal, it was approved on July 19, 1932, by the secretary of war as a replacement for an earlier award, the "Citation Star," from the Great War. Authorization for the award was placed into law by two acts of Congress in 1942; approval for Army recipients began on December 15, 1942. The award is for gallantry in action against the enemy. For Army ground troops, this generally means singular acts of valor, or heroism over a brief period, such as one or two days of an extended battle. It was far more difficult to win a Silver Star than a Bronze Star, especially for enlisted soldiers.

Any other military person could recommend a soldier for a Silver Star (i.e., you cannot nominate yourself). During the war, division commanders are the approval authority; they often established review committees to read award recommendations and then forward an opinion to the commander for final decision. Because the committees had not personally witnessed most of these acts, and because some committee members were not infantrymen, it was crucial that the originating unit selected an officer who was a proficient writer to complete the forms. In Company B, Jack Jewell was that go-to officer. However, a successful submission included more than a good narrative, as a June 12, 1944, memo from Gen. Eisenhower emphasized:[46]

> It is essential that each recommendation includes all available evidence to support the case. Emphasis will be placed upon the supporting evidence and data, rather than on the citation. In appropriate cases, supporting evidence in the form of affidavits or official records should be enclosed.

The first award of the Silver Star was the medal itself; a soldier receiving a subsequent second award would receive a bronze Oak Leaf Cluster to put on the ribbon; any soldier who received a fifth award of the medal would receive a silver Oak Leaf Cluster, but winning even two was rare. Roughly 1,789 Silver Stars are awarded to soldiers in the 9th Infantry during the entire war. Some twenty-six Silver Stars went to men in Company B during this late-war period.

SNIPERS

Whether a soldier is peering over the edge of his foxhole, treading gingerly on the edge of a village street, or crossing an open field, the thought of an enemy sniper always lurks in the back of his mind. A German sniper killed Paddy Flint in Normandy, and countless other AAAO guys went down to the single shot since. German, especially Austrian, snipers are superb shots, and while the Mauser K98k rifle may not have had the world's fastest rate of fire, no one ever questioned its accuracy. Then there are sniper scopes, some made by Carl Zeiss, a renowned optics company in Jena; a sniper peering through a Zeiss six-power scope can tell the last time you shaved.

To make matters worse, German *Scharfschützen* (sharpshooters) use special sniping ammunition with extra-carefully measured propellent and seated full-metal-jacketed boattail, match-grade bullets; the overall effect of the ammunition is to improve the ballistic coefficient of the round. To the GI, all that gobbledygook means is that a sniper can take your head off from a long way away. German snipers could qualify for their Sniper's Badge, which comes in three grades: Third Class for twenty kills, Second Class for forty kills, and First Class for sixty kills. Close-quarter kills do not count; every kill has to be witnessed and reported to the battalion commander, who records each in an individual "sniper's book." US soldiers do not know it, but several German snipers are able to achieve kills at 1,100 yards and run up scores in the hundreds, such as Austrian Matthäus Hetzenauer, who rings up 345.

BEWARE, TRAITOR . . . THE WEREWOLF WATCHES

The Harz Mountain region of Germany is a strange place, and home for many a legend. Twelve hundred years ago, when Charlemagne campaigned to brutally convert pagans and unbelievers, one of the last bastions of defiance was in the Upper Harz Mountains, where witches celebrated Walpurgis Night every April 30 on Brocken Mountain—the area's highest peak. Belowground, trolls, goblins, dwarves, and maybe a *Nibelung* or two prowled their subterranean realm. Now the region has another troubling tale. Back in 1943, the evil leader of the wicked SS, Heinrich Himmler, began to doubt if the Third Reich would win the war. Poring through German legends, the *Reichsführer* found a 1910 novel by Herman Löns titled *Der Wehrwolf.* The story, set in the Thirty Years' War, 1618 to 1648, describes bloody revenge of Saxon peasants against invading marauding soldiers. Although the story was fiction, that actual war was not—bloody with eight million violent deaths, as well as several simultaneous famines and plagues.

Himmler's fantasies concerning armed resistance against an invading army went on the back burner, like so many of his other ideas, such as searching for the origin of the Aryan race in the Himalayas. But as Germany's fortunes plummeted by the fall of 1944, Himmler began Operation Werwolf, resolute fanatics who would spread terror behind enemy lines, selecting SS general Hans-Adolf Prützmann, who already had the blood of tens of thousands on his hands for his killing programs in Russia, as general inspector of special defense. With a headquarters in Berlin, they would adopt guerrilla tactics of Soviet partisans that Prützmann had fought earlier.

With the fall of Aachen in October 1944, Himmler learned that a new civil government, led by Mayor Franz Oppenhoff, was collaborating with the Allies—and for that, Oppenhoff had to die. By late November, Prützmann had five thousand recruits, stiffened with a cadre of Waffen-SS officers and sergeants, training at Hülchrath Castle near Grevenbroich. From this force, Prützmann selected six personnel for the assassination, code-named Operation Karneval.

At 2100 hours on March 20, 1945, the six reportedly board a captured B-17, operated by the Luftwaffe's 200th Special Operations Wing, at an airfield outside Hildesheim; just before midnight, the commandos parachute into the night air over a Belgian forest close to Aachen. Five days later, they arrive at the mayor's home, where an SS sergeant—screaming, "Heil Hitler"—fires a fatal bullet to Oppenhoff's head from a silenced pistol; the team then escapes. But not far; the group unwisely elects to travel through the Hürtgen Forest, and near Rollesbroich, SS sergeant Josef "Sepp" Leitgeb, the assassin, steps on a mine and is killed.

But the fuze of resistance is lit, and on April 1, Propaganda Minister Josef Goebbels begins airing "Radio Werwolf." The broadcasts begin with a shrill howl of a wolf, brag of assassinating Oppenhoff, and announce the resurgence of medieval Germanic Vehmic courts, secret tribunals that had carried out death sentences long ago. Their credo is "Destroy the enemy or destroy yourself!," and in many villages, ghostly writing appears: "Beware, Traitor, the Werewolf Watches." Now the werewolf is in the Harz, preparing to create a Werwolf Festung (Werewolf Fortress) led by fanatical wounded Waffen-SS sergeants from local military hospitals.[47]

CHAPTER NINE

"Show Me the Way to Go Home"

How many points ya got?
—Asked daily by three million American soldiers after VE-day

The war in Europe is over, but it feels like limbo. Two days after VE-day, the Army's adjutant general sends Grace MacLean a telegram: "The Chief of Staff of the Army directs me to inform you your son Private First Class Myron D. MacLean is being returned to the United States within the near future and will be given an opportunity to communicate with you upon arrival."

Returning home is on everyone's mind. "How many points have ya got?" It is the most frequently asked question from one American soldier to another, not only in Europe but around the world. In 1943, Gen. George Marshall realizes that once the war ends, not only will the American public demand demobilization, but soldiers will want an orderly effort of deployment home that recognized their sacrifices, not just whom they know, or what rank they are.

There are three million military personnel in Europe, but they cannot be sent home willy-nilly. Some units will occupy Germany for an undefined period. Other units must reorganize; still others will redeploy to the Pacific to fight the Japanese. Rather than send soldiers home as individual returnees, reminiscent of individual replacements—its downside already known—soldiers returning to the States will be assigned to units heading back. But how to determine when soldiers go back? The answer is not long in coming. On May 10, 1945, the same day that Grace receives confirmation that her son is coming home, the War Department announces a point system for demobilization and discharge of Army enlisted personnel. Termed the "Advanced Service Rating Score," it has the goal of achieving equity in demobilization and discharge—objective criteria, not subjective.

Soldiers receive one point for each month of military service after September 16, 1940. If you had enlisted two years earlier (May 1943) than the current time, for example, that would give you 24 points. You receive one additional point for every month you have served overseas, because that is considered a hardship. It does not matter where that service occurred, as long as it's overseas. Therefore, a soldier deployed to England from the States in January 1944 will accrue 16 overseas points by VE-day. Those 16 points would be in addition to the points for overall military service and increase each month like clockwork. A soldier in Europe thus receives two points every month—one for overall military service, and one for being overseas.

That sort of grates on combat soldiers, who feel that actually fighting should be worth something—and the brass agrees. So, a soldier also receives 5 points for each of the following decorations received: Medal of Honor (although this was actually managed as its own category), Distinguished Service Cross, Distinguished Service Medal, Legion of Merit, Silver Star Medal, Distinguished Flying Cross, Soldier's Medal, Bronze Star Medal, Air Medal, and Purple Heart. A soldier with a Silver Star, Purple Heart with Oak Leaf Cluster (indicating two total awards of the Purple Heart), and Bronze Star, for example, would pick up 20 points.

Immediately, the infantry grasps that this list does not include the CIB—intentional, in part, because the Army knows—but does not broadcast—that a future invasion of Japan is going to take a whole lot of infantrymen with valuable combat experience. Then the Army examines battle stars issued to units, which denotes an individual's participation in a specific campaign, and determines a soldier will receive 5 points for participating in each. The 39th Infantry, for example, is credited with participating in the following eight campaigns during the war:

Algeria–French Morocco	November 8, 1942–November 11, 1942
Tunisia	November 17, 1942–May 13, 1943
Sicily	July 9, 1943–August 17, 1943
Normandy	June 6, 1944–July 24, 1944
Northern France	July 25, 1944–September 14, 1944
Rhineland	September 15, 1944–March 21, 1945
Ardennes-Alsace	December 16, 1944–January 25, 1945
Central Europe	March 22, 1945–May 11, 1945

Thus, a soldier who landed in Normandy with the 39th and remains in it until the end of the war would have participated in five campaigns, worth 25 points. Finally, the Army decides that family responsibility should enter the system. Soldiers receive 12 points per dependent child up to a maximum of three children, but no points for marital status, or for children over age eighteen.

Balancing the needs of the service with desires of the soldiers, the Army can determine a fair cutoff point to allow troops to go home. Initially, although it would later change several times, this figure will be a total of 85 points needed to head home. Therefore, our sample soldier who joined the Army in May 1943, arrived in Britain in January 1944, participated in every battle campaign after that, and received a Silver Star, a Bronze Star, and two Purple Hearts and had no young children at home would be authorized 24 + 16 + 20 + 25 + 0 = 85. Bingo! And that young soldier would ensure that the company first sergeant saw him every day, just as a reminder! Jack Jewell is sitting on 71 points, so he will have a while to wait.[1]

Mac MacLean arrives in Boston on a hospital ship on May 13. He then technically goes AWOL, traveling to nearby Norton and to Wheaton College to visit Julie Lane.

Returning to Boston, Mac then takes a train to Chicago. In Indiana, the train stops to take on passengers from another train, and to both their surprise, Julie Lane steps aboard. The two continue to Chicago and board the "Peoria Rocket" train to their hometown. Mac then takes a cab to St. James Place; opening the door, "Mums" sees that her little "Sunny" is finally home—a little thinner, but safe.

Mac writes Bob Pettigrew in Aichach, Bavaria, to inquire what has happened to the platoon. Bob's letter back on June 3 describes the unit:

Dear Mac, Received your letter of May 20th and was sure glad to hear from you. Also, glad to hear that you are back in the good old USA. Thank your Mom for the swell note she added to your letter. Boy that made me feel good. I am now working in the Personnel Section back at the regiment in a clerical job, which is right up my alley. Always thought I was too old for that tramping around in the woods, Mac, and I guess they got wise to themselves and put me back at a job that is easy on the legs.

Will never forget that day, Mac, because our trio combination was well broken up, with Ken being wounded and you taken prisoner. Well, it turned out OK anyway and the Good Lord sure was on our side. I am forwarding your letter to Ken or better still will bring it up with me to the company on pay day. Glad to hear that you met your one and only even if you had to go AWOL to do it. Believe I would have done the same.

Sorry to report, Mac, that Lieutenant Benoist died up there as we couldn't get up to him. You would never know the outfit, Mac, as there are only a few of us present right now; Ken, Daniels, Billie Flowers, Holman, Holdren, and Wasnick along with yours truly out of the 3rd Platoon. Some wounded and some killed; Boy, and to think I got through without a scratch. Can't believe it myself. By the way, Turner went home on rotation about 5 weeks ago and probably will get his discharge under the point system. Sorry you were not with us when we were taking town after town right after crossing the Rhine. I know you would have enjoyed it as the looting was good and the eats better. We took hams, eggs, and all kinds of preserves and gave the Krauts our "C" rations to eat and they liked it (They had to.)

Well, Mac, time to sign off once again so let me say: God Bless You and all the luck in the world to a swell guy and a real buddy. Know your Julie and your Mom are all glad that you are back. And here's hoping you stay there as I believe you have done your share. Luck to you Mac and get well soon. Bob

On May 21, 1945, the morning report includes "Six (6) EM left for the good old United States today." Six more leave the next day. Jack Jewell assumes temporary command of Company B on May 26. Jack Dunlap returns from the hospital on May 31 and takes over from Jewell, who writes home on June 5 that the 9th Infantry is assigned to Third Army and General Patton. Jack discusses another lesson from the Army: "An outfit doesn't have to stay in the same army. All it takes to change you is a good type-writer."[2] On June 7, from Ingolstadt, Germany, Ken writes to Mac in Peoria:

Dear Mac, Julie, and Mrs. MacLean, Received your May 23rd letter two days ago and was happy for all five of us: Bob [Pettigrew] and I for getting the letter and for you three for being together. I got the letter, Mac, but Bob came down to the Company the next day, so he as well as some of the other boys you know read it. We are on detached duty guarding German SS and WACS. Something like that memorable January 30, 1945, when we were attached to the 3rd Battalion. The rest of the regiment is 60 miles away taking life easy—playing ball. Personally, I have no complaints, as a jeep driver I have little or nothing to do.

Horton will soon be going home so I can have his T/5 if I want it—I don't know for sure as yet though, as I had an interview at regiment the other day in regard to a position in Special Services as athletic director for the regi-ment—which would be a nice racket as well as a T/4. They called me up because of my service record listing me as a Pro-ball player. Bob isn't too happy with his new job—not feeling well [sic] either. Too much inside work. You should see the boys now; tan and handsome, shoes shined, and all their "fruit salad." Mac, you could do like I did when I bought Mary Ellen her engagement ring. Pick out at least a five-dollar one, but just make the down payment of a dollar; worry about the rest later. Since Julie says she may insist on the $4.00 one, she is sure to be very happy and surprised to get such an expensive one. I can't see why Mac is getting engaged to you, Julie. Just because he used to keep me awake until midnight telling me about you and him.

Mac, I wish you would do something for me; call or write to my mother. She would be very glad to hear from you because she knows what good friends we are and still are (ain't we?) Willie Flowers says tell you hello. Burt hasn't come back from the hospital yet. I'm going to let Millar (now mail clerk) write you a few lines—'member him: BAR in Rush's squad—little English runt. Guess you know your old buddy Osborne [Osbourn] got hit pretty bad back at Remagen, didn't you?

[James Millar] We were certainly sweating you out, Mac, and we really were relieved to hear you came through OK. As usual Ken has everything all messed up. I'm certain you remember I was in Osborne's [Osbourn's] squad and the ancestry is Scotch. Ken's done a pretty good job of describing our present set-up except to mention that I have a Jerry CP tent for my mail room and private quarters. You can see the postal department has suffered a re-naissance. I guess I've written all I can about me, so I'll wish you and Julie all the luck I can. Say I haven't read any new books lately and turn the whole mess over to Wasnick.

[Lloyd Wasnick] Hi, Mac, remember me the little Russian that used to sleep with Jones? Well, I don't look as rugged now as I did. I had to shave off my beard and now I even comb my hair once in a while. Sure, am getting chicken, ain't I? Seaman is my boss now, but I straighten him out whenever he starts in getting rough. All for now, Mac; be good and good luck from the mad Russian. Love and Kisses, Russian

[Kenny Seaman] PS. Drink a C.C. for me."

The company guards 3,500 POWs near Ingolstadt. Writing home on "liberated" stationery—Jack Jewell slipped past a guard and crawled through a window, the naughty officer. It's from the Gaststätten zum Bürgerbräukeller, where Hitler launched his November 1923 Beer Hall Putsch, and Jack notes that the *Stars & Stripes* says that the 9th Infantry will be a "Division of Occupation" in Europe and that commissioned officers will need 85 points to get home. Jack says he is sitting on 81 points, and a year or two in Germany would be OK with him if he can stay out of the Pacific. Then Jack scares his mother half to death: "It looks like the best thing to do is marry one of these Dutch girls. They work like mules and are a lot easier to handle. They say that soldiers will be permitted to have their wives and future wives come to Germany in a year or so, but I don't know who I could get to come over here."[3]

On June 27, Company B moves to Klingen, just south of Aichach. The troops discover a captured motorcycle, and Jack Jewell gets his first ride on one. His mother would never allow him to have one at home, but Jack kids her by writing: "I guess it's a little difficult for you to do much now—Hah!"[4] A Dutch wife? A motorcycle? Mama Norma is probably not amused back in Kansas, but at least Jack has the good sense not to rub it in by adding: "Toto, I've a feeling we're not in Kansas anymore."

Mac convalesces, chowing down on everything in sight. On June 28, a special agent from the War Crimes Office of the Judge Advocate General's Office interviews Mac at home, asking about Stalag VI G and if he witnessed anything that might have been a war crime. Mac describes the two severely burned airmen shot down over Flamersheim, who did not receive medical care. Mac also states that the Germans beat an Army Air Corps major in the camp for answering their questions in a "wise-ass" manner. Jack Dunlap goes on leave to Paris for several days in early July. On July 7, division issues *GO #120*, awarding a Silver Star to Mac:

Private First Class Myron D. MacLean, 16122373, Infantry, United States Army, who distinguished himself by gallantry in action against the enemy on 30 January 1945 in the vicinity of Kalterherberg, Germany. At this time Pfc. MacLean's platoon was forced to reorganize and redeploy after a bitter enemy counterattack. In diverting enemy fire, two members of Pfc. MacLean's automatic rifle team were wounded. To cover his unit and to enable his injured comrades to return safely for aid, Pfc. MacLean employed automatic rifle fire incessantly against the enemy, and by so doing drew the hostile machine gun and rifle fire to his own position. With outstanding gallantry and total disregard for his personal safety, Pfc. MacLean moved from place to place, drawing the enemy's fire until his platoon had safely regrouped. Pfc. MacLean's devotion to duty and heroic actions contributed immeasurably to his unit's success in repulsing the enemy attack which followed. Entered service from Illinois.

Jack Jewell sends photographs taken at the Dachau concentration camp home to his parents on July 13. Two days later, he sits on a court-martial as a juror.[5] Mac is told that after he completes his furlough in Peoria, he will travel to Miami, Florida, to await orders. That scares his mother. The schoolteacher widow, who has almost lost a son and a son-in-law, reads every newspaper in sight. She knows that Japan must be defeated, and that the Army will need a whole lot of infantry to do that. Mac may be one of them.

War planners in Washington estimate that the initial invasion of Japan will cost 109,000 killed and 347,000 wounded Americans; an additional 161,000 men will be killed and 583,000 wounded during the second phase. But don't worry, Grace: for phase 1, Gen. Douglas MacArthur's staff believe that the US would suffer only 125,000 casualties and later reduce that to 105,000—by confidently subtracting from the losses those wounded soldiers who would return to combat after being stitched up.[6]

Blissfully unaware of these ominous estimates, beginning August 17, Mac is living large in South Florida. Early in the war, hotel proprietors there and the US military agreed to house troops at empty resorts; by October 1942, more than 78,000 troops are housed in three hundred hotels (eighty on the beach) such as the Palm Beach Breakers and Miami Biltmore. In September 1944, the Army Service Forces open "redistribution centers" at well-known hotels around the country at Lake Placid, Asheville, Hot Springs, and Santa Barbara, as well as those in Florida. Uncle Sam makes a few changes to the joints, such as taking out the two civilian beds per room, often replacing them with bunk beds that will accommodate six GIs, but it's still easy street.

Mac belongs to the Army Ground and Services Forces Redistribution Station, Miami Beach, in effect a holding detachment for former POWs, and lives in one of the hotels. Duty is nice; the Army's mission is to monitor the physical and mental healing of the men, who are often allowed to go out on the town. Mac notices that there are more lieutenants around than you can shake a stick at, so in the best traditions of scroungers everywhere, Mac "appropriates" an Air Corps lieutenant's uniform and can be seen late afternoons in his room ironing the outfit, so that he can look sharp and have a hotsy-totsy time in the many officers' clubs in the area.

Mac is never caught in his subterfuge, although one evening he thinks he is a "goner." Strolling into the main dining room of an officers' club like he owns the place, the twenty-one-year-old notices that all present suddenly rise from their seats and stand at attention. "They know who I am," the stealth Pfc. quakes inside, believing that at any second, MPs will slap him in handcuffs. But his worries are unfounded; unknown to him, walking in behind him is an Air Corps major general, who smiles as he passes

Mac, now at a nervous halt—the general telling all present to please take their seats and continue their meals.

Back in Illinois, Mac's mother is having none of this "redistribution center" nonsense; redistribution to where? The Pacific? She has already read that Japanese premier Kantarō Suzuki declared that Japan will fight to the very end, rather than accept unconditional surrender. That doesn't sound good. So, she starts writing letters to her member of Congress, Representative Everett McKinley Dirksen. Everett answers. But what Dirksen does not know is that American technology will make everything a moot point, if a special bomb proves successful at a test at Los Alamos, New Mexico. That occurs on July 16, 1945—while Mac was home on furlough—but almost no one knows about it, just as the current president of the United States, Harry Truman, who knew nothing about the project when he was the vice president. But everyone will soon.

Capt. Robert M. Hall replaces Jack Dunlap in command. Hall was with the Sixty-Fifth US Infantry Division, in Third Army. Company B dedicates "Olive Field" in memory of Ray Olive; it is supposed to improve morale, but Jack Jewell writes home on July 24: "Day by day we are getting more like garrison soldiers. We wear ODs [olive drab, noncombat uniform] and now stand retreat and reveille. The men are really disgusted and out of sorts most of the time."[7]

The Allies demand Japan's unconditional surrender on July 26 in the "Potsdam Declaration." Jack Jewell writes on July 28:[8] "The news in the Pacific sounds good, and I sure hope they can end that conflict soon. I know there are a lot of men sweating out that situation." He writes again on July 30. Company B will participate in a parade in two days, and after a short hike in the morning, the unit practices marching all afternoon. Jack comments on the upcoming event: "Old General Patton is supposed to have a division review for us in a few days, and we are supposed to be our best for the old stinker. I am sure glad of one thing and that is we were not under him in combat. They worked the socks off of us as it was, no telling what he would have had us doing."[9] Gen. George Patton reviews the division on July 31 at Manching Airport near Ingolstadt. At the parade's conclusion, he talks—as only George Patton can:

> We should not be sorry that these men died so much as we should be glad that they were born and lived. There are probably few Divisions in the world in your class. . . . I can hardly think of another Division that has written its name so large upon the scroll of history.

Jack writes home and says that the rumor going around is that the number of points required for a discharge might be lowered, which could then include him. He also described the review:[10]

Well, we had our parade yesterday with Patton and all. It was a nice parade, but I didn't feel as impressed as I have at other times. Patton made a short speech which I thought was pretty good. He didn't use all the strong talk and blood-and-guts stuff he is noted for. He also made a short inspection of the troops on the parade ground. It must be nice to be a four-star general. We were all (9th Division) on the parade grounds ready for him and at the exact moment a big C-47 flew in, and he got out ready for the show.

The world changes forever on August 6, 1945, when one B-29 Superfortress bomber, the "Enola Gay," drops one bomb, nicknamed "Little Boy," on Hiroshima, killing between 45,000 and 80,000 Japanese that day. Equal numbers will die of the effects over the next several months. Twenty Allied POWs in Hiroshima die as well. The Soviets, not wanting to miss the spoils of war, declare hostilities and invade Manchuria. On August 9, another B-29, "Bockscar," drops a more powerful atomic weapon on Nagasaki that kills another 80,000. Emperor Hirohito and Prime Minister Suzuki ignore hardcore generals wishing to fight on, and Suzuki seeks an immediate peace with the Allies. Jack reads about the first bomb but knows nothing of Hirohito's discussion with his generals and sends a letter home: "The war in the Pacific looks more promising than it has for some time. I wish those Japs throw in the towel. I think it is almost certain now that I will remain here and probably for a year."[11]

On August 14, Jack Jewell writes from the company's new digs at Friedberg, just east of Augsburg. Jack does not know the details about Japan's unconditional surrender: "Right now the news sounds good, and I only hope it works out. If they don't surrender, they should drop so many atomic bombs that there won't be anything left of Japan, and I have a good idea that's what they will do."[12] And Jack is not alone in those views. Meanwhile, nothing will stop the flow of Army paperwork, not even an unconditional surrender. On August 20, the Army publishes orders awarding Mac a Purple Heart for wounds received at Kalterherberg. Points do not affect him, since liberated POWs have been sent home for medical treatment in the same manner as seriously wounded soldiers. The next day, Bob Pettigrew writes Mac from Aichach:

Received your letter of August 11 and was glad to hear from you. Glad to hear that you received the award papers and now all you have to do is go out and get the medal. Don't contact the boys much lately since I am the company clerk and only see them once a month or so. Hope you get a break and get out of the Army now that the war is over, and start burning the midnight oil on other things besides writing, or are you better in the dark?

Thought you knew about "Noodles," and I write Jay [Lavinsky] once in a while and hope he gets his discharge too. Don't need a thing ole dear right now except some loving but am waiting patiently to get home to get that lovin. Stud is gone home, and all the boys are now sweating out trying to get a point here and there to increase their total. Consequently, more headaches for the Company Clerk, but I don't mind and would like to get enough points for everybody to get home. Think the Infantry boys deserve that much of a break anyway but you being an old Air Corps man probably don't agree with me. See Ken more often than I see anyone of the boys as he comes up to Aichach in <u>his</u> jeep once in a while and stops over to see me.

Pickard went home Sunday last, and he was one happy guy. Guess they will go to work on all of us guys pretty soon and try to send us home. Well, Mac old dear, think I will sign off for now with love and kisses to Mom, Julie, and yourself but you wouldn't want to be bussed by me, or would you. Hope to get back to the Good Old US one of these days. No joking though; lots of luck to you all, and I hope I can write to you and Julie real soon as Mr. and Mrs. Love and kisses, Bob.

Jack Jewell is offered the opportunity to command a company but declines. He tells his parents that there is restlessness among the soldiers, since now that the war is over, all want to go home. "Many of them are hard to control; there is nothing for them to do and they have no interest in any type of training."[13] Although everyone knows that it is only a matter of time before the end of the war in the Pacific—and thus the end of World War II around the world—the Army promotes Pfc. Myron D. MacLean to corporal on August 30. In later years, Mac concludes that this was a "charity" promotion or a good old-fashioned snafu. In an equally momentous occasion as Mac's promotion, on September 2 Japanese officials—humbled and bowed—come aboard USS *Missouri* and sign the surrender documents. President Truman declares Victory over Japan (VJ) Day.

On September 1, Jack Jewell sends his last letter home from Company B—he is going to another outfit the next morning and may be able to return home in October. One of the last chapters of wartime Company B is closing. In mid-September, 9th Infantry headquarters moves to Wasserburg-am-Inn, 35 miles east of Munich and Camp Gabersee, a former insane asylum. Army clerks continue to be industrious, issuing orders on September 23, awarding Cpl. Myron D. MacLean a Purple Heart for wounds received near Monschau, Germany, on November 25, 1944, obviously an error, since Mac was not wounded during that month. Events now hurtle to the finish line. AAAO sets up at the Bavarian village of Rosenheim on the Inn River on October 2. On October 9, the Army issues instructions to allow the newly minted corporal to report to Fort Sheridan, Illinois, for discharge. Mac is crushed the next day, when the Detroit Tigers defeat his beloved Chicago Cubs in game 7 of the 1945 World Series. Mac and millions of other Cubs fans adopt the view "wait till next year." But next year for the Cubs will elude Mac for the rest of his life.

Back in Europe, life becomes better, and on October 27 the AAAO football team wins the 9th Infantry Division championship in Germany. Since the end of the war, the division has been concentrated around Ingolstadt performing occupation duties and will do so until January 1947, when it is inactivated. What the German army in

North Africa, Sicily, Normandy, the Hürtgen, Hohes Venn, Merode Castle, Elsenborn Ridge, and the Remagen Bridge could not do with bullets and bombs, the American army is doing with a typewriter. Finally, on November 7, 1945, Cpl. Myron D. "Mac" MacLean, with his Army Air Corps lieutenant's uniform permanently "retired," is discharged at Fort Sheridan, Illinois.

For Mac, the war is finally over.

SCHOOL OF THE SOLDIER

OPERATION DOWNFALL

There are a whole lot of "Macs" needed to invade Japan. First developed early in 1945 by the Combined Chiefs of Staff at the Argonaut Conference on the Mediterranean island of Malta, the invasion plan receives the ominous code name of Operation Downfall, to be commanded by General Douglas MacArthur against the homeland of Japan. Phase 1 of Olympic will be to assault the southern island of Kyushu and is slated to begin December 1, 1945. The seizure of Kyushu will provide air bases from which to launch massive airstrikes to support the later main effort, Operation Coronet, a landing on Honshu—the largest and most populous island of Japan, slated for March 1, 1946. A major Army unit of the attack will be the First Army—Mac's old outfit. The Joint Chiefs of Staff approves Operation Olympic on May 25, 1945.

"I won't forget the men who died, who gave that right to me."

The rifleman fights without promise of either reward or relief. Behind every river there's another hill—and behind that hill, another river. After weeks or months in the line only a wound can offer him the comfort of safety, shelter, and a bed. Those who are left to fight, fight on, evading death but knowing that with each day of evasion they have exhausted one more chance for survival. Sooner or later, unless victory comes, this chase must end on the litter or in the grave.

—Omar Bradley, commander, Twelfth US Army Group,
A Soldier's Story

Brad's sobering conclusion is confirmed by Company B. From June 10, 1944, to VE-day—a period when America is clearly winning—Company B suffered 88 killed in action / died of wounds, 453 wounded in action, 41 seriously injured in action, and 231 nonbattle casualties—a stunning 813 total casualties, over four and a half times the daily average number of soldiers assigned. According to 1Sgt. Joe Gravino, who was there at Company B's formation in 1941, only a dozen men of that original group remained in the company at the end of the war—equating to just one squad out of an entire company. A small number received promotions that led to transfers, but most not present in May 1945 had been killed or were so badly wounded that they went stateside to noncombat jobs or extensive rehabilitation or were discharged.

The previous fall, back in the Hürtgen, at a battalion aid station, a soldier noticed the area where the dead have been placed. "The bodies were stacked [in rows] three or four [bodies] high and forty to fifty feet long—there may have been many more, but I saw two such stacks."[1] Doing some grisly math, each stack may have contained 133 bodies. Graves Registration sections bury the dead in the 9th Infantry plot at the temporary corps cemetery at Berg, Belgium, northeast of Brussels. Later, the division dead are interred at the temporary Belgian cemetery Henri-Chapelle #1 in graves dug continuously from mid-September 1944 to the end of March 1945. Graves registration personnel place each body inside a mattress cover—not a wooden casket—with identification, such as the soldier's Army serial number marked on various clothing items, which will facilitate the process of later permanent interment. It is from this temporary cemetery that the first shipments of remains of war dead will be returned home for permanent burial.

This repatriation program begins on July 27, 1947. For those remains staying in Europe, the permanent American cemetery Henri-Chapelle, located at Plombières, Belgium, will hold 7,992 American soldiers, many from the 9th Infantry. Seventy-six brothers rest side by side, and three brothers from one family are buried next to one another. Ninety-four graves are unidentified, marked with crosses that read "Here Rests in Honored Glory A Comrade in Arms Known but To God." A colonnade at the cemetery entrance lists 450 servicemen whose bodies have never been recovered.

The remains of all but one Company B soldier killed in those last months now rest with those of their comrades in American cemeteries in Belgium and the Netherlands, or in family plots from California to Maine. Out of necessity, grave markers often record only their names, ranks, date of birth, date of death, home state, and regiment. The paucity of information is not due to a lack of facts, or a shortage of skilled stone masons; the reason is far more significant: there is simply not enough marble and granite on God's green earth upon which to truly record the sacrifice that American soldiers made for their comrades, their families, their fellow citizens, and millions of people they never knew around the world.

Pfc. Henry A. Ambrose: Buried at the Church Hill Cemetery, Wilkins Township, Allegheny County, Pennsylvania.[2]

Pvt. James W. Arnold: Received a sucking chest wound from artillery shrapnel. Although doctors sew up a hole in his lung, James dies of his wounds on March 30 and is buried at Margraten American Cemetery, plot B, row 6, grave 19.[3]

Pfc. Leslie J. Bacon: Remains sent home; buried in the East Bloomfield Cemetery, East Bloomfield, New York, on July 10, 1949.[4]

Pfc. Michael J. Baran Jr: Born in what later became the Czech Republic, buried in the Epinal American Cemetery and Memorial at Arches, France, plot A, row 46, grave 10.[5]

Pfc. Alan H. Bauer: Buried at Henri-Chapelle American Cemetery, plot D, row 3, grave 27.[6]

Pvt. Paul B. Bean: Buried in the Lawn Area in section F, tier 36, grave 4, Santa Rosa Odd Fellows Cemetery, Sonoma County, California. Left a widow, Marjorie B. Henley.[7]

Pfc. Albert D. Bittino: Buried at Saint Thomas Cemetery, Ogdensburg, New Jersey.[8]

Pfc. John H. Boyle: Interred at 1700 hours, February 9, 1945, temporary cemetery Henri-Chapelle #1 in plot KKK, row 6, grave 101. Remains transferred in 1948 to Saint Joseph Cemetery, Ashtabula, Ohio.[9]

Pfc. Deloss J. Bradshaw: Interred at 1000 hours, March 18, 1945, temporary cemetery Henri-Chapelle #1 in plot D-4, row 3, grave 43. On May 7, 1948, remains returned to America aboard US Army transport ship *Lawrence Victory* and buried at Leeds Cemetery, Washington County, Utah. His gravestone reads "He Gave His Life in Freedom's Cause."[10]

Sgt. Roy L. Burchwell: Buried at Newman Cemetery #1, Hi Hat, Floyd County, Kentucky.[11]

Pvt. Walter S. Burke: Interred at 1500 hours, February 8, 1945, temporary cemetery Henri-Chapelle #1, plot MMM, row 10, grave 188. On August 1, 1945, Walter's mother, Mary Loretta, writes the War Department, in this unedited letter: "I am writting about are Son Walter S. Burke, 35613408. That was killed February 5, 1945. when could we get the remains of are Son back. as you say there grave are propely marked recorded to preserve their identity I would thank you to let us know when we could and all about it and if it would be are Son. We only wont are boy and soon as the could possible get remains and we could get things ready for that time. Please let me know when and all about it. I Thank you. Your Truly, This is Walter Mother." The remains are buried August 4, 1948, at Henri-Chapelle American Cemetery in plot C, row 10, grave 57. Walter left a daughter, Phyllis Eilene, in Dayton, Ohio.[12]

Pfc. Theodore S. Clinker: Although Stan received a blood transfusion after massive artillery shrapnel wounds, he died, and he is buried at Henri-Chapelle American Cemetery in block H, row 4, grave 24. Left a widow, Mary.[13]

Pvt. Benedict J. Conrad: Buried at Saint John the Baptist Cemetery, New Brighton, Minnesota. Ben left behind a widow, Ruby, and a daughter, Virginia.[14]

Cpl. Lafie Crabtree: Buried at Oak Hill Cemetery, Webbville, Lawrence County, Kentucky. Left a widow, Dora Ethel, and a son, Charles Glenn.[15]

Pfc. Carl D. Erickson: Interred at 1500 hours, April 7, 1945, temporary cemetery Margraten in plot H, row 5, grave 92. Concerning the final disposition of his grave, Carl's parents write the Army: "If the cemetery at Margraten, Holland, is to be continued—would like to have him left there. If religious services are held—Please have them in Lutheran." Carl is buried at the Margraten American Cemetery, Netherlands in plot I, row 8, grave 9.[16]

Pvt. Willard D. Frase: Interred at 1400 hours, December 26, 1944, temporary cemetery Henri-Chapelle #1 in plot UU, row 2, grave 27. The remains are transferred to the Henri-Chapelle American Cemetery, Plombières, Belgium, in plot A, row 8, grave 24.[17]

SSgt. Pedro Gonzalez: Interred at 1500 hours, February 5, 1945, temporary cemetery Henri-Chapelle #1 in plot MMM, row 10, grave 190. Remains returned to Texas, where his father buries him at the Calvary Catholic Cemetery in Laredo in 1948.[18]

SSgt. John Gourlay: Interred at 1600 hours, October 16, 1944, in temporary cemetery Henri-Chapelle #1 in plot M, row 2, grave 39. Remains later transferred to the Henri-Chapelle American Cemetery in plot A, row 12, grave 36.[19]

SSgt. Albert M. Handy: Interred at Henri-Chapelle #1 in plot M, row 2, grave 34. Remains buried December 19, 1947, at Arlington National Cemetery, section 12, site 1627.[20]

Pvt. Charles H. Irish: Buried at Normandy American Cemetery and Memorial at Colleville-sur-Mer, Basse-Normandie, France, in plot E, row 8, grave 11.[21]

Pfc. John J. Jablonski: Buried in the Epinal American Cemetery and Memorial at Arches, France, in plot A, row 7, grave 124.[22]

Pfc. William A. Karko: Interred at 1600 hours, October 18, 1944, temporary cemetery Henri-Chapelle #1 in plot N, row 1, grave 6; later buried at Henri-Chapelle American Cemetery in plot C, row 3, grave 47. Left a widow, Lorraine. His daughter, Andrea Marie, was born two months after his death.[23]

T/5 William E. Kelley: Interred at 1600 hours, March 8, 1945, temporary cemetery Henri-Chapelle #1. Buried at the Henri-Chapelle American Cemetery in plot C, row 12, grave 5.[24]

Pfc. Joseph M. Kelly: Buried at Mount Calvary Cemetery, Wheeling, West Virginia. The carpenter left a widow, Alice.[25]

Pfc. John Koches: Buried at Brittany American Cemetery and Memorial, Montjoie-Saint-Martin, Saint James, France, in plot C, row 13, grave 12.[26]

Pfc. Joseph J. LaChance: French Canadian, he was buried at Saint Joseph Cemetery, Chelmsford, Middlesex County, Massachusetts, in section A, lot 20.[27]

Pfc. Warren S. Lorio: Interred in temporary cemetery Henri-Chapelle #1 at 1700 hours, February 13, 1945, in plot KKK, row 6, grave 102. In 1949, USATS *Carroll Victory* transports the remains of 3,333 American soldiers home, including his. On July 31, 1949, Warren is laid to rest at Cypress Grove Cemetery, New Orleans, in location 56, Cypress Jessamine Rose. Warren left behind a mother, three brothers, and three sisters.[28]

Pvt. Raymond A. Madison: Temporarily buried in Belgium. In 1948, his remains are returned home and buried at the Fairlawn Cemetery, Stillwater, Oklahoma.[29]

Pvt. Jerome Magluilo: Buried at Holy Cross Cemetery, Brooklyn, New York, in the St. Edmund section, row 4, plot 28.[30]

Pfc. Milton Marlatt: Buried at Morrow Cemetery, Morrow, Warren County, Ohio.[31]

Sgt. George C. Mavis: Buried at Greenleaf Cemetery, Marion, Wisconsin.[32]

Pfc. Chester A. McClurg: In January 1949, a train chugs into the station at St. Matthews, Kentucky. The "bad boy" of Company B is coming home. Initially buried at the American Military Cemetery at Margraten, his family wants him closer. A hearse picks up the wooden casket at the station, and a simple procession transfers it to the Zachary Taylor National Cemetery, plot 1393, in Louisville, Kentucky. The cemetery clerk misspells Chester's name and misses his date of birth by three years. The clerk was extremely fortunate that the scrapper was not alive to see the errors.[33]

Pfc. James T. McCulloch: Buried Rosemound Cemetery, Waco, McLennan County, Texas, in section K 110.[34]

Pvt. Frederick C. McInnis: Buried at the Henri-Chapelle American Cemetery in plot D, row 3, grave 53. Left a widow, Nora.[35]

Pvt. John T. McIntyre: Buried at Margraten American Cemetery, plot F, row 4, grave 27.[36]

SSgt. John J. McPherson: Interred in Belgium. Remains are returned home and buried in the Veterans' section, grave 62, Forest Lawn Cemetery, Greensboro, North Carolina.[37]

Pfc. Willard J. Meadows: Buried at Normandy American Cemetery and Memorial, Colleville-sur-Mer, France, in plot I, row 17, grave 32.[38]

Pfc. Ernie Miguel: Interred in Belgium. Remains returned home and buried by the Veterans of Foreign Wars with full honors in the Quechan Indian Cemetery (Fort Yuma Quechan Cemetery,) Winterhaven, Imperial County, California.[39]

Sgt. Chester C. Miller: Buried at Northview Cemetery, Dublin, Georgia. Left a widow, Robbie.[40]

Pvt. Parry J. Miller: Buried at Memorial Park Cemetery, Bethlehem, Pennsylvania, in section E. Left a widow, Ruth.[41]

Pvt. Odie Z. Mitchell: Buried at Holly Creek Cemetery, Idabel, Oklahoma. Left a widow, Pauline Gladys.[42]

Pfc. Thomas J. Monaghan: Buried at Brittany American Cemetery and Memorial, Montjoie-Saint-Martin, Saint James, France, in plot I, row 9, grave 8.[43]

Pfc. Walter E. Muehleman: Buried in the Long Island National Cemetery, East Farmingdale, New York, in plot H, grave 7992. Left a widow, Laurie Mae, and a son, Walter Ellsworth, whom he had never seen.[44]

Pfc. Lester L. Neal: Buried at Holcomb Memorial Gardens, Bickmore, Clay County, West Virginia.[45]

Pfc. Arnold L. Odette Jr.: Buried at Spring Hill Cemetery, Huntington, West Virginia.[46]

SSgt. Raymond L. Olive: Buried at Henri-Chapelle American Cemetery in plot D, row 13, grave 27. Left a widow, Pearl, and a son, Kenneth. "Buddy" had a brother Richard, killed in action on *USS Maddox* off Sicily on July 10–11, 1943.[47]

Pfc. Alphonse A. Poni: Buried at Normandy American Cemetery and Memorial at Colleville-sur-Mer, Basse-Normandie, France, in plot B, row 19, grave 10.[48]

Pvt. Joseph D. Pratt: Buried at Jeanette Cemetery, Jeannette, Decatur County, Tennessee. Left a widow, Byrda, and a daughter, Kathleen, who was born a month after her father died.[49]

Pvt. Tony Raskell: From West Virginia. Buried at Brittany American Cemetery and Memorial, Montjoie-Saint-Martin, Saint James, France, in plot F, row 28, grave 19.[50]

Pfc. Israel L. Reese: Buried at Henri-Chapelle American Cemetery, plot D, row 12, grave 30. A memorial stone at the Mount Vernon Baptist Church Cemetery, Baxley, Georgia, reads "He gave his all."[51]

SSgt. John E. Reiser: On the morning of March 30, 1945, John Reiser's parents receive his letter. "This war will be over soon, and I will be home to wear my medals so have them ready for me!" Four hours later, his parents receive a telegram stating that their son had been killed in action, while John's wife, Margaret, receives a similar telegram. John's remains are initially interred in Belgium but are later returned to the US and buried at Saint Mary's Cemetery, Hanover Township, Luzerne County, Pennsylvania.[52]

Pfc. Harold Rinebolt: Interred at Henri-Chapelle #1 in plot KKK, row 6, grave 103. Remains later returned home and after cremation are buried at Graham Cemetery, Wayne, Ohio.[53]

Pfc. Gaspar Ruiz: Buried at Cemeterio Municipal, Bayamo, Municipio de Bayamo, Granma, Cuba.[54]

Sgt. James W. Russell: Interred at Henri-Chapelle American Cemetery. In 1957, family members request a flat granite marker be placed at Gray Cemetery, Gray, Maine, where James's remains are later reinterred.[55]

Pfc. Melvin B. Schneider: Buried at Mount Zion Cemetery, Flanagan, Livingston County, Illinois.[56]

Pfc. Anton J. Semrov: Buried at Saint Joseph Cemetery, Joliet, Will County, Illinois.[57]

SSgt. Charles G. Somers: Buried at Riverview Cemetery, Baldwinsville, Onondaga County, New York, in plot B-40 RV.[58]

Pvt. Carlas Tomes: Buried at Lincoln Memorial Park, Portland, Oregon. An only child, he left behind a widow and two sons: Donald, age nine, and David, age two.[59]

Pfc. William Uveges: Buried at Henri-Chapelle American Cemetery, plot E, row 2, grave 62.[60]

Pfc. James S. Vaught: From Dandridge, Tennessee, he is buried at Henri-Chapelle American Cemetery in plot E, row 9, grave 50.[61]

Pfc. Lloyd R. Vunk: Buried at Henri-Chapelle American Cemetery in plot A, row 7, grave 21. Lloyd left behind a widow, Agnes, and a son, Norman Charles.[62]

Pfc. Irving J. Wahl: Buried at Margraten American Cemetery, plot A, row 7, grave 9. Irving left behind a widow, Josephine.[63]

Pfc. Raymond O. Wahlstrom: From Cook County, Minnesota, he is buried at Fort Snelling National Cemetery, Minneapolis, Minnesota, in section C-26, site 14588. Left a widow, Evelyn Florence, and a son, David Peter, age twenty months.[64]

Pvt. Ralph W. Wallace: Buried at Eastlawn Cemetery, Beloit, Rock County, Wisconsin.[65]

Pvt. Noel P. Waters: Buried at Henri-Chapelle American Cemetery, plot E, row 2, grave 72.[66]

Pfc. Roy Weaver: Buried at Oakdale Baptist Church Cemetery, Moultrie, Colquitt County, Georgia.[67]

Pfc. John R. Williams: Buried at Brownville Cemetery, New Lyme, Ashtabula County, Ohio.[68]

Pvt. John S. Wood: Buried at Alderson Cemetery, Alderson, Greenbrier County, West Virginia. Probably died of wounds right after being captured by the Germans on August 11, 1944.[69]

Pvt. Carl D. Wright: Buried at Ashland Cemetery, Ashland, Boyd County, Kentucky.

Pfc. Newton L. Yount: Born on November 2, 1921, in Toledo, Ohio, son of Clarence Albert Yount and Fay E. Millan Yount. He is buried at Toledo Memorial Park, Sylvania, Ohio. Left a widow, Eunice Elsie, and two daughters, Carole, age two, and Gloria, age fourteen months.[70]

Pfc. Theodore Zajac: From Chicago, he is buried at the Normandy American Cemetery and Memorial at Colleville-sur-Mer, Basse-Normandie, France, in plot E, row 12, grave 44.[71]

Pfc. Harry C. "Noodles"/"Brooklyn" Nodell: The soldier who woke up every morning in his foxhole cheerfully announcing, "It's a wonderful day in Germany," is buried in a temporary grave in Belgium. Remains later exhumed, returned to the US, and buried on April 19, 1948, in the Long Island National Cemetery, East Farmingdale, New York, in plot H, 8458. Survived by his widow, Mollie, and two young daughters, Susan Leslie and Barbara June. The family, who moved to Queens after the war, missed their father, referring to him as "the Late Great Harry C." Barbara died in 2012, and Susan in 2017; both left wonderful families of their own. Mollie died in Phoenix, Arizona, on April 3, 2001. She never remarried.[72]

2Lt. Louis A. Benoist III: Interred at an American military cemetery in Belgium, reinterred at the Natchez City Cemetery on November 13, 1947 (section case plot #3, lot #554). His widow wrote a family friend a few months later: "When he died, something in me went too." She later remarried. Louis, the son he never saw, served as an orthopedic surgeon for the Veterans Administration and now lives in Dallas, Texas.[73]

But we shouldn't just be left with only General Omar Bradley's assessment, since it has an edge that the "Soldier's General" probably never intended. It is too linked to numbers, not feelings. For that, let us go to Ernie Pyle, known as "the Old Man" by the troops he covered:[74]

That is our war, and we will carry it with us as we go one from one battleground to another until it is all over, leaving some of us behind on every beach, in every field. We are just beginning with the ones who lie back of us here in Tunisia. I don't know whether it was their good fortune or their misfortune to get out of it so early in the game. I guess it doesn't make any difference, once a man has gone. Medals and speeches and victories are nothing to them anymore. They died and others lived, and nobody knows why it is so. They died and thereby the rest of us can go on and on. When we leave here for the next shore, there is nothing we can do for the ones beneath the wooden crosses, except perhaps to pause and murmur, "Thanks, pal."

Col. Harry A. "Paddy" Flint, the old colonel, who understood the grit of the American soldier, was not assigned to Company B, but he was part of them—and they were part of him. After his death, his widow received his second Distinguished Service Cross:

To Colonel Harry A. Flint, 39th Infantry Regiment, US Army, for extraordinary heroism in action against the enemy on July 24, 1944, in France. Fierce enemy resistance consisting of heavy tanks, artillery, mortar, machine gun, machine pistol, and small-arms fire was delaying the advance of his regiment in the vicinity of LaCour des Landes, France. Convinced that a determined infantry could push through the hostile positions, Colonel Flint went to the battle command post of the Second Battalion to urge the troops forward. Fearlessly exposing himself to heavy enemy fire, he moved ahead of the assault elements of the battalion to observe positions for his troops to occupy. Calling for a tank, Colonel Flint moved along its side and directed fire on a heavily defended hedgerow and then continued alone to a group of buildings just evacuated by the enemy.

Far in advance of his troops, Colonel Flint remained in the dangerous position personally firing at the enemy and urging his men to follow his example. While in this advanced position, Colonel Flint was mortally wounded by sniper fire. During the engagement, Colonel Flint's absolute fearlessness under enemy fire and his dogged determination to show his men by personal example how to dislodge the enemy, so inspired his troops that the objective for which his unit had been fighting for several days was captured. The brilliant leadership, unflinching devotion to duty, and extraordinary heroism displayed by Colonel Flint was [*sic*] in keeping with the highest traditions of military service of the United States and reflect great credit upon himself, his unit, and the United States Army."

It was bound to happen, and perhaps Colonel Flint knew it. With D-day on the horizon, on April 30, 1944, Paddy wrote Omar Bradley, including with it a copy of a letter he had just sent his troops:[75]

Dear Brad, You can read this with no foreboding. A regiment is about the biggest unit, I think, which can have a personal touch. There is a chain of command, though, Brad, and we use it here. I wish it were found in all echelons, including the higher ones. Give that a thought, Brad. Anyway, the [attached] letter tells you honestly what I think, and in all fairness, it is said to the men because it kept them perhaps more content to know as much as they could.

Anyway, Brad, I am content with "Suicide Ranch," ~~AAA~~O. It is certainly a grand fighting unit today and I have a top-hole "segundo" to run it when I have gone. Equipment, supplies, knowledge how to use them and conserve them must be, but when all is said and done, Brad, it is the guts to drive on in that will finish the way. Anyway, that's what we think. Probably won't be seeing you again, Brad, but just wanted to have a personal talk with you and tell you how glad I am to be on your team. Good luck and thank you for being my friend as I am yours, Paddy. This needs nor expects an answer. It's only a wave to cheer you up!

In addition to doing the big things in war, Paddy took care of the little details. When one of his soldiers was wounded or sick and evacuated to a field hospital, Paddy wrote a note to the trooper, telling him that his old spot in the regiment would always be open for him and that no one would take his place. One soldier recalled his own personal meeting with "the Old Man":[76]

> I went to the medics with an infected tooth. I had just emerged from the tent after the extraction with a mouthful of blood, and still wobbly from the shot. I came face to face with Paddy Flint. I saluted him and went on my way. Suddenly I heard him shout "Corporal, wait a minute." "Yes Sir," I replied and stood my ground. "Corporal, I want you to close your eyes and walk about twenty-five yards straight ahead until I stay stop." This I did. Then he told me to do it once more. By this time, my mouth was full of blood from the extraction.
>
> Stopping, I spit out the blood. He walked over and asked me: "What's wrong?" I told him that due to the extraction my mouth was full of blood, and I didn't want to swallow it. He said, "I'll be damned, corporal, why the hell didn't you say so?" I replied, "Hit don't make no difference [a famous Paddy saying]." He smiled and said "OK, take off and take care of yourself." I never did find out what experiment he had in mind with that walking bit, but I did know that while walking back to my outfit, I liked this "old guy."

The remains of "the Fighting Irishman" were interred in Normandy, were later transported home, and are buried on September 13, 1948, at section 2, site 310, Arlington National Cemetery. There is no special gravestone inscription, such as ~~AAAO~~, but Paddy's influence was far more influential than just four letters.

Col. Harry Flint knew that soldiers didn't win just with their smarts, or their equipment, or even their leaders; they won with their heart, which started a special chain reaction that would prove unstoppable: "A soldier can be a hero and a hero can be a legend and a legend can make a superman out of a soldier."[77] Paddy made ordinary soldiers extraordinary and motivated more than a few Willies and Joes to achieve that which they thought they never could, which ultimately became part of the legend called "the Greatest Generation."

I'll Be Seeing You.
—Billie Holiday

The Silent Generation

Perhaps he will change back again when he returns, but never completely. If he is lucky, his memories of those sharp, bitter days will fade over the years into a hazy recollection of a period which was filled with homesickness and horror and dread and monotony, occasionally lifted and lighted by the gentle, humorous, and sometimes downright funny things that always go along with misery.

—Bill Mauldin, *Up Front*

Victory came for the rest, and they were met by Doris Day and "Sentimental Journey" when they returned home. The sacrifices made by their buddies propelled many to finish an education, get a job, and raise a family. Some achieved "that which they thought they never could." One later appeared in *Vogue*; another won an Emmy and an Academy Award. Another Company B soldier founded a teaching journal and developed a "Mechanical Manipulation Test," while still another became a biochemist and discovered the molecular heterogeneity of D-amino oxidase—and to think they all had once been called "dogfaces." Regardless of the life's path they took, however, they largely remained tight lipped for the rest of their lives about what they experienced in the dark forests, deep snow, and windswept ridges. But they didn't retreat from the outdoors: playing golf, fishing, planting Christmas trees, hunting, farming, beekeeping—because they never retreated from anything.

Now known as Dad, Pop, Gramps, Grandpa, or Papaw, they watched *Combat*, saying that every episode had a moral lesson that you should learn. They shook their heads in dismay, viewing the "shenanigans" in a POW camp in *Hogan's Heroes*. For those who made it to 1998, they walked out of theaters by the dozen during scenes in *Saving Private Ryan*—not because the movie was too Hollywood, but because it brought back too many terrible memories. And because they knew never to quit, they turned around, walked back in, and watched the rest of it.

Each of them had his own, unique, memory—or nightmare—concerning the Hürtgen that would never leave his subconscious, always ready to crawl up from his guts and grab his throat. Too many buddies had died hard. They wouldn't tell their families what really happened, because if they did, it would have gone something like this, and they didn't want their loved ones having nightmares of their own:[1]

You can't get all of the dead because you can't find them, and they stay there to remind the guys advancing as to what might hit them. You can't get protection. You can't see. You can't get fields of fire. The trees are slashed like a scythe by artillery. Everything is tangled. You can scarcely walk. Everybody is cold and wet, and the mixture of cold rain and sleet keeps falling . . . and soon there are only a handful of the old men left.

Or maybe it was the things they had to do, such as this from a Silver Star citation in 1943 in North Africa to Company B's Pvt. Jesus C. Flores, from El Paso, Texas:[2]

Private Flores, as a scout, was moving up a hill under heavy machine gun fire, when he observed Private [Harold] Rogers, another scout, engaged in hand to hand combat with the enemy. Promptly, and without any regard of his own safety, Private Flores rushed the German, shot him, and then broke his neck with a vertical butt stroke.

Jay Lavinsky went through five operations before departing England on May 10, 1945. He later recalled that in the hospital, as soldiers reached a certain level of recovery, nurses sometimes invited them into a closet for "further treatment." During his return home on a hospital ship, Jay won $7,000 playing poker—he gave $5,500 to his parents when he arrived in the US on May 24. But Jay was still not fully healthy and went into another hospital on Staten Island. He received an honorable discharge on September 22, 1945, at Camp Upton, the recipient of two Bronze Stars for Valor and the Purple Heart. On October 1 in Ventnor City, New Jersey, Jay wrote Mac MacLean after a visit to Brooklyn to see the widow of Noodles Nodell: "I also stopped up to see Noodles' wife, and she was glad to see me as she still had a slight feeling, he was still alive. It sure is a shame as his kids are out of this world."

Returning to Philly, Jay graduated from the Tyler School of Art, Temple University, in 1950. Memories of the war haunted him, and he briefly considered suicide—later joking that he changed his mind when he saw that the gas oven into which he was about to put his head was actually an electric one. His father changed the family name to Lavin, as Jay headed west.[3] Jay Lavin became a successful high-end jewelry designer in California with Peter J. Bentley, Ltd., winning numerous awards, appearing in *Vogue* magazine, and receiving a Chevalier-grade French Legion of Honour in 2016, both for his professional success and military service.

In 1998 he was inducted into the Contemporary Design Group Hall of Fame. In his personal life, he was best friends with Timmy S. Woods (Beverly Hills designer), so much so that they got married—twice! Jay helped raise Timmy's son, Briny, although not his biological son, and loved him as his own.

"I wanted to be good to my country," he later said. And he had been. Once, while his squad provided covering fire, Jay charged and captured a farmhouse occupied by ten German soldiers. In another instance, he carried a wounded soldier off a hill to medical support, undoubtedly saving that soldier's life.

Jay's physical wounds plagued him for life. Worse, in 1994, a psychiatrist diagnosed him with posttraumatic stress syndrome, beginning in 1945, which led to "chronic sleep disturbance, nightmares, recurring/re-experiencing various war-related traumatic events, depression, mood instability, anger outbursts, dissociative events, decreased concentration, hypervigilance, and exaggerated startle responses."[4] Even worse were memories of the German family killed at Berg: "After that, I have never shed tears for any reason and to this day I carry guilt that I can't shake. I lost respect for myself even though the Germans killed many families. No matter what happens around me to my family or friends, I cannot shed tears."

But because, deep down, Jay was a mensch, he softened that opinion for Briny's thirteen-year-old son, Dean: "If you are in combat, that stays with you for your whole life, no matter what type of person you are, or where you push it [your memories]." And while his memories remained, so did his compassion, and he helped disabled veterans for decades.[5] In 2023, Jay sustained a severe fall, after which he needed constant care to eat, bathe, and climb into a wheelchair, and then back to his final foxhole—a hospital bed. Seeing his need, the Veterans Administration quickly rode to the rescue and admitted Jay to their long-term facility in West Palm Beach. Jay is still alive.

Willie White received the Combat Infantryman Badge at the end of the war and later the Bronze Star. On June 30, 1945, he was promoted to staff sergeant.[6] He separated from the service in March 1946, but Army life was now in his blood. Willie attended Tennessee Agricultural & Industrial State College in Nashville, where he played football. He rejoined the Army on October 12, 1950, and married Jo Ann Douglas in Dallas on November 13, 1952; the couple would have four children: Kenneth, James, Marcellina, and Anna. From 1952 to 1954 and from 1958 to 1961, he was stationed in West Germany. Anna recalled that he loved golf, music, dancing, and spending precious free time with his family. Sgt. Maj. Willie Scott White was assigned to South Korea on August 4, 1967, and died of coronary artery insufficiency there on January 15, 1968, serving in the 2nd Infantry Division. He is buried at Arlington National Cemetery, section 51, site 2485.[7]

Jack Dunlap was offered the French Croix de Guerre before he left Europe. He declined this honor, insisting that it be awarded to an officer continuing to serve in the theater. Col. Dunlap served in the Korean Conflict, winning three Battle Stars, later becoming the G1 personnel officer in Okinawa. He became a paratrooper, serving thirteen years with the 82nd and 11th Airborne Divisions. Throughout his career, Col. Dunlap jumped approximately 150 times in military maneuvers and air shows.[8] Jack later deployed to the Vietnam Conflict. After retiring from the Army with thirty years' service, he worked as a tax assessor for Charleston County and was a real estate salesman for Everett-Smith Realty. An avid fisherman and golfer, he moved to Hesperia, California, in the early 1980s. In 1994, he and his family moved to Las Vegas, where he died on November 1, 2005. Jack was interred with full military honors in South Carolina at the Beaufort National Cemetery, section 35, site 52.

Jack Jewell returned to Kansas and was released from active duty on October 30, 1945; just before, at a USO dance, Jack met Jane. He and Marion "Jane" Palmer married in Dallas, Texas, on May 25, 1946. The couple would have four sons and two daughters. Jack became the manager of the Branch Flour Mill for several years before returning to the Army. He served in the Ordnance Section, Eighth US Army in Korea, 1951–52, and the Tokyo Ordnance Depot, 1952–54, and supervised ordnance research at Duke University, 1954–56. Later assignments included being stationed at Aberdeen Proving Grounds, serving as an ordnance officer in the Vth Corps in Frankfurt, Germany, and attending the Army Command and General Staff College, Fort Leavenworth.

Jack returned in 1962 to the University of Kansas, obtaining a BA in international relations before revisiting Aberdeen and Korea again. He was assigned to the Commander in Chief Pacific Office in Honolulu, Hawaii, 1966–69. Unfortunately, his son John died at age fifteen at Tripler Armey Medical Center in Hawaii in 1966.

Col. Jewell retired in 1972 and then attended KU a third time, earning a BS in education; from 1975 to 1978 he taught in Taif, Saudi Arabia, as the program manager of the Saudi Arabian Army Ordnance Corps School. He later served as cross-cultural coordinator for Saudia, the national airline of Saudi Arabia. In the 1980s, Jack and Jane purchased a wooded rural property near Lawrence and built a home, known to the family as "The Land."

With a spirit of adventure and desire to see the world, encouraged by reading Richard Halliburton's *The Royal Road to Romance*, he and Jane returned to countries where they had lived—Germany, Japan, and Saudi Arabia—and visiting the special families they had befriended. In 2010, he traveled to Europe with daughter Kathy for the dedication of a 9th Infantry plaque on the remains of the Ludendorff Bridge at Remagen, the only Company B soldier present. Jack died on November 2, 2011, in Topeka; his ashes were buried five days later at Fort Leavenworth National Cemetery with full military honors in section T, site 298. Jack once said that after the war, he had a hard time looking at flowers, because in France in 1944 he had seen so many dead bodies covered with flowers along the roads, placed by the local people.

"Grandpa Jack" shared his favorite pastimes and values with his eight grandchildren, including morel-mushroom-hunting expeditions, promising a chocolate milkshake to whoever located the first one. He offered a crisp 100-dollar bill to any grandchild who could recite the Gettysburg Address from memory. His grandchildren recalled that when they visited Grandpa Jack on "The Land," he took them on hayrides and let the older kids drive a Mule all-terrain vehicle and, if they were well behaved, shoot a BB gun. He loved grilling barbecue ribs, beer in a frosted mug, black walnuts, licorice, peanut brittle, pickled onions, horseradish, fried eggplant, fried mush, Chet Atkins, *Hee Haw*, accordion music, fishing, photography, delivering truckloads of firewood to friends and family members, supporting KU and Wellsville High basketball and football, working hard, and being a good neighbor. Years after Jack died, Kathy found a letter revealing a hidden side of her father, written on October 5, 1945, before he departed France:[9]

Last Friday [September 28], I was given a 2½-day pass to visit Paris, and I never had any time better in my life. I didn't buy anything this time, but I sure didn't miss seeing anything and I only spent $40. I met a girl the first afternoon I was there, and she was my guide for the rest of the time. I can't tell you all we did now but will tell more when I see you. She had me to her home for dinner and I went to a horse race with her father and brother. Went to Versailles, dance shows (front seats always). What a time was had by all—if we stay here any length of time, I'm going back. I wanted to marry her while I was there but just didn't have time.

Jack ran out of time and went home just days later. Kathy and other family members insist that Jack was not one to kid around about something this serious, and that he probably did indeed have thoughts of marrying the French girl he met, similar to thoughts of thousands of other GIs about girls they fell in love with overseas.

Stanley Mills returned to Fort Douglas, Utah, in early 1945. Not only had Marie learned to walk again despite multiple sclerosis, but she and Stanley would have two children, Judith "Judy" and Anita. Stanley toyed with the idea of buying a farm but became an accountant in Garfield, Washington. The work was boring compared to his wartime days, and Stan returned to the service, retiring as a lieutenant colonel. Anita recalled that her dad was orderly and always followed the rules. With two daughters, Stanley checked up on arriving dates, although in typical fashion, he often forgot their names. But he never forgot to take his family fishing at Lake Coeur d'Alene, his favorite fishing hole. The couple had nine grandchildren; one, Heidi Marie, recalled: "He never really talked to me about the war. He was quiet and always well-dressed— slacks and cardigans—except when he went fishing, which he loved to do. And he was quite tolerant even with nine grandchildren running around!"

The war stayed with Stanley, especially his constant rumbling cough, a "souvenir" from the Hürtgen. "When we were at the store, if I couldn't find Dad, I just stopped, stood still, and listened for his cough, which surely would occur within a few minutes," said Anita. Mere died in 1988, while Stanley passed away in Tacoma, Washington, on November 16, 1992. Stanley Mills is buried in the Moscow Cemetery, Moscow, Idaho (Old Section, block 3).[10]

Joe Gravino went home on furlough and married Grace Mary Pronest, a recent graduate of Nazareth College, on February 21, 1945, at St. Patrick's Church, Fairport, New York. He returned to Company B on May 14, 1945, and departed Europe for a final time on June 14 and was discharged on June 28 at Fort Dix.

Like many other soldiers, Joe later ran up against government bureaucracy after a massive 1973 fire at the National Personnel Records Center in St. Louis. In the conflagration, Joe's file was destroyed. In his attempt to receive a copy of his records, he documented that he had been wounded twice and should have two Purple Hearts, a

CIB, and a Bronze Star. Despite letters from two company commanders, the Army Board for Correction of Military Records did not accept much of his information. His old buddy, Ben Murrell wrote on Joe's behalf, revealing the nature of the combat that the paper-pushers back home could never know:

> In the Hürtgen Forest, Germany. His company command post was built out of fallen trees, cut off by artillery bursts. During an attack, a log broke loose and landed on Sergeant Gravino, pinning his left leg. It took 30 minutes to free him. I do not remember whether I made out a battle casualty report as at that time no sick calls were allowed.... Unless you were shot or had shrapnel wounds there were no sick calls. He was in pain for a few days but came out of it.

The board was unmoved. Exasperated, the old first sergeant wrote back: "If there is any question regarding the stone fragments embedded in my hip, the stone fragments were propelled by the concussion grenades thrown by the Germans." Joe and Grace had nine children: Joseph, Charles, James, John, Teresa, Thomas, Bernard, Donald, and Mary Lou. Joe bought a "mom and pop" butcher shop / grocery store from his father-in-law, renamed it Gravino's, and ensured that each child learned responsibility by working there. He retired in 1974 to spend more time outside, becoming a groundskeeper at the Rochester Country Club.[11] Grace died in February 1994. Joe and Al DiRisio stayed close during the postwar years. He would later say that the conflict had turned the soldiers in Company B into a brotherhood. When Joe died in Macedon, New York, on November 19, 2007, he had fourteen grandchildren and several great-grandchildren. First Sergeant Joseph Francis Gravino received a funeral mass at St. Patrick's Church in Macedon, with interment at the Macedon Village Cemetery. In the middle of Macedon, Gravino Park and baseball field, named for Joe, salutes his accomplishments. Top Gravino was a soldiers' soldier.

Frank Randall survived his life-threatening wounds; initially hospitalized at Kennedy General Hospital, Memphis, he carried a German machine gun bullet in his left pelvis for the rest of his life. An Army medical board offered him medical retirement. "I told them to shove it," he said, and he remained in the service and was promoted to captain later in 1945; elevated to the Regular Army in 1946, he returned to Germany and took command of the same Company B, but the old soldiers were gone. Frank attended the US Army Command and General Staff College (CGSC) in 1951 and served as chief advisor, Joint Task Force, Chinese Nationalist Army. Frank married Marilyn Josephine Johnson in 1955 in Lordsburg, New Mexico.[12] Retiring from the Army on July 31, 1964, he died on February 6, 2006, and was buried in the Resurrection Chapel Mausoleum in Jefferson City, Missouri. When Frank retired, he said to his wife, "I didn't get the star." Her reply: "You didn't get the ulcer either." Frank would forever call the company "Fireball B."[13]

Phil Holman was discharged at Camp Beale, California, on April 4, 1946. Later returning to Lincoln, Nebraska, he enrolled in the University of Nebraska, using the GI Bill. By then he had met the love of his life, Arvilla "Pete" Petersen, who was also active with the university. She had taught all grades in a one-room school in Nance County, until she entered the Nursing Corps at Methodist School of Nursing in Omaha, graduating in 1947. The couple met on a blind date when she worked as a nurse in training at a hospital psychiatric ward. Phil would spend the rest of his life using that experience as a punch line for a joke. They married on November 28, 1947.

In 1953, Phil was the editor of the Cornhusker Alumnus Association. The couple had two sons, James and John Paul, and three daughters, Patricia, Linda, and Ann Elizabeth. Phil joined the US Army Reserves, receiving a commission in the 89th Infantry Division. He attended CGSC at Fort Leavenworth, later taught there, and retired a colonel. Arvilla and Phil visited Hawaii, Greece, Italy, Switzerland, Germany, Denmark, Norway, Sweden, the Caribbean, and Germany. Arvilla died in 2014; she was a true lady, which is appropriate since he was a true gentleman. Phil Holman died on October 8, 2020. A year prior, Phil provided something that he wanted each of you to know:[14]

You wanted a story, something that happened to me in World War II. Something that stands out in my memory. What I write about still haunts me sometimes when thinking about what happened some 70 years ago. I have not told this story to anyone before. Perhaps now is the time to do so, to put it to rest, so to speak. It is not a pleasant story, but then war is not pleasant. A day I can still remember. A day I can still see in my mind. Here is what happened.

It was a nice warm spring day in Germany. The war was mostly over, or so we thought. The squad had made it through the deadly Hürtgen Forest screwup, the Battle of the Bulge, the battles for the Roer River dams, and the crossing of the Rhine River at Remagen. The Ninth Infantry Division and the rifle squad of which I was a part was rushing across Germany riding tanks and trucks, but sometimes on foot, especially when we took small-arms fire. But generally, it was a time to relax from the brutal battles during the worst winter weather in the country's recent history. The squad, down to eight men (12 is normal) from losses during the winter, was sent on patrol to see what was ahead.

The sun was shining, a few clouds in the otherwise clear sky—a perfect day for a stroll on the tree-covered hills of central Germany. We could see a column of smoke rising lazily from the chimney of a small brick farmhouse nestled in the valley below us, next to a small creek flowing past (like a *Saturday Evening Post* cover). All was quiet—too quiet. No birds singing, no guns rumbling their thunder. Just quiet. I was the assistant squad leader (Sergeant), 19 years old and scared. Combat veterans were scared most of the time. Those who said they were not are dead or liars. A recon patrol in front of your parent unit's lines was apt to turn into a combat patrol at a moment's notice.

We, the eight of us, tired and a little jittery, rested on the hill, searching for signs of the enemy, but finding none. Across from our vantage point, on the other side of a gravel and mud road leading past the farmhouse, was a higher hill that could give us a better view of the terrain ahead. The road had to lead somewhere, probably to another city to be fought for and a river to be crossed—all things our commanders needed to know. So, we headed to the higher hill, not without some grumbling since we were in a nice lazy spot. We ran across the road—no problem and regrouped on the other side and began to move up the new hill. Before we reached the top, however, we ran into a problem—a German patrol doing the same thing we were—recon.

For some reason, probably because the assistant squad leader was responsible for the rear, I looked back at the road we had just crossed and saw a German walking down the far side toward us. I turned around to signal the squad leader only to see him signal enemy in sight. We all hit the dirt. I could see through the trees in front of me, about 100 yards away, gray trench coat and all, a German soldier. I shot him. After a brisk but short fire fight the squad, unharmed, returned to our first hill and then back to our platoon headquarters to report. Another ho-hum day in the life of an infantryman and still a good day for a stroll in central Germany. After all, we could count on a hot meal from our kitchen this day.

Oliver Osbourn was discharged on December 5, 1945, in Chickasha, Oklahoma. He married Hermione Juanita "Dickie" Hawkins on November 20, 1948, in Montgomery, Alabama. The couple had two sons, John and Michael. Over the years he served in a variety of jobs, including a messenger; a yard clerk for the Gulf, Mobile and Ohio Railroad; and a machine operator for the Cardinal Pest Control Company. Oliver died on June 10, 1992.[15]

Jessie Slaughter returned to the States on September 18, 1945, discharged on October 23, and returned to Texas to see his son Billie Joe for the first time and to find work at the Dickson Weatherproof Nail Company in Houston. He and Eva Marie had a second son, Thomas Claude, in 1947. Billie Joe served in the Vietnam Conflict in First Battalion, 13th Armored Regiment, and later was mayor of Trinity, Texas. Jessie died of cancer on October 22, 1980, in Walker County, Texas, and is buried at Cedar Grove Cemetery in Trinity. Billie Joe said of his father: "He wouldn't talk about the war. I guess he was trying to forget the things he saw."[16] Eva Marie died twenty years later and is buried next to him. The words on their grave read "My Love Goes with You and My Soul Waits to Join You."

Langley Turner returned to the US, furloughed after many arduous years overseas. He was discharged on May 27, 1945, at Camp Atterbury, Indiana, returned to Kentucky, and married Violet Sparkman. The couple had two sons, Gary Langley—who died at birth—and Larry Michael, and one daughter, Myra Gail (Elliott); his grandkids (Myranda Grace and John Michael) called him "Papaw." Langley became a railroad engineer with the Chesapeake and Ohio Railway; in thirty-six years, he missed only one week of work. He was an avid raccoon hunter, raising treeing Walker coonhounds, including a 1984 hunting champion named "Goofy." As his family said, "Papaw worked hard but always found time for his favorite recreation, coon hunting. He would often work a sixteen-hour shift, come home, get his dogs, and hit the hills. Sometimes he napped, while the dogs were running, by leaning back against a tree until they would bark that they were on a coon, and he would wake up and go to them."

The family also remembered what a stickler Papaw was for punctuality; "fashionably late" just didn't cut it: "He believed that you were never, ever to be late. He would arrive ahead of schedule at least one hour. If you arrived on the appointed time, it meant you were late. We had to eventually tell him later dinner times because he would show up two hours ahead of schedule and would want to know why you weren't ready."

Violet died of cancer in 1994. Langley had open heart surgery in 2007, but the tough old soldier insisted on driving his old Chevy pickup soon afterward, demanding Jimmy Dean sausage biscuit sandwiches every breakfast. Myranda described Papaw as "the strongest, toughest person I ever knew. I loved spending time with him, including hiking up and down Kentucky hills looking for new hunting areas. He was stubborn, had an impeccable memory, and kept everything he ever bought, but was generous and would give anything to someone in need. And he loved his grandchildren no matter what we did." Residing in Prestonsburg, Lang died on May 6, 2014; he was buried at the Turner Cemetery in Dema, Knott County. Phil Holman said of his platoon sergeant: "[He was] one of the best men I've ever met."[17]

Jim Rush returned to the States with a Purple Heart and went to Camp Joseph T. Robinson, Arkansas. He developed pneumonia and came under the care of an Army medical technician, Virginia Frances Perry—who "stalls" his recovery for three months, until the war is over. Jim separated from the Army on November 8, 1945, graduated from college, and married Virginia; they had two daughters, Glenna Louise and Alison Edith, and a son, James Joseph III. The family lived in Chester and Media, Pennsylvania, where he was employed as an engineer, and then moved to Alexandria, Virginia, to work for the Navy. Virginia died in 1988. Jim, who liked to sail and garden and was a beekeeper, later moved to North Carolina. He disliked the sound of fireworks his entire life; watching *Saving Private Ryan*, he shuddered hearing the squealing sound of the tank tracks. Jim Rush died in New Bern on March 20, 2000, and was cremated.[18]

Ken Seaman received the Bronze Star and the Purple Heart. On December 27, 1945, he sent a telegram from Nürnberg, Bavaria, to Mary, saying that he hoped they would never spend another Christmas or New Year's apart. Returning home on April 6, 1946, he became the Mattoon streets superintendent, managed the American Legion baseball team, and was the commander and club manager of American Legion Post 88. Nobody but nobody tells the veterans in Post 88 that they can't have illegal, two-bit slot machines in the legion hall, and Ken is one step ahead of the law, setting up an "intelligence service" so that minutes prior to every police raid, the machines simply "disappear"—to a barn on his parents' farm; the machines are never confiscated.[19]

An avid sports fan, Ken enjoyed listening to broadcasts of the Chicago Cubs, the Chicago Bears, and the University of Illinois. His love of the Cubs later turned to anxiety, and after a few innings he would have to stop listening—waiting till the next day for the results in the *Chicago Tribune*. Ken also loved golf, baseball, and bowling. His two daughters, Gail and Jeanne, had children of their own, and he never missed his grandchildren's baseball games; at last count he had sixteen great-grandchildren. Mary developed dementia, and Ken insisted that she remain home so he could care for her, feeding her every meal and carrying her to the bathroom until the day she died in 2001. Ken maintained his own independence until he died of a heart attack in Mattoon on February 16, 2007, while he was sitting in his car waiting for the windows to defrost. He was buried in Dodge Grove Cemetery. Before his death, Ken implored his two grandsons to never join the military, on the basis of his own wartime experiences. Grandson David summed up Ken's life: "I can't imagine a better grandfather."

Herman Eichel, as a good marksman and promoted in May 1945 to communication sergeant, might have made the Army a career after the war, but he did not. He returned to Ohio, was separated on March 15, 1946, and graduated from the University of Dayton with a BS in chemistry in 1948. Grandson of German immigrants, Herman later received a PhD in biochemistry from the University of Cincinnati. He married Margaret Ann Ens; the couple had four sons and a daughter. Dr. Eichel was an extraordinarily successful biochemist at the C. F. Kettering Foundation, Abbott Laboratories, and National Cash Register Company, and he was a member of the Ohio Academy of Science. He also determined the molecular heterogeneity of D-amino oxidase enzyme. Herman never spoke much about the war to his children. But he did something even better—he brought back his M1903 Springfield rifle! After a life of wonderful achievements, Herman died in Albuquerque, New Mexico, on September 5, 1994. He is buried at Graceland Cemetery, Sidney, Shelby County, Ohio.[20]

Edward Pickard undoubtedly thought that the Hürtgen was rough, but his postwar future was even rougher. He reenlisted as staff sergeant on October 17, 1945, at Fort Oglethorpe, Georgia, for duty in Hawaii. He and Martha Perdue soon divorced, and he married Dorothy Marie Kelly in 1946; a son, Edward "Skip," was born in 1947. Sergeant Pickard later joined the Twenty-Fifth US Infantry Division, the "Tropic

Lightning Division," for occupation duty in Japan, which was shattered on June 25, 1950, when North Korea launched a surprise invasion of South Korea. On July 5, 1950, SSgt. Pickard and his unit were ordered to the conflict.

On January 3, 1951, enemy troops captured Edward Pickard and held him prisoner at Camp Ch'ang-Song. En route to prison camps, North Korean guards allowed their captives to drink only standing water at rice paddies—which had been fertilized with human excrement. Nicknamed "Death Valley," the Ch'ang-Song huts had mud walls; the prisoners had no access to medicine and were poorly fed. Firing squads executed prisoners attempting to escape. In winter, temperatures fell to −20°F.[21] Over 2,800 American soldiers died in the camps.

Edward was repatriated on September 5, 1953, and spent five months in a hospital. He was discharged from the Army as a sergeant first class on August 1, 1963. After the breakup of his second marriage, he married Mary Francis Barber. Edward A. Pickard died on February 14, 1989, at Texarkana, Texas; he is buried at Greenwood Community Cemetery, Greenwood Texas.[22]

Billie Flowers got into one more scrap after the war in Germany, duking it out with William Spano in Company B for some unknown reason—but when did a true scrapper ever need a cause for throwing a punch? He was discharged on January 5, 1946, at Fort Bragg and later married Thetus Grace Cox. The couple had a son, Billy Joseph, on September 26, 1948, as well as sons Douglas and Ted. They also had a daughter, Hilda, on September 14, 1950, but she died of acute stomach flu on October 3 of that year. The couple divorced in 1967. Shortly afterward, son Billy was drafted and sent to Crailsheim, Germany, and the 1-51st Infantry, making Spec 5. Billie, who was bothered by foot issues after the war, gave this advice to his son, the future infantryman: "Whatever you do, you wash your feet every day." Billie worked at the North Carolina Division of Roads, retired, and then opened a small rural grocery store called the "Red Barn Grocery." He loved to hunt and fish and kept up with baseball. Grace remarried and died on December 14, 2012. Billie died of liver cancer at the Veterans' Administration Hospital at Durham, North Carolina, on July 24, 1981, at age fifty-seven. The Company B scrapper is buried at the New Hollywood Cemetery in Lumberton, North Carolina.[23]

Thomas Naud was promoted to corporal and returned home. He went on to be a reporter and producer with *The Today Show*, *The Tonight Show*, and *The Jonathan Winters Show*, winning an Emmy and an Academy Award and interviewing Marilyn Monroe and Rocky Marciano. He died on September 24, 2016, and is buried at Riverside National Cemetery, Riverside, California, in section 61A, site 497.[24]

Kermit Lockridge returned to the US on April 8, 1946, and departed the service as a T/5 four days later.[25] Dale, nicknamed "Cuz," worked for his cousin at Lockridge Lumber Company until 1954 and then built industrial air conditioner units with Westinghouse in Staunton, Virginia, until 1985. Dale married Lennis Anne Bussard on May 5, 1953, at Staunton. They had a daughter, Debra Kaye, born in 1957, and two grandchildren, Ashley and Daniel. Both youngsters loved him very much, whether it was fishing, hunting, or appreciating his jokes—"Granddaddy" would often tie his grandchildren's shoes together or tie knots in the laces! Dale served as a deacon at the Third Presbyterian Church in Staunton. At his funeral, Dale was described as a "silent saint," always cleaning the parking lot and sidewalks during winter and neatly trimming the shrubs year-round, usually when no one was around, since he did not like to be in the limelight. He once told his daughter that Germany was beautiful, and that he would love to go back and see it again, but Dale never did. Dale Lockridge died on February 24, 2009, at Fishersville, Virginia. He is buried at Augusta Memorial Park in the Garden of Devotion.[26]

George Holdren returned to West Virginia and married Fern Myla Dudley in Mercer County in 1946; the couple had one daughter, Jane (Shorter). George died on July 18, 1982, in Princeton, West Virginia. He was buried in Belcher Cemetery in Princeton. Fern remarried after George's death, died in December 2010, and was buried in the same tiny cemetery.[27]

Seymour Berry recovered from his wounds, returned home, and worked for the Department of the Treasury. In 1953, he received a law degree from George Washington University Law School. Moving up through the ranks, he became the director of the Bureau of Engraving and Printing in 1977. He died in Silver Springs, Maryland, on December 6, 2008.[28]

Manley Fuller, like all GIs, was forbidden to fraternize with Germans, but after the war he befriended a German woman, Rosa Wagner; they secretly dated before Manley received orders for home in late 1945. He promised to write her, but the trauma he suffered during the war left him depressed, and he never did, a failure that nagged him his entire life—and he always wondered how her life had turned out. Waiting in a camp in Normandy for his turn to leave, his tent mate was a man in terrible condition—unshaven and filthy, he wore the same tattered clothes every day, while his spare clothing was all perfectly clean and unworn. Manley told him that they'd be going home soon. The man just looked through him and said, "We're never going home." Departing Le Havre, France, eight days later, Manley's ship, the *Athos II*, was hit by a hurricane near the Azores Islands and stranded. He recalled: "The ship rolled so hard that the galley freezers wouldn't stay shut and disgorged their contents, spewing melted ice cream and Christmas turkeys everywhere."[29] The passengers were finally transferred to USS *Enterprise* and made it to New York.

Manley received an envelope from his mother, containing the allotment money he had sent home, a good start for his civilian life. But it wasn't to be. Manley worked in a shoe factory, but his hands shook badly from his wartime experiences. The foreman moved him between several stations, requiring less manual dexterity, but to no avail, and Manley was released after a few weeks. He used a GI loan to buy a new truck but couldn't afford the payments and sold it, buying a used vehicle. He drifted between jobs, spending one cold winter living in a box truck on the side of the road. Drinking heavily, he picked fights to cope with his anger. Losing track of most of his buddies, he met just once with Howard Kaufman. Manley married a woman he met at a tavern; after a brief marriage, they divorced.

But you can't keep a good man down. Amber, a waitress at a local Belfast, Maine, diner, set her sights on the young man staring into his dinner plate, lost in thought. One day at lunch, she asked, "So, Manley, when are you going to ask me out?" Manley left without saying a word but returned after working up his courage. In the best decision he will ever make, he married Amber L. Philbrook on December 6, 1952; they have two children, a daughter, Debra A. (O'Connor), and a son, Douglas. Manley started his own painting business and drove trucks, one of the loves of his life. Debra died in 1992, Amber in 2012. In April 2013, Manley contacted a son of John Boyle, and the talk set the old soldier's mind at ease. Manley Fuller overcame his demons and after a long life died on April 18, 2015, at the HealthAlliance Hospital in Leominster, Massachusetts. He is buried at Glenwood Cemetery in Natick, survived by his son and five grandchildren. During the last three years of his life, Manley stayed with granddaughter Sarah, finally discussing the war; in return, she ensured that he avoided climbing ladders. Sarah said this about her beloved grandfather:[30]

World War II was the defining point of Manley Fuller's life. It irrevocably changed him. From a barefoot boy who grew up without electricity and running water, he shook hands with Russian soldiers and saw medieval castles while carrying the most sophisticated equipment his country could offer. It also left him with shaking hands and nightmares that he tried to suppress…. Manley's unit was once ordered to advance out of a wooded area across a field and into a small village. The order was passed to fix bayonets. Manley looked down at his bayonet and prayed he wouldn't have to use it. He had joined because it was his patriotic duty, but he didn't want to actually have to kill anyone. That moment was when the reality of his situation sank in…. The repressed trauma led to heavy drinking through much of the 1950s and early '60s, but he tried to keep it under control for his family's sake. His wartime mementos were locked away in a cabinet and not to be discussed or touched.

Al DiRisio was discharged on June 24, 1945. Al married Beatrice Jane Alles on July 19, 1947. The former mess sergeant established Hawk's Hamburgers, in Fairport, New York, specializing in hamburgers and piles of french fries, becoming a local legend. Always an entertainer, he wrote and performed a skit titled "Why was I ever drafted?" Al also sang the solo "Madamina" from Mozart's *Don Giovanni* with the Verdi Opera Society of Rochester. In 1980, Al appeared in the first of thirty-nine columns in a local newspaper over the next two years—most about Army life, witty and entertaining. Not a single column was about the Hürtgen.

Hawk served as master of ceremonies at many Company B reunions; the most notable gathering occurred in June 1977, a four-day event at the Gatehouse Motor Inn of Rochester; eighty veterans and guests attended, swapping stories—all exaggerated over the years. According to an article in the *Herald-mail* of Fairport, titled "Company B in 25th Reunion" and written—naturally—by Al, the highlight of the banquet was belly dancers Natasha and Kasscima. In 1981, Al wrote the National Personnel Records Center in typical Hawk style: "Would you please send me all medals, ribbons and decorations I have coming to me?" The letterhead indicated that Al was a licensed real estate broker with Perinton Realty in Fairport. Jane died on September 10, 1998. Al DiRisio died on August 18, 2000, and is buried at Saint Mary's Roman Catholic Cemetery in Fairport.[31]

James Millar, son of Scotch immigrants, completed his duties as mail clerk in a satisfactory manner and was discharged on March 10, 1946, at Newark, New Jersey, and became a watchman for a construction company. He married Jean Wallace in Newark in October 1950. The couple had a daughter, Christine. James died on August 30, 2001, in Morris Plains, New Jersey. Jean died on November 23, 2013.[32]

Al Baccile returned home, married Lucy D'Orio, and worked for Remington Rand for many years before becoming code enforcement officer for the City of Elmira. He was also active in Elmira's Italian American Veterans Club. The couple had two sons, Alfred and Nicholas; Lucy died in 1980, son Alfred in 2012. Albert Baccile died at St. Joseph's Hospital on January 2, 2010, in Elmira. He was buried in the city's Saint Peter and Paul's Cemetery. Nicholas, who attended several reunions with his father, recalled his experiences:[33]

> He loved to go to the company reunion as often as he could, especially so he could see Joe Gravino and Hawk DiRisio. I called them the "Big Three" because they were always there. Hawk ran a great greasy-spoon hamburger joint in Fairport and was a real entertainer, singing and playing piano. But after a few drinks the guys started remembering things from the war that maybe they didn't want to remember. Dad didn't take crap from anybody. He could be laughing one minute and then his mood would turn in a minute; several guys were like that. We went to Normandy, France, and visited several of the villages, where the company had fought. Dad had been wounded near one in July 1944 by mortar shrapnel while he was under a tree. A film crew was shooting some scenes for *Saving Private Ryan* and asked Dad if he wanted to be an extra, but he wanted to get to Germany to see the Hürtgen one more time, because he said that place was the worst of all.

Lloyd Wasnick was discharged on February 13, 1946, at Camp McCoy, Wisconsin, and returned to Minneapolis; he married Marianne Lucille Pribble, oldest of eight children, in 1948, after she graduated from the University of Minnesota. Lloyd, an excellent artist, found a job working for the Soo Line Railroad in 1951. A registered civil engineer, he conducted surveys of railroad intersections. The couple had a daughter, Linda Jeanne, and two sons, Jeffrey Lloyd—who graduated from the University of Minnesota and played on the Gophers' ice hockey team—and Larry Jay. Lloyd became assistant vice president for operations for the Soo Line.

Nicknamed "Ludy" back home, Lloyd doted on his family, as recalled by grandson Alex: "He did not talk about his service, but he was injured at least two times. He was also an excellent painter in his free time. I remember my time 'up north' with him at the cabin learning how to fish and spending the day out on the lake."[34] Russian Wasnick, the kid who was an artist in his soul and who always came back into the line to help his buddies, died on December 10, 1996. Marianne died in 2006. They are buried together at the Glen Haven Memorial Gardens in Crystal, a suburb of Minneapolis.[35]

Bob Pettigrew served as the Company B clerk and in the Personnel Section, 39th Infantry, in occupied Germany, becoming a clerk-typist. Promoted to corporal on August 28, 1945, he transferred to the 801st Tank Destroyer Battalion and the 118th Infantry Regiment for his journey home, passing through Camps Defrost, Norfolk, Cleveland, Bordeaux, and Phillip Morris in France. However, Corporal Pettigrew had one more major obstacle in his path on his way home. He departed from Le Havre on December 13, 1945, on the *Athos II*, the same ship as Manley Fuller. Bob picks up the adventure: "The trip home on the *Athos II* when we hit a hurricane that topped 120 miles an hour and we leaked and rolled for about 40–50-degree angle. Finally, the transferring to the great carrier USS *Enterprise* [January 8, 1945] by tug-pulled barges and finally arrived home at last on January 14, 1946." Later, Bob's thoughts returned to Company B, and what he wanted to always remember, as only the "old man" from the Bronx could put it:

THINGS I WANT TO REMEMBER: Never to get in the Army again. To stay out of the Infantry. To try to forget not remember the suffering and hardship endured by the men as we fought thru forests, towns, cities, and hills. That the German soldier was a good soldier and the only things that beat him were we were just a little better and had more equipment than they did. They had been fighting a long war too. The Battle of the Bulge when many of my buddies and friends were wounded and killed. The exchanging of our C-rations for ham and eggs with the German people. The "88" and Burp gun.

Arriving at Pier 13, Staten Island, he then spent one day out-processing at Camp Kilmer. Bringing home a Luger as a souvenir, Robert Pettigrew received his final papers and discharge at Fort Dix on January 19, 1946. As he later wrote, "Arrived home at 3:40 p.m. and was met by Mary, Bob & Jim, who had the place all decorated for me. Finally, home to my sweetheart after a 16-month stretch overseas. At times I thought that I would never make it, but their never-ending prayers brought me through okay."

Bob and Mary welcomed daughter Jean into the world in November, as Bob returned to his old job, while Mary worked at their one-bedroom apartment on Marion Avenue in the Bronx. On his Separation Qualification Record, the Army listed his military qualifications that might translate into civilian life. The clerk must have had a sense of humor, since he included "Rifleman. Was a member of a 12-man rifle squad. Fired M1 rifle, carbine, BAR, and other weapons. Experienced forest, village, hill, and open-terrain fighting."[36] Yep, the civilian sector was probably just rarin' to get in line to hire "Rifleman Robert" from the Bronx. Working days, Bob again attended New York University at night so he could better take care of his family someday.

But sometimes legends don't have fairy-tale endings, and that day never came. Bob Pettigrew died at home of a massive heart attack on November 3, 1947—less than two years after returning to the States. His premature death devastated Mary and left his three young children fatherless, including little Jean, just eleven months old. Crushed, and bitter toward the Army in which Bob had spent much of his last years away from the family, Mary worked for the Union Bag and Paper Company, starting at the bottom of the wage tree. There was no one to really help. Even little Jim pitched in, sorting bottles at a local mom-and-pop grocery store until old enough to work at a dry cleaners; ultimately the tough Bronx family survived.

Jim went into the Army in the 1960s and again Mary worried, but Jim came home safe and sound. Mary died in 1985 at age sixty-eight. She was buried next to Bob in section 47 in the Gate of Heaven Cemetery in Valhalla, New York, along with Jim's infant son Michael, who passed away at three days old. Bob Pettigrew—he could have avoided military service, and once in, he could have avoided the infantry. But he didn't because that would mean that some young kid might have to stand in that foxhole instead.

Leonard Pourchot received a week's leave on May 2, 1945, to the US Riviera Recreational center. Later, as a first sergeant, he departed Europe, arriving at New York on January 14, 1946, and was discharged at Camp Grant on January 19. Leonard entered Eastern Illinois State College at Charleston, Illinois, receiving a bachelor of science degree in education in 1948. More importantly, he married Mary Ellen Orr, a writer from Normal, Illinois. The couple would have four sons: Patrick, Thomas, Eric, and Regan. Then it was on to the University of Wisconsin, where he earned a master of science degree in 1951. He taught English and speech at high school in Mendota, Illinois, and at a junior high school in Ripon, Wisconsin, before heading to Colorado State College, teaching there, and receiving a doctorate in education, and then became director of Lassen Junior College in Susanville, California.

Professor Pourchot was a man of many talents. A prolific writer, he could quote passages from Dostoevsky's *Crime and Punishment* and could discuss the nature of man making moral choices. Before retiring at Northern Illinois University in 1982, he helped found and served as editor for a teaching journal, *Thresholds in Education*, and developed the "Pourchot Mechanical Manipulation Test," measuring hand-tool dexterity. Mary Ellen died in 1991; Leonard remarried, to Delores J. "Dee" Gregory, who worked for the University of Illinois and at Virginia Tech. The pair lived in Lincoln, Illinois, until his death in nearby Springfield on March 7, 2013. Dee died a month later. He was buried with military honors next to Mary Ellen at Mount Repose Cemetery in Friendship, Wisconsin. Perhaps it was Leonard's experiences in the Hürtgen that throughout his life he loved fir trees; his sons estimate that he planted 500,000 Christmas trees.[37]

That is in his obituary. What is not included is that the quiet, bespectacled school-teacher, who organized desserts in college, had once led an infantry squad—that had just lost its veteran squad leader—in a desperate battle of life and death, and through his personal bravery he saved the lives of ten of his soldiers.

Mac MacLean married Julie Lane, the girl who sent him her ring, her letters, and her prayers the entire war, on August 6, 1947, after she graduated from Northwestern University. Fulfilling the "demands" of Julie's uncles, who wanted her to marry the "right" guy, Mac graduated from the University of Illinois and obtained a job at Caterpillar Tractor Company in Peoria. Mac's high school friend Bob Michel recovered from his wounds and returned to Peoria, attending Bradley University, and served thirty-eight years in the US House of Representatives. Another close friend, David Connor, returned safely as well. Dave left Yale University during the war—as did his friend and classmate George H. W. Bush—to join the Navy and had his own close brush with death in the Pacific on the fleet oiler USS *Caribou*, as a lieutenant (j.g.) on the night of July 29–30, 1945, when the skipper of the Japanese sub *I-58* apparently declined to waste a torpedo on the 3,665-ton ship; six hours later, the *I-58* sank USS *Indianapolis*.[38]

Mac and Julie had two sons: French, born in 1952, and David, born in 1957; both graduated from West Point and retired from the Army as colonels. When the boys were growing up, Mac—recalling a German sergeant at Stalag VI G, would pound on their bedroom door each morning, throw it open, enter their room, turn on the overhead light, and fling open the curtains and shades, all the while yelling, "Raus, Raus!" to waken his sons for school. He also used the war to bring up lessons on life. At Stalag VI G, he had seen prisoners die. "They'd just sit down in the dirt and die after a few days, maybe of exhaustion, maybe of malnutrition. They just gave up. You can't ever quit. You quit once, and the next time things get rough, it's easier to quit again, and soon you're a quitter, and that's the worst thing you can be." As for the German soldiers he fought, Mac would only say, "They were tough bastards." Then he'd shut up.

In 1975, Mac, Julie, and David visited French, then a second lieutenant in Germany. The four go to the Hürtgen, staying at a hotel in Kalterherberg—the owner had been a German POW in Missouri, volunteering to catch rattlesnakes and being paid for each one he caught. He took those American dollars back to Germany and purchased the hotel they were now in! The two old POWs talked well into the night. Later, visiting Euskirchen, Mac found that the city was rebuilding the jail. Mac identified the building immediately, walked inside to an interior courtyard, found the cell in which he had been held, and "liberated" a chain from its door.

On November 26, 1984, the Army belatedly awarded Mac the Bronze Star Medal for his service in World War II; on May 19, 1988, he received the Prisoner of War Medal, which allowed him to receive an "Ex-Pow" license plate from the state of Illinois, which not only was free but would have unintended benefits as well.

Once, as Mac and Julie traveled south to avoid a brutal Illinois winter, he was driving east in Louisiana on the interstate and was pulled over for speeding by a state trooper. The officer looked at the license plate and then strolled up to the driver's window, while Mac sweated inside. He informed Mac that he had been speeding, and asked him when and where he had been a POW. Mac explained Stalag VI G to the officer, secretly hoping the fine might be reduced a bit. The patrolman mentioned no fine, cutting straight to the chase by asking Mac where the couple was headed—to which Mac rasped, "Florida." The officer replied: "Sir, the way I figure it is that guys like you own this country, so follow me to the Mississippi line." So, with lights flashing in the lead patrol car, Mac followed—going about 80 in his recollection. Over the next 200 miles, Mac was escorted by two additional troopers, one meeting him at each successive state line at Mississippi and Alabama, and he arrived in Florida in record time!

Because the Germans had taken his boots, leaving him with wooden shoes through the frigid winter of 1945, Mac was declared in the 1990s to be a disabled veteran because of severe frostbite to his feet. In later years, "the Ear" seems to have become hard of hearing—especially when Julie gave him household instructions. Julie died in Decatur, Illinois, on July 28, 2008; Mac died exactly seven years later to the day. French put both urns of their ashes next to the television in 2016 so they could see the Cubs finally win the World Series. At Pawleys Island, South Carolina, on July 28, 2018, French, David, and their families placed the couple's ashes in the ocean as their parents had wished.

Mac had no regrets about his service. Asked later in life if he lamented not joining the Army Air Corps as a gunner on a B-17 Flying Fortress, he replied, "Heck no. Those guys had it really rough with all that flak and German fighters." And when asked what rank he might have attained had he stayed in after the war, Mac mused: "I might have made buck sergeant, but they also might have found out about that lieutenant's uniform!" And the advice he gave the night before French entered West Point: "Never volunteer and never play cards with sergeants."

What was Mac talking about concerning card playing? Was it a delightful round of bridge or perhaps whiling away a comfortable afternoon of whist? It was neither;

playing cards, usually poker or pinochle, with sergeants, or doughboys of any rank, or swabbies, or flyboys, or jarheads involved good old-fashioned, nut-cuttin' gamblin', during which it was almost expected that at least one player—and maybe everyone—is a "four-flusher," low-down cheater. This springs from the common assumption that every poker player believes that he is the best who ever played since Bat Masterson. Thus, if he is losing, someone has to be up to no good.

First you'll need an army blanket and a deck of cards. Good old Uncle Sam provides the first, and often your mom—thinking her little boy might like to play solitaire while he's thinking of home—will send you a deck from your hometown Walgreens. Heck, the Red Cross even distributes cards to soldiers in hospitals, and Red Cross doughnut wagons have been known to have a few decks on hand along with the crullers. Next, determine what type of poker you all are playing. There are almost unlimited variants: Draw, Follow the Queen, High Chicago, Stud, Omaha Hold 'Em, Texas Hold 'Em, Wild Cards, Fixed Limit, No Limit—and everyone seems to have his own favorite.

The key is understanding the rules, because a winning hand in one type of poker may not be a winning hand in another. And if you don't know what wins, the other players aren't going to help you, unless it's to "let" you win the first hand, so—over-confident—you stay in the game, Bat—especially if somebody thinks you might have some jack in your pocket. But remember, as any sergeant will tell you: "If you're playing in a poker game and you look around the table and can't tell who the sucker is, it's you." So, listen to your old man; don't play cards with sergeants.

Lots of GIs also play craps. It is so popular that gambling authority John Scarne, for *YANK* magazine, works out the odds and determines that it is almost the perfect gambling game, and that American soldiers gamble $300 million a month. So, *YANK* prints two million small cards with the odds in craps so that soldiers can paste them inside their helmets. The cards become known as the "Official Army Odds." Scarne also determines that most GI crap games are on the level. But remember, shaving even a tiny, almost undetectable, sliver off an edge of a die will change the odds that only the owner of the dice will know.

Warren Ridgeway. On February 10, 1945, the *Oswego Palladium Times* and the *Pulaski Democrat* reported that Mr. and Mrs. John Ridgeway of Lacona, New York, had received a message from the War Department stating that their son Warren E. Ridgeway was missing in action. On May 27, 1945, Sandy Creek held a large memorial service for the young men, including Warren, who never came home; his name is also on the Tablets of Missing in Action at the American Military Cemetery at Neupré, Belgium. Timber's three brothers also fought in the war: Aaron, a paratrooper; Paul, in the Army in Europe; and John as a tail gunner in the 8th Air Force. In January 1946, the Army declared Warren to be dead. The War Department sent a letter concerning that to the family on September 4, 1946:[39]

I have the honor to inform you that by direction of the President, the Bronze Star Medal has been awarded to your son by the commanding general, for distinguishing himself by heroic achievement in action against the enemy on 17 July 1944. In addition to the above decoration S/Sgt. Ridgeway was entitled to the Combat Infantryman Badge, American Defense Service Medal, American Theatre Ribbon, European-African-Middle Eastern Theater Ribbon with one Silver and one Bronze Service Star for the Tunisia, Sicily, Algeria-French Morocco, Normandy, Rhineland, and Ardennes Campaigns. Also, the Distinguished Unit Badge with one Bronze Oak Leaf Cluster, for service with the 39th Infantry Regiment, when it was cited in the name of the President for outstanding performance of duty, 6–9 August 1944, and 18 June 1944: Bronze Arrowhead for the invasion of North Africa, World War 2 Victory Ribbon.

Timber's mother, Anna, died in 1983; John had died in 1962. In 1980, Hawk DiRisio recalled Timber in an interview for the *Fairport Herald Mail*. Al explained that he was with a group of guys in Company B in 1941 at Fort Bragg, discussing professional wrestling back home.[40]

Timber popped over while I'm telling this story to say he remembered when the carnivals came annually to Lacona. Timber continues, in his southern drawl, "Ah was borke and ah was listnin' to this barker's askin' afor challengers to take on this big animal for three minutes and ah would git five dollars. Ah decided ah would git in the ring with this wrestler and run like hell for three minutes in order to git my five dollars. And if ah could stay away from him for three minutes, ah would have my five dollars. So, ah got in the ring and ah ran and ah ran, and ah ran Hawk, but the #&+%@ caught up with me and almost broke my neck."

Timber Ridgeway is the only Company B soldier in that last period of the war whose remains have never been found, but memories of him certainly returned with the soldiers of Company B to be told and retold in their hometowns of Fairport, Mattoon, Peoria, Sylacauga, Lumberton, Mumford, Scranton, and even Philadelphia, Brooklyn, and the Bronx.

So what exactly did happen to Timber on that cold January day? A January 21, 1945, the 9th Infantry *G2 Journal* stated that "1st Battalion patrol went to find supply trail and 4 green communication line wires and set up an ambush. Soon saw two Germans coming along the creek to [grid] 945107 dragging sleds, fired on them but enemy escaped." The First Battalion's *Unit Journal* recorded that the combat patrol departed at 1410 hours, found the enemy wire, and cut it. The patrol reached a location known as Point #1 at 1500 hours and was ordered to return at 1600 hours. That location was on the edge of thick woods 200 yards north of a small creek feeding into the

Schwalmbach River. After Timber went missing, possibly Pfc. James M. Thurston took charge of the patrol and safely returned, since 9th Infantry *GO #57*, dated April 30, 1945, awarded James M. Thurston a Bronze Star for Heroism on January 21, 1945.

Belgian Jean-Phillippe Speder of the Missing in Action Project, which specializes in finding missing-in-action soldiers from both sides in the Elsenborn area, located two key statements concerning the incident. The first was provided by Jack Jewell on January 29, 1945, to 1Lt. Lawson M. Kateley, assistant adjutant (assistant S-1) of the battalion:[41]

On 21 January 1945, Co. B, 39th Infantry, located near Kalterherberg, Germany, was ordered by higher headquarters to form a Combat patrol to operate behind enemy lines. The mission assigned the patrol was as follows: To capture or kill Germans to secure identification, to cut communication wire and ambush wire men. To establish location of enemy supply route. SSgt. Warren E. Ridgeway, ASN 32025844, as a member of the patrol left his platoon area at 1400 hours, 21 January 1945, with the patrol to accomplish the assigned mission. During the action which followed, the patrol encountered the enemy and S/Sgt. Ridgeway became separated from the patrol. When the patrol started to withdraw, he was last seen firing at the enemy, and it was believed at the time he would return with the patrol. After returning to the company area, it was discovered that SSgt. Ridgeway could not be found. Several men were sent back to the point where he was last seen, but no trace of SSgt. Ridgeway was found."

This statement is pretty benign; however, another declaration made James M. Thurston on the same day to 1Lt. Kateley lays bare what transpired.[42]

On 21 January 1945, near Kalterherberg, Belgium, I was with S/Sergeant Warren E. Ridgeway, Company B, 39th Infantry, when we were briefed about noontime by Cpt Perry and when we were briefed about an hour later by Lieutenant Lucas, just before the patrol left. I was with Ridgeway all the time from the time we left, and I was the last man to see him. Me and him were leading this patrol. We got out to where me and Ridgeway cut this Jerry line. And there was two Jerries came up the trail; and when they came up the trail, somebody fired on them. And it seemed like when the firing started, Ridgeway just went nuts—crazy, I'd put it. I have known Ridgeway as long as I have been in this company, and I know he spoke several times about going nuts.

When the firing started, the patrol withdrew. And when we got back to Point #1, Ridgeway wasn't with us. Me and a boy named Stein went back to look for him, and we found him up on this Jerry trail, standing up. He had thrown his rifle, helmet, everything away. We tried to get him to come back with us; he just wouldn't do it, just stood there, looking like he had gone off his top. While we were trying to get him to come back, another Jerry came down this trail. We tried to get this Jerry to surrender; we hollered at him; and this Jerry took off running. Well, I shot eight times at him and left him lying there. And I told Ridgeway, "Let's leave here; let's get out of here." Ridgeway was about ten yards from me then. So, me and Stein took off again; and when we got back to Point #1, where the rest of the patrol was, Ridgeway wasn't with us. That's about all I can say about it; that's all I know. He just didn't come back with us when we came back the second time. I thought he was going to run back with us, but he didn't.

I wouldn't say that Ridgeway was under the influence of alcohol. I think he was perfectly sober. I didn't see him drinking at all that day. Didn't drink anything out of the bottle he took with him, didn't touch it at all. I wasn't going to say anything about the bottle; but he was going to drink it after he got back off the patrol. I saw the bottle, and nothing had been taken out of it. It had never been opened.

Capt. Edwin Perry, now the battalion intelligence officer, briefed SSgt. Ridgeway, and Pfc. Thurston—apparently the assistant patrol leader—about 1200 hours on what to accomplish on the patrol. About 1300 hours the two soldiers received further instructions from 1Lt. Lucien L. Lucas, 1st Platoon leader. There was no mention of the size of the combat patrol or its equipment; every soldier was armed, and they had at least one set of wire cutters. Given that a private first class was the assistant patrol leader, there were probably no noncommissioned officers except Ridgeway on the patrol; there likely were five to eight men on the mission, of which we know four. The soldier identified as Stein was almost certainly Donald C. Stine. Manley Fuller was also on the patrol and later confirmed Thurston's story.

The patrol started between 1400 and 1410 hours, passing point #1 on their map and observing two Germans moving along a small creek at grid coordinate 945107, dragging sleds. One soldier—not Ridgeway or Thurston—opened fire and the Germans ran. During this encounter, Ridgeway "went nuts—crazy" probably hollering conflicting orders. Thurston took charge; the patrol withdrew to point #1 and then realized that Ridgeway was missing. Thurston and Stine returned to where the engagement had been, and found Ridgeway in the middle of a trail, having thrown down his rifle, helmet, and load-bearing equipment. The two soldiers attempted to persuade him to return with them, but he looked like "he had gone off his top."

During this discussion, they observed another German soldier coming down the trail. Thurston yelled at him to surrender, and the German began to run away before Thurston fired eight rounds at him, striking the German at least once. Ridgeway was 10 yards away from Thurston, who told Timber, "Let's leave here; let's get out of here." Thurston, Fuller, and Stine quickly returned to point #1, where the rest of the patrol was, but Ridgeway was not with them. At 1600 hours, the patrol departed point #1, heading back to the battalion.

And Timber? The Germans never reported him as a POW. It was almost dark. Not wanting to be discovered by the Germans, Timber probably did not start a warming fire or make any noise. He may have tried to head west to rejoin the company, but at some point he just sat down, and by dawn Timber had frozen to death. Or maybe a random artillery shell scored a direct hit on him. As to his remains, who knows? Maybe the wolves got them in the spring after the snow melted. Maybe local villagers found them scattered after the war and just gave them a hasty burial—especially if there were no dog tags remaining.

Timber had been the embodiment of moxie. Sure, he got into a rhubarb every now and then, but going off the deep end? Leonard Pourchot of 1st Platoon wrote in his small notebook that he had gone on six patrols in January and that "Number 5 was a combat mission. Lost Staff Sergeant Ridgeway."[43] Was Porky Pourchot on the patrol? If so, that would make six identified, and he could have been the actual assistant patrol leader and taken the rest of the patrol to a rally point, while Thurston and Stine went back to look for Timber.

In 1945, Lord Moran (Charles McMoran Wilson Moran) published *The Anatomy of Courage*, examining the psychological effects of war, specifically fear. Concentrating on the Great War, Moran asked the question that can never be fully answered: Why can a person appear to be as brave as a lion one day and break the next? Lord Moran concluded that courage is willpower; no individual has an unlimited stock of courage, and fear contributes to the degradation of that courage. In everyday terms, courage is like a bank account. Every stressful moment is a debit on your account. When your account reaches zero, you will break down. You cannot borrow from any other source; you cannot go into debt. And worst of all, no one ever knows exactly how much is in their account, and how much is being withdrawn over time.[44]

Even a very brave person has limits, and once exceeding those limits that person will succumb to fear. Timber had been a little braver for a little longer than the enemy he faced all these years in Africa, Sicily, Normandy, the Hürtgen, and now Elsenborn, Belgium. Did Timber's willpower to fight fear finally break that cold afternoon in the snow as the shadows began to lengthen, as the evidence seems to suggest? Is that how the "legend" of Timber Ridgeway died?

There had been so much mystery underneath his rough demeanor: the fight with 1Sgt. Gravino, climbing into the ring with a professional wrestler, duck hunting with Gehrig and Ruth. Decades after their deaths, photographs emerged of the baseball immortals duck hunting in 1927 at the Farmers Gun Club in Cypress, California; in 2009, original grainy home movies of the event surfaced as well. The same year, the Long Beach Police Historical Society reported on the outing: "Duck blinds were readied and [Glenn] Thomas said he spent the first night of the hunt in the Babe's blind. Ruth got so drunk that Thomas was afraid that Ruth might accidentally shoot him.

Thomas reported that on the second night of the hunt, he stayed with Gehrig in his blind."[45]

The two sluggers were also thought to have hunted together on another occasion out west at the Lomita Gun Club.[46] A photograph exists of Babe Ruth after he shot two deer and a black bear, reportedly in the 1930s. Another photo, circa 1930, shows Babe after successfully bagging a turkey in a snowy field with woods in the background. And photographs exist of the Babe hunting at Camp Bryan in Craven County, North Carolina, and at Greenwood Lake, New York. Given Timber's age, any guiding for Ruth and Gehrig, which he had claimed, would have occurred between 1936 and 1939—this study has found a photograph dated November 28, 1937, showing Ruth near a cabin, with a shotgun tucked under his left arm and holding three ducks in his right hand. Babe Ruth and Lou Gehrig hunting with Timber? Maybe, just maybe . . .

. . . because there was so much we never knew about this "Silent Generation." And whether they died hard on the battlefield or passed away decades after the war, the young men of Company B have moved on to their great reward. Given the sacrifices they made for their country, their families, and each other, one hopes that there is indeed a heaven, so they can meet again, perhaps at something like this . . .

・・・

"Je suis Le Capitan Lindsey Nelson de le Neuvieme Division—I am Captain Lindsey Nelson of the Ninth Division. I speak Fractured French, New Yorkese, Tennessee, and fluid Fayetteville.[47] Welcome today to the Harry M. "Paddy" Flint Ballpark for another wonderful day of baseball—an intra-squad game of Company B, the Anything, Anytime, Anywhere, Bar Nothing, scrapping, kick-ass boys of the 39th Infantry" flows the elegant voice as smooth as Tennessee sippin' whiskey, from Lindsey's normal position up in the booth overlooking the field.

・・・

As always, Lindsey is wearing one of his marvelously loud and colorful plaid sport coats. NBC-TV press agents used to say that the average American male listens to his wife, to his boss, and to Lindsey Nelson. And on Saturday after-noons, he won't listen to his boss or his wife.[48] That's because over the years, Lindsey broadcasts twenty-six Cotton Bowls, five Sugar Bowls, four Rose Bowls, hundreds of other college football games, and over two thousand Major League Baseball games. Lindsey likes doing those games—but he loves doing this game.

・・・

"Lou Gehrig and the bambino, Babe Ruth, will pick sides, and again Top Gravino will serve as catcher for both teams," announces Lindsey. Babe and Lou are batting 1.000. Gravino is beaming in his St. Louis Cardinals uniform; more so as Lou tells him again that he has big-league talent. "And as a reminder, after the game, you are all invited to the Town Pump, where the drinks and food are always on the house—as are the broken doors and the smashed plate-glass windows!" At that, Chester McClurg perks up. Lou walks over to Timber Ridgeway, puts his arm around the big lumberjack's shoulder, laughs, and says hello. Dang—those hunting stories were true! In 1939 at Yankee Stadium, Lou said a final goodbye to the fans as he was dying of a terrible disease, stating, "Today I consider myself the luckiest man on the face of the earth." Now, Lou knows he'll never have to say goodbye again.

...

As he's talking to Timber, "the Iron Horse" hears a rising crescendo of cheering from the stands—spreading out like a tidal wave throughout the stadium. Lou has heard plenty of ovations in his day, but he knows that this one is not for him. And it's not for the Babe. It's for Timber. Because everyone whoever served in Company B now knows what Timber went through that final, endless, freezing January night in 1945, and they want him to know that they sure are glad he's finally back.

...

Not everyone plays every day, and those who don't, sit up in the stands with their loved ones. There's Noodles Nodell right next to Mollie; she was a widow for fifty-six years, but not anymore; Harry is holding the little baseball glove he gave to his baby daughter before he left home for the last time. Who knows? He might get lucky and shag a foul ball. Doc Slaughter is always standing by in case someone gets a charley horse, but that never happens on this field of dreams. Holding Doc's hand is his little son Jessie, who's always smiling—now that he's with his dad.

...

Hawk DiRisio caters the games from the ballpark outlet of Hawk's Hamburgers, and the cold beer and dogs are always free here too. Jay Lavinsky often invites a few Hollywood stars, and his uncle "Battling Levinsky" always ensures that several boxing greats are in attendance—sometimes even Joe Louis and Rocky Marciano—posing for pictures and reliving the memories of their greatest bouts for Billie Flowers, Chester McClurg, Timber, Jay Lavinsky, Willie White, and all the other scrappers—but nobody gets decked in the fun!

...

The grass is bright green, and the sky is light blue. There's never any snow here, and no games ever get rained out. Nobody carries an M1 Garand or a Browning Automatic Rifle; the most lethal piece of equipment is that Louisville Slugger that looks like a tree trunk, when the Babe ambles to the plate, but like they say, you can't hit a home run with a toothpick. Kenny Seaman is hovering around .400, and when he plays, Ted Williams shows up to watch. Maybe because Ted's there, the ump never calls a strike when it's just "close," because this gang knows better than anyone that "close" counts only in horseshoes and hand grenades.

. . .

There aren't any silent land mines or booby traps, or clanking tanks, or hissing flamethrowers, or screeching planes. There aren't any young men dying hard, crying for their mothers with their last breath. There's no razor-sharp barbed wire, jagged shrapnel, or snapping guard dogs. There aren't any shattered bodies buried in bloody mattress covers. And there aren't any soldiers holding mortally wounded friends in their last moments of life.

. . .

But there is one of those little Weasels delivering snacks and drinks out to the bleachers, and a second one, driven by Manley Fuller joyriding with his buddy John Boyle and company mascot, Buff, now scurrying in with a relief pitcher from the bullpen, while the "Black Market Band" strikes up "The Wabash Cannonball," and the thoughts of Noodles, Jay, Mac, Kenny, Bob, Phil, and all the rest of the gang go back to a place long ago and far away, as they all begin softly singing, "We'll have our Christmas dinner, in a big Berlin hotel . . ."

Company B Personnel
(October 1, 1944–May 8, 1945)

The following soldiers have documentary proof in the National Archives that they served in Company B during the last nine months of the war; some from before. Hundreds more were in the company from 1941 to mid-1944. Absence of a remark says nothing about the effort of the soldier. Almost every soldier here fought in direct combat with the enemy—and fought well.

LEGEND

* In Company B since 1941

KIA: killed in action

DOW: died of wounds

WIA: wounded in action

2 WIA: wounded twice

3 WIA: wounded three times

4 WIA: wounded four times

SIA: serious injury in action

POW: prisoner of war

NAME	ARMY SERIAL NO.	RANK	REMARKS
Abbey, Henry A.	42078401	Pvt.	*WIA* (9/19/44)
Absher, George C.	14030196	Pfc.	*WIA* (7/10/44)
Adams, Calvin M.	33772113	Pvt.	*2 WIA*
Adkins, William G.	33660848	Pvt.	*2 WIA*
Akers, Paul C.	36959945	Pfc.	*3 WIA*
Alexander, Vallis R.	34715127	Sgt.	
Allen, Dewey	35077330	Pvt.	
Allen, Paul E.	36767837	Pfc.	**KIA** (8/11/44)
Ambrose, Henry A.	33439188	Pfc.	weapons platoon: light-mortar crewman [607]; *WIA* (3/3/45); **KIA** (4/02/45)
Anderson, Robert L.	[35802939]	Pfc.	*WIA* (6/12/44)
Ansley, John W.	34681008	Pfc.	
Armstrong, Samuel H.	33715557	Pvt.	leg infection (11/4/44)

Arndt, August L.	36960112	Pfc.	
Arnold, James W.	39463059	Pvt.	*WIA*; **DOW** (3/30/45)
Atkins, Claude B.	37630791	Sgt.	*2 WIA*
Austen, Emmett V.	35272534	Pfc.	
Baccile,* Albert J.	32025778	SSgt.	company supply sergeant [821]; *WIA* (7/21/44)
Bachman, Walter R.	38693036	Pvt.	*WIA* (10/13/44)
Bacon, Leslie J.	32937415	Pfc.	2 *WIA*; **KIA** (12/12/44); Silver Star (12/12/44)
Baer, Carl J.	35106970	Sgt.	weapons platoon: light machine gunner [604]; *2 WIA*
Ballard, James	35812503	Pvt.	*WIA* (3/2/45)
Baran, Michael J., Jr.	39614941	Pfc.	**DOW** (9/1/44)
Barnett, Raymond H.	34514204	Pvt.	**KIA** (9/19/44)
Batalaris,* Christopher G.	32029922	Pvt.	*3 WIA*
Beauchamp, Robert N.	12152399	Cpl.	
Bauer, Alan H.	37533907	Pfc.	**KIA** (3/4/45)
Bauman, John A.	36309340	Sgt.	
Bean, Paul B.	39144832	Pvt.	**KIA** (10/13/44)
Becker, Alvin P.	32623618	Sgt.	1st Platoon: Collins's/Reiser's squad; ammo bearer; BAR; *WIA* (12/15/44); Silver Star (3/17/45)
Benoist, Louis A., Jr.	0514473	2nd Lt	3rd Platoon leader [1542-9]; **KIA** (1/30/45)
Benton, Merl H.	0406013	1Lt.	2nd Platoon leader [1542-9]; *2 WIA*
Benyo,* Frank	32029960	SSgt.	*WIA* (9/1/44)
Berry, Cecil	38401319	Pfc.	*WIA* (7/44)
Berry, Seymour	13075155	Pvt.	*WIA* (10/13/44)
Bittino, Albert D.	32607111	Pfc.	**DOW** (10/12/44)
Blanchard, Edward G.	38657615	Pvt.	*WIA* (3/17/45)
Blue, Wilbur E.	37753441	Pfc.	
Boden, John X.	33809672	Pvt.	
Bodenheimer, Eddie J.	38658166	Pfc.	
Bojorquez-Montijo, Ramon	39865793	Pvt.	
Bolton, Lewis E.	33562904	Pfc.	*WIA* (9/14/44)
Bowman, Gail S.	35696399	SSgt.	3rd Platoon; took over Rush's squad in March 1945; *WIA* (10/11/44)
Boyle, John H.	35830330	Pfc.	1st Platoon: Collins's/Reiser's squad; **KIA** (2/9/45)

Bradshaw, Deloss J.	39916542	Pfc.	3rd Platoon: Rush's squad; *WIA* (1/30/45,) **KIA** (3/12/45)
Brady, Ruben J.	35830945	Pfc.	1st Platoon: Collins's/Reiser's squad; *WIA* (1/26/45); trench foot (1/26/45)
Brady, William N.	34799428	Pvt.	*2 WIA*
Branchfield, Frank B.	36952567	Pfc.	Bronze Star (10/13/44)
Branham, Mitchell	35777410	Sgt.	*WIA* (4/4/45)
Braun, Walter W.	35584314	Pfc.	
Britt, Leo H.	33928349	Pfc.	
Bryla, Edward	36469222	Pfc.	
Buckner, Perle J.	15054548	SSgt.	*WIA* (10/13/44)
Bucklin, Archer W.	31318937	Pfc.	
Budd, Lester J.	35236833	Pfc.	
Buff			mascot / guard dog
Bulaski, John M.	16069092	Pfc.	company medic; *WIA* (1/31/45); Bronze Star (1/31/45)
Bullock, Charles G.	38636039	Pvt.	
Burchwell, Roy L.	16054789	Sgt.	**KIA** (6/12/44)
Burd, Chester N.	33615001	Pvt.	appendicitis (11/25/44)
Burke, Spegiel M.	34975644	Pvt.	*WIA* (10/12/44)
Burke, Walter S.	35613408	Pvt.	**KIA** (2/5/45); Silver Star (2/5/45)
Buscemi, Stephen S.	42131267	Pvt.	*WIA* (1/15/45)
Byron, John H.	31262110	T/5	
Campbell, Donald E.	33424845	Pfc.	*WIA* (9/14/44)
Cannon, Mack	34570142	Pfc.	*WIA* (6/12/44)
Capoziello, Luciano J.	32014891	T/5	light vehicle driver [345]; *WIA* (6/13/44)
Carl, Clyde L.	35631048	Pvt.	
Carlone, Michael	31445357	Pfc.	*WIA* (10/8/44)
Carlsen, Kenneth A.	32605132	Sgt.	
Carroll, Charles E.	35243194	Pvt.	*WIA* (10/10/44)
Carter, James T.	42127886	Pvt.	frostbitten feet (1/11/45)
Carter,* Lawrence E.	15055458	SSgt.	Silver Star (8/7/44); *2 WIA*
Cascio,* Noel J.	32029924	Pfc.	light-vehicle driver (Jeep) [345]; *WIA* (7/15/44)
Castañon, Nieves, Jr.	18102904	Pfc.	*WIA* (4/17/45)
Chamberlain, Basil B.	35080409	Pfc.	1st Platoon: Collins's/Reiser's squad
Chandler, Everett R.	38693239	Pfc.	*WIA* (10/13/44)

Cherry,* Lawrence L.	15044623	TSgt.	platoon sergeant [651];Bronze Star (12/20/44); *3 WIA*
Chisholm, Charles E.	34724761	Pfc.	
Chew, Clifford R.	35928407	Pvt.	*WIA* (10/9/44)
Chin, Bing San	42131139	Pvt.	
Christal, Meyer	32343736	Pfc.	*2 WIA*; ammunition handler [504]
Ciccone,* Salvatore P.	32057150	TSgt.	1st Platoon sergeant [651]; *2 WIA*
Cinker, Theodore S.	33706686	Pfc.	**DOW** (9/19/44)
Claxton, Aubury J.	38075634	Pfc.	
Collins, James F.	31287362	SSgt.	1st Platoon: squad leader [653]; *WIA* (12/21/44)
Collins, Jim R.	6969054	Pfc.	
Conrad, Benedict J.	37586916	Pvt.	**KIA** (10/13/944)
Constant, Madison A.	36695682	Pfc.	*WIA* (7/44)
Coy, Joseph M.	35263153	Pfc.	weapons platoon: light machine gunner [604]; *3 WIA*
Crabtree, Lafie	15054579	Cpl.	**DOW** artillery shrapnel (7/23/44)
Cusimano, Alfred	32745947	Pfc.	*WIA* (8/9/44)
Daniels, Napoleon A.	32748030	SSgt.	3rd Platoon; *WIA* (10/12/44)
Davala, Joseph J.	32018953	Pvt.	*WIA* (6/18/44)
Davis, James I.	18007303	Pfc.	*WIA* (10/12/44)
Dawkins, Asbury	34304326	SSgt.	1st Platoon: 3rd Squad leader
Debaran, John Serdinola	39235085	Pfc.	weapons platoon: light machine gunner [604]
Decker, Robert D.	39577014	Pfc.	*WIA* (12/15/44)
Deller, James E.	34390969	Pvt.	
Demery, Chester C.	37114849	Pvt.	
DiBenedetto, John	33317028	Pfc.	
DiCriscio, Michael C.	33051356	Pvt.	
Di Mauro, Philip F.	32902435	Pfc.	Bronze Star (7/25/44); *WIA* (7/25/44)
Dietrich, Robert J.	36964844	Pfc.	1st Platoon: Collins's/Reiser's squad; BAR; Silver Star (2/6/45)
DiRisio,* Albert P.	32029918	SSgt.	company mess sergeant [824]
Dolan, Elwyn J.	39588504	Pvt.	former shop maintenance machinist [114]
Dollar, James E.	34390989	Pfc.	*WIA* (7/21/44)
Donald, William O.	38416397	Pfc.	*WIA* (7/20/44)
Dotson, Lawrence	35655727	Pfc.	*WIA* (8/7/44)
Douvanis, Daniel	33623620	SSgt.	*WIA* (3/25/44)
Driskell, Louie E.	34449222	Pfc.	Bronze Star (1/45)

Dunlap, Jack A.	01294635	Capt.	company commander [1542-7]; Silver Star (6/16/44); Silver Star (7/25/44); WIA (12/6/44)
Duvall, Rex V.	34605534	Pvt.	WIA (3/12/45)
Dzierga, Robert F.	42086239	Pfc.	WIA (2/5/45)
Eannace, Carmine V.	32445753	Cpl.	former supply clerk [835]; WIA (4/17/45)
Eckardt, Albert P.	36965212	Pfc.	1st Platoon: Collins's/Reiser's squad
Edwards, Earnie W.	15012364	SSgt.	WIA (12/44)
Eelman, Samuel	42006884	Pfc.	
Eggelston, Thomas C.	32856087	Sgt.	squad leader [653]
Eichel, Herman J.	15303048	Pfc.	bugler [803]; hernia (10/20/44); frostbite (1/29/45)
Eiken, Elmer G.	37026257	Pvt.	WIA (9/26/44)
Ellsworth, Leonard J.	32294439	TSgt.	Silver Star (12/12/44); 2 WIA
Erickson, Carl D.	37581215	Pfc.	KIA (4/7/45)
Ervin, Eugene M.	6931906	SSgt.	1st Platoon; 3 WIA
Ewalt, Sidney M.	15333663	Pfc.	3rd Platoon: Rush's squad; WIA (2/7/45)
Faa, Leland M.	37429226	Pfc.	
Falbo,* Frank F.	32025498	SSgt.	2 WIA
Farinella, Tony J.	36638508	Pfc.	
Farmer, William R.	36894317	Pvt.	WIA (10/10/44)
Ferguson, Jeremiah M.	12217541	Pvt.	WIA (10/14/44)
Fickbohm, Louis F.	17017302	SSgt.	3 WIA; Bronze Star (6/12/44)
Finerd, Charles F.	35299260	Pvt.	
Fink, Victor G.	35045235	Sgt.	SIA (10/10/44)
Fleming, Broadus	34892696	SSgt.	
Fleming, Lawrence D.	37587966	Pvt.	WIA (10/13/44)
Flickinger, Ralph L.	35247665	Pfc.	1st Platoon
Flores, Jesus C.	39252935	SSgt.	Silver Star (4/43); 3 WIA
Floriano, Leroy N.	0404002	1Lt.	company commander [1542-7]; Silver Star
Flowers, Billie S.	34851110	Pfc.	3rd Platoon: Ridgeway's/ Osbourn's squad; WIA (9/18/44)
Foley, Patrick J.	42086421	Pvt.	WIA (10/13/44)
Frankel, Phil M.	12096935	Pfc.	2 WIA; Silver Star (2/28/45)
Frase, Willard D.	35232723	Pvt.	1st Platoon: 3rd Squad; KIA (12/26/44)
Fraundorfer, Joseph L.	33570020	SSgt.	

Fredendall, Verdun H.	37426850	Pfc.	*2 WIA*
Freedman, Melvin J.	01822984	1Lt.	
Fried, Joseph D.	32900883	Pfc.	
Frost, Norman M.	42024306	Pvt.	*WIA (9/26/44)*
Frueauf, Walter H.	35867491	Pfc.	ammunition handler [504]; *2 WIA*
Fuller, Manley G.	31282498	Pfc.	1st Platoon: Collins's/Reiser's squad; *2 WIA*
Fuller, Ralph A.	34798818	Pvt.	*WIA (9/30/44)*
Gamble, John F.	33844841	Pvt.	*2 WIA*
Gartland, Donald W.	32025670	Pfc.	*3 WIA*
Garner, Thomas E.	34466865	Pfc.	*2 WIA*
Gasper, Howard E., Jr.	39263492	Pvt.	weapons platoon: light-mortar crewman [607]
Gaunt, Cecil C.	35754222	Sgt.	*WIA (9/20/44)*
Gellman, Herman P.	37385024	Pfc.	
Genaro, Joseph	35283304	Cpl.	
Gerbliss, John J.	33412062	Pfc.	*2 WIA*
Getsy, Paul J.	33081229	Pfc.	*WIA (9/26/44)*
Gladis, William S.	32025812	Sgt.	squad leader [653]; *WIA (10/12/44)*
Glenn, Andrew J.	38057355	Cpl.	3rd Platoon: Bowman's squad; former company cook [060]
Glenn, Curtis R.	33140717	Pfc.	3rd Platoon: Rush's squad
Glick, Alexander	33601193	Pfc.	*WIA (6/19/44)*
Golden, Joseph E.	39326506	Pfc.	ammunition handler [504]; *WIA (9/28/44)*
Gonzalez, Pedro	38074678	SSgt.	*WIA (07/44)*; **KIA** (2/5/45); Bronze Star (06/44)
Goodrich, Edward C.	33525800	Pfc.	*WIA (10/8/44)*
Goodwin, Ray H.	35272469	Pfc.	weapons platoon: light machine gunner [604]; *3 WIA*
Gordon, Ulies C.	34581108	Pfc.	*WIA (8/12/44)*
Gordon, William C.	35720142	Pfc.	weapons platoon: light machine gunner [604]; *2 WIA*
Gore, Rush	15054769	TSgt.	**KIA** (7/19/44); 2 Bronze Stars
Gore, Seben J.	38616922	Pfc.	3rd Platoon: Bowman's squad
Gould, Charles, Jr.	12204099	Cpl.	
Gourlay,* John	32039947	SSgt.	squad leader [653]; *WIA (6/12/44)*; **KIA** (10/11/44)
Graham, Hanson M.	33530082	Pfc.	
Grashel, Paul R.	35411460	Sgt.	

Gravino,* Joseph F.	32025804	1Sgt.	company first sergeant [585]; *2 WIA*; Silver Star (8/12/44); Silver Star (10/13/44)
Griffin, Truman L.	34579999	Sgt.	assistant squad leader [653]
Griffis, Dennis W.	34795367	Pfc.	weapons platoon: light machine gunner [604]; *WIA* (8/17/44)
Grofford, Frank J.	42104401	Pfc.	*WIA* (3/15/45)
Gronkiewicz, John P.	36626230	Pfc.	*2 WIA*
Grove, William A.	33845452	Pvt.	
Guinn, Ewing E.	35698474	Pfc.	
Haga, Kyle	33049007	Pfc.	*WIA* (4/43); SIA (8/6/44)
Hall, John O.	35752009	Pfc.	*WIA* (1/31/45)
Hall, Luther J.	20363167	Pfc.	WIA (6/12/44)
Halpin, John M.	32237142	Pfc.	1st Platoon: Reiser's squad; *WIA* (2/6/45)
Hammond, Dwight H.	37477668	SSgt.	
Handy, Albert M.	33049003	SSgt.	*2 WIA*; **KIA** (10/13/44)
Harms, Albert R.	36548326	Pfc.	*WIA* (1/30/45)
Harmon,* Howard H.	15055124	Sgt.	assistant squad leader [653]
Harris, Howard G.	32588276	Pfc.	
Harris, William T.	6397958	Pvt.	bugler [803]; division stockade; *WIA* (4/45)
Heiderman, Frederick H.	33555499	Pfc.	*WIA* (7/17/44)
Helmer, Edward A.	37038174	Cpl.	company clerk [055]
Henry, John C.	01325495	1Lt.	
Hess, Roy E.	33102105	Sgt.	former light vehicle driver [345]
Hill, John L., Jr.	16012248	Sgt.	assistant squad leader [653]; *WIA* (3/4/45)
Holdren, George H.	35135658	Pfc.	3rd Platoon
Holman, Jay P.	39707361	Sgt.	3rd Platoon: Rush's squad / Bowman's squad; assistant squad leader [653]
Homan, Dale L.	15013203	Pvt.	truckmaster [668]; assigned as rifleman
Honea, Berry L.	38154585	Pfc.	*WIA* (2/5/45)
Hooper, Harold H.	34689546	Pfc.	*WIA* (9/26/44)
Horton, William M.	38063724	T/5	light-vehicle driver [345]; *2 WIA*; Bronze Star
Houck, Loyd H. O.	38525506	Sgt.	
Houk, Charles E.	37514410	Sgt.	
Houlihan, Donald K.	35679233	Pfc.	

Hoyt, Harold J. J.	38601245	SSgt.	
Hribal, Charles E., Jr.	33440555	Pfc.	*WIA (6/12/44)*
Hubbs, Donald E.	12101172	Pfc.	trench foot (10/21/44)
Hudson, John W.	44017327	Sgt.	SIA (4/7/45)
Hughes, Ralph, Jr.	35593532	Pfc.	*3 WIA*
Hyman, Arthur M.	12220740	Pfc.	*WIA (2/5/45)*
Irish, Charles H.	31369282	Pvt.	**KIA** (6/18/44)
Jablonski, John J.	33684028	Pfc.	**KIA** (9/1/44)
Jacobs, Bernard	42024290	Pfc.	*WIA (4/2/45)*
Jenyk, Andy A.	35319042	Pfc.	3rd Platoon: Bowman's squad
Jerome,* Patsy	32025810	TSgt.	*WIA (4/1943);* Silver Star (10/12/44)
Jewell, Jack F.	01283969	1Lt.	weapons platoon leader [1542-9]; company executive officer [1542-8]; Silver Star (9/1/44)
Johnson, Charles W.	37678036	Pfc.	*WIA (6/19/44)*
Johnson, Harry M.	31454388	Pvt.	*WIA (10/10/44)*
Johnson, Hayden E.	33662160	Pfc.	*2 WIA*
Johnston, George A.	32797072	Pfc.	SIA (2/24/45)
Jones, Bert O.	39156647	Pvt.	3rd Platoon: Ridgeway's/ Osbourn's squad; *WIA (3/12/45)*
Jones, Henry D., Jr.	34464941	Pfc.	automatic rifleman [746]; *2 WIA*
Jones, Wira R.	36885138	Pfc.	ammunition handler [504]; SIA (3/4/45); *WIA (8/17/44)*
Kacmar, John J.	33349520	Pvt.	*WIA (2/27/45)*
Kalinowski,* John	32014615	SSgt.	*2 WIA*
Kalvitz, Robert	35913420	Pfc.	*WIA (10/8/44)*
Kane, Leonard K.	01284884	1Lt.	platoon leader [1542-9]; Silver Star (3/18/45)
Karko, William A.	36714215	Pfc.	**KIA** (10/16/44)
Kaufman, Howard E.	35591625	Pfc.	1st Platoon: Collins's/Reiser's squad; *WIA (9/20/44)*
Kavchak, Joseph J.	33678744	Pvt.	
Kelley, William E.	32842938	T/5	company clerk [055]; **KIA** (3/3/45)
Kelly, Joseph M.	35741679	Pfc.	**KIA** (8/5/44)
Kelly, Michael O.	33256824	Pfc.	*WIA (6/12/44);* SIA (3/18/45)
Kenda, Julius A.	35253880	SSgt.	*2 WIA;* Bronze Star (8/9/44)
Kenward, Louis R.	32141128	Pfc.	*WIA (6/12/44)*
Kerns, Raymond L.	37245927	Pfc.	*WIA (10/44)*
Kessler, Saul	32950905	Pvt.	acute rhinitis (12/18/44)

King, Irving L.	32029897	SSgt.	*WIA* (6/12/44)
Kinner, Stephen G.	01325132	2Lt.	platoon leader [1542-9]; *2 WIA*
Kinney, Clarence M.	12059340	Pfc.	*WIA* (2/27/45)
Kinrade, James R.	36306187	Pfc.	*WIA* (8/43)
Koches, John	36873147	Pfc.	**KIA** (8/9/44)
Kompanik, Charles G.	36781759	Pvt.	
Kossives, Leo G.	37668322	Pvt.	*WIA* (2/13/45)
Koziol, Joseph	36642702	Pfc.	*2 WIA*
Kreager, Charles B.	36587126	Pfc.	
Kryger, Frank S.	31454171	Pvt.	*WIA* (10/8/44)
Lance, Ben J.	34573679	Pfc.	*2 WIA*
LaChance, Joseph J.	31184010	Pfc.	**KIA** (6/12/44)
Landman, Elvin	32693931	Pvt.	ammunition handler [504]
Lane, William N.	20106638	Pfc.	ammunition handler [504]
Laprairie, Norris H.	42085662	Pvt.	*WIA* (10/13/44)
Lavinsky, Jay H.	33594370	Pfc.	3rd Platoon: Ridgeway's/ Osbourn's squad; BAR; *WIA* (3/4/45); *WIA* (grenade); 2 Bronze Stars with "V" for Valor
Lawrence, George W.	36918459	Pvt.	
Lawrence, Robert C.	33159683	SSgt.	*WIA* (6/12/44)
Lay, Marvin D.	38110355	Pvt.	
Leach, Eugene K.	39183857	Pvt.	frostbite (11/20/44); frostbite (12/11/44)
Ledford, Claud	38512688	Pfc.	*3 WIA*
Ledford, George W.	44036447	Pvt.	1st Platoon; *2 WIA*
Lee, George C. M.	30111658	Pfc.	
Lee, Soon Shin	30111488	Pvt.	*WIA* (4/1/45)
Legate, Charles H.	36446629	Sgt.	BAR; Silver Star (10/13/44); *WIA* (10/13/44)
Lekutis, William T.	35284818	Pfc.	BAR; Silver Star (2/28/45); *2 WIA*
Leonard, Edward A.	33202503	SSgt.	
Lewis, Keith W.	6666452	1Sgt.	company first sergeant [585]; *2 WIA*
Lewis, Kenneth K.	30111822	Pfc.	automatic rifleman [746]
Lewis, Robert J.	39210057	Pfc.	
Liberman, Fred	42061494	Pfc.	*2 WIA*; Bronze Star (12/22/44)
Lim, Joseph	30111489	Pvt.	*WIA* (4/1/45)
Little, Luther	38081480	Pfc.	*WIA* (4/1/45)
Lockridge, Kermit D.	33848494	Pfc.	3rd Platoon: Rush's squad

Lockwood, Acie	39726662	Pfc.	*WIA* (3/13/45)
Lombardi, James C.	32598663	Pvt.	1st Platoon; *WIA* (3/11/45)
Long, Gleason R.	14203506	Pfc.	3rd Platoon: Bowman's squad
Longenecker, John A.	33874903	Pvt.	*WIA* (10/23/44)
Lopez, Antonio M., Jr.	39852555	Pfc.	Silver Star (9/19/44)
Lopez, Lee	37712802	Pvt.	
Lorio, Warren S.	14013101	Pfc.	**KIA** (2/9/45)
Lucas, Lucien L.	01314507	1Lt.	1st Platoon leader [1542-9]; *2 WIA*
Lyons,* Timothy	32014573	SSgt.	*2 WIA*
Mabry, Robert H.	36263354	Pfc.	
Machacz, Theodore J.	31082288	Pfc.	
MacLean, Myron D.	16122373	Pfc.	3rd Platoon: Ridgeway's/ Osbourn's squad; squad scout; *WIA*/POW (1/30/45); Silver Star (1/30/45); frostbite (Stalag 6 G)
Maddin, John D.	35782617	Pvt.	
Madison, Raymond A.	39338563	Pvt.	1st Platoon: Collins squad; squad scout; **KIA** (10/12/44)
Magluilo, Jerome	42183837	Pvt.	1st Platoon; *WIA* (4/7/45); **DOW** (04/10/45)
Magrino, Rocco P.	33419878	Pfc.	SIA (8/9/44)
Mahorney, Verne M.	37702173	Pvt.	1st Platoon; *WIA* (10/24/44)
Maliongas, George L.	36671264	Pvt.	1st Platoon: Collins's/Reiser's squad; squad scout; burned/ evacuated (1/15/45)
Mantos, Vasilios	42128259	Pfc.	
Marcinkowski, James	42092659	Pfc.	*2 WIA*
Maresca,* Albert A.	32014810	Pfc.	messenger [675]; *WIA* (10/11/44)
Mariano, Lawrence L.	30112197	Pvt.	*WIA* (4/8/45)
Marti, Harold D.	37753625	Pvt.	*WIA* (4/8/45)
Marlatt, Milton	35668180	Pfc.	messenger [675]; *WIA* (8/7/44); **KIA** (9/14/44)
Martin, Francis L.	33102689	Pvt.	*WIA* (3/13/45)
Martin, Lionel E.	31358792	Pvt.	general court-martial, desertion
Martinez, Charles	39579140	Pfc.	
Martinez, Gilbert	39409000	Pfc.	
Mathies, Robert A.	35812241	Sgt.	*WIA* (3/3/45)
Matulevich, Edward	36958388	Pfc.	*2 WIA*
Mavis, George C.	36834724	Sgt.	*WIA* (2/16/45); **KIA** (4/19/45)
Maxwell, William	38389581	Pfc.	

Mayer, Charles E.	31447657	Pfc.	*2 WIA*
McAfee, Alexander	34975110	Pvt.	trench foot (10/31/44)
McCamey, Albert N.	33435702	Pfc.	*WIA* (3/3/45)
McClanahan, Robert L.	37753632	Pfc.	3rd Platoon: Bowman's squad
McClurg, Chester A.	15054563	Pfc.	1st Platoon: Collins's/Reiser's squad; division stockade; **KIA** (4/19/45)
McCollum, William E.	36982182	Pvt.	
McConnell, Ernest C.	37710287	Pvt.	
McCulloch, James T.	38534278	Pfc.	**KIA** (8/7/44)
McDonald, Carl E.	37753611	Pfc.	
McDonough, Edmund J.	32826829	T/5	light-vehicle driver [345]
McGarvey, Joseph A.	33768019	Pfc.	3rd Platoon: Bowman's squad
McInnis, Frederick C.	31453345	Pvt.	1st Platoon; **DOW** (10/24/44)
McIntyre, John T.	44047859	Pvt.	**KIA** (4/1/45)
McLaughlin, Ernest D., Jr.	0437724	1Lt.	platoon leader [1542-8]; company executive officer [1542-8]; *WIA* (8/9/44)
McMahon,* James E.	32025836	T/5	company cook [060]
McNamee, William H.	33312059	Sgt.	assistant squad leader [653]; *WIA* (9/14/44); Bronze Star (2/12/44)
McPherson, John J.	20466249	SSgt.	**DOW** (3/17/45)
McQueen, Joe	35474584	Pfc.	*2 WIA*
Meadows, Willard J.	35638806	Pfc.	**KIA** (6/12/44)
Mear, Morris	32791288	T/5	armorer [511]; Bronze Star (6/12/44)
Metkoff, Meyer M.	42061700	Pfc.	
Meyer, David R.	33574696	Pfc.	*WIA* (8/11/44)
Meyer, Joseph	42044767	Pfc.	*WIA* (9/28/44)
Mickelson, Norman S.	01318993	1Lt.	platoon leader [1542-9]
Miguel, Ernie	19044241	Pfc.	**KIA** (9/26/44)
Milas, John C.	35007256	T/5	light-vehicle driver [345]
Millar, James L.	32927389	Pfc.	3rd Platoon: Ridgeway's/Osbourn's squad, then Rush's squad; BAR; company mail clerk after war
Miller, Charles E.	32888778	Pfc.	influenza (5/44)
Miller, Chester C.	34099964	Sgt.	**KIA** (9/26/44)
Miller, Gilbert E.	33048769	SSgt.	*3 WIA*
Miller, Howard J.	33174054	Pfc.	*2 WIA*

Miller, Joseph L.	32949010	Pvt.	1st Platoon: Reiser's squad
Miller, Parry J.	33927929	Pvt.	**KIA** (10/13/44)
Mills, Stanley R.	0463314	1Lt.	weapons platoon leader [1542-9]; company executive officer [1542-8]; *WIA* (10/8/44)
Minor,* Wayne R.	15012370	Pfc.	*3 WIA*
Mitchell, Odie Z.	39724900	Pvt.	**KIA** (10/13/44)
Moen, Richard S.	37024518	Pfc.	weapons platoon: light machine gunner [604]; died (05/19/45), alcohol poisoning
Molinari, Steve J.	36774317	Pvt.	*WIA* (8/17/44)
Monaghan, Thomas J.	31447799	Pvt.	**KIA** (8/6/44)
Montague, Lewis A.	34889495	Pfc.	*2 WIA*
Montalchi, Joseph D.	32056656	Pvt.	*WIA* (10/11/44)
Monte, Leroy	33705171	Pfc.	*WIA* (9/20/44)
Montoya, Louis A.	38348593	Pfc.	*3 WIA*
Moore, Alva M.	34449422	Sgt.	headquarters platoon; communications chief [542]; *WIA* (10/8/44)
Moore, John A.	38661794	Pfc.	
Moore, John J.	33606749	Pvt.	*WIA* (10/8/44)
Moore, Ralph P.	35902336	Pvt.	*2 WIA*
Moriarty, Dennis J.	31126320	Pvt.	automatic rifleman [746]
Morman, Rufus A.	34973638	Pfc.	
Morris, Jesse A.	15056277	Sgt.	assistant squad leader [653]; *WIA* (9/14/44)
Morris, Mack	38095354	Pfc.	
Mosley, Howard C.	34831875	Pfc.	*WIA* (2/6/45)
Moyer, David R.	33574696	Pfc.	*2 WIA*
Muehleman, Walter E.	32344668	Pfc.	ammunition handler [504]; *WIA* (7/17/44); **KIA** (9/28/44)
Mullaney, Justin P.	42003396	Pfc.	ammunition handler [504]
Murphy, David F.	39344642	Pvt.	WIA (10/13/44)
Murrell, Benjamin A.	32040833	T/5	company medic; Silver Star (4/43); *2 WIA*
Myers, Melvin J.	33660465	Pfc.	*WIA* (3/13/45)
Naud, Thomas H., Jr.	42182829	Pfc.	weapons platoon: light machine gunner [604]; *WIA* (4/20/45)
Naugle, Frederick B.	32807615	Sgt.	*2 WIA*
Naylor, Merl F.	42085816	Pvt.	*WIA* (7/13/44)
Neal, Lester L.	15054779	Pfc.	**KIA** (6/18/44)

Nelson, James	35656311	Pvt.	WIA (10/8/44)
Nielsen, John B.	37679552	Pfc.	trench foot (2/2/45)
Nill, Charles L.	35046313	Pfc.	WIA (12/15/44)
Nodell, Harry C.	42056919	Pvt.	3rd Platoon: Ridgeway's/ Osbourn's squad; **KIA** (2/28/45)
Nuhn, William W., Jr.	33592358	Pfc.	WIA (7/17/44)
O'Brian, Richard L.	35770189	Pvt.	
Odette, Arnold L.	35658362	Pfc.	**KIA** (10/6/44)
Olive, Raymond L.	20911369	SSgt.	1st Platoon; **KIA** (2/4/45); Silver Star (10/21/44)
Oliver, Herchel H.	34160009	Pfc.	WIA (8/9/44)
Olsen,* Arnold J.	32014397	Sgt.	squad leader [653]; WIA (10/12/44)
Osbourn, Oliver J.	34905155	SSgt.	3rd Platoon: took over squad leader [653] of 3rd squad for Timber Ridgeway; WIA (2/27/45)
Ott, Claradon L.	35742689	Pvt.	
Pawlik, John P.	36761086	Pfc.	WIA (10/9/44)
Pellock, Donald J.	39919202	Pfc.	
Pemberton, Frank B., Jr.	35219682	Pvt.	general court-martial, desertion
Perry, Edwin A.	01290805	Capt.	company commander [1542-7]; 3 WIA; 4 Bronze Stars
Pettigrew, Robert S.	42127964	Pfc.	3rd Platoon: Ridgeway's/ Osbourn's squad; BAR
Phillips, Bertrum R.	44041434	Pfc.	weapons platoon: light machine gunner [604]
Pickard, Edward A.	34503151	Sgt.	3rd Platoon: Ridgeway's/ Osbourn's squad: assistant squad leader
Poni, Alphonse A.	32029939	Pfc.	WIA (3/43); **KIA** (6/18/44)
Ponzurick, George	33617096	Pvt.	
Poole, Jack E.	36847256	Pfc.	weapons platoon: light machine gunner [604]; WIA (4/15/45)
Porter, Harold W.	36464815	Pfc.	
Pourchot, Leonard L.	16122523	SSgt.	1st Platoon: Collins's/Reiser's squad; assistant squad leader; Silver Star (3/16/45); WIA (12/15/44)
Prado, Jesus	39579454	Pvt.	WIA (10/12/44)
Pratt, Joseph D.	34495056	Pvt.	WIA (8/4/44); **KIA** (8/5/44)
Pratt, Karl L.	01297586	1Lt.	3rd Platoon leader; WIA (6/17/44); SIA (10/12/944)

Preuss, Arthur M.	36847217	Pvt.	weapons platoon: light-mortar crewman [607]
Prophet, Delbert R.	39141699	Pfc.	
Raboin, Alan L.	36834636	Pvt.	
Randall, Frank J.	01316669	1Lt.	3rd Platoon leader [1542-9]; *WIA* (12/12/44)
Rapuano, Richard E.	31407251	Pfc.	BAR; *WIA* (3/2/45)
Raskell, Tony	35741670	Pvt.	**KIA** (6/12/44)
Ray, Albert	36412343	Pfc.	*2 WIA*
Reber, George E.	36835961	Pfc.	*2 WIA*
Redden, Robert F.	32669137	Pfc.	*WIA* (10/8/44)
Redmond, Floyd	6851985	SSgt.	*2 WIA*
Reed, Clifton L.	14031114	Pfc.	*3 WIA*
Reese, Israel L.	34974024	Pfc.	3rd Platoon: Rush's squad; BAR; **KIA** (1/30/45)
Reeves, Roger E.	01306145	2Lt.	platoon leader [1542-9]; *WIA* (8/6/44)
Reiser, John E.	33349982	SSgt.	1st Platoon: squad leader [653]; *2 WIA*; **KIA** (3/17/45)
Reisinger, Clarence P.	33243490	Pfc.	*WIA* (6/17/44)
Renda, Paul R.	42182673	Pvt.	weapons platoon: light-mortar crewman [607]
Rhoden, Arthur	34057608	Pfc.	*2 WIA*
Richardson, William C.	42182629	Pvt.	weapons platoon: light-mortar crewman [607]; *WIA* (4/7/45)
Ridgeway, Warren E.	32025844	SSgt.	3rd Platoon: 3rd Squad leader; 1st Platoon: squad leader [653]; Bronze Star (7/17/44); **MIA/KIA** (1/21/45)
Rinebolt, Harold	35765726	Pfc.	**KIA** (2/9/45)
Riser, James W.	34079189	SSgt.	*WIA* (8/10/44)
Ritter, Edward	32758486	Pfc.	BAR; *WIA* (12/15/44)
Roden, Grady F.	39722587	Pvt.	
Rodrigues, John C.	31455393	Pvt.	Silver Star (1/30/45); *WIA* (1/30/45)
Rogers,* Harold W.	15055116	Sgt.	*2 WIA*
Rojo, Charles	42046168	Pfc.	*2 WIA*
Rolewski, Henry J.	36710294	Pfc.	*3 WIA*
Rose, Charles W., Jr.	62085797	Pvt.	
Rose, Raymond J.	16125909	Pfc.	*WIA* (2/5/45)

Rosen, George	32014166	Sgt.	assistant squad leader [653]; *4 WIA*; Silver Star (12/27/44); Bronze Star (9/15/44)
Rosencrance, Lester	33611657	Pvt.	*WIA* (7/13/44)
Rouse, Paul B.	34898204	Pvt.	*WIA* (10/14/44)
Rowland, Omer E.	36692087	Pvt.	*WIA* (8/7/44)
Rudd, George N.	34921247	Pvt.	*WIA* (12/13/44); white phosphorus (01/45)
Ruiz, Gaspar	31210236	Pfc.	**KIA** (6/19/44)
Runyon, Archie	35735433	Pvt.	*WIA*
Rush, James J., Jr.	33778981	SSgt.	3rd Platoon: squad leader [653]; *WIA* (3/17/45)
Russ, Robert I.	01317131	1Lt.	weapons platoon leader
Russell, Herbert E., Jr.	31431883	Pvt.	*WIA* (2/11/45)
Russell, James W.	31318897	Sgt.	squad leader [653]; *WIA* (1/26/45); **KIA** (3/15/45)
Russell, William A.	34147447	SSgt.	*WIA* (10/20/44)
Russo, Frank	32066414	Pfc.	*WIA* (10/9/44)
Rutledge, Melvin W.	39466834	Sgt.	*WIA* (2/5/45)
Rynearson, Harold E.	36478105	Pfc.	*WIA* (7/23/44)
Sacco, James L., Sr.	32847417	T/5	transferred to Company L
Sanchez, Gabriel	32000947	Pvt.	
Sandifer, Edward S.	35781140	Pvt.	
Sands, George W.	34794661	Pfc.	
Santi, Peter J.	32025826	SSgt.	*WIA* (6/12/44); Bronze Star (6/12/44)
Sapp, Clarence M.	33563412	Pfc.	*WIA* (3/17/45)
Sapp, Paul R.	14028056	Pfc.	*4 WIA*
Scafaro, Joseph J.	32172638	Pfc.	
Scates, James R.	37624274	Pvt.	*WIA* (7/12/44)
Scheffel, Charles	0446059	1Lt.	weapons platoon leader; Silver Star (8/10/44); Bronze Star; *5 WIA*
Schell, Glenn W.	33872476	Pvt.	*WIA* (2/10/45)
Schmidt, Harold	36732328	Pfc.	*WIA* (8/4/44)
Schneider, Melvin B.	36044227	Pfc.	*WIA* (7/7/44) **KIA** (09/19/44)
Schoenwald, Benjamin	36382703	Pfc.	*WIA* (10/13/44)
Schopper, John E.	35235864	Sgt.	weapons platoon: light machine gunner [604]; *WIA* (8/7/44)
Schtucka, Edward	35272545	Pfc.	*WIA* (6/16/44)
Schultz, John M., Jr.	33574479	T/5	*WIA* (2/27/45)

Seaman, Kenneth	36960664	Pfc.	3rd Platoon: Ridgeway's/ Osbourn's squad; *WIA* (1/30/45)
Semrov, Anton J.	36773153	Pfc.	**DOW** (9/15/44)
Shafron, Walter	33773416	Pvt.	1st Platoon; *2 WIA*
Shew, Robert J.	36418359	Pfc.	*2 WIA*; Bronze Star (4/17/45)
Shields, James S.	33418819	Pvt.	*WIA* (2/27/45)
Shockley, Arthur W.	36839682	Pvt.	*WIA* (10/10/44)
Sim, Michael	36479333	Pfc.	SIA (4/19/45)
Singer,* Victor	32014915	SSgt.	*WIA* (9/27/44)
Skelly, Walter F.	36672383	Pvt.	
Skinner, Gerson L.	32535585	Pvt.	*WIA* (10/11/44)
Slack, Harold E.	35247118	Pfc.	*WIA* (12/21/44)
Slaughter, Jessie D.	38303340	T/5	3rd Platoon; medic; *2 WIA*
Small, William R.	34779649	Pvt.	ammunition handler [504]; *WIA* (7/44)
Smetana, Stephen S.	36890660	Pfc.	*WIA* (12/21/44)
Smith, Glenn, Jr.	35556781	Pvt.	
Smith, Marvin A.	36526796	Cpl.	*WIA* (3/4/45)
Solano, Ambrosio A.	37704796	Pvt.	*2 WIA*
Soltis, George T.	33088671	SSgt.	company supply sergeant [821]
Somers,* Charles G.	32025807	SSgt.	**KIA** (9/1/44)
Spaan,* John A.	32029965	Sgt.	*2 WIA*
Spanguolo, William J.	6880020	Pvt.	*WIA* (10/10/44)
Spano, William P.	32715540	Pfc.	3rd Platoon; broke back 11/45; hospital to 9/46
St. Peter, Robert J.	36566578	Pfc.	Silver Star (10/13/44)
Sternlicht, Sam	32117214	Pfc.	*2 WIA*
Stevens, Harold A.	36462808	T/4	company cook [060]
Stine, Donald C.	35348110	Pfc.	1st Platoon: Ridgeway's squad; *WIA* (2/5/45)
Stock, Carl V.	35247128	Pfc.	*2 WIA*
Strang, John H.	32269413	Pvt.	*WIA* (artillery shrapnel 7/44)
Sullivan, Paul H.	34984013	Pfc.	ammunition handler [504]
Swan, Herbert E.	36461998	T/5	*WIA* (3/17/45)
Swedo, Ted J.	16101411	SSgt.	*2 WIA*
Szymanik, Francis	32266893	Cpl.	former general clerk [055]
Szollosy, Michael	32240858	SSgt.	*3 WIA*
Taluba, Leonard E.	33606186	Pfc.	
Tanem, Johan	37159756	Pfc.	Bronze Star (8/12/44)

Taylor, Eugene D.	01305499	1Lt.	company commander [1542-7]; Silver Star; Bronze Star (9/28/44); Bronze Star (2/3/45); *WIA* (9/28/44)
Taylor, Marshall L.	38662394	Pvt.	SIA (3/45)
Taylor, Paul L.	38153949	Pvt.	*WIA* (10/8/44)
Tedeschi, Arthur L.	32238453	Pfc.	*WIA* (10/13/44)
Temple, Kenneth E.	36671427	Pfc.	1st Platoon: Collins's/Reiser's squad
Terchak, Irving H.	36217184	Cpl.	*2 WIA*
Terek, Frank	35067825	T/5	company armorer [511]
Thompson, Oscar H.	0333774	Capt.	company commander [1542-7]; Bronze Star (5/3/43); Bronze Star (10/30/44)
Thompson, Shelby J.	6298154	Pvt.	*WIA* (10/6/44)
Thompson, Warren S.	39044733	Pfc.	*WIA* (9/21/44)
Thornton, Waldo L.	34686112	Pfc.	*WIA* (10/13/44)
Thurston, James M.	6662080	Sgt.	1st Platoon: Ridgeway's squad; *2 WIA*; Bronze Star (1/21/45)
Tierney, Richard J.	31426063	Pvt.	*WIA* (9/21/44)
Timmons, Lafayette F.	42080816	Pfc.	*2 WIA*
Tindale, Merrill M.	14044623	SSgt.	*WIA* (12/12/44)
Tome, Thomas R.	33581372	Pvt.	
Tomes, Carlas	39471995	Pvt.	**KIA** (12/12/44)
Townsend, Ralph	35731829	Pvt.	*WIA* (9/26/44)
Trine, Robert E.	36450437	Sgt.	
Trzecinski, Frank A.	7032052	TSgt.	*WIA* (6/18/44)
Turner,* Langley	15054785	TSgt.	3rd Platoon: platoon sergeant [651]; *2 WIA*; Silver Star (1/31/45)
Uveges, William	33081112	Pfc.	**KIA** (3/12/45)
Valencia, Hipolito F.	38552831	Pfc.	company cook [060]
Vanderzanden, Elmer W.	39333882	Pfc.	
Vargas, Lorenzo J.	37445976	Pfc.	3rd Platoon: Bowman's squad
Vaught, James S.	14120867	Pfc.	**DOW** (10/12/44)
Vickers, Gordon L.	33556494	Sgt.	*2 WIA*
Vito, Alfred	31447848	Pfc.	3rd Platoon: Rush's squad
Voltin, Francis J.	37586896	Pvt.	*WIA* (10/13/44)
Voyles, L. G.	34629961	Pfc.	*WIA* (9/27/44)
Vunk, Lloyd R.	32663760	Pfc.	**DOW** (12/22/44)
Wahl, Irving J.	39472168	Pfc.	**DOW** (4/6/45)
Wahlstrom, Raymond O.	37589300	Pfc.	**DOW** (3/4/45)

Walden, John A.	31429721	Pvt.	
Wallace, Ralph W.	36838535	Pvt.	KIA (10/12/944)
Wasnick, Lloyd	37566632	Pfc.	3rd Platoon: Ridgeway's/ Osbourn's squad; WIA (4/4/45)
Waters, Noel P.	39693650	Pvt.	WIA (9/26/44); KIA (2/28/45)
Weaver, Roy	34084919	[Pfc.]	KIA (6/19/44)
Weber, Robert S.	6918052	TSgt.	platoon sergeant [651]; 2 WIA
Weiner, Edward	32901788	Pfc.	WIA (9/1/44)
Weiner, Leon H.	12192834	Pfc.	WIA (4/4/45)
Wetovsky,* Louis	32014739	Pfc.	2 WIA
Whatley, George O.	6969786	TSgt.	2 WIA
Wheeler, Jesse L.	0520913	1Lt.	2 WIA; Silver Star [10/13/44 in Company L]
Whitcombe, Warren L., Jr.	42018799	Pfc.	2 WIA; SIA (1/30/45)
White, Willie S.	38535383	SSgt.	3rd Platoon: Bowman's squad
White, Thomas C.	01315624	1Lt.	
Widdis, William E.	42005523	T/5	WIA (3/18/45)
Wieland, Charles F.	01320799	2Lt.	2 WIA
Wienhoff, Joseph W.	36955384	Pvt.	frostbite (12/23/44)
Wilhoite, Walter	35881375	Pfc.	WIA (10/10/44)
Williams, John R.	35173549	Pfc.	KIA (9/15/44)
Williamson, Edison B.	35762683	Pfc.	
Wilson, Arthur K.	42081501	Pfc.	WIA (10/14/44)
Wilson, Floyd L.	38452614	Sgt.	
Wilson, Luther D.	15055040	Sgt.	2 WIA; Silver Star (2/3/45)
Wlodarczyk, Walter F.	32581088	Pfc.	accidentally shot (3/14/45)
Wolfe, George M.	39102383	Pfc.	WIA (2/27/45)
Wood, John S.	35775888	Pvt.	KIA (8/11/44)
Wright, Carl D.	35262614	Pvt.	KIA (6/18/44)
Yannuzzi,* Anthony J.	32025833	T/4	company cook [060]
Yates, Patrick E., Jr.	32450607	Pfc.	2 WIA
Yeakel, Clarence F.	33834360	Pfc.	WIA (10/8/44)
Youles, Robert G.	34832603	Pvt.	weapons platoon: light-mortar crewman [607]; WIA (8/6/44)
Young, Warren J.	37681581	Pvt.	WIA (10/8/44)
Yount, Newton L.	35248197	Pfc.	DOW (12/28/44)
Yunis, George	12072330	Pfc.	DOW (6/21/44)
Zajac, Theodore	6920323	Pfc.	DOW (7/18/44)
Zolnowski, Chester R.	33033145	Pfc.	WIA (8/6/44)
Zimmermann, Elmer J.	36297971	Pfc.	WIA (12/15/44)

Note 1: Soldiers without Army specialty (e.g., 060, 504, 607, 651) are 745–rifleman.

Note 2: In 1947, the US government authorized the retroactive awarding of the Bronze Star Medal to World War II veteran soldiers who had been awarded the Combat Infantryman Badge. These Bronze Stars are not shown in this table, since many were issued decades later; however, for discharged veterans it was often a hassle to find paperwork that would support this award, and many never received it at all. The small bronze stars on the European–African–Middle Eastern Campaign Medal ribbon designate individual campaigns in which the soldier participated. They are not Bronze Star Medals.

ENDNOTES

INTRODUCTION

1. Casualty figures rely on Nese F. De Bruyne, "American War and Military Operations Casualties: Lists and Statistics" (Washington, DC: Congressional Research Service, April 26, 2017); and Edward G. Miller, "To Build Infantry for the Future, Look First to the Past," Modern War Institute, West Point, NY, October 15, 2018.

2. Ernie Pyle, *Here Is Your War: Story of GI Joe* (Lincoln: University of Nebraska Press, 2004), 246.

3. Ancestry.com, PFC Richard Sidney Moen.

PREFACE

1. Kurt Vonnegut, *Slaughterhouse-Five* (New York, Delacorte, 1961), chap. 1.

CHAPTER 1

1. Thanks to Charles Dickens for initial sentence from *A Tale of Two Cities*. Eisenhower White House American Legion "Back-to-God" Program.

2. Joseph B. Mittelman, *Eight Stars to Victory: A History of the Veteran Ninth US Infantry Division* (Washington, DC: Ninth Infantry Division Association, 1948), 30.

3. Ibid., 16, 30, 31.

4. Ancestry.com, Langley Turner.

5. Mittelman, *Eight Stars to Victory*, 32.

6. Discussion, Myron MacLean.

7. Ancestry.com, Chester A. McClurg.

8. William Bradford Huie, *The Execution of Private Slovik* (New York: Delacorte, 1970), 15.

9. James Gravino, April 30, 2020; Albert A. Colacino, "We Remember . . . Gravino brothers," *Courier-Gazette* (Newark, NY), April 28, 1995, 4; Baseball Reference, www.baseball-reference.com; Personnel File [PF], Joseph Gravino, 32025804; and Ancestry.com, Joseph Francis Gravino.

10. William M. Kreye, *The Pawns of War* (New York: Vintage, 1983), 26.

11. Headquarters, 39th Infantry Regiment, APO 9, *GO* #2 (January 31, 1944).

12. Ancestry.com, Albert Paul DiRisio; John Doser, "Singing Waiter Hawk Wows 'Em at the Piano," *Fairport (NY) Herald Mail*, June 18, 1980; John Doser, "The Hawk Recalls: The Induction Center," *Fairport (NY) Herald Mail*, July 9, 1980; John Doser, "The Hawk Recalls: Carnival Wrassling No Game for the Puny," *Fairport (NY) Herald Mail*, April 30, 1980; Donovan Shilling, *Rochester's Marvels & Myths: Twenty-Four Very Remarkable Stories about Some Very Unusual People, Events, and Places* (Victor, NY: Pancoast, 2011), 71; John Doser, "The Hawk's First Love, Woodchuck Hunting, " *Fairport (NY) Herald Mail*, 1980; and John Doser, "The Hawk Displays His Marksmanship," *Fairport (NY) Herald Mail*, 1980.

13. PF, Oscar H. Thompson, O-333774.

14. John Doser, "Pearl Harbor Ends the Hawk's Romance," *Fairport (NY) Herald Mail*, August 27, 1980.

15. John Doser, "The Hawk Obeys Orders Promoted to Sergeant," *Fairport (NY) Herald Mail*, September 3, 1980.

16. John Doser, "Laughing Cooks Spoil the Menu," *Fairport (NY) Herald Mail*, July 23, 1980.

17. Thaddeus Holt, "Relax—It's Only a Maneuver," *MHQ Magazine*, Winter 1992.

18. Kreye, *Pawns of War*, 33, 39.

19. Discussions, Myron MacLean.

20. Ancestry.com, Warren Earle Ridgeway.

21. "Lindsey Nelson's Speech Captured Mood of Reunion," *Octofoil* 37, no. 3 (May–July 1982): 1.

22. Westbrook Pegler, "As Pegler Sees It: Kicked Out of 2 Schools, Matt Eddy Rose to General," 2.

23. Steven Attanasio, *Untouched Heroics: Anecdotes from the Life of a World War II Veteran* (Middletown, DE: Steven Attanasio, 2014), 39.

24. Mittelman, *Eight Stars to Victory*, 45–53.

25. Letter, Charles A. Bodnar to *Octofoil*, November–December 1997, 7.

26. War Department, *Field Manual (FM) 23-5, Basic Field Manual: US Rifle. Caliber .30, M1*, issued on July 20, 1941, chaps. 2, 5.

27. Walter Cronkite (Scripps-Howard), "They Threatened Hitler," *Octofoil* 5, no. 2 (May 1947): 7.

CHAPTER 2

1. Pyle, "The God-Damned Infantry," *Scripps-Howard*, May 2, 1943, found at the Media School, Indiana University.

2. Doser, "The Hawk Obeys Orders Promoted to Sergeant."

3. Shilling, *Rochester's Marvels*, 72; and Mittelman, *Eight Stars to Victory*, 56.

4. Myranda Elliott, granddaughter of Langley Turner, March 2020; and Peter R. Mansoor, "The Development of Combat Effectiveness in the United States Army during World War II," MA thesis, Ohio State University, 1992, 86. The division secured 22,977 pounds of hay and 85,416 pounds of barley for the animals.

5. Mittelman, *Eight Stars to Victory*, 97–99; "Report on Operation Conducted by 9th Infantry Division, United States Army, Southern Tunisia, 26 March–8 April 1943," Headquarters, 9th Infantry Division, APO #9, 1943, 9; and PF, Joseph Gravino.

6. Rick Atkinson, *An Army at Dawn: The War in North Africa, 1942–1943* (New York: Henry Holt, 2003), 502.

7. "Report on Operation Conducted by 9th Infantry Division, United States Army, Southern Tunisia," 10–11.

8. *Fairport (NY) Herald-Mail*, April 29, 1943, 1.

9. Pyle, "The God-Damned Infantry."

10. Mittelman, *Eight Stars to Victory*, 109.

11. "Report on Operation Conducted by 9th Infantry Division, United States Army, Southern Tunisia," 23.

12. Attanasio, *Untouched Heroics*, 92.

13. Hal Boyle, "Yank Unit Peeved; Never Hits a City—Ninth Division Gets to See Only Europe's Back Alleys," *Deseret News* (Salt Lake City, UT), October 10, 1944.

14. A 1939 movie about the Foreign Legion, starring Gary Cooper.

15. French L. MacLean, *Custer's Best: The Story of Company M, 7th Cavalry at the Little Bighorn* (Atglen, PA: Schiffer, 2011), 37; Thomas J. Gibbs, "Venereal Disease and American Policy in a War Zone: 39th Infantry Regiment in Sidi Bel Abbès, Algeria, May of 1943," University of New Orleans theses, Fall, December 18, 2015; Scheffel, Charles, segment 1, Digital Collections of the National WWII Museum; William Butler, *The Cage: Memoirs of a Medical Officer with the 39th Infantry Regiment in World War II* (William Butler); 9th Infantry, GO #62 (September 1, 1944); and Red Phillips, "Different as CGs, but Both Top Performers," *Octofoil* 56, no. 1 (January–February 2001), 5.

16. Shilling, *Rochester's Marvels*, 72–73.

17. Headquarters, 39th Infantry Regiment, *GO* #2 (January 31, 1944).

18. Mittelman, *Eight Stars to Victory*, 126–27.

19. Jack Toffey, KIA, 3rd Infantry Division, on June 3, 1944, near Rome, Italy.

20. Mittelman, *Eight Stars to Victory*, 127–30.

21. USNA Virtual Memorial Hall, Harry A. Flint; Robert A. Anderson, *Paddy: The Colorful Story of Colonel Harry A. "Paddy" Flint* (Westminster, MD: Heritage Books, 2006), 29, 32, 44, 46–47, 52, 57; Joseph Driscoll, "Paddy Flint, Cherbourg's Captor," *New York Tribune*, 1945; Rick Atkinson, *The Day of Battle: The War in Sicily and Italy, 1943-1944* (New York: Macmillan, 2008), 155; and Omar N. Bradley, *A Soldier's Story* (New York: Modern Library, 1999), 153.

22. Kreye, *The Pawns of War*, 138.

23. Bradley, *Soldier's Story*, 153. Nelson's eye / turning a blind eye, attributed to Admiral Horatio Nelson, blind in one eye. At the Battle of Copenhagen, Nelson was signaled to withdraw; putting his telescope to his blind eye, he said he couldn't see it.

24. Atkinson, *The Day of Battle*, 155.

25. William M. Kreye, "The Pawns of War," *Octofoil* 25, no. 1 (January–February 1970): 3; Anderson, *Paddy*, 89; USNA Virtual Memorial Hall, Harry A. Flint; and Summary of 39th Infantry Regiment Decorations, NARA.

26. "'Black Market' Band Leader Writes Col. Flint's Widow," *Octofoil* 18, no. 6 (May–June 1965): 6; and Anderson, *Paddy*, 102.

27. Anderson, *Paddy*, 105.

28. All witness statements are in PF, Joseph Gravino.

29. Ancestry.com, Jack Alexander Dunlap.

30. *Octofoil* 34, no. 1 (January–February 1979): 4; Ancestry.com, Edwin A. Perry; and Headquarters, 39th Infantry Regiment, *GO* #2 (January 31, 1944).

31. *GO* #2 (January 31, 1944).

32. Discussions, Judith Mills Porter, Anita Mills Thompson, and Heidi Marie Thompson; and *GO* #2 (January 31, 1944).

33. *Octofoil* 32, no. 1 (January–February 1977): 2; and "'Black Market' Band Leader Writes Col. Flint's Widow," 6. Bennie received a Bronze Star for improving morale on October 1, 1943.

34. Anderson, *Paddy*, 112.

35. Attanasio, *Untouched Heroics,* 131.

36. "39th Infantry Regiment," Faces beyond the Graves website.

37. "Private Snafu": Looney Tunes Wiki.

38. Miller, "To Build Infantry for the Future."

39. Gerald Astor, *The Bloody Forest: Battle for the Huertgen; September 1944–January 1945* (Novato, CA: Presidio, 2000), 209.

40. Miller, "To Build Infantry for the Future."

41. Section I, *War Department Circular* 269 (October 27, 1943).

42. Bob Hope, *I Never Left Home: Bob Hope's Own Story of His Trip Abroad* (New York: Simon and Schuster, 1944).

43. Ibid., 173.

44. Astor, *Bloody Forest*, 209.

CHAPTER 3

1. Study unable to find the name of the whiny German general involved.

2. 9th Infantry, *GO* #94 (October 30, 1944).

3. Ancestry.com, Jessie Dale Slaughter; interviews, Billie Joe Slaughter; and PF, Jessie D. Slaughter, 38303340.

4. Discussion, Nicholas Baccile, son Albert Baccile, June 8, 2020.

5. Edwin A. Perry, "Operations of the 1st Battalion, 39th Infantry (9th Infantry Division) North of St. Jacques De Nehou, Cotentin Peninsula, 18 June 1944 (Normandy Campaign) (Personal Experience of a Company Commander)," Fort Benning, GA, 1949.

6. PF, Billie S. Flowers, 34851110; and Ancestry.com, Billie S. Flowers.

7. Kreye, *Pawns of War*, 186.

8. Mansoor, "Development of Combat Effectiveness," 113.

9. *Fairport Herald-Mail*, July 20, 1944, 8.

10. Perry, "Operations of the 1st Battalion, 39th Infantry (9th Infantry Division)."

11. Henry Gerard Phillips, *Remagen: Springboard to Victory* (Penn Valley, CA: Henry Gerard Phillips, 1995), 97.

12. James Richardson, "Operations of the 1st Battalion, 39th Infantry Regiment (9th Infantry Division) at Cherence le Roussel, France, (German Attack on Avranches), 4–10 August 1944 (Northern France Campaign) (Personal Experience of a Battalion S-3)," Fort Benning, GA, 1948, 14.

13. 9th Infantry, *GO* #81 (October 1, 1944).

14. Richardson, "Operations of the 1st Battalion," 16.

15. PF, Joseph Gravino.

16. Jewell, V-mail, August 15, 1944.

17. Ancestry.com, Jack F. Jewell; PF, Jack F. Jewell, 0283969; and "Jack Jewell Timeline," Watkins Museum of History, Douglas County Historical Society.

18. Ancestry.com, Edward Arnold Pickard.

19. Jewell, V-mail, August 19, 1944.

20. Ibid., August 20, 1944.

21. Ibid., August 23, 1944.

22. Ibid., August 25, 1944.

23. Company B Morning Report, August 27, 1944; and Ancestry.com, Alfred Cusimano.

24. Mansoor, "The Development of Combat Effectiveness," 113.

25. "Earned Silver Star," *Wellsville (KS) Globe*, April 26, 1945.

26. Martin Blumenson, *Breakout and Pursuit* (Washington, DC: Office of the Chief of Military History, 1961), 694.

27. Jewell, letter, September 11, 1944.

28. Sebastian D. Andriello, narrator, New York State Military Museum, interviewers Michael Russert and Wayne Clark, October 7, 2006, Holiday Inn, Kingston, NY.

29. 9th Infantry, *GO* #89 (October 15, 1944).

30. PF, Billie S. Flowers; and Ancestry.com, Billie S. Flowers.

31. Rolls-rough: play on "Rolls-Royce."

32. Ancestry.com, Manley G. Fuller; and discussions, Sarah O'Connor Collins, grand-daughter Manley Fuller.

33. Ancestry.com, Kermit Dale Lockridge.

34. Ancestry.com, Israel Lafayette Reese.

35. "Ax Blow on Head Kills Child," *Salt Lake (UT) Tribune*, December 16, 1941, 9.

36. Ancestry.com, Deloss J. Bradshaw.

37. ewell, V-mail, September 24, 1944.

38. Ibid., September 30, 1944.

39. *Army Talks* II, no. 39 (September 27, 1944), folder title: Ground Force Reinforcement Command, chapter VI, box 157, Records Group 498, NARA, College Park, MD.

40. Jewell, letter, September 30, 1944.

41. Mansoor, "The Development of Combat Effectiveness," 113.

42. Jewell, letter, September 18, 1944.

43. Ancestry.com, Leonard Pourchot; conversations, Regan Pourchot, Leonard's son, May 2020; and Pourchot notebook.

44. Discussions, Linda Wasnick Browning, daughter of Lloyd L. Wasnick, June 2020; Ancestry.com, Lloyd Ludwig Wasnick; and PF, Lloyd Ludwig Wasnick, 37566632.

45. Jay Philip Holman, "The Day I Ran Faster"; telephone conversation, April 8, 2019; *Omaha Central High School Yearbook*, 1943; and Jay Philip Holman, letter to Linda, July 28, 1995.

46. PF, James J. Rush, 33778981; and Ancestry.com, James Joseph Rush.

47. Ancestry.com, Francis J. Randall; and Astor, *Bloody Forest*, 80–81.

48. Ancestry.com, Louis Armand Benoist; conversations with Louis Benoist, son of Lt. Louis Benoist, and other family members 2019; and letter from Louis Benoist to friend Paul, August 1944.

49. Ancestry.com, Robert S. Pettigrew; discussions, Jim Pettigrew, son of Robert S. Pettigrew 2019–22; and "Robert S. Pettigrew Service Record," written by Bob Pettigrew, January–February 1946, provided by Jim Pettigrew, February 21, 2019.

50. Interview, David Basham, grandson of Ken Seaman, October 24, 2019; and Ancestry.com, Kenneth Ray Seaman.

51. Ancestry.com, Harry C. Nodell.

52. Letter from David Frankel, grandson of Harry Nodell, November 29, 2019; conversations, Kelly Lieber, granddaughter of Harry Nodell, 2020; and Ancestry.com, Harry C. Nodell.

53, Mac MacLean diary 1944.

54. *Yank—the Army Weekly*, 1942.

55. Butler, *The Cage*, 2.

56. Discussion, Scott Woodard, US Army Medical Service Corps, April 30, 2019.

57. Paul Dickson, *War Slang: American Fighting Words and Phrases from the Civil War to the War in Iraq* (New York: Bristol Park Books, 2007), 187.

58. Astor, *The Bloody Forest*, 135.

59. Edward G. Miller, *A Dark and Bloody Ground: The Hürtgen Forest and the Roer River Dams, 1944–1945* (College Station: Texas A&M University Press, 1995), 42.

60. Todd Smith, "How a World War I Jazz-Playing Marine Gave Us the Best Weapon Name Ever," *Marine Times*, September 3, 2021; "Bazooka (Musical Instrument)," in *The Encyclopedia of Arkansas History & Culture*; Robert H. Scales (US Army), "Edward Uhl," *Time Magazine*, May 31, 2010; Gordon L. Rottman, *The Bazooka* (Oxford: Osprey, 2012), 14–15; and Paul Huard, "The Bazooka: A History," Real Clear Defense, March 13, 2015.

61. Discussion, Vernon Carlson's nephew Sam Carlson, captain, AUS (Ret.), 2020.

62. *Octofoil* 37, no. 3 (May–June 1982): 1; Douglas C. Haines, Franklin D. Haines, and Jeffrey A. Haines, *This Cockeyed War: An Infantry Platoon Leader's Days with G CO 2nd BN 47th RGT 9th DIV in WWII* (CreateSpace, 2018), 34, 241; and Stefanie Van Steelandt, "The Georgie Patton, the New Old Fashioned," The Cereal Reader, March 26, 2020.

63. Miller, *Dark and Bloody Ground*, 77.

64. "Rocket, Air-to-Surface, 5-Inch, HVAR," Smithsonian National Air and Space Museum.

65. Jewell, letter, September 30, 1944.

CHAPTER 4

1. US Army, 1944, Germany, 1:25,000 *Sheet 5303, Rötgen*, coordinates 952288.

2. Ibid., coordinates 904287.

3. All times are military time: 0001 is 12:01 a.m., 1000 is 10:00 a.m., 1400 is 2:00 p.m., 1900 is 7:00 p.m., 2400 is midnight, etc. Combat strength is number of soldiers available for combat. Soldiers absent or unable to fight are not included. Thompson received a Bronze Star with Oak Leaf for Tunisia as the commander of Company B. Served as the S-3 (operations officer) and XO (executive officer) for Second Battalion before assuming battalion command. Jewell, V-mails, October 1, 1944, and October 2, 1944.

4. Jewell, letter, October 3, 1944.

5. *Sheet 5303, Rötgen*, coordinates 994337.

6. Eric William Klinek, "The Army's Orphans: The United States Army Replacement System in the European Campaign, 1944–1945," PhD diss., Temple University, May 2014.

7. *Sheet 5203, Stolberg*, coordinates 977355.

8. Ibid., coordinates 957367.

9. Astor, *Bloody Forest*, 9.

10. Sylvester Fourre, "The Green Hell of Huertgen Forest," *Man's Conquest* 8, no. 4 (October 1963).

11. Ibid.; Jewell, letter, December 4, 1944; Charles B. MacDonald, *The Battle of the Huertgen Forest* (Philadelphia: J. B. Lippincott, 1963), 2–5; Astor, *Bloody Forest*, 9, 37, 41; Ernest Hemingway, "War in the Siegfried Line," *Collier's*, November 18, 1944; and interview, Kathy Scroggins, grandfather of James J. Rush.

12. *Sheet 5303, Rötgen*, coordinates 994337.

13. Haines et al., *Cockeyed War*, 13.

14. *Sheet 5303, Rötgen*, coordinates 004336.

15. Ibid., coordinates 007339 to 008347.

16. Frank Buchholz and Thomas Brüggen, *German Machine Guns: Development, Tactics, and Use from 1892 to 1918* (Vienna: Verlag Militaria, 2019).

17. *Sheet 5303, Rötgen*, coordinates 003336.

18. *Sheet 5304, Nideggen*, coordinates 014332.

19. *Sheet 5303, Rötgen*, coordinates 995343.

20. *Sheet 5304, Nideggen*, coordinates 014332 and 015333.

21. Headquarters, 39th Infantry Regiment, *Combat Report*, October 6, 1944, 2400 hours, Dwight D. Eisenhower Presidential Library, Abilene, KS.

22. *Sheet 5304, Nideggen*, coordinates 021336.

23. Ibid., coordinates 020334.

24. Astor, *Bloody Forest*, 83.

25. *heet 5304, Nideggen*, coordinates 020333.

26. Ibid., coordinates 021331.

27. Ibid., coordinates 010337.

28. Ibid., coordinates 021332 to 021329.

29. Ibid., coordinates 021336.

30. Exact date undetermined.

31. *Sheet 5304, Nideggen*, coordinates 021329 to 020332.

32. Joris Nieuwint, "The Self Propelled 155 mm "Doorknocker" or "Bunker Buster—You Would Not Believe the Holes This Could Punch!," War History Online.

33. Astor, *Bloody Forest*, 154.

34. Ernest Hemingway, *Across the River and into the Trees* (London: Readers Union, 1950), chap. XXXI.

35. *Sheet 5304, Nideggen*, coordinates 021336.

36. Ancestry.com, John P. Pawlik.

37. *Sheet 5304, Nideggen*, coordinates 022330.

38. *New York Times*, Monday October 9, 1944.

39. *Sheet 5304, Nideggen*, coordinates 013330.

40. "Robert S. Pettigrew Service Record."

41. *Sheet 5304, Nideggen*, coordinates 022328.

42. Headquarters, 9th Infantry Division, *G-2 Periodic Report*, daily report, November 21, 1944, Dwight D. Eisenhower Presidential Library, Abilene, KS.

43. Miller, *Dark and Bloody Ground*, 58.

44. Boyle, "Yank Unit Peeved."

45. *Sheet 5304, Nideggen*, coordinates 013330.

46. Ibid., coordinates 018324.

47. Ibid., coordinates 024327.

48. William C. Sylvan and Francis G. Smith Jr., *Normandy to Victory: The War Diary of General Courtney H. Hodges and the First US Army* (Lexington: University of Kentucky Press, 2008), entry for Thursday, October 26, 1944.

49. *Sheet 5304, Nideggen*, coordinates 016337.

50. Ibid., coordinates in order 015334, 017340, and 021340.

51. Organization: Battle Group 1/12—"Battalion Boehm" (500 soldiers; commander, Captain Friedrich Wilhelm Boehm); Battle Group 3/12—"Battalion Weinen" (500 soldiers, commander, Major Albert Weinen); and Battle Group 2/12—Army Noncommissioned Officers School Saarlautern (1,000 soldiers).

52. *Sheet 5304, Nideggen*, coordinates 017335.

53. Ibid., coordinates 015337.

54. Ibid., coordinates 016337.

55. Ibid., coordinates 014337 to 017337.

56. Ibid., 016337. Morning report had coordinate as 016377, certainly in error.

57. *Sheet 5304, Nideggen*, coordinates 013339.

58. Headquarters, 9th Infantry, *GO* #113 (July 2, 1945).

59. Ibid., coordinates 017340, 018339, and 019339.

60. Headquarters, 9th Infantry, *GO* #120 (July 7, 1945).

61. Headquarters, 9th Infantry, *GO #9* (January 16, 1945).

62. PF, Jessie D. Slaughter; and interviews with his son Billie Joe.

63. Astor, *Bloody Forest*, 80–81.

64. *Sheet 5304, Nideggen*, coordinates 016340.

65. Ibid., coordinates 019338, 020339, 021339 to 023339.

66. Roger A. Freeman, *Mighty Eighth War Diary* (London: Janes, 1981), 364.

67. Sylvan and Smith, *Normandy to Victory*, entry for October 14, 1944.

68. Astor, *Bloody Forest*, 83.

69. Ancestry.com, Jay H. Lavin (Lavinsky); discussion, Jay H. Lavin, February 25, 2019; and discussions, Dr. Gerald Marks, lifelong friend of Jay H. Lavin.

70. *Sheet 5304, Nideggen*, coordinates 028332.

71. Individual Deceased Personnel File (IDPF), William A. Karko, 36714215.

72. Jewell, letter, October 16, 1944.

73. Haines et al., *This Cockeyed War*, 28.

74. *Sheet 5304, Nideggen*, coordinates 028332.

75. Haines et al., *This Cockeyed War*, 29.

76. *Sheet 5304, Nideggen*, coordinates 028332.

77. Klinek, "The Army's Orphans," 250.

78. *Sheet 5304, Nideggen*, coordinates 028332.

79. Emails, Herman's grandson Carl; and Herman Eichel's *Report of Examination of Enlisted Personnel Prior to Discharge, Release from Active Duty or Retirement*, March 14, 1946.

80. Holman, "The Day."

81. Astor, *Bloody Forest*, 130; and Holman, "The Day."

82. Jewell, letter, October 20, 1944.

83. *Sheet 5304, Nideggen*, coordinates 028332.

84. Bill Mauldin, *Up Front* (New York: W. W. Norton, 1945), 132.

85. Jewell, letter, January 1, 1945.

86. *Sheet 5304, Nideggen*, coordinates 028332

87. Hemingway, *Across the River*, 215.

88. Pourchot, notebook.

89. Miller, "To Build Infantry for the Future."

90. Jewell, letter, October 22, 1944.

91. *Sheet 5304, Nideggen*, coordinates 028332.

92. Pourchot, notebook.

93. Jewell, V-mail, October 24, 1944.

94. *Sheet 5304, Nideggen*, coordinates 028332.

95. Pourchot, notebook; and Jewell, V-mail, October 24, 1944.

96. *Sheet 5303, Rötgen*, coordinates 994337.

97. David Higgins, *Roer River Battles: Germany's Stand at the Westwall, 1944–45* (Havertown, PA: Casemate, 2010), 92.

98. Sandy Mazza, "Once Nashville's Biggest Business, the Sock Mill That Clothed Astronauts and Fought Nazis Is Transforming," *The Tennessean*, May 27, 2019.

99. Lieutenant Colonel Carey A. Clark et al., *Armor in the Hurtgen Forest* (Fort Knox, KY: Armored School, 1949), 21; Astor, *Bloody Forest*, 83; and Headquarters, 39th Infantry Regiment, *Combat Report*, October 7, 1944, 1200 hours, 1800 hours, and 2400 hours.

100. Haines et al., *This Cockeyed War*, 105.

101. Headquarters, 9th Infantry Regiment, *G-2 Periodic Report*, October 18, 1944.

102. Mac MacLean experienced the painful result numerous times.

103. Astor, *Bloody Forest*, 112.

104. John Boyd Coats, Ebbe Curtis Hoff, and Phebe M. Hoff, *Preventive Medicine in WWII*, vol. 4, *Communicable Diseases, Transmitted Chiefly through Respiratory and Alimentary Tracts* (Washington, DC: Office of Surgeon General, Department of the Army, 1958), table 34—Admissions for Primary Atypical Pneumonia in the US Army, 1942–45, and table 35—Admissions for Pneumonia.

105. Mauldin, *Up Front*, 215–16.

106. Astor, *Bloody Forest*, 122.

107. Richardson, "Operations of the 1st Battalion," 13.

108. Jewell, letter, November 28, 1944.

CHAPTER 5

1. *Sheet 5503, Elsenborn*, coordinates 915130.

2. Sylvan and Smith, *Normandy to Victory*, entry for October 11, 1944.

3. *Sheet 5503, Elsenborn*, coordinates 896084.

4. Ibid., coordinates 913123.

5. Ibid.

6. Jewell, V-mail, October 27, 1944.

7. Ibid., October 28, 1944.

8. Ibid., October 29, 1944.

9. "Warren Ridgeway Is Awarded Bronze Star," *Sandy Creek (NY) News*, December 6, 1944, 1.

10. Letter, Harry Nodell to Larry and Francis Lewis, January 2, 1945, Kelly Lieber.

11. Headquarters, Ninth Infantry Division, *Report of Operation, 1–31 October 1944*; Headquarters, Ninth Infantry Division, Office of the Surgeon, APO #9, *Report of Medical Activities for the Month of October 1944*, November 1, 1944; and Robert R. Palmer, Bell I. Wiley, and William R. Keast, *The Army Ground Forces: The Procurement and Training of Ground Combat Troops, United States Army in World War I* (Washington, DC: Center of Military History, 2003), 72. The Boys' Crusade was first discussed in those terms by Paul Fussell in *The Boys' Crusade: The American Infantry in Northwestern Europe, 1944–1945* (New York: Modern Library, 2003).

12. Jewell, V-mail, November 1, 1944.

13. Jewell, letter, November 2, 1944.

14. Mac MacLean.

15. *Sheet 5503, Elsenborn*, coordinates 977047.

16. *Sheet 5504, Hellenthal*, coordinates 005046.

17. Astor, *Bloody Forest*, 94.

18. *Sheet 5503, Elsenborn*, coordinates 999051.

19. Ibid., coordinates 911042.

20. Jewell, letter, November 5, 1944.

21. *Sheet 5503, Elsenborn*, coordinates 999051.

22. Jewell, V-mail, November 6, 1944.

23. Klinek, "The Army's Orphans," 297.

24. *Sheet 5503, Elsenborn*, coordinates 999051.

25. Headquarters, 9th Infantry Division, *G-2 Periodic Report*, November 7, 1944.

26. Pourchot, notebook.

27. Jewell, V-mail, November 9, 1944.

28. *Sheet 5403, Monschau*, coordinates 915130.

29. Klinek, "The Army's Orphans," 287.

30. *Sheet 5503, Elsenborn*, coordinates 924077.

31. Ibid., coordinates 896084.

32. Jewell, letter, November 13, 1944.

33. Jewell, V-mail, November 14, 1944.

34. PF, Jay H. Lavinsky, 33594370.

35. APO 9, *GO* #23 (November 15, 1944).

36. Discussions, Sarah O'Connor Collins, granddaughter of Manley Fuller.

37. Ibid.

38. Freeman, *Mighty Eighth War Diary*, 382.

39. Pourchot, notebook.

40. Miller, *Dark and Bloody Ground*, 72.

41. "Sgt. 'Joe' Gravino Twice Wounded, Gets Purple Heart," *Newark (NY) Courier-Gazette*, November 16, 1944, 1.

42. Jewell, letter, November 16, 1944.

43. Tom F. Whayne and Michael E. DeBakey, *Cold Injury, Ground Type, in World War II* (Washington, DC: Office of Surgeon General, Department of the Army, 1958).

44. Jewell, letter, November 18, 1944.

45. Ibid., November 19, 1944.

46. Pourchot, notebook.

47. Ibid.

48. Headquarters, 9th Infantry, *G-2 Periodic Report*, November 21, 1944.

49. Pourchot, notebook.

50. Mac MacLean letter.

51. Haines et al., *This Cockeyed War*, 129. Snafu—Situation normal, all fouled up.

52. Whayne and DeBakey, *Cold Injury*, table 25.

53. Jewell, V-mail, November 25, 1944.

54. Ibid.

55. Headquarters, Ninth Infantry Division, *G-2 Periodic Report*, November 28, 1944.

56. PF, Frank B. Pemberton, 35219682.

57. Ibid.

58. French L. MacLean, *The Fifth Field: The Story of the 96 American Soldiers Sentenced to Death and Executed in Europe and North Africa in World War II* (Atglen, PA: Schiffer, 2013).

59. Jewell, V-mail, November 30, 1944.

60. Headquarters, Ninth Infantry Division, Office of the Surgeon, *Report of Medical Activities for the Month of November 1944*, December 2, 1944.

61. Whayne and DeBakey, *Cold Injury*, table 25.

62. Jewell, letter, December 1, 1944.

63. Ibid., December 2, 1944.

64. Tessa Robinson, "How the Army-Navy Game of 1944 Stopped World War II," We Are the Mighty, December 11, 2021.

65. Ibid.

66. Jewell, letter, December 3, 1944.

67. Ibid., December 4, 1944.

68. Pourchot, notebook.

69. *Sheet 5204, Lendersdorf*, coordinates 020445.

70. *Sheet 5103, Eschweiler*, coordinates 977467.

71. Pourchot, notebook.

72. *Sheet 5204, Lendersdorf*, coordinates 035435.

73. Ibid., coordinates 029445.

74. Sylvan and Smith, *Normandy to Victory*, entry for December 6, 1944.

75. Whayne and DeBakey, *Cold Injury*, table 25.

76. Jewell, letter, December 9, 1944.

77. Arthur Fields's 1919 song "How Ya Gonna Keep 'em Down on the Farm (After They've Seen Paree?)."

78. Headquarters, Ninth Infantry Division, Office AC of S, G-2, *Journal*, December 9, 1944, 1135 hours.

79. *Sheet 5204, Lendersdorf*, coordinates 035435.

80. Pourchot, notebook.

81. Sylvan and Smith, *Normandy to Victory*, entry for Wednesday, December 10, 1944.

82. Letter, Seaman to MacLean, June 7, 1945.

83. *Sheet 5204, Lendersdorf*, coordinates 050453.

84. Headquarters, 39th Infantry Regiment, *Combat Report*, December 11, 1944, 2000 hours.

85. Tour guides annual Merode Castle *Christkindlesmarkt.*

86. *Schloss Merode Romantischer Weihnachtsmarkt.*

87. Headquarters, 39th Infantry, *Combat Report*, December 11, 1944, 2000 hours.

88. Pourchot, notebook.

89. *Sheet 5204, Lendersdorf,* coordinates 058439.

90. IDPF, Leslie J. Bacon, 32937415.

91. *Sheet 5204, Lendersdorf,* coordinates 057444, 058439.

92. Letter, Frank Randall to author 2004.

93. Astor, *Bloody Forest*, 312.

94. Headquarters, 39th Infantry Regiment, *Combat Report*, December 12, 1944, 2000 hours.

95. Jewell, letter, December 14, 1944.

96. Pourchot, notebook.

97. *Sheet 5204, Lendersdorf,* coordinates 058439.

98. Sylvan and Smith, *Normandy to Victory*, entry for December 13, 1944.

99. *Sheet 5204, Lendersdorf,* coordinates 058439.

100. *Sheet 5104, Düren,* coordinates 050454.

101. Jewell, letter, December 14, 1944.

102. Pourchot, notebook.

103. Letter, Harry Nodell to Larry and Francis, January 2, 1945, Kelly Lieber.

104. Whayne and DeBakey, *Cold Injury*, table 25.

105. Pourchot, notebook.

106. Ibid.

107. *Sheet 5104, Düren,* coordinates 040475.

108. Ibid., coordinates 104455.

109. Ibid., coordinates 103457.

110. *Sheet 5204, Lendersdorf,* coordinates 099453.

111. Enlisted Record/Report of Separation, Louis A. Montoya, November 7, 1945.

112. Headquarters, 39th Infantry Regiment, *Combat Report*, December 17, 1944, 2000 hours.

113. Jewell, letter, December 18, 1944.

114. Jay Philip Holman, email, May 6, 2019.

115. Astor, *Bloody Forest*, 166.

116. Discussion, James Gravino, son of Joseph Gravino, April 30, 2020.

117. Scott Mall, "FreightWaves Classics: Red Ball Express Supplied American Troops Fighting the Nazis (Part 3)," FreightWaves.

118. Haines et al., *This Cockeyed War*, 21.

119. Ibid., 34.

120. Jewell, V-mail, August 19, 1944.

121. Telephone interview, Jay Philip Holman, 2019.

122. Gordon L. Rottman, *World War II Axis Booby Traps and Sabotage Tactics* (Oxford: Osprey, 2011).

123. Jay Philip Holman, email, May 6, 2019.

124. Haines et al., *This Cockeyed War*, 22; and Manley Fuller recollections to his granddaughter Sarah.

125. Jewell, letter, September 30, 1944.

126. Astor, *Bloody Forest*, 42.

127. Discussions, Sarah O'Connor Collins, granddaughter of Manley Fuller.

128. Mac MacLean heard a rumor of a soldier in Company B but never knew whom.

129. Astor, *Bloody Forest*, 101.

130. Milton Wainwright, "Hitler's Penicillin," *Perspectives in Biology and Medicine* 47, no. 2 (Spring 2004), 189–98.

131. French L. MacLean, *Waffen-SS Tiger Crews at Kursk: The Men of SS Panzer Regiments 1, 2, and 3 in Operation Citadel, July 5–15, 1943* (Atglen, PA, Schiffer, 2020).

132. Headquarters, 9th Infantry Division, *G-2 Periodic Report*, December 23, 1944.

CHAPTER 6

1. *Sheet 5503, Elsenborn*, coordinates 945083.

2. John Sperry, *9th Infantry Division* (Paducah, KY: Turner, 2000), 15.

3. *Sheet 5503, Elsenborn*, coordinates 894116.

4. Ibid., coordinates 933110 to 953081.

5. *Sheet 5502, Malmedy*, coordinates 850103.

6. Pourchot, notebook.

7. *Sheet 5503, Elsenborn*, coordinates 945083.

8. Pourchot, notebook.

9. *Sheet 5503, Elsenborn*, coordinates 943106, 951097, and 955122, respectively.

10. *Sheet 5402, Ternell*, coordinates 837242.

11. Pourchot, notebook.

12. Headquarters, Ninth Infantry Division, Office AC of S, G-2, *Journal*, December 20, 1944, 2132 hours.

13. *Sheet 5503, Elsenborn*, coordinates 945083.

14. Ibid., coordinates 946116.

15. Gerhard Dieckhoff, *3. Infanterie-Division, 3. Infanterie-Division (mot.), 3. Panzergrenadier-Division* (Cuxhaven, Germany: Erich Borries Verlag, 1960), 375–80.

16. Sources, December 24: Holman, "The Day"; Mansoor, "The Development of Combat Effectiveness," 100; Sperry, *9th Infantry Division: Old Reliables*, 16; "Battle of the Bulge: The Greatest American Battle of the War," National Veterans Memorial Museum, December 16, 2020; and Whayne and DeBakey, *Cold Injury*, table 25.

17. *Sheet 5503, Elsenborn*, coordinates 945083.

18. Headquarters, Ninth Infantry Division, G-2, *Journal*, December 24, 1944, 1527 hours.

19. *Sheet 5403, Monschau*, coordinates 894137.

20. Haines et al., *This Cockeyed War*, 226.

21. *Sheet 5503, Elsenborn*, coordinates 956089.

22. Ibid., coordinates 945083.

23. Jewell, letter, December 25, 1944.

24. Haines, *This Cockeyed War*, 228.

25. Jean-Paul Pallud, David Parker, and Ron Volstad, *Ardennes, 1944: Peiper and Skorzeny* (London: Osprey, 1987), 29.

26. IDPF, Willard D. Frase, 35232723; and Pourchot, notebook.

27. Pourchot, notebook.

28. Jewell, letter, December 27, 1944.

29. Phillips, *Remagen*, 134.

30. Whayne and DeBakey, *Cold Injury*, table 25.

31. Jewell, letter, December 30, 1944.

32. Haines et al., *This Cockeyed War*, 237.

33. Headquarters, Ninth Infantry Division, Office of the Surgeon, APO #9, *Report of Medical Activities for the Month*, December 1944, January 2, 1945.

34. *Sheet 5503, Elsenborn*, coordinates 934083.

35. Haines et al., *This Cockeyed War*, 243.

36. Ibid., 240.

37. *Sheet 5402, Ternell*, coordinates 825245.

38. Letter, Mac MacLean, January 1, 1945.

39. Jewell, letter, January 1, 1945.

40. Ibid., January 2, 1945.

41. Haines et al., *This Cockeyed War*, 245.

42. Astor, *Bloody Forest*, 206.

43.   Letter, Harry Nodell to Larry and Francis, January 2, 1945, Kelly Lieber.

44. *Sheet 5503, Elsenborn*, coordinates 934083.

45. Louis Benoist, letter to Myra Leake, sister of Paul Eason, January 4, 1945, Brook Eason, Paul's son, May 7, 2019.

46. *Sheet 5403, Monschau*, coordinates 915130.

47. Haines et al., *This Cockeyed War*, 253.

48. Whayne and DeBakey, *Cold Injury*, table 25.

49. Jewell, letter, January 8, 1945.

50. *Sheet 5503, Elsenborn*, coordinates 943112.

51. Whayne and DeBakey, *Cold Injury*, table 25.

52. *S heet 5503, Elsenborn*, coordinates 943112.

53. Ibid., coordinates 946111.

54. First Battalion, 39th Infantry Regiment, *Unit Journal*, monthly log of events, January 13, 1945, NARA, College Park, MD.

55. Jewell, letter, January 13, 1945.

56. *Sheet 5503, Elsenborn*, coordinates 946106.

57. Jewell, V-mail, January 15, 1944.

58. Ibid., January 16, 1945.

59. First Battalion, 39th Infantry Regiment, *Unit Journal*, January 17, 1945.

60. Ibid., January 18, 1945.

61. Jewell, V-mail, January 18, 1945.

62. John "Mike" Dykes, support platoon leader, 1-51 Infantry, 1975, Crailsheim, Germany, observing that veteran mess sergeants make wholesale quantities of coffee.

63. Jewell, letter, November 28, 1944.

64. Mac MacLean.

65. Sources, January 19: Haines et al., *This Cockeyed War*, 281; First Battalion, 39th Infantry Regiment, *Unit Journal*, January 19, 1945; Whayne and DeBakey, *Cold Injury*, table 25; discussions, Mac MacLean; and Jewell, V-mail, January 19, 1945.

66. First Battalion, 39th Infantry Regiment, *Unit Journal*, January 20, 1945.

67. Ibid.

68. Shilling, *Rochester's Marvels*, 74.

69. *Sheet 5503, Elsenborn*, coordinates 940103.

70. First Battalion, 39th Infantry Regiment, *Unit Journal*, January 23, 1945.

71. Jewell, V-mail, January 24 and 25, 1945.

72. *Sheet 5503, Elsenborn*, coordinates 944110.

73. bid., coordinates 943112.

74. Sources, January 26: Pourchot, notebook; Whayne and DeBakey, *Cold Injury*, table 25; and Jewell, V-mail, January 26, 1945.

75. *Sheet 5403, Monschau*, coordinates 926137.

76. Jewell, letter, January 28, 1945.

77. *Sheet 5403, Monschau*, coordinates 926149.

78. Ibid., coordinates 913167.

79. Jewell, letter, January 29, 1945.

80. Herman Eichel's Report of Examination of Enlisted Personnel.

81. Emails, Herman Eichel's son Carl, March 2020.

82. *Sheet 5403, Monschau*, coordinates 927147.

83. Ibid., coordinates 954135.

84. PF, Israel L. Reese, 34974024.

85. Haines et al., *This Cockeyed War*, 302.

86. *Sheet 5403, Monschau*, coordinates 953144.

87. Donald E. Lavender, *Nudge Blue: A 9th Infantry Division Rifleman's Memoir of World War II* (Bennington, VT: Merriam, 2012), 38–39.

88. *Sheet 5403, Monschau*, coordinates 951146.

89. Telephone discussion, Ken Seaman, 2004.

90. Letter, Anne Benoist to Paul, dated August 20, 1945.

91. PF, Israel L. Reese, 34974024.

92. Lavender, *Nudge Blue*, 39.

93. Michael Haft and Harrison Suarez, "The Marines Secret Weapon: Coffee," *New York Times*, August 16, 2013

94. Tom Huntington, "Captain Swing," America in WWII.

95. Visit with Alexander Sommer, University of Heidelberg, to dueling matches.

96. "Battle of the Bulge: The Greatest American Battle of the War."

97. Haines et al., *This Cockeyed War*, 14.

98. Sources, Continental Stockade: MacLean, *Fifth Field*; and interview, Tom Ward, DTC supply sergeant.

99. Astor, *Bloody Forest*, 212.

100. Sources, Victory Mail: "V-Mail," Smithsonian National Postal Museum.

CHAPTER 7

1. Klaus-Dieter Gernert and Helmut Wolff, *Das Geheimnis der Versöhnung heißt Erinnerung: Zur Situation von Kriegsgefangenen und Fremdarbeitern während des Zweiten Weltkrieges in Rösrath und andere zeitgeschichtliche* (Rösrath, Germany: Geschichtsverein für die Gemeinde Rösrath und Umgebung e.V., 1991).

2. War Department, HQ Army Air Forces, "Missing Air Crew Report" (B-17G, 42-97164, Rebel Queen, January 28, 1945), Fold 3.

3. Info on Stalag VI G: Gernert and Wolff, *Das Geheimnis der Versöhnung heißt Erinnerung.*

4. Astor, *Bloody Forest*, 159.

5. Government of the United Kingdom, National Archives, RAF History Bomber Command, Campaign Diary, March 1945.

6. "46th Tank Bn History," in *13th Armored Division—46th Tank Battalion* (Baton Rouge, LA: Amy & Navy Publishing, 1946), 106.

7. Ibid.

8. Telegram, Army provost marshal general to Grace MacLean, April 5, 1945.

9. "46th Tank Bn History," 106.

10. Ibid., 107.

11. Ibid.

12. Patricia Kollander and John O'Sullivan, *I Must Be a Part of This War: A German American's Fight against Hitler and Nazism* (New York: Fordham University Press, 2005).

13. Vic J. Wojtas, "Final Chapter of P.O.W. Diary," *Octofoil* 4, no. 3 (March 1949): 8.

14. Ibid.

CHAPTER 8

1. *Sheet 5403, Monschau*, coordinates 980149.

2. Whayne and DeBakey, *Cold Injury*, 138.

3. *Sheet 5403, Monschau*, coordinates 002125.

4. Pourchot, notebook.

5. US WWII Hospital Admission Card Files, 1942–1954, George Rosen.

6. PF, Raymond L. Olive, 20911369; and "Four War Dead Listed by Army," *San Bernardino County Sun* (Ontario, CA), March 14, 1945.

7. IDPF, Walter S. Burke, 35613408; and 9th Infantry, *GO #57* (April 30, 1945).

8. IDPF, Pedro Gonzalez, 38074678.

9. PF, Patsy Jerome, 32025810.

10. 9th Infantry, *GO #120* (July 7, 1945).

11. Ibid.

12. Sources, Manley Fuller and John Boyd: discussions, Sarah O'Connor Collins, 2020; IDPF, John H. Boyle, 35830330; and Find a Grave, Pfc. John H. Boyle.

13. Jewell, V-mail, February 11, 1945.

14. PF, George C. Mavis, 36834724.

15. Letter, Ltc. Marvin O. Larson, Hospital Plant #4272, 176th General Hospital, to Ken's wife, February 15, 1945.

16. Sources, February 22–24: Jewell, letters, February 22, 23, and 24, 1945; and Headquarters, 9th Infantry, "Administrative Order #36," February 23, 1945, 1.

17. Sources, February 28: *After Action Report*, 746th Tank Battalion, February 1945; discussion, Jay Lavin (Lavinsky), February 25, 2019, Lavin papers, February 2023; and 9th Infantry, *GO #120* (July 7, 1945).

18. IDPF, William E. Kelley, 32842938.

19. *After Action Report*, 746th Tank Battalion, March 1945.

20. Discussion, Jay Lavin (Lavinsky), February 25, 2019; PF, Jay H. Lavinsky; and discussions, Dr. Gerald Marks, lifelong friend of Jay H. Lavinsky (Lavin).

21. PF, Jack A. Dunlap, 0294635.

22. Sources, March 10: *After Action Report*, 746th Tank Battalion, March 1945; Phillips, *Remagen*, 57; and Holman, "The Day."

23. Jay Phillip Holman, email, May 6, 2019.

24. IDPF, Deloss J. Bradshaw, 39916542.

25. Jewell, letter, March 14, 1945.

26. Telephone calls, Scott Blanchard, son of Edward Blanchard, December 2019.

27. "Sgt. L. Pourchot Captures Germans, Gets Silver Star," *Taylorville (IL) Daily Breeze Courier*, June 21, 1945.

28. Phillips, *Remagen*, 98.

29. Jewell, V-mail, March 21, 1945.

30. Ibid., March 22, 1945.

31. Headquarters, Ninth Infantry Division, *Report of Operation, 1–31 March 1945*, file 309-0.3, (NB3) 427, Records Group 407, NARA, College Park, MD.

32. US Army World War II Enlistment Records, Soon Shin Lee, via Ancestry.com.

33. IDPF, Henry A. Ambrose, 33439188.

34. Ancestry.com, Bernard Jacobs; and Ancestry.com, Dominic Buongermino.

35. *After Action Report*, 746th Tank Battalion, April 1945.

36. Narrative from Phil Holman.

37. Jewell, letter, April 6, 1945.

38. Sources, April 7: *After Action Report*, 746th Tank Battalion, April 1945; and IDPF, Carl D. Erickson, 37581215.

39. Joe Wilson, *The 761st "Black Panther" Tank Battalion in World War II* (Jefferson, NC: McFarland, 1999), 53; PF, Edgar E. Zeno, 38501025; Elliott Vanveltner Converse, *The Exclusion of Black Soldiers from the Medal of Honor in World War II* (Jefferson, NC: McFarland, 2008), 83; "Patton's Panthers: The Story of the 761st Tank Battalion," Warfare History Network; and Headquarters, Ninth Infantry Division, *GO #58* (May 5, 1945).

40. Service record, Willie Scott White, 38535383, NARA, St. Louis, MO.

41. Jewell, letter, April 9, 1945.

42. Ibid., April 11, 1945.

43. Headquarters, 39th Infantry Regiment, APO 9, Special Orders #46, April 15, 1945.

44. Video, Manley Fuller, from Sarah O'Connor Collins.

45. Headquarters, Ninth Infantry Division, *Report of Operation, 1–30 April 1945*, NARA, file 309-0.3, (NB3) 427, Record Group 407.

46. Headquarters, ETO, US Army, Memorandum, *Awards and Decorations*, June 12, 1944.

47. Perry Biddiscombe, "The Last Ditch: An Organizational History of the Nazi Werwolf Movement, 1944–45," doctoral diss., London School of Economics; Kelly Bell, "Werewolves of Aachen," Historynet, July 2017; and Gerhard Rempel, *Hitler's Children: The Hitler Youth and the SS* (Chapel Hill: University of North Carolina Press, 1989), 244–48.

CHAPTER 9

1. Jewell, letter, May 23, 1945.

2. Ibid., June 5, 1945.

3. Ibid., June 8, 9, and 23, 1945.

4. Ibid., June 23, 1945.

5. Ibid., July 13 and 17, 1945.

6. C. N. Trueman, "Operation Downfall," The History Learning Site, May 19, 2015.

7. Jewell, V-mail, July 24, 1944.

8. Ibid., July 28, 1945.

9. Ibid., July 30, 1945.

10. Ibid., August 1, 1945.

11. Ibid., August 9, 1945.

12. Ibid., August 14, 1945.

13. Ibid., August 27, 1945.

CONCLUSION

1. Astor, *Bloody Forest*, 130.

2. Ancestry.com and Find a Grave, Henry A. Ambrose.

3. Ancestry.com and Find a Grave, James W. Arnold.

4. Ancestry.com and Find a Grave, Leslie J. Bacon.

5. Ancestry.com and Find a Grave, Michael J. Baran Jr.

6. Ancestry.com and Find a Grave, Alan H. Bauer.

7. Ancestry.com and Find a Grave, Paul B. Bean.

8. Ancestry.com and Find a Grave, Albert B. Bittino.

9. IDPF, John H. Boyle, 35830330.

10. IDPF, Deloss J. Bradshaw, 39916542.

11. Ancestry.com and Find a Grave, Roy L. Burchwell.

12. IDPF, Walter S. Burke, 35613408.

13. Ancestry.com and Find a Grave, Theodore S. Clinker.

14. Ancestry.com and Find a Grave, Benedict J. Conrad.

15. Ancestry.com and Find a Grave, Lafie Crabtree.

16. IDPF, Carl D. Erickson, 37581215.

17. IDPF, Willard D. Frase, 35232723.

18. IDPF, Pedro Gonzalez, 38074678.

19. IDPF, John Gourlay, 32029947.

20. IDPF, Albert M. Handy, 33049003.

21. Ancestry.com and Find a Grave, Charles H. Irish.

22. Ancestry.com and Find a Grave, John J. Jablonski.

23. IDPF, William A. Karko, 36714215.

24. IDPF, William E. Kelley, 32842938.

25. Ancestry.com and Find a Grave, Joseph M. Kelly.

26. Ancestry.com and Find a Grave, John Koches.

27. Ancestry.com and Find a Grave, Joseph J. LaChance.

28. Ancestry.com and Find a Grave, Warren S. Lorio.

29. Ancestry.com and Find a Grave, Raymond A. Madison.

30. Ancestry.com and Find a Grave, Jerome Magluilo.

31. Ancestry.com and Find a Grave, Milton Marlatt.

32. Ancestry.com and Find a Grave, George C. Mavis.

33. Ancestry.com and Find a Grave, Chester A. McClurg.

34. Ancestry.com and Find a Grave, James T. McCulloch.

35. Ancestry.com and Find a Grave, Frederick C. McInnis.

36. Ancestry.com and Find a Grave, John T. McIntyre.

37. Ancestry.com and Find a Grave, John J. McPherson.

38. Ancestry.com and Find a Grave, Willard J. Meadows.

39. Ancestry.com and Find a Grave, Ernie Miguel.

40. Ancestry.com and Find a Grave, Chester C. Miller.

41. Ancestry.com and Find a Grave, Parry J. Miller.

42. Ancestry.com and Find a Grave, Odie Z. Mitchell

43. Ancestry.com and Find a Grave, Thomas J. Monaghan.

44. Ancestry.com and Find a Grave, Walter E. Muehleman.

45. Ancestry.com and Find a Grave, Lester L. Neal.

46. Ancestry.com and Find a Grave, Arnold L. Odette Jr.

47. Ancestry.com and Find a Grave, Raymond L. Olive.

48. Ancestry.com and Find a Grave, Alphonse A. Poni.

49. Ancestry.com and Find a Grave, Joseph D. Pratt.

50. Ancestry.com and Find a Grave, Tony Raskell.

51. Ancestry.com and Find a Grave, Israel L. Reese.

52. "4 Hours Separate Son's Letter and Death Notice," *Wilkes-Barre (PA) Times Ledger*, March 30, 1945; and Ancestry.com and Find a Grave, John E. Reiser.

53. Ancestry.com and Find a Grave, Harold Rinebolt.

54. Ancestry.com and Find a Grave, Gaspar Ruiz.

55. Ancestry.com and Find a Grave, James W. Russell.

56. Ancestry.com and Find a Grave, Melvin B. Schneider.

57. Ancestry.com and Find a Grave, Anton J. Semrov.

58. Ancestry.com and Find a Grave, Charles G. Somers.

59. Ancestry.com and Find a Grave, Carlas Tomes.

60. Ancestry.com and Find a Grave, William Uveges.

61. Ancestry.com and Find A Grave, James S. Vaught.

62. Ancestry.com and Find A Grave, Lloyd R. Vunk.

63. Ancestry.com and Find A Grave, Irving J. Wahl.

64. Ancestry.com and Find A Grave, Raymond O. Wahlstrom.

65. Ancestry.com and Find A Grave, Ralph W. Wallace.

66. Ancestry.com and Find A Grave, Noel P. Waters.

67. Ancestry.com and Find A Grave, Roy Weaver.

68. Ancestry.com and Find A Grave, John R. Williams.

69. Ancestry.com and Find A Grave, John S. Wood.

70. Ancestry.com and Find A Grave, Newton L. Yount.

71. Ancestry.com and Find A Grave, Theodore Zajac.

72. Letter, David Frankel, November 29, 2019; conversations, Kelly Lieber, 2020; and recording of Jay Lavin by Dean Woods, 2017.

73. Multiple discussions with Louis Benoist family members.

74. Pyle, *Here Is Your War*, 246.

75. Anderson, *Paddy*, 117.

76. Robert E. Mautte, "An Ex-Sergeant's Memoirs," *Octofoil*, March 1953, 1.

77. "Legends of Paddy Flint," *Octofoil* 7, no. 12 (December 1952–January 1953): 1.

EPILOGUE

1. Interview, T/5 George Morgan.

2. Headquarters, 9th Infantry, *GO* #57 (April 30, 1945).

3. Discussion, Jay H. Lavin (Lavinsky), February 25, 2019.

4. Examination by a Dr. Jay Singer.

5. Discussions, Briny Woods, February–March 2023; written recounts by Jay Lavin (Lavinsky); and interview with Dean Woods, 2017.

6. Headquarters, 39th Infantry Regiment, APO 9, Special Orders #86, June 30, 1945.

7. Ancestry.com, Willie Scott White.

8. Find a Grave, Jack Alexander Dunlap.

9. Sources, Jack Jewell: PF, Jack F. Jewell; Ancestry.com, Jack F. Jewell; and Jewell, letter, October 5, 1945.

10. Sources, Stanley Mills: Discussions, Mills's family; and Ancestry.com, Stanley R. Mills.

11. Sources, Joe Gravino: Ron Holdraker, "Old Soldiers' Memories Never Die," *The Times* (Walworth, NY), June 14, 1994, 5; PF, Joseph Gravino; and discussion, James Gravino, son of Joseph Gravino, on April 30, 2020.

12. Source, Frank Randall: Astor, *Bloody Forest*, 374; and letter, Frank to author in 2004.

13. Letter from Frank Randall, April 12, 2002.

14. Jay Philip Holman, untitled manuscript, dated November 18, 2014.

15. PF, Oliver J. Osbourn, 34905155; and Ancestry.com, Oliver J. Osbourn.

16. Text, Billie Joe Slaughter to author, March 13, 2020.

17. Sources, Langley Turner: Myra Elliott and Myranda Elliott, March 2020; and April 1945 photograph, Phil Holman.

18. PF, James J. Rush, 33778981; Ancestry.com, James Joseph Rush; Alison Rush, daughter of James Rush; and Kathy Scroggins, granddaughter of James Rush.

19. PF, Kenneth R. Seaman, 36960664; and interviews, David D. Basham, November 2019.

20. Emails, Herman's son Carl March, 2020.

21. Ancestry.com, Edward A. Pickard.

22. Ibid.

23. PF, Billie S. Flowers; Ancestry.com, Billie S. Flowers; and discussions with son Billy.

24. Ancestry.com and Find a Grave, Thomas H. Naud Jr.

25. PF, Kermit D. Lockridge, 33848494.

26. Emails, Debbie Lockridge Pitsenbarger, daughter of Kermit Lockridge, September 2, 2021.

27. PF, George H. Holdren, 35135658; and Ancestry.com, George Henry Holdren.

28. Ancestry.com and Find a Grave, Seymour Berry.

29. Discussions, Sarah O'Connor Collins.

30. Ibid.

29. Sources, Al DiRisio: "Vocal Concert to Feature Local Singer, Albert DiRisio," *Herald-mail* (Fairport, NY), April 12, 1956, 1; Al "Hawk" DiRisio, "Company B in 25th Reunion," *Herald-mail* (Fairport, NY), June 29, 1977, 3; and PF, Al DiRisio, 32029918.

31. PF, James L. Millar, 32927389; and Ancestry.com, James Lunn Millar.

32. Ancestry.com and Find a Grave, James Millar.

33. Discussion, Nicholas Baccile, son of Albert Baccile, June 8, 2020.

34. Email, Alex Wasnick, grandson of Lloyd Wasnick, June 8, 2020.

35. Ancestry.com and Find a Grave, Lloyd Wasnick.

36. Sources, Robert Pettigrew: "Robert S. Pettigrew Service Record"; and US Army Separation Qualification Record, Pettigrew, Robert S.

37. Discussions, Regan Pourchot, son of Leonard Pourchot, 2020.

38. Discussions, David E. Connor.

39. "Family to Receive Awards Won by S-Sgt. Ridgeway," *Sandy Creek (NY) News*, September 4, 1946.

40. Doser, "The Hawk Recalls: Carnival Wrassling No Game for the Puny."

41. Emails, Jean-Phillipe Speder, February 2020, on statements of Ridgeway's patrol, dated January 29, 1945.

42. Statement, Pfc. James M. Thurston, January 29, 1945.

43. Pourchot, notebook.

44. Lord Moran, *The Anatomy of Courage* (New York: Carroll & Graf, 2007).

45. Chris Epting, "In the Pipeline: Local Babe Ruth Footage Unearthed," *Los Angeles Times*, August 15, 2012.

46. Ibid.

47. *Octofoil* 37, no. 3 (May–July 1982): 1.

48. "Lindsey Nelson Is All-American Sportscaster," *Octofoil* 13, no. 5 (June–July 1960): 4.

BIBLIOGRAPHY

PRIMARY PERIOD SOURCES

Army Talks II, no. 39 (September 27, 1944), Folder title: Ground Force Reinforcement Command, chapter VI, box 157, Records Group 498. NARA, College Park, MD.

Company B, 39th Infantry Regiment. *Company Morning Reports*. Microfilm (located at the National Archives and Records Administration, NARA, St. Louis, MO).

June 1944	File 27058	December 1944	File 22959
July 1944	File 15614	January 1945	File 11017
August 1944	File 27630	February 1945	File 25251
September 1944	File 25715	March 1945	File 20329
October 1944	File 14115	April 1945	File 08884
November 1944	File 03713	May 1945	File 14201

First Battalion, 39th Infantry Regiment. *Unit Journal*. Monthly log of events from October 1, 1944, to May 8, 1945. NARA, College Park, MD.

Headquarters, 39th Infantry Regiment. *Combat Report*. Daily reports from October 1, 1944, to May 8, 1945. Dwight D. Eisenhower Presidential Library, Abilene, KS.

Headquarters, 39th Infantry Regiment. *General Orders*. Lists of soldiers receiving Combat Infantryman Badge. NARA, College Park, MD.

Headquarters, 39th Infantry Regiment. *Operations, 39th Infantry*. Monthly reports from October 1944 to May 1945. Dwight D. Eisenhower Presidential Library, Abilene, KS.

Headquarters, 39th Infantry Regiment. *Unit Journal*. Event log by month, October 1, 1944, to May 8, 1945. Dwight D. Eisenhower Presidential Library, Abilene, KS.

Headquarters, 9th Infantry Division. *G-2 Periodic Report*. Daily reports, October 1, 1944, to May 8, 1945. Dwight D. Eisenhower Presidential Library, Abilene, KS.

Headquarters, 9th Infantry Division. *General Orders*. List of soldiers receiving Bronze Stars and Silver Stars. NARA, College Park, MD.

Headquarters, 9th Infantry Division. *Journal, Ninth Division G2*. Daily reports, October 1, 1944 to May 8, 1945. Dwight D. Eisenhower Presidential Library, Abilene, KS.

Headquarters, 9th Infantry Division, Office of the Surgeon. APO #9, *Report of Medical Activities for the Month*. October 1944 to May 1945.

Headquarters, 9th Infantry Division. *Report of Operation*. Monthly reports, October 1944 to May 1945. Records Group 407/409, file 309-0.3, (NB3) 427. NARA, College Park, MD.

Headquarters, ETO, United States Army, Memorandum. *Awards and Decorations*. June 12, 1944. https://www.afhra.af.mil/Portals/16/documents/Timelines/World%20War%20II/WWIISilverStarMedalCriteriaandPolicyGuidance.pdf?ver=2016-08-30-150742-177.

Interview, T/5 George Morgan, 1st Battalion, 22nd Infantry, 4th Infantry Division Combat. Interviews, box 24021, Record Group 407, NARA.

"Report on Operation Conducted by 9th Infantry Division, United States Army, Southern Tunisia, 26 March–8 April 1943." Headquarters, 9th Infantry Division, APO #9, 1943.

War Department Circular 269 (October 27, 1943).

POSTWAR OFFICIAL US ARMY DOCUMENTS

Perry, Edwin A. "Operations of the 1st Battalion, 39th Infantry (9th Infantry Division) North of St. Jacques De Nehou, Cotentin Peninsula, 18 June 1944 (Normandy Campaign) (Personal Experience of a Company Commander)." Fort Benning, GA, 1949.

Richardson, James. "Operations of the 1st Battalion, 39th Infantry Regiment (9th Infantry Division) at Cherence le Roussel, France (German Attack on Avranches), 4–10 August 1944 (Northern France Campaign) (Personal Experience of a Battalion S-3)." Fort Benning, GA, 1948.

PRIMARY ARCHIVAL DOCUMENTS

Individual Deceased Personnel Files (IDPF). NARA, St. Louis, MO (currently available for research only for those individuals whose last name begins with A–L).

Personnel Service Record Files (called Personnel Files [PF]). NARA, St. Louis, MO.

US WWII Hospital Admission Card Files, 1942–1954. (For many wounds, and for many nonbattle injuries and disease, detailing extent of these casualties and resulting stay in a hospital; also available in PF at NARA, or Ancestry.com.)

MILITARY MAPS, US ARMY, 1944, GERMANY 1:25,000

Sheet 5103, Eschweiler	*Sheet 5104, Düren*	*Sheet 5203, Stolberg*
Sheet 5204, Lendersdorf	*Sheet 5303, Rötgen*	*Sheet 5304, Nideggen*
Sheet 5402, Ternell	*Sheet 5403, Monschau*	*Sheet 5502, Malmedy*
Sheet 5503, Elsenborn	*Sheet 5504, Hellenthal*	

BOOKS

Anderson, Robert A. *Paddy: The Colorful Story of Colonel Harry A. "Paddy" Flint.* Westminster, MD: Heritage Books, 2006.

Astor, Gerald. *The Bloody Forest: Battle for the Huertgen; September 1944–January 1945.* Novato, CA: Presidio, 2000.

Atkinson, Rick. *An Army at Dawn: The War in North Africa, 1942–1943.*New York: Henry Holt, 2003.

———. *The Day of Battle: The War in Sicily and Italy, 1943–1944.* New York: Macmillan, 2008.

Attanasio, Steven. *Untouched Heroics: Anecdotes from the Life of a World War II Veteran.* Middletown, DE: Steven Attanasio, 2014.

Blumenson, Martin. *Breakout and Pursuit.* Washington, DC: Office of the Chief of Military History, 1961.

Bradley, Omar N. *A Soldier's Story.* New York: Modern Library, 1999.

Buchholz, Frank, and Thomas Brüggen. *German Machine Guns: Development, Tactics, and Use from 1892 to 1918.* Vienna: Verlag Militaria, 2019.

Butler, William. *The Cage: Memoirs of a Medical Officer with the 39th Infantry Regiment in World War II.* William Butler, 1996.

Coats, John Boyd, Ebbe Curtis Hoff, and Phebe M. Hoff. *Preventive Medicine in WWII.* Vol. 4, *Communicable Diseases, Transmitted Chiefly through Respiratory and Alimentary Tracts.* Washington, DC: Office of Surgeon General, Department of the Army, 1958.

Dickson, Paul. *War Slang: American Fighting Words and Phrases from the Civil War to the War in Iraq.* New York: Bristol Park Books, 2007.

Dieckhoff, Gerhard. *3. Infanterie-Division, 3. Infanterie-Division (mot.), 3. Panzergrenadier-Division.* Cuxhaven, Germany: Erich Borries Verlag, 1960.

"46th Tank Bn History." In *13th Armored Division—46th Tank Battalion.* Baton Rouge, LA: Army & Navy Publishing, 1946.

Freeman, Roger A. *Mighty Eighth War Diary.* London: Janes, 1981.

Gernert, Klaus-Dieter, and Helmut Wolff. *Das Geheimnis der Versöhnung heißt Erinnerung: Zur Situation von Kriegsgefangenen und Fremdarbeitern während des Zweiten Weltkrieges in Rösrath und andere zeitgeschichtliche.* Rösrath, Germany: Geschichtsverein für die Gemeinde Rösrath und Umgebung e.V., 1991.

Griffith, Robert K., Jr., and Richard H. Kohn. *The Exclusion of Black Soldiers from the Medal of Honor in World War II.* Jefferson, NC: McFarland, 1997.

Haines, Douglas C., Franklin D. Haines, and Jeffrey A. Haines. *This Cockeyed War: An Infantry Platoon Leader's Days with G CO 2nd BN 47th RGT 9th DIV in WWII.* CreateSpace, 2018.

Hemingway, Ernest. *Across the River and into the Trees.* London: Readers Union, 1950.

Higgins, David. *Roer River Battles: Germany's Stand at the Westwall, 1944–45.* Havertown, PA: Casemate, 2010.

Hope, Bob. *I Never Left Home: Bob Hope's Own Story of His Trip Abroad.* New York: Simon and Schuster, 1944.

Huie, William Bradford. *The Execution of Private Slovik.* New York: Delacorte, 1970.

Kollander, Patricia, and John O'Sullivan. *I Must Be a Part of This War: A German American's Fight against Hitler and Nazism.* New York: Fordham University Press, 2005.

Kreye, William M. *The Pawns of War.* New York: Vantage, 1983.

Lavender, Donald E. *Nudge Blue: A 9th Infantry Division Rifleman's Memoir of World War II.* Bennington, VT: Merriam, 2012.

MacDonald, Charles B. *The Battle of the Huertgen Forest*. Philadelphia: J. B. Lippincott, 1963.

———. *The Siegfried Line Campaign*. US Army in World War II, European Theater of Operations. Washington, DC: Office of the Chief of Military History of the Army, 1963.

MacLean, French L. *Custer's Best: The Story of Company M, 7th Cavalry at the Little Bighorn*. Atglen, PA: Schiffer, 2011.

———. *The Fifth Field: The Story of the 96 American Soldiers Sentenced to Death and Executed in Europe and North Africa in World War II*. Atglen, PA, Schiffer, 2013.

———. *Waffen-SS Tiger Crews at Kursk: The Men of SS Panzer Regiments 1, 2, and 3 in Operation Citadel, July 5–15, 1943*. Atglen, PA: Schiffer, 2020.

Matloff, Maurice, gen. ed. *American Military History*. Washington, DC: Office of the Chief of Military History, United States Army, 1969. Reprinted and partially revised 1973.

Miller, Edward G. *A Dark and Bloody Ground: The Hürtgen Forest and the Roer River Dams, 1944–1945*. College Station: Texas A&M University Press, 1995.

Mittelman, Joseph B. *Eight Stars to Victory: A History of the Veteran Ninth US Infantry Division*. Washington, DC: Ninth Infantry Division Association, 1948.

Moran, Lord. *The Anatomy of Courage*. New York: Carroll & Graf, 2007.

Morgan, David T. *Murder along the Cape Fear: A North Carolina Town in the Twentieth Century*. Macon, GA: Mercer University Press, 2005.

Omaha Central High School Yearbook, 1943.

Pallud, Jean-Paul, David Parker, and Ron Volstad. *Ardennes, 1944: Peiper and Skorzeny*. London: Osprey, 1987.

Palmer, Robert R., Bell I. Wiley, and William R. Keast. *The Army Ground Forces: The Procurement and Training of Ground Combat Troops, United States Army in World War II*. Washington, DC: Historical Division, Department of the Army, 1948. Reproduced, Washington, DC: Center of Military History, 2003.

Phillips, Henry Gerard. *Remagen: Springboard to Victory*. Penn Valley, CA: Henry Gerard Phillips, 1995.

Pyle, Ernie. *Here Is Your War: Story of GI Joe*. Lincoln: University Nebraska Press, 2004.

Rempel, Gerhard. *Hitler's Children: The Hitler Youth and the SS*. Chapel Hill: University of North Carolina Press, 1989.

Rottman, Gordon L. *The Bazooka*. Oxford: Osprey, 2012.

———. *World War II Axis Booby Traps and Sabotage Tactics*. Oxford: Osprey, 2011.

Shilling, Donovan. *Rochester's Marvels & Myths: Twenty-Four Very Remarkable Stories about Some Very Unusual People, Events, and Places*. Victor, NY: Pancoast, 2011.

Sperry, John. *9th Infantry Division: Old Reliables*. Paducah, KY: Turner, 2000.

Sylvan, William C., and Francis G. Smith Jr. *Normandy to Victory: The War Diary of General Courtney H. Hodges and the First US Army*. Lexington: University of Kentucky Press, 2008.

Vonnegut, Kurt. *Slaughterhouse-Five*. New York, Delacorte, 1961.

War Department. *Field Manual (FM) 23-5, Basic Field Manual: US Rifle. Caliber .30, M1.* Issued on July 20, 1941.

Whayne, Tom F., and Michael E. DeBakey. *Cold Injury, Ground Type, in World War II.* Washington, DC: Office of Surgeon General, Department of the Army, 1958.

Wilson, Joe. *The 761st "Black Panther" Tank Battalion in World War II.* Jefferson, NC: McFarland, 1999.

MAGAZINES AND NEWSPAPERS

"Ax Blow on Head Kills Child." *Salt Lake (UT) Tribune*, December 16, 1941.

Boyle, Hal. "Yank Unit Peeved; Never Hits a City—Ninth Division Gets to See Only Europe's Back Alleys." *Deseret News* (Salt Lake City, UT), October 10, 1944.

Colacino, Albert A. "We Remember . . . Gravino Brothers." *Courier-Gazette* (Newark, NY), April 28, 1995.

DiRisio, Al "Hawk." "Company B in 25th Reunion." *Herald-mail* (Fairport, NY), June 29, 1977.

Doser, John. "The Hawk Recalls: Carnival Wrassling No Game for the Puny." *Fairport (NY) Herald Mail*, April 30, 1980.

———. "The Hawk Recalls: The Induction Center." *Fairport (NY) Herald Mail*, July 9, 1980.

———. "The Hawk Obeys Orders Promoted to Sergeant." *Fairport (NY) Herald Mail*, September 3, 1980.

———. "Laughing Cooks Spoil the Menu." *Fairport (NY) Herald Mail*, July 23, 1980.

———. "Pearl Harbor Ends the Hawk's Romance." *Fairport (NY) Herald Mail*, August 27, 1980.

———. "Singing Waiter Hawk Wows 'Em at the Piano." *Fairport (NY) Herald Mail*, June 18, 1980.

Driscoll, Joseph. "Paddy Flint, Cherbourg's Captor." *New York Tribune*, 1945.

"Earned Silver Star." *Wellsville (KS) Globe*, April 26, 1945.

"Family to Receive Awards Won by S-Sgt. Ridgeway." *Sandy Creek (NY) News*, September 4, 1946.

"4 Hours Separate Son's Letter and Death Notice." *Wilkes-Barre (PA) Times Ledger*, March 30, 1945.

"Four War Dead Listed by Army." *San Bernardino County Sun* (Ontario, CA), March 14, 1945.

Fourre, Sylvester. "The Green Hell of Huertgen Forest." *Man's Conquest* 8, no. 4 (October 1963).

Haft, Michael, and Harrison Suarez. "The Marines Secret Weapon: Coffee." *New York Times*, August 16, 2013.

Hemingway, Ernest. "War in the Siegfried Line." *Collier's*, November 18, 1944.

Holdraker, Ron. "Old Soldiers' Memories Never Die." *The Times* (Walworth, NY), June 14, 1994.

Holy Cross Alumnus Newsletter 18, no. 1 (October 1943).

"Most-Decorated Newark Soldier, 2½ Years at Front, Tells of Fighting." *Newark (NY) Courier-Gazette*, February 12, 1945.

Octofoil Newsletter. Weehawken, NJ: Ninth Infantry Division Association, 1946–2004.

"Reverend Edward T. Connors, Former Immaculate Conception Pastor." *Telegram & Gazette* (Worcester, MA), January 29, 1986.

Scales, Robert H. (US Army). "Edward Uhl." *Time Magazine*, May 31, 2010.

"Sgt. Gravino Given Silver Star for Heroism, Medal for Wounds." *Newark (NY) Courier-Gazette*, January 4, 1945.

"Sgt. 'Joe' Gravino Twice Wounded, Gets Purple Heart." *Newark (NY) Courier-Gazette*, November 16, 1944.

"Sgt. L. Pourchot Captures Germans, Gets Silver Star." *Taylorville (IL) Daily Breeze Courier*, June 21, 1945.

Smith, Todd. "How a World War I Jazz-Playing Marine Gave Us the Best Weapon Name Ever." *Marine Times*, September 3, 2021.

"Vocal Concert to Feature Local Singer, Albert DiRisio." *Herald-mail* (Fairport, NY), April 12, 1956.

Wainwright, Milton. "Hitler's Penicillin." *Perspectives in Biology and Medicine* 47, no. 2 (Spring 2004).

"Warren Ridgeway Is Awarded Bronze Star." *Sandy Creek (NY) News*, December 6, 1944.

Yank—the Army Weekly, 1942.

PHOTOS

All photos from the National Archives (NARA) were taken by US Army Signal Corps.

THESES

Biddiscombe, Perry. "The Last Ditch: An Organizational History of the Nazi Werwolf Movement, 1944–45." Doctoral diss., London School of Economics.

Gibbs, Thomas J. "Venereal Disease and American Policy in a War Zone: 39th Infantry Regiment in Sidi Bel Abbès, Algeria, May of 1943." University of New Orleans theses, Fall, December 18, 2015. http://scholarworks.uno.edu/cgi/viewcontent. cgi?article=3191&context=td.

Klinek, Eric William. "The Army's Orphans: The United States Army Replacement System in the European Campaign, 1944–1945." PhD diss., Temple University, May 2014.

Mansoor, Peter R. "The Development of Combat Effectiveness in the United States Army during World War II." MA thesis, Ohio State University, 1992.

ONLINE SOURCES

Andriello, Sebastian D., narrator. New York State Military Museum, Interviewers Michael Russert and Wayne Clark, October 7, 2006, Holiday Inn, Kingston, NY. https://dmna. ny.gov/historic/veterans/transcriptions/Andriello_Sebastian_D.pdf.

"Battle of the Bulge: The Greatest American Battle of the War." National Veterans Memorial Museum, December 16, 2020. www.nationalvmm.org/ battle-of-the-bulge-the-greatest-american-battle-of-the-war.

"Bazooka (Musical Instrument)." In *The Encyclopedia of Arkansas History & Culture*. http:// www.encyclopediaofarkansas.net/encyclopedia/entry-detail.aspx?entryID=2186.

Bell, Kelly. "Werewolves of Aachen." Historynet, July 2017. https://www.historynet.com/ werewolves-of-aachen.htm.

De Bruyne, Nese F. "American War and Military Operations Casualties: Lists and Statistics." Washington, DC: Congressional Research Service, April 26, 2017. www.census.gov/ history/pdf/wwi-casualties112018.pdf.

Epting, Chris. "In the Pipeline: Local Babe Ruth Footage Unearthed." *Los Angeles Times*, August 15, 2012. https://www.latimes.com/socal/daily-pilot/ocnow/tn-hbi-0816-pipe-line-20120813-story.html.

Government of the United Kingdom. National Archives, RAF History Bomber Command, Campaign Diary, March 1945. https://webarchive.nationalarchives.gov. uk/20070706060012/http://www.raf.mod.uk/bombercommand/mar45.html.

Holt, Thaddeus. "Relax—It's Only a Maneuver" *MHQ Magazine*, Winter 1992. www. historynet.com/relax-its-only-a-maneuver.htm.

Huard, Paul. "The Bazooka: A History." Real Clear Defense, March 13, 2015. www.real-cleardefense.com/articles/2015/03/14/the_bazooka_a_history.html.

Huntington, Tom. "Captain Swing." America in WWII. www.americainwwii.com/articles/ captain-swing/.

Mall, Scott. "FreightWaves Classics: Red Ball Express Supplied American Troops Fighting the Nazis (Part 3)." FreightWaves. https://www.freightwaves.com/news/ freightwaves-classics-red-ball-express-supplied-american-troops-fighting-the-nazis-part-3.

Mazza, Sandy. "Once Nashville's Biggest Business, the Sock Mill That Clothed Astronauts and Fought Nazis Is Transforming." *The Tennessean*, May 27, 2019. https://www. tennessean.com/story/money/2019/05/27/ may-hosiery-mill-nashville-sock-factory-readies-tech-future/3692995002/.

Miller, Edward G. "To Build Infantry for the Future, Look First to the Past." Modern War Institute, West Point, NY, October 15, 2018. www.mwi.usma.edu/ build-infantry-future-look-first-past/.

Missing in Action Project: J. P. Speder. http://www.miaproject.net/.

Nieuwint, Joris. "The Self Propelled 155 mm "Doorknocker" or "Bunker Buster"—You Will Not Believe the Holes This Could Punch!" War History Online. www.warhistoryonline. com/author/joris?chrome=1.

9th Infantry Division in World War II: Yuri Beckers. https://9thinfantrydivision.net.

"Patton's Panthers: The Story of the 761st Tank Battalion." Warfare History Network. https://warfarehistorynetwork.com/article/pattons-panthers-the-story-of-the-761st-tank-battalion.

"Private Snafu": Looney Tunes Wiki. https://looneytunes.fandom.com/wiki/Private_Snafu.

Pyle, Ernie. "The God-Damned Infantry." *Scripps-Howard*, May 2, 1943. Found at the Media School, Indiana University. https://sites.mediaschool.indiana.edu/erniepyle/.

Robinson, Tessa. "How the Army-Navy Game of 1944 Stopped World War II." We Are The Mighty, December 11, 2021. wearethemighty.com/mighty-history/army-navy-wwii/.

"Rocket, Air-to-Surface, 5-Inch, HVAR." Smithsonian National Air and Space Museum. https://airandspace.si.edu/collection-objects/rocket-air-to-surface-5-inch-hvar/nasm_A19820116000.

Scheffel, Charles, segment 1. Digital Collections of the National WWII Museum. www.ww2online.org/view/charles-scheffel#segment-1.

Schloss Merode Romantischer Weihnachtsmarkt. https://www.weihnachtsmarkt-merode.de/en/.

"39th Infantry Regiment." Faces beyond the Graves. facesbeyondthegraves.com/pagina67.html.

Trueman, C. N. "Operation Downfall." The History Learning Site, May 19, 2015. www.historylearningsite.co.uk.

USNA Virtual Memorial Hall: Harry A. Flint. https://usnamemorialhall.org/index.php/HARRY_A._FLINT,_COL,_USA.

Van Steelandt, Stefanie. "The Georgie Patton, the New Old Fashioned." The Cereal Reader, March 26, 2020. https://thecerealreader.com/2020/03/26/the-georgie-patton-the-new-old-fashioned/.

"V-Mail." Smithsonian National Postal Museum. https://postalmuseum.si.edu/exhibits/past/the-art-of-cards-and-letters/mail-call/v-mail.html.

War Department, HQ Army Air Forces. "Missing Air Crew Report." B-17G, 42-97164, Rebel Queen, January 28, 1945. Fold 3. https://www.fold3.com/image/1/46711947.

INTERVIEWS

Telephone interviews, Jay Philip Holman, 2019–20.

Telephone interview, Ken Seaman, 2004.

Telephone interviews, Jay Harvey Lavinsky (now Lavin), 2019.

Discussions, David E. Connor, ca. 2012.

Letter, Frank J. Randall, April 12, 2002.

Discussions, Myron D. MacLean, ca. 1958–2015.

"Jack Jewell Timeline." Watkins Museum of History, Douglas County Historical Society.

The following relatives provided verbal descriptions, personal diaries and papers, photographs, and video interviews concerning their soldiers who served in Company B:

Nicholas Baccile / Lisa Baccile Navone: son/granddaughter, SSgt. Albert Baccile

David Basham: grandson, Pfc. Kenny Seaman

Louis Benoist: son, 2Lt. Louis Benoist

Scott Blanchard: son, Pvt. Edward Blanchard

Linda Wasnick Browning / Alex Wasnick: daughter/grandson, Pfc. Lloyd Wasnick

Sarah O'Connor Collins: granddaughter, Pfc. Manley Fuller

Anita Eannace: daughter, Cpl. Carmine Eannace

Carl Eichel: grandson, Pfc. Herman Eichel

Myra Elliott / Myranda Elliott: daughter/granddaughter, TSgt. Langley Turner

Billy Flowers: son, Pfc. Billie Flowers

James Gravino: grandson, 1Sgt. Joseph Gravino

James Holman / Matthew Holman: son/grandson, Sgt. Phil Holman

Kathy Jewell Schilmoeller / Glenn Jewell: daughter/son, 1Lt. Jack Jewell

Kelly Lieber / David Frankel: granddaughter/grandson, Pfc. Harry Nodell

Debra Kaye Lockridge Pitsenbarger: daughter, Pfc. Kermit Lockridge

Scott Lucas: grandson, 1Lt. Lucien Lucas

David MacLean: son, Pfc. Myron MacLean

James Pettigrew: son, Pfc. Robert Pettigrew

Judith Mills Porter / Anita Mills Thompson / Heidi Marie Thompson: daughters/granddaughter, 1Lt. Stanley Mills

Regan Pourchot: son, Sgt. Leonard Pourchot

Nancy Ridgeway: niece, SSgt. Warren Ridgeway

Alison Rush / Kathy Scroggins: daughter/granddaughter, SSgt. James Rush

Billie Joe Slaughter: son, Medic Jessie Slaughter

Anna White Blair / Lauriekim White: daughter/niece, Sgt. Willie S. White

Timmy Woods / Briny Woods / Dean Woods / Dr. Gerald Marks: wife / stepson / Briny's son / lifelong friend, Pfc. Jay H. Lavinsky (Lavin)

US ARMY

Anderson, Conrad V., 37

Andriello, Sebastian, 66–67

Arnold, Henry H. "Hap," 88

Ayers, Loren "Little Patton," 161

Barnes, Gladeon M., 83

Benedict, Arnold F., 144–145

Bond, Van H., 24, 62–63, 97, 99, 105, 107, 113, 130, 180–182, 183, 186, 188–190, 213

Boyes, Wallace F. Jr. "Wally," 204

Bradley, Omar N. "Brad," 14, 42, 44–45, 51, 63, 110, 133–134, 136, 150, 197, 211, 251, 257–258

Brown, J. Trimble, 36–37

Caffey, Benjamin, 30

Carpenter, Charles M. "Bazooka Charlie," 83

Cheatham, Charles H., 36

Chernitsky, John, 133

Collins, J. Lawton "Lighting Joe," 62, 99, 148, 150, 160

Craig, Louis A., 64, 91, 93, 99, 101, 104–105, 109, 114, 131, 180–184, 186–187, 189, 191, 196, 232

Craig, Malin, 104

Crosby, Herbert B., 43

Dalessandro, Peter J., 176

Delnore, Victor E., 206–207

Devers, Jacob L. "Jake," 23, 27–28, 43

Duckworth, Willie Lee, 87

Eddy, Manton S. "Matt," 30, 36, 44–45, 48, 51, 62, 64

Eisenhower, Dwight D. "Ike," 14, 42, 44, 50, 53, 110, 134, 136–137, 160, 211, 238

Fausset, Calvin Basil, 62

Felgenhauer, Elmer W., 204

Flint, Harry "Paddy," 14, 42–46, 48, 50, 62, 107, 238, 258–259, 284

Flowers, James Jr., 178

Fredendall, Lloyd R., 44

Gerow, Leonard T., 136, 172

Hodges, Courtney H., 14, 63, 104, 110, 114, 140, 148, 155, 160, 211

Honeycutt, Francis W., 23

Houston, Jack A., 135, 149

Kateley, Lawson M., 281

Larson, Marvin, 217

Lee, John C. H., 43

MacArthur, Douglas, 14, 33, 246, 250

MacDonald, Charles B., 91

Marshall, George C., 32, 104, 137, 241

Mayberry, Hugh T., 172

McNair, Leslie J., 43, 66

Nardone, Bennie "The Deacon," 50

Nelson, Lindsey, 29, 39, 50, 83, 103, 231, 284

Patton, George S. "Old Blood and Guts," 24, 42–44, 46, 48, 52, 62, 84, 110, 211, 231, 243, 247–248

Pershing, John J. "Black Jack," 40

Quesada, Elwood "Pete," 87, 114, 155, 185

Readey, John, 80

Richardson, James, 113

Ritter, William L., 37, 40–42

Rosenfeld, A. H., 35–36

Ryder, Gordon, 178

Sherwood, Robert, 104

Shields, James R., 97

Simpson, William H., 110

Skinner, Leslie, 82

Slovik, Edward G. "Eddie," 145

Stroh, Donald A., 37

Stumpf, Robert H., 194–195

Thompson, Oscar H., 66, 97, 125, 141, 148, 178, 184, 312

Tinley, Phil, 57

Toffey, John J., 41, 308

Tucker, Henry P., 57

Turner, Merritt D., 204

Twiggs, James W., 198

Uhl, Edward, 82

Ulio, J. A., 203

Wade, Wallace, 171

Westmoreland, William C., 45, 109

Womble, James, 40–41

Woods, John C., 198

Young, Charles, 196

Zeno, Edgar E., 231

US NAVY

Bush, George H. W., 277

Connor, David E., 277

Heiden, Ray, 134

US MARINES

Carlson, Vernon Lyman, 83

US WAR CORRESPONDENTS

Boyle, Hal, 103

Hemingway, Ernest M., 92–93, 100, 117

Mauldin, Bill, 11, 17, 80, 117, 129, 261

Pyle, Ernest T. "Ernie," 15, 35, 38, 257

US PERSONALITIES

Atkins, Chet, 264

Baker, Newton, 40

Barrow, Clyde, 125

Barrow, Joseph L. (Joe Louis), 46, 285

Basie, William J. "Count," 21, 197

Beneke, Gordon Lee "Tex," 197

Berlin, Irving, 26

Blanc, Mel, 52

Blanchard, Felix A. "Doc," 147

Blyth, Ann, 130

Brown, Les, 142

Burns, Bob, 82

Bryant, Paul "Bear," 201

Cagney, James F. "Jimmy," 79

Calhoun, John C., 70

Capra, Frank, 52

Cole, Nathaniel "Nat King Cole," 52

Cooper, Frank J. "Gary," 308

Cooper, William Walker, 25

Costello, Francesco "Frank," 78

Crosby, Harry L. "Bing," 116–117, 130

Davis, Glenn, 147

Day, Doris, 142, 261

Dean, Jimmy Ray, 269

Devine, Andy, 130

DiMaggio, Joseph P. "Joe," 16, 197

Dirksen, Everett McKinley "Ev," 247

Dorsey, Thomas F. "Tommy," 21

Ellington, Edward K. "Duke," 21

Fields, Arthur, 317

Flynn, Errol, 139

Gehrig, Henry L. "Lou," 28, 283–285

Geisel, Theodor "Dr. Seuss," 52

Goddard, Robert H., 82

Goldberg, Rube, 126

Goodman, Benjamin D. "Benny," 21

Grable, Elizabeth R. "Betty," 197

Halliburton, Richard, 264

Harper, Paul, 15

Hayworth, Rita, 54

Hermann, Woodrow C. "Woody," 21

Holiday, Billie, 21, 259

Hope, Leslie Townes "Bob," 54–55, 69

Horne, Lena Mary, 21

Johnson, Charles V. "Van," 86

Johnson, Edward "Noon," 82

Jones, Lindley A. "Spike," 73

Kendrick, Sanford, 82

Key, Francis Scott, 13

Krishnamurti, Jiddu, 213

Krupa, Eugene B. "Gene," 199

Lansky, Meyer, 78

Lebrowitz, Barney "Battling Levinsky," 111

Lee, Bruce, 21

Marciano, Rocco F. "Rocky," 285

Masterson, Bartholemew "Bat," 279

May, Jacob, 121

McGuire, Dorothy H., 38

Michel, Robert H. "Bob," 78–79, 218, 277

Miller, Alton Glen "Glenn," 21, 73, 83, 196

Monroe, Marilyn, 271

Parker, Bonnie, 125

Peck, Eldred G. "Gregory," 38

Pegler, Westbrook, 30

Post, Emily, 81

Rickey, Branch, 15

Rice, Grantland, 146

Roosevelt, Franklin D., 208

Ruth, George H. "Babe," 28, 283–286

Ryan, Margaret O. "Peggy," 130

Scarne, John, 279

Shore, Dinah "Fanny," 110

Sitting Crow (Kangi Iyotanke), 233

Smith, Kathryn E. "Kate," 21

Southworth, William H. "Billy," 25

Truman, Harry S., 247, 249

Turner, Julia J. "Lana," 54

Vonnegut, Kurt, 57

Whitmore, James A., 86

Williams, Theodore Samuel "Ted," 286

Wilson, Thomas Woodrow, 40

Wrigley, Philip K., 16

Zanuck, Darryl F., 38

AUSTRALIAN PERSONALITIES

Chain, Ernst, 169

Florey, Howard, 169

Heatley, Norman, 169

BARBARIANS

Atilla the Hun, 83

BELGIAN PERSONALITIES

De Merode, Jean, 148

De Pinto, Count and Countess, 104

King Leopold II, 148

BRITISH PERSONALITIES

Churchill, Winston L. S., 50, 171

Fleming, Alexander, 169

King George VI, 110

Moran, Lord Charles M. W., 283

Nelson, Horatio, 44, 308

Tennyson, Lord Alfred, 15

FRENCH PERSONALITIES

Charlemagne, 239

Clemenceau, Georges, 40

Giraud, Henri H., 43–44

Napoleon, 26, 172

GERMAN ARMY

Bremm, Josef Benedikt, 183

Denkert, Walter, 173

Hetzenauer, Matthäus, 238

Hindenburg, Paul von, 129

Lemcke, Gerhard, 123–124

Manteuffel, Hasso von, 157

Model, Walter, 157

Paulus, Friedrich, 173

Rommel, Erwin, 113

Rundstedt, Gerd von, 157

Schmidt, Hans, 110

Scholze, Georg, 60

Stegmann, Rudolf, 59

Strachwitz, Hyacinth Graf von, 62

Türke, Gerhard, 175

Wegelein, Helmuth, 105, 110

Weise, Karl-Heinz, 175

GERMAN AIR FORCE (LUFTWAFFE)

Becker, Karl Heinz, 152

Schimpf, Richard, 221

GERMAN WAFFEN-SS

Dietrich, Josef "Sepp," 157

Leitgeb, Josef "Sepp," 239

Peiper, Joachim, 169

Prützmann, Hans-Adolf, 239

Skorzeny, Otto, 197

GERMAN PERSONALITIES

Bach, Johann Sebastian, 135

Beethoven, Ludwig van, 135

Brothers Grimm, 93, 168

Dannert, Horst, 199

Frankenstein, 132

Goebbels, Josef, 239

Himmler, Heinrich, 239

Hitler, Adolf, 13, 32, 46, 157, 169, 245

Löns, Herman, 239

Oppenhoff, Franz, 239

Schmeling, Max, 46

Zeiss, Carl, 238

ITALIAN PERSONALITIES

Alighieri, Dante, 93

Mussolini, Benito, 13, 197

JAPANESE PERSONALITIES

Emperor Hirohito, 248

Suzuki, Kantarō, 246, 248

Tojo, 13

MACEDONIAN LEADERS

Alexander the Great, 52

PRUSSIAN PERSONALITIES

Frederick II "Frederick the Great," 26, 85

Scharnhorst, Gerhard Johann David von, 191

Schill, Ferdinand Baptista von, 191

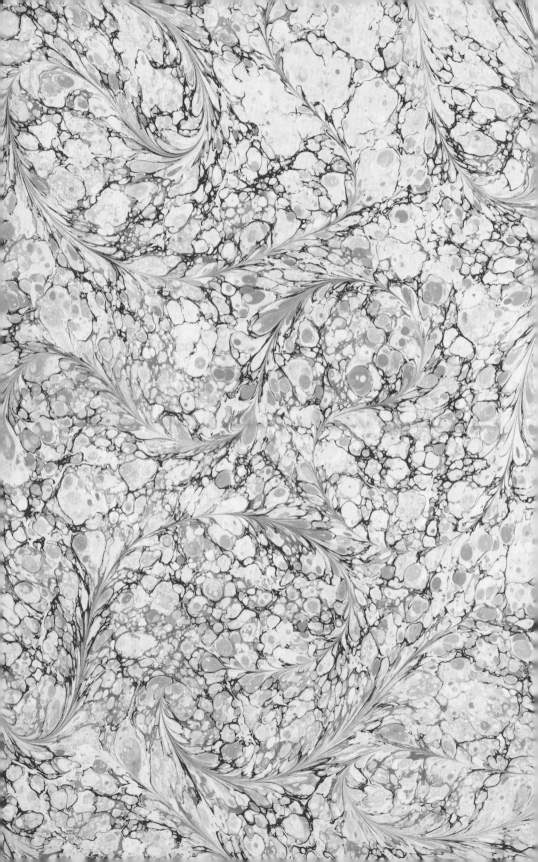